CARIBBEAN
THE LESSER ANTILLES

DEDICATION

For Phyllis
and
our family, growing with glee

ACKNOWLEDGEMENTS

This book incorporates the wisdom and advice of a great many West Indians and others, all gracious and helpful in the extreme. My special thanks to: Marty Flaherty and Amoret Bethel in Anguilla; Maryse Romney and Bernadette Davis in Saint-Martin; "Baby" in Sint Maarten; Elise Magras and David Henderson in Saint-Barts; Wilma Hassell in Saba; Pat Riley and Peter Titley in St. Kitts; Dr. Adly Abdel-Megud, Elmeader Prentice, and Fitzroy "Teach" Williams in Nevis; Elizabeth Mason in Antigua; James "Mango" Frith in Montserrat; Guy Claude-Germaine, Sylvia Schwarzer, and "Serge of Gosier" in Guadeloupe; Marie-José Edwards, Glenroy Espirit, and Zoltan Csete in Dominica; Annie Merlande, Georgie Vernes, and Roland Cupit in Martinique; Maria Monplaisir and John Jeremie in St. Lucia; Celia Ross and "Bam" in St. Vincent; Anadene Casimir and Sitah Singh in Trinidad; and Van Richards of San Francisco, once of Barbados.

In the U.S., my appreciation for helping me put my travels together is owed to the diligent Myron Clement, Tim Benford, Lauren Thomas, Marcella Martinez, Frank Connelly, Regina Henry, Peter Rothholz, Joan Medhurst, Catherine van Kempen, and Betty Tahir at LIAT.

As well, many thanks to Peter "Acid Bath" Zimmerman, my editor, who lived up to his name and helped form a book from a mountain of text. And, to Magnus Bartlett and the staff at The Guidebook Company, thanks for the very professional support.

CARIBBEAN
THE LESSER ANTILLES

KARL LUNTTA

British Library Cataloguing-in-Publication Data

A catalogue record of this book is available from the British Library

Distribution by Hi Marketing, 38 Carver Road, London, SE24 9LT, UK

Editor: Peter Zimmerman
Illustrations Editor: John Oliver
Designer: Harvey Symons
Maps: Tom Le Bas and Louis Papachristou

Front cover photography: Catherine Karnow
Photography courtesy of Catherine Karnow, except for the following: Barnabys
Picture Library 10; Mary Evans Picture Library 35, 58–9, 62, 108–9, 236, 237,
320; Illustrated London News Picture Library 318–9; National Maritime Museum
98–9, 328; the syndics of Cambridge University Library 107; Royal Geographical
Society 234–5, 324–5

Production House: Twin Age Ltd
Printed in China

Contents

ISLAND MAPS

TOWN PLANS

'A Negro Festival drawn from Nature in the Island of St Vincent,
from an original picture by Agostine Brunyas'

The Lesser Antilles: The People

Introduction

The Lesser Antilles is the sort of place that lends itself well to stereotypes. Balmy breezes, swaying palms, limpid blue water and elegant people of all hues and tongues create the standard pictures, the clichés of the Lesser Antilles. And, as we all know, clichés are what they are precisely because they are so often true. The Lesser Antilles is a region of great and, in places, singular beauty, with equally beautiful people descended from Arawak and Carib Amerindian groups, European colonizers, slavers and slaves and the nouveau entrepreneurs of this century. Lesser Antilles languages reflect a heady swirl of Patois and Creoles, the Queen's English, French, Dutch, Portuguese, Spanish and Amerindian and African holdovers. The cultures, religions, cuisines and architecture of the Lesser Antilles reflect the rich amalgam of its various conquerors and visitors.

Yet the antithesis of this beauty, the cliché of "trouble in paradise," also rings true. Whether one calls the Lesser Antilles a Third World region, a developing region or some variation on the theme, the fact is that it is generally a poor region. In places the average annual per capita income is less than a tourist might spend during a week's stay at a luxury resort. Once the domain of sugar barons and the landed gentry, the Lesser Antilles today is a disparate group of struggling economies, in some cases loosely banded together for economic and regional growth, but in many cases reliant on the tourist dollar for foreign exchange.

Modern problems have also taken their toll. Social plagues such as crime, racial disenfranchisement, drug use and sexually transmitted diseases, including AIDS, are threats and threads in the fabric of Antillean life. Political corruption has found its place in several governments and phrases such as coup d'etat and military intervention have become part of the regional lexicon.

The Lesser Antilles is, in other words, a very pretty picture with a deeper story to tell. The region is, pound for pound, one of the most intriguing and deeply exquisite hideaways on earth, yet its seductiveness is wrapped in a cloak of harsh history and some pain—doubtless much the same as the place from which you came.

Except it probably has better beaches.

Defining Terms

The terms "West Indies," "Caribbean Islands" and their attendant subgroups—the Greater Antilles, Lesser Antilles, Windward Islands, Leeward Islands, French West Indies and Netherlands Antilles, among others—represent the myriad political and cultural influences the nations of the world have had on this relatively tiny region. It can be a labyrinth of terminology, difficult to discern which island is where, which island is politically affiliated with what country, which languages and currencies are used.

To make sense of it, a West Indies primer:

The West Indies is an archipelago, some 1,500 miles (2,400 kilometres) from head to toe, that roughly divides the Atlantic Ocean and the Caribbean Sea. The total land mass of the hundreds of islands in the archipelago is about 91,000 square miles (236,000 square kilometres), roughly the size of Uganda or the state of Oregon. Cuba represents just under half the total West Indies' land area. Some 50 islands of the group are inhabited.

The West Indies comprises the Bahamas and Turks and Caicos islands in the Atlantic Ocean and the Greater and Lesser Antilles islands of the Caribbean. It lies between 10° and 27° north and 55° and 85° west, generally east and south of Florida, east of Central America and north of the coast of South America.

The Greater and Lesser Antilles form a sweeping arc, stretching from Cuba to the southeast, creating the string of islands ending north of the Venezuelan coast. The body of water encompassed by these islands is the Caribbean Sea, an area of more than one million square miles (2.6 million sq km). The Greater and Lesser Antilles lie south of the Tropic of Cancer, placing these islands firmly in the tropics.

The Greater Antilles islands are, in order of descending size, Cuba, Hispaniola (the island shared by Haiti and the Dominican Republic), Jamaica and Puerto Rico, plus smaller adjacent islands.

The Lesser Antilles were known as the more lyrical "Caribbee Islands" in the 17th century. Its two main divisions are called the Leeward Islands and the Windward Islands, which would be fine—if everyone would agree on which islands are which. Agreement often depends on the nationality of the speaker. The Dutch, for instance, refer to Saba, Sint Eustatius and Sint Maarten, their three islands in the north, as the Netherlands Antilles Windward Islands. The statement is true enough in that they do lie, in fact, windward of Aruba, Curaçao and Bonaire, the Dutch islands to the southwest. However, they also lie in the island group generally known as the Leeward Islands. For some time the British used the terms Windward and Leeward Islands for administrative purposes, as in British Leeward Islands. Yet the terms applied to their own possessions and commonwealth affiliates and not, for instance, the French islands that lie in the same waters. The French do not use the terms at all. Today the terms Leeward and Windward are considered to be locative and carry no political significance.

Farthest north are the British Virgin Islands and U.S. Virgin Islands. South of the Virgins is the Leeward Islands group, consisting of Anguilla, Saint-Martin/Sint Maarten, Saba, Sint Eustatius, Saint-Barthélémy, St. Kitts and Nevis, Antigua and Barbuda, Montserrat, Guadeloupe and adjacent islands. Next come the Windward Islands: Dominica, Martinique, St. Lucia, St. Vincent and the Grenadines, Grenada and adjacent islands. Barbados, Trinidad and Tobago, the Venezuelan islands plus Aruba, Curaçao and Bonaire, commonly known as the ABC Islands, complete the Lesser Antilles roster.

The other divisions among the Caribbean islands rely on politics, not geography. The French West Indies, sometimes called the French Antilles, and the Netherlands Antilles define political groups of islands with past and present affiliations. The territories of Puerto Rico and the U.S. Virgin Islands have political, and some cultural, ties to the United States.

The largest group of politically affiliated islands are those that were the British colonies, at one time collectively called the British West Indies. Today they have become either direct possessions or Commonwealth nations. The direct British possessions, throughout the Lesser Antilles, are the British Virgin Islands, Anguilla and Montserrat. The Commonwealth nations are Antigua and Barbuda, Barbados, Dominica, Grenada, St. Kitts and Nevis, St. Lucia, St. Vincent and the Grenadines and Trinidad and Tobago. By and large they are distinguished by British influence in their cultures and government and by the official use of English (and, unofficially, a wide range of Patois and Creole languages)—and by the fact that one can universally catch a good cricket game in any of these places. English is also the official language of the U.S. Virgin Islands.

The French West Indies is a smaller group. The islands are: Guadeloupe, which counts as its dependencies Marie-Galante, La Désirade and Les Saintes, as well as Saint-Barthélémy and Saint-Martin to the north; and Martinique. French is widely spoken on these islands and they are administered as *départments d'outre mer,* or overseas departments of France. Their citizens are considered French citizens and travel between the French West Indies and France doesn't require heavy documentation.

The Netherlands Antilles is also a small group, consisting of Bonaire, Curaçao, Sint Maarten (which shares island space with the French Saint-Martin), Sint

Eustatius and Saba. These islands are, as a unit, part of the Kingdom of the Netherlands, and Dutch culture is evident. Dutch is the official language, although English and other languages, such as Papiamento, are widely spoken. Aruba withdrew from the Netherlands Antilles in 1986 and became an autonomous member of the Kingdom of the Netherlands, enjoying the same status as the rest of the Netherlands Antilles combined.

The Lesser Antilles is covered in this book. For our purposes, this area will include the islands from the British and U.S. Virgin Islands in the north, through Trinidad and Tobago in the south. The ABC Islands and the Venezuelan islands, because of their distance from the main island chain, have not been included.

Regional History

INDIGENOUS PEOPLE

Slavers and slaves, owners and the owned: the history of the Lesser Antilles is inexorably linked to Europeans and Africans. For centuries, sugar and slavery drove each other and the economies of these small islands. The human mix formed the basis for the cultures, art, music and the social stratification you'll find in the present-day Lesser Antilles. Yet before sugar, and before Ferdinand and Isabella sent Columbus on his way to the New World, native peoples had inhabited the region for a good 4,000 years.

The first were Stone Age hunters and gatherers, of whom little is known beyond that they hunted and gathered, using tools made of flint and stone. Beyond that, they left few other artifacts. We know them today as the Ciboney (also spelled "Siboney") and that name is reflected in hotel and place names throughout the Lesser Antilles.

The Ciboney were followed by the Arawaks, a daring group of seafarers who crossed the Caribbean in two waves, so to speak—the first sometime between the death of Christ and AD 500 and the second from AD 850 to 900. They came from the Amazon and Orinoco regions of northern Brazil and Venezuela and settled the Antilles in groups from Trinidad to Cuba, where Christopher Columbus would first encounter them in his late-15th century voyages. A smaller Arawak sub-group, called the Taino, settled areas of Puerto Rico, Haiti and eastern Cuba.

The Arawaks appear to have been relatively peaceful. They were a fishing and farming culture, fond of ceremony and organized games and had little history of attacking others. They settled in large villages of up to 1,000 huts and 3,000 people, generally by the sea or near rivers, yet skilled Arawak artists left paintings on cave walls that indicate they also lived in the central and upland areas of certain islands. They shaped and milled their "canoes," an Arawak word that made its way to English via Spanish.

The Arawaks grew "tobacco"—the word derived from the name of their pipes—and used it both socially and ritually. They also grew fruit and vegetables, including maize and cassava (yuca), the starchy staple of the tropics. The Arawaks grew two types of cassava, commonly known as the sweet and bitter varieties. The now-famous pepperpot stew, popular throughout the Lesser Antilles, is also Arawak in origins.

In addition, the Lesser Antilles' first inhabitants were responsible for the introduction of the words "hammock," "barbecue," "hurricane" and "manatee," a large sea mammal, into various languages.

For centuries the Arawaks existed unperturbed until the arrival of the bellicose Caribs, another seagoing indigenous group from the Orinoco region of South America.

The Caribs, possibly distant relatives of Arawak groups, had, over the years, made their way from South America to the Lesser Antilles, leaving depredation and conquered islands in the wakes of their war canoes. According to evidence, they captured and destroyed entire villages. Although it's disputed by scholars, the Caribs reportedly ate their adversaries. In fact, the word "cannibal" is derived from Caribal, the Spanish word for the Caribs.

By the mid-15th century, the Caribs had reached as far north as Puerto Rico, Cuba and Hispaniola. Such was the extent of their influence that the waters around them eventually acquired their name—the Caribbean Sea.

COLUMBUS AND EUROPEAN EXPLORATION

Meanwhile, in another part of the world, events were taking place that would change the destiny of the tiny islands of the Lesser Antilles.

In his relentless, largely ego-driven quest for riches and a route to the New World, the Italian explorer Christopher Columbus (Cristoforo Colombo, in his native language) sailed into both fame and a bit of infamy on his four voyages to the Americas (1492–3, 1493–6, 1498–1500 and 1502–4).

The premise of his daring plan, which inspired the Spanish sovereigns Ferdinand and Isabella to supply sponsorship, was that the ever-growing European demand for Asian luxuries necessitated a simpler and more efficient route to obtain them. The current overland routes were dangerous, time-consuming and costly. It was part of Columbus' grand scheme, the "Enterprise of the Indies," to find an ocean route west from Spain to Asia and to secure any discovered land for Spain's empire. He did not know, of course, that the Americas lay uncharted between Europe and Asia. It took years and no small effort for Columbus to convince his patrons that he could find this shorter route and thus enrich the Spanish empire and its sovereigns.

Columbus, with the title "Admiral of the Ocean Sea, Viceroy and Governor," and his crew of 90 sailed from Palos, Spain, on 3 August 1492 with a fleet of three caravels: the *Nina,* the *Pinta* and his flagship the *Santa Maria.* Columbus was optimistic that Asia was less than 2,800 miles (4,480 km) to the west. In fact, due to a miscalculation of the earth's size and an overestimation of Asia's easternmost point, his calculations fell drastically short. The actual distance between Spain and easternmost Asia, as the plane flies, is about 10,000 miles (16,000 km).

On 12 October, Columbus and his crew sighted land. It was an island the native inhabitants called Guanahani, renamed San Salvador or "Holy Savior" by Columbus, and was most likely today's Watling Island of the Bahamas. Later, on this first voyage, Columbus went on to explore Cuba and Espaniola, or "Little Spain" (today's Hispaniola).

For the native Arawaks Columbus encountered, his plan was simple. He would begin the process of converting them to Christianity and, ultimately, enslave them for Spain. The enslavement of the Arawaks on Hispaniola began almost instantly, as Columbus established a garrison there to protect Spain's new-found interests.

It is a small part of Columbus' legacy that when he landed he erroneously believed he was in the Indies, near the coasts of Japan and China. It would be his lifelong belief that he had discovered islands off the coast of Asia, gateway to the lands traveled by Marco Polo more than two centuries earlier. His lifelong quest was to make contact with the emperor of China, the Great Khan. He never succeeded, of course. Nevertheless, his discoveries tagged the moniker "West Indies" to the islands of the region and the people who inhabited them became known as "Indians." The momentum of history carries those names today.

On his second voyage, now bearing the title "Viceroy of the Indies," Columbus discovered Jamaica, Puerto Rico, Dominica, Guadeloupe, Antigua and several other Lesser Antilles islands. It was on these trips that he first encountered the Caribs, already settled in the Lesser Antilles. In his journal the great explorer wrote: "As for monsters I have found no trace of them except at one point on the second island [Puerto Rico] on the way to the Indies; it is inhabited by a people considered throughout the island to be most ferocious."

On his third voyage, Columbus sailed as far south as Trinidad and the Venezuelan coast, but by the time of his fourth voyage the travels had taken their toll. The Great Khan had remained elusive and no substantial amounts of gold had been discovered. Ferdinand and Isabella began to question their support, at one point deposing Columbus as governor of the islands and there were arguments over Columbus' compensation. During this last voyage, his old caravels gave way and sank and he and crew members were marooned on Jamaica for over a year. When finally rescued, Columbus returned to Spain a broken and defeated man, plagued by illness and constant bickering with King Ferdinand over title and recompense. Within two years of his return, on 20 May 1506, he died at Valladolid.

The early discoveries of Columbus opened the floodgates of European exploration. All this settlement spelled doom for the hapless Arawaks and Caribs. During the 16th and 17th centuries, they were in turns enslaved, murdered, diseased and zealously converted to death. Many committed suicide rather than submit to European domination. Entire communities were eliminated, either in battle or by their own hands. Today only a few of these indigenous people survive; most live on the islands of St. Vincent and Dominica.

THE COLONIES

During the 16th and 17th centuries, Europeans established major ports in the Greater and Lesser Antilles. Small settlements grew larger with the introduction of sugar, coffee and other crops. With the absence of Arawak slave labor, African slaves were imported in increasing numbers, thus ensuring the ethnological and sociological makeup of the Caribbean today.

The European ports and outposts in the Lesser Antilles were by no means, however, permanent. Eager to find footholds in the New World and for expansion and commerce (and in some cases religious freedom), the principal European countries vied for power and possessions. Spain, which controlled the seas and the major islands of Puerto Rico, Cuba, Hispaniola and, briefly, Jamaica and Trinidad, was targeted by French, Dutch and English ships of war, as well as by privateers and assorted scalawags who roamed the Caribbean in search of easy riches. The Danes, who ruled the Virgin Islands for two centuries, and Swedes, who later occupied Saint-Barthélémy from 1786–1878, were also players in the acquisitions game. The rattling of sabers in the Caribbean was part and parcel of the continuing European wars of domination, where treaties were signed and alliances rearranged—and islands changed hands repeatedly.

The late 17th century was also a time of unbridled recklessness and, possibly, a smattering of heroics, perpetrated by some of the Caribbean's more colorful malcontents, the buccaneers. A loose association of sailors, pirates, thugs and some truly evil people, outcasts who'd given up their nationalities for the lure of the sea and quick wealth, the buccaneers (the name evolved from the French boucan, for a wooden rack used to dry meat) were bound together by a unwavering distrust for authority and a particular distrust of Spain.

Nominally employed as privateers by the likes of England, the mercenary buccaneers waged war on the Spanish Main, particularly in Panama, as well as the Spanish ports of San Juan, Havana and Cartagena, in Colombia. Names such as Francis Drake, Henry Morgan, Calico Jack Rackham, Edward Teach (also known as Blackbeard), Mary Read and Anne Bonney rank among the better known privateers of the time.

The War of Spanish Succession, fought mainly in Europe, was brought to an end by the 1713 Treaty of Utrecht. During that war France and Spain, then allies, battled with and lost to England and the Netherlands in a familiar skirmish over property and trade rights. Spain was divested of its European possessions and England was in turn awarded France's Asiento, or contract, to supply the Spanish New World possessions with slaves. The buccaneers were left without a united front. England no longer needed them and most buccaneers reverted to whence they came—a small group of marauding pirates, aligned to no one but themselves and hunted down like dogs. Others, such as the then Sir Francis Drake and Sir Henry Morgan, were to become wealthy aristocrats and landholders.

It wasn't until the end of the Napoleonic Wars, when the 1815 Treaty of Vienna was signed after the defeat of Napoleon at Waterloo, that the Lesser Antilles settled down into a semblance of orderly rule. Ultimately, the history of the islands demonstrates numerous changes of rule. The island of St. Lucia, for example, was discovered and first colonized by Spain, then ruled by France; it changed hands 14 times before it finally emerged as a British colony. Present day Saint-Martin/Sint Maarten is half-French, half-Dutch. The U.S. Virgin Islands have known Spanish, Dutch, French, Danish and U.S. rule, as well as a brief stint under the Knights of Malta.

PLANTER SOCIETY

Emerging from the European rivalries of the 17th and 18th centuries was a Antillean society economically steeped in agriculture and the slave trade. Within the "triangle" of trade, stretching from West African ports where slaves were bought and loaded onto cargo ships, to various European ports and to the sugar-producing ports of the Antilles (and Brazil), commerce was brisk and profitable. Fortunes were made, often by absentee landholders, and the great plantocracies of the Caribbean created the basis for the multi-tiered, multiracial society that we know today.

During the 18th and early 19th centuries, sugar reigned in the Caribbean. Over 10 million African slaves were imported to the Americas, most from western, central and eventually eastern Africa, most ending up in the Greater Antilles and Brazil, where large land masses favoured the production of sugar. Still, virtually all the islands of the Lesser Antilles produced sugar and other crops and slaves provided the backbone for building roads, ports and the infrastructures of the day.

The planter society was characterized by a mix of landed plantation owners, overseers, merchants and, of course, Africans bound by slavery. In white society brutality, ignorance and illiteracy were rife, the result of years of settling by European misfits and criminals. The masters were more often than not unrepentant bigots and their methods of disciplining slaves were harsh—beheadings, live burnings and mutilations were not uncommon. Slaves outnumbered their masters by the thousands and the society was one where too few, who were none too lenient, held too much power—a perfect recipe for tension and failure.

Slave life itself was tragic. Beginning with the infamous Middle Passage from Africa, chained and relegated to the stench-filled bowels of cargo ships, a slave's lot was one virtually without hope. During the 12-week Atlantic passage, many died of starvation or dehydration. Upon arrival, slaves were typically stripped and exhibited for sale, some even branded, not the last affront to dignity they would encounter. Their labor in the sugarcane fields was the most difficult and grinding possible and many died while working or were beaten to death by overseers. Others died as a result of suicide or open rebellion. Others simply ran away and were often recaptured and executed. Planters could expect an average of six deaths to occur for every live birth among slaves and the need to import more Africans increased with the expansion of trade and planter society.

Black slaves consorted—most often by force—with whites to produce a new "brown" layer of society, mixed-race offspring who held the unintentionally peripheral position between the whites and Africans. In cases, the mixed-race class was called "free coloreds," unable to function in a racist white society that saw them as inferior and pretenders, yet considered by whites to be superior to black Africans. The emergence of a brown class so fueled the planters' fears that miscegenation would kick in the door of white supremacy, that a bizarre and ultimately futile system of racial classification emerged throughout the islands. A person of mixed race in the English-speaking colonies would be classified as musteefino, octaroon, quadroon, mulatto, sambo and so on, depending on the percentage mix of white and black heritage. In the French Antilles official and complicated gradations of color numbered more than one hundred. Today, although official classifications no longer exist and the islands' mottoes and tourist brochures proclaim multiracial societies existing in ebony-and-ivory harmony, one needn't look very hard to find that informal color classifications remain strong.

The planter society lived in constant and justified fear of slave uprisings. If, for no other reason, the sheer numbers of slaves wasn't enough cause for concern, the planters found themselves dealing with a people they had clearly misjudged in terms of intellect and ability to organize. Slaves customarily and relentlessly sabotaged their masters' plantations by ruining farm equipment, holding forbidden meetings and plotting reprisals. Rebellions erupted in Barbados, Jamaica, Trinidad and Antigua and were put down with frightening brutality. The black Haitian leader Toussaint L'Ouverture, borrowing ideas and impetus from the French Revolution, led a successful 1794 uprising and became the first leader of a free black state—with over 450,000 newly freed slaves—in the New World. In America, the slave preacher Nat Turner led black slaves on a wide-scale rebellion in 1831.

For years, particularly during the 18th century, many in mainstream European society had been horrified by the spectacle of slavery in the Antilles. Guided by abolitionist movements and the clergy, protests and calls for an end to the practice were common. Finally, during the early 1800s, the reprisals exacted on rebellious slaves in the New World reached the ears of an already agitated Europe. Finally, after much debate (and, in the case of America, a civil war) slavery was abolished in the New World. The British outlawed the ownership of slaves in 1834, the French in 1848 and the Dutch in 1863. The Spanish, who then operated large sugar plantations in Brazil and Cuba, followed in 1886.

LIFE AFTER SLAVERY

The end of slavery signaled the death knell for the heyday of the West Indian planter society. Many former slaves went on to farm small parcels of land, while others remained on the plantations as indentured, paid laborers. Eventually, planters imported more laborers from West Africa, Europe, India and Asia. Yet even this new labor force was not enough to save the large plantations. Rising production costs and competition from other countries, notably Brazil's massive sugar plantations on which slavery remained intact until the late 19th century, destroyed the large plantocracy, which was not accustomed to either paying its help or even treating them as equals. Some plantations gave way to smaller, more profitable farming enterprises. Some were gobbled up by emerging agricultural production companies. In effect, the great plantocracy of the West Indies became a wistful memory in the colonial mind and its absence paved the way for the islands' turbulent 20th-century battles for racial equality and viable economies.

THE 20TH CENTURY

The late 19th century and early parts of this century saw a worldwide move in agrarian societies toward forms of industrialized activity. In the Lesser Antilles, this shift was first to the industrial centers, the emerging cities such as Bridgetown in Barbados and Port of Spain in Trinidad. Wage-paying oil refineries in Trinidad and large sugar production plants fueled the urban move. Agricultural production had diversified to include coffee, cocoa, bananas and other profitable crops, while the infrastructures needed for processing and exporting the crops employed thousands.

The influence of the United States in the Caribbean increased in the 20th century, starting with the acquisition of Puerto Rico in the Spanish-American War of 1898. After the completion of the Panama Canal in 1914, the U.S. purchased the Virgin Islands from Denmark, primarily to use as a strategic and military base.

World War I brought profound changes in the international makeup of the world. No longer innocent or isolated, and for the most part shunned by their colonial rulers, the islands of the Lesser Antilles were caught up in worldwide movements fomenting a wide range of human rights, including the all-important voting privilege. The islands and islanders began to define their emerging national identities and a growing sense of pride in local cultures also emerged. This was in marked contrast with the prevailing European attitude of the time, which saw the islands as little more than pitiable ghettos and ready-made markets for expensive European technologies. By and large the typical Creole (in this sense, born in the West Indies) islander of the early 19th century was a disenfranchised worker, a source of cheap labor for foreign-owned industries, yet one whose past and future was linked to the island itself—a true native. And a captive audience, in a sense. These imperfect conditions led to conflict between the islanders and former colonial masters and to nascent movements for independence.

The worldwide depression of the 1930s touched the Lesser Antilles in no small way. Islanders who had migrated in the thousands seeking employment in Central and South America and the U.S., now returned home to find stagnant economies and neglected paradises. Despair and poor working conditions in turn led to widespread worker riots in 1935-38, primarily in the British islands. The result of these riots, besides correcting some immediate wrongs within the workplace—the reformation of child labor laws and formal acknowledgment of trade unions, among others—was the birth of organized and recognized political parties. If nothing else, political parties within the colonies signaled the advent of new, self-governing islands of the Lesser Antilles, if not an independent Lesser Antilles.

Tourism, most often in the form of cruise ships, existed in the islands during the early part of the century. In the postbellum Fifties many of the islands, having made a shaky shift from primary agrarian to industrial activity, took stock of their natural resources and saw the dollar signs written on the wall and those dollar signs spelled "tourism." The crystal Antillean waters and swaying palms were the allure. Accelerated promotion brought tourism to the Caribbean in a way that hadn't been seen previously. Today, in many Lesser Antilles islands, tourism earns more foreign currency than any other industry.

The Fifties and Sixties also saw the ripening of inchoate political movements. A clamoring for island self-rule and independence became louder than ever and colonialism finally began to relinquish its strong grip, sometimes grudgingly, sometimes with great relief. For the British in particular, the islands had ceased to be profitable since the emancipation of slaves in 1834 and independence, along with Commonwealth status, came somewhat easily to her islands. Jamaica and Trinidad and Tobago, the two largest states, became independent in the early Sixties. The Dutch Kingdom Statute of 1954 gave the Netherlands Antilles islands direct representation in the Dutch government as districts of the Kingdom of the Netherlands. Likewise, laws passed by the Paris National Assembly in 1946 granted the French Antilles islands status as *départments d'outre mer,* or overseas departments of France. As such, they enjoy all the privileges of French citizenry.

Yet the independence movements of the Lesser Antilles have not always been without discord. Britain, for instance, had in 1825 attached the island of Anguilla to St. Kitts and Nevis for administrative purposes. She granted the three islands internal self-government in 1967. Anguilla objected to the collective agreement and formed a breakaway political party that demanded independence from St. Kitts and Nevis. By 1969, in the midst of failed talks and increasingly violent agitation, the situation became dangerous. British troops invaded Anguilla, establishing an interim rule that remained on the island until 1972. Anguilla is now a crown colony of Great Britain.

In 1983 Grenada, faced with a continued reliance on Cuba for technical and financial aid and rocked by anarchic internal political strife, was invaded by a U.S.-Caribbean force that restored order to the island. In 1984 the French government in Guadeloupe banned the Caribbean Revolutionary Alliance, a radical independence group, after a series of bombings convulsed the island.

Trinidad was a surprise news item in 1990, when an attempted coup organized by a Muslim fundamentalist group was put down. And as recently as November 1993, the normally stable St. Kitts was rocked by protest during general elections.

Today's Lesser Antilles societies still struggle with borderline economies, high unemployment and social stratification of wealth and power, often related to ethnicity. The concept of "pan-Caribbeanism"—a united Caribbean state or status borne primarily of economic need and similar ethnic and historical backgrounds—has been a recurring theme in discussions of the future of the region. For most in the region pan-Caribbeanism does not seem feasible today, given the evolution of myriad and distinct Antillean cultures. There do exist, however, collective regional organizations that deal with trade, tourism and culture throughout the Caribbean, such as the Caribbean Community and Common Market (CARICOM) nations, the Caribbean Tourism Organization (CTO), the Eastern Caribbean States Export Development Agency (ECSEDA) and the Caribbean Development Bank (CDB).

ANTILLEAN PEOPLE

With the dawn of the 20th century, the influx of peoples from the world over had turned the Lesser Antilles into a unique amalgam of races, languages, religions, music, cuisines and cultures. Blacks, whites, Jews, Asians, East Indians and smatterings of exoticism from the far corners of the globe formed the new creole societies that form our image of the Caribbean today. Yet, as we've noted, to characterize the Lesser Antilles as rainbow societies living in multiracial harmony would be ambitious and naive—despite frequent tourism slogans that portray the islands as long limbo lines of ethnic assimilation.

The reason, of course, hearkens back to slavery. The bedrock of Antillean society, the literal back upon which nations were built, consisted of displaced and ultimately disenfranchised Africans and their descendants. In the early days of slavery Africans outnumbered whites by the thousands, particularly on major sugar-producing islands such as Barbados. By some estimates more than 10 million slaves were brought to the West Indies during the heyday (17th and 18th centuries) of the planter society. The descendants of those slaves form the current majority population throughout the Lesser Antilles.

As mentioned earlier, the early emergence of a mixed race class, spawned most often by forced miscegenation, added layers to society which, to this day, maintain a political and economic presence somewhat distinct from those of pure African descent.

After the demise of slavery, planters turned to other sources for labor with which to keep their sprawling plantations alive. Among their first sources of paid laborers were, ironically, more Africans, this time as indentured (ostensibly free) laborers. East Indians (from India, as opposed to West Indians), Chinese and Europeans all found their way to various islands. In Trinidad and Tobago, East Indians make up nearly 40 per cent of the population, on equal par with African Trinidadians. In Dominica, some of the few remaining Caribs occupy a territory on the eastern side of the island. Descendants of Scottish Highlanders and the Irish deported in Oliver Cromwell's 17th-century purges can be found in Barbados. St. Vincent is host to descendants of Portuguese indentured laborers, brought in after the demise of slavery. Descendants of Dutch settlers are found on the tiny island of Saba. Other Europeans, some of whom have resided in the islands for generations, are evident throughout the islands, particularly in the French Antilles.

The people of the Lesser Antilles, in other words, present a diverse and exotic human face that in many ways defines the energy of the islands.

RELIGIONS

Modern religions in the Lesser Antilles follow patterns similar to those of widely diverse nations. Religious tolerance is expected and practiced to large degree. On any given Sunday, or Saturday in some cases, the small wooden structures of the rural areas and the towering city cathedrals seem to expand with the lung power of the faithful.

Because of widespread Christian proselytizing during the early days of Caribbean settlement, particularly in the slave quarters, organized religion took a somewhat early but tentative hold in the lives of Antillean peoples. It was partially missionary zeal that first drove the converters to the slaves, but later it became an act of self-preservation—it did not take long for the planters to discover that Christian slaves were easier to control than pagan slaves. Present-day religious beliefs of Antilleans reflect a blend of deity-based New World beliefs and ancient, African cosmologies.

Africans, most often from West African areas, had retained their own strong religious beliefs through the dreaded transition from free men to slaves. These beliefs consisted of various spirit worship and animist tenets, reflected in devotion to ancestors and other revered spirits. The actual practices involved invoking these ancestors through the ritualistic behavior of drumming, dancing, offerings and prayer. Europeans (conveniently ignoring the equally spiritual elements attributed to the Christian God, as well as the deeply ritualistic behavior involved in Christian church services and masses), deplored the African religions as paganistic magic and drove them quickly underground. As the early missionaries began the process of winning souls for the church, the Africans in turn began the process of disguising their ancient beliefs and syncretizing them with the new rules of Western theology.

It remains so today. While Anglican, Roman Catholic, Lutheran, Methodist and other Protestant religions predominate throughout the region, African-Caribbean peoples are hedging their bets. Arcane and mystical practices, commonly described under the umbrella term obeah, literally produce the magic that fills in the gaps where Western religions fall short. The word is thought to have originated with obayi, an Ashanti (West African) word meaning priest or sorcerer. The use of obeah and other forms of magic became stronger during the post-emancipation period, when free West Africans were brought to the Lesser Antilles as indentured laborers and in turn reinvigorated existing African beliefs.

Not everyone in the Lesser Antilles practices obeah, nor does everyone believe in it (nor are all believers of African descent). The practice is more widespread on some islands than others and called by many names, such as the famous voodoo of Haiti. Obeah is illegal in most places and designated practitioners are either respected or feared, but certainly sought out. Magic employs a combination of rum, tobacco, herbs, fetishes, drumming, chanting, spirits called jumbies and duppies (among other names)—a literal witches brew of ingredients—and is sometimes evil; it might seek to alter the natural courses of the universe by eliminating, or causing, disease, wealth, good fortune or even death. But whatever obeah is or is not, it is seen by many as a vital and dynamic force, the magic that hums below the surface of everyday Antillean life. The use of magic forms, combined with traditional Christian practice, is strong in several island cults. The Shango sect of Trinidad utilizes ritual practices of the Yoruba group (from today's Nigeria, Togo and Benin): drumming, frenzied dancing and some animal sacrifice.

Meanwhile, on the surface, the Lesser Antilles are peppered with the religions of their various conquerors and settlers. Among the churches are the Anglican, Roman Catholic, Methodist, Baptist and offshoot Baptist groups, Seventh-Day Adventist, various Evangelical movements, Jewish, Moravian, Society of Friends (Quaker) and Mormonism, officially the Church of Jesus Christ of Latter-day Saints. Not surprisingly, Catholicism is strong in the French Antilles. The Church of England and Protestant sects remain dominant in former British colonies such as Antigua and Barbuda and Barbados. The exception is Montserrat, where Catholicism dominates, due to the island's origins as a refuge for Irish settlers fleeing religious oppression in St. Kitts and Nevis. In Dominica, St. Lucia, St.

Vincent and the Grenadines and Grenada, the French influence is evidenced by the large number of adherents to Catholicism, who coexist with several Protestant sects. Trinidad and Tobago host a wide range of religions, from Catholic and Anglican to Hindu and Muslim.

Rastafarianism, the quasi-religious sect that grew out of Jamaica's Kingston ghettos in the 1930s, has attracted an increasing number of adherents throughout the Caribbean and the world since the 1970s, including famous acolytes such as the late reggae singer, Bob Marley. Rastafarianism is based on the strong belief that Africa, particularly Ethiopia, is "Zion," or heaven on earth, and the rest of the world's countries and systems are the undesirable "Babylon." Adherents believe that the late ruler of Ethiopia, Haile Selassie I, whose ordination name was Ras Tafari, was a living messiah, born to lead all displaced Africans back to the promised land. At the very least, Rastafarianism espouses a strong message of African pride and borrows from the teachings of Jamaican Marcus Garvey, an early advocate of pan-Africanism. Rastafarianism has, in places, become more a fashion statement than a true set of beliefs; heavy identification with the more stylish bits, such as reggae and the ritual use of marijuana ("the herb"), can overshadow the spiritualism of the sect. Rastas are recognized by their dreadlocks and clothing, often sporting the Ethiopian national colors of red, gold and green.

LANGUAGES

Two or three minutes on any island in the Lesser Antilles should clear up any worries you'll have about communicating in the local dialect. You can't.

Not that you won't be able to communicate at all. Islanders do speak excellent English and French, the two most common western languages in the Lesser Antilles. And they'll speak it readily—with you. But among themselves, you'll most likely hear an accelerated and lyrical version of a language that is at once familiar and indiscernible. It incorporates, again, the history of the region.

The languages of the Lesser Antilles are descendants of English, French, Spanish, Dutch, African and various pick-up languages that wove their way through the islands during their wartime exchanges and agricultural heydays. Called Patois, Creole (which here denotes a French Patois, but also refers to people, food and culture originating in the West Indies) and Papiamento, a Patois with heavy Spanish and some Portuguese influences, the languages evolved as a practical method for communication among slaves, who had come from numerous African linguistic groups. Over the years, as islands changed hands, new languages were introduced and incorporated into the local Patois. Each island has developed its own distinct version of Patois, yet it would be a mistake to assume that the current political affiliations of the islands also dominate their languages. French is an official language of Martinique, Guadeloupe and Saint-Barthélémy, but French Creole is the people's language. English is spoken, though a working knowledge of French would greatly enhance your visit. Saint-Martin, a dependency of Guadeloupe, uses French, Creole and some Papiamento from next-door Sint Maarten. English, however, is widely spoken.

In general, the former British colonies and dependents use English and English-based Patois. Exceptions are St. Lucia, Dominica and St. Vincent which, because of numerous political exchanges during the colonial days, use a Patois heavily laced with French Creole and some Spanish. Trinidad's Patois retains some Spanish influences.

In Sint Maarten, Saba and Sint Eustatius Dutch is the official language, but most everyone speaks fluent English. Papiamento is popular with locals on these islands, but is much more common in Aruba, Bonaire and Curaçao.

The Arts

MUSIC AND DANCE

The music of the Lesser Antilles is, in many ways, the music of the Caribbean. The common forms—reggae, calypso, soca, beguine and zouk—have been made accessible by modern inter-island movement and exchange and, to an extent, by tourism. Grouped together, they define an island sensibility by their upbeat tempos and heavy reliance on the often bawdy and satirical lyrics of love, sex and politics. But it would be a mistake to categorize any one of them as a generic West Indian sound.

Modern Antillean music, folksongs and dance emerged from the blend of cultures and people that were its first settlers. Today's Caribbean music has evolved through centuries of settlement and is, at this point, purely creole—original West Indian music born in the blue-green waters and tropical sun of the islands.

Africa has exerted the strongest influence, from the drumming that recalls ancient rituals to the dances of modern day carnivals. African drumming, in fact, is responsible for the overtly rhythmic quality of today's calypso and reggae.

Trinidad, a country with a relatively large population and a world-class carnival, was responsible for pioneering two musical innovations in the 20th century—calypso and the steelband.

Calypso may be the most widely recognized island music outside the West Indies. In its original form it is thought to have been a type of call-and-response song, originating in the slave fields of 18th century Trinidad. The name itself is a source of debate, but many posit that it comes from kaiso, derived from a West African word meaning "well done."

Calypsonians today have not only brought their music to the international arena (anyone who has heard the standards "All Day, All Night, Mary Ann" or "Day-o" already knows two calypso songs, the latter popularized by Harry Belafonte), but are an integral part of the Trinidad Carnival celebrations. You'll find calypso competitions in tents throughout the two islands, with calypsonians belting out their seemingly extemporaneous lyrics laced with ribald sexual innuendo, competing for cash prizes and notoriety. The grand prize is that of Calypso Monarch and the winning song will become the anthem of the year, the Road March. Calypsonians take stage names like Atilla the Hun, Lord Kitchener, Cro Cro and Watchman, names that are not a small part of their appeal.

One of the most popular calypsonians worldwide is the venerable Mighty Sparrow, of late known simply as Sparrow. Sparrow has cut an estimated 300 albums, testament to his talent and an almost insatiable desire for calypso throughout the world. Throughout the Lesser Antilles calypsonians are popular; Invader No. 3, a past winner of Barbados' Calypso Monarch crown, and calypso-soca crossover king Arrow, of Montserrat, are two examples.

Trinidad also claims responsibility for the development of another ubiquitous island sound, the steelband, also called tinpanny. A steelband is an ensemble group of tuned percussion instruments called pans, made from steel oil drums. Their development recalls the harsh days of post-emancipation colonial life, when, in their efforts to suppress local gatherings, the British governors of Trinidad banned African and East Indian drumming at street processions and festivals. The aim was to ban the festivals altogether. From this ban evolved "tamboo-bamboo" bands, where musicians substituted the thumping of hollow bamboo for their drums. In fact, musicians began to bang on just about everything they could lay their hands on—other than the forbidden drums. By the 1930s and 1940s, with Trinidad's oil industry in overdrive, a copious supply of oil drums apparently seemed to beg for artistic expression.

They got what they wanted and musicians sank, pounded, grooved and tuned the tops of oil drums to form the prototype of today's instrument. They then sawed off the barrels to the proper length to create "ping-pongs" (tenor pans), rhythm pans (including double pans and cello pans) and "tuned-booms" (bass pans). Initially used to accompany the Carnival, the unique sound of the steel pans quickly found their way into the mainstream music scene. Trinidadians today claim that the pan is the only musical instrument to have been invented in this century. While that claim may be based more in national pride than in fact, the prevalence of steel bands worldwide may indeed prove that it is one of the few internationally accepted instruments new to the scene. Today few carnivals, hotels, nightclubs, musical venues or even schools do not feature the instruments in some form. The players are highly trained, sophisticated and adept; in concert halls you might hear tunes from calypso to Tchaikovsky to Chuck Berry.

A popular hybrid musical form said to have its roots in Trinidad is soca, taken from the first two letters of soul and calypso. Soca combines calypso with an American rhythm and blues back beat and originated with a younger generation of calypsonians who were exposed to R&B and merged the sounds and styles of the two musical forms. Soca is also extremely popular throughout the islands and hosts its own competitions and concerts.

No one can say for sure when or from what the term reggae originated. Some say it came from the Jamaican slang terms rege rege, meaning rags or ragged clothing, or raga raga, meaning ragamuffin. According to Timothy White's official biography of Bob Marley, Catch A Fire, its first appearance in print came in 1968 on a single by Jamaican legends Toots and the Maytals called "Do The Reggay." Some even credit Frederick "Toots" Hibbert with creating the form. Whatever the word's origins, however, most would agree that reggae is a Jamaican original and is today one of the standards of the island and international music scene.

Jimmy Cliff, the reigning king of Jamaican pop in the Sixties and Seventies and today one of Jamaica's best known singers, had put the singles "Wonderful World, Beautiful People," "Wild World" and the popular "You Can Get It If You Really Want" on the charts in 1969 and 1970 respectively. Cliff would later star in one of the few Jamaican films to be internationally known, The Harder They Come, a story about the "rude boy" underworld and music scene of Kingston.

Still, the recognized reggae spokesman and premier performer, without whom reggae might have ended its days as a standard on Jamaica's oldies charts, was Bob Marley. In fact, still is Bob Marley, more than ten years after his death from cancer in 1981. Marley's success with the Wailers in the Seventies, and with other bands in the late Seventies and early Eighties, established reggae as an international behemoth. Its choppy beat and lyrics heavy on love and politics have carried it worldwide, with bands like UB40 and Third World taking up the mantle after the Wailers' demise. Also popular throughout the Lesser Antilles are the reggae spin-offs, dub and dancehall, which combine the heavy bass and beat of reggae with the lyric-dense style of rap.

Somewhat less universal, the Afro-Spanish sounds of the Cuban congo and rumba, the plena and bomba of Puerto Rico and the Dominican Republic's merengue still have influence beyond their shores, particularly in the Spanish-speaking world, but can be heard in the Lesser Antilles in concert and on radio stations.

The French Antilles gave us the African-inspired zouk and the beguine, with its lush arrangements and inspired quasi-ballroom dancing styles. The Virgin Islands originated fungi bands, consisting of guitars, bass, drums and bamboo instruments.

Antillean dance styles emulate the disparate regional cultures. Most creole dance evolved from traditional African drumming and dancing, later combined with European planters' dances such as the quadrille and the waltz. These dances were used in celebrations, the most important of which were the widespread carnivals throughout the islands. In St Lucia, kutumba drumming and dancing was and still is most frequently seen at ceremonies for the recently deceased. On the Grenadian island of Carriacou, the tradition of "big drum" dancing continues today; dancers in elaborate costumes parade and sing to the drums and "chac-chac" rattles.

Today several Lesser Antilles islands, notably Martinique's Les Grands Ballets de la Martinique and the U.S. Virgin Islands' Caribbean Dance Company, host national dance troupes that perform at carnivals and other festivals.

LITERATURE

Early Caribbean storytelling was oral rather than written. Pre-Columbian Indian groups, primarily the Arawaks and Caribs, left rock carvings and petroglyphs that have indicated a tradition of storytelling and folk tales. With the elimination of the Amerindian groups by Europeans by the 17th century, virtually all traces of this culture—and language, for that matter—disappeared.

The West Africans who, in turn, replenished the New World labor force brought their own stories and folk tales that survived the journey on the slavers' ships. Again the tradition was oral and the African folktales have since been passed along to the West Indian-born generations, who've kept many of them, or variations, alive until today.

The folk tales, steeped in mysticism and morality, have over the years adapted the West Indian milieu but are no less powerful than their African antecedents.

The vivid characters in the folk tales originate in the environment and the characters are often anthropomorphized animals such as rabbits, turtles, dogs and spiders. Often humorous and instructional, the tales and are popular with children. In several island folktales the quick-witted Anancy, (also Ananse, Anansi), a half-human, half-spider huckster, outwits foolish and bumbling humans (not surprisingly, often a harsh plantation master) and manages to escape from his self-instigated troubles in hilarious ways.

Early Caribbean literature is, in many ways, not Caribbean at all, but tended to follow the conventions of the European narrative traditions from which it flowed. After all, the early settlers did not consider themselves "Caribbean" in any real sense, but rather temporary residents of the colonies. Contemporary Caribbean literature emerged with the labor union movement of the 1920s, which provided the impetus for the birth of political parties and the formation of strong nationalist movements. As Caribbean people began to define their identities, they embraced their nationalism and regionalism and literature began to reflect Caribbean values and language, often with an emphasis on the African heritage.

One major theme in contemporary Caribbean literature is the writer's struggle for a multitude of identities—personal, national, racial—within the context of the diverse Caribbean heritage. The initial and often harsh displacement of the peoples of the Caribbean—the Africans, East Indians, Asians and even Europeans—created within the society a sense of rootlessness that, to a certain extent, exists today. Caribbean writers have long explored the powerful insecurity engendered by that displacement, with a need to either embrace or reject their exile and then to forge their own sense of place. That place remains, for many, a sort of "incorporated" Caribbean, or a Caribbean that has truly become home, where the wistful longing for and identification with a mother country remains strong yet not easily resolved.

Another important and recurrent theme in Caribbean literature, and perhaps a more contemporary one, is that of the ongoing Caribbean diaspora. Since the turn of the century, when industry began to replace agriculture as the world's economic bedrock, millions of West Indians have migrated to the U.S., U.K. and Canada in search of better jobs and opportunities. Entire West Indian communities have been established in foreign cities and entire generations have never returned to the Caribbean. Writers, too, descended on the industrial world's urban areas during the 1950s and 1960s, to places where publishing industries flourished and readers were plentiful. This "double" exile has taken writers farther from the cradle, far enough from their Caribbean roots to create the need to examine the exposure that envelops strangers in a strange land.

In fact, a number of the Lesser Antilles' preeminent writers have spent much of their lives outside the region. These include living writers Derek Walcott, V.S. Naipaul and Jamaica Kincaid, as well as Jean Rhys.

Modern Caribbean literature invokes aspects of West Indian life. Patois and other lilting languages, as well as the music, food, family life, religion and race, are all strong components of Caribbean writing. Some of the best examples of West Indian fiction are, in fact, better resources than nonfiction textbook analyses for understanding life in the Lesser Antilles.

The French-speaking West Indies, including Haiti, produced writers who early on embraced the recognition of African and Caribbean cultural heritage in their work. Their literary movement was called Négritude, a term attributed to the Martiniquan poet, playwright and politician Aimé Césaire. Négritude called for the recognition and advancement of black cultural values and black heritage worldwide—black humanism—and further rejected the French colonial influences. The movement, in both its literary and political forms, became a strong force in Africa, where it inspired a generation of leaders to call for independence from France. Among them was the Senegalese leader and poet Leopold Senghor.

Césaire, who was born in 1913, studied in Paris, where Négritude was born among the black expatriates of the 1930s. His works often incorporate a surrealistic style and include the epic poem *Cahier d'un retour au pays natal* (Return to My Native Land; 1939). Césaire once served as the mayor of Fort-de-France and is considered an influential political philosopher.

Nationalism and the voice of black culture came somewhat later, during the 1930s and 1940s, to the English-speaking Caribbean. With several notable exceptions, much English literature originates from the islands of Barbados, Trinidad and Jamaica, presumably because of their larger populations, excellent universities and literary traditions.

Novelist George Lamming, born in Barbados in 1927, has been an expatriate university lecturer and writer for much of his life. His work often explores the dilemmas of race and culture confronting Caribbean peoples living overseas. Lamming's works include a critically acclaimed first novel, In the Castle of My Skin (1953), and Season of Adventure (1960).

Frank Collymore (1893–1980), a Barbadian poet and short story writer, was influential in the Caribbean literary scene during the heyday of 1930s nationalism. Aside from several volumes of poetry, including Beneath the Casuarinas (1945) and Flotsam (1948), and a recent posthumous collection of short stories called *The Man Who Loved Attending Funerals and Other Stories* (1993), his major legacy to West Indian writing is the literary magazine Bim, which he established in 1942 and edited for most of his life. Over its long life (Bim is still published) the magazine has printed and promoted the work of nearly every major West Indian literary talent.

Barbadian Edward Brathwaite, born in 1930, is known for poetry that incorporates West Indian rhythms and prose. His works include *Rights of Passage* (1967), *Islands* (1969) and *Sun Poem* (1982). A noted historian and professor at the University of the West Indies, Brathwaite has written extensively on the history of Africans in Jamaica.

The novelist Jean Rhys (1894-1979) is considered by some to be less Caribbean than European influenced, yet she was born in Dominica and used a Caribbean setting for one of her most famous works, *The Wide Sargasso Sea* (1966). The novel utilizes an interesting conceit, being a fictionalized account of the Jamaican youth of the madwoman, Mrs. Rochester, from Charlotte Bronte's Jane Eyre. The novel also deals with post-emancipation West Indian life and the dwindling years of the colonial period. Other works by Rhys, particularly several short stories, use intricate West Indian speech rhythms.

A perhaps lesser known Dominican writer was a contemporary of Jean Rhys. Phyllis Shand Allfrey (1907-86) left Dominica for education in the U.S. and England when she was a teenager. She returned in the early Fifties, having established a reputation as a writer and politician in England. In Dominica she edited several newspapers and was a founding member of the radical Dominica Labor Party. On Dominica she wrote her one and only novel *The Orchid House* (1953), a loosely autobiographical story of the decline of colonialism, as seen through the lives of three Dominican sisters over a twenty-year span. The novel is noted for its rich descriptions of the island's tropical setting and its faculty in linking the passions of the sisters with the mystical forces of the island. The novel was made into a film in 1990.

Trinidad's writers have flourished under a long tradition of literature and publishing that includes a fairly rigorous free press. The multicultural setting of Trinidad is unique, with its large numbers of East Indians, Africans, and Asians— a situation Trinidadian writers have found ripe with drama and passion.

V(idiadhar) S(urajprasad) Naipaul, born in Trinidad in 1932 and now living in the U.K., is possibly the most celebrated regional writer, although he is often critiqued as British rather than Caribbean. His later work, much of it non-fiction and travel writing, takes him far from the Caribbean, particularly to the India of his heritage, as in 1991's India: A Million Mutinies Now. Yet his early works often draw from his West Indian roots, reflecting Caribbean themes and sensibilities and a sharp wit. Among them: *The Mystic Masseur* (1957) and *A House for Mr. Biswas* (1961), which deals with the breakdown of a West Indian family and its culture in the face of insipid colonial values and life.

Naipaul's younger brother, Shiva Naipaul (1945–85), was a well-regarded novelist and journalist until he died unexpectedly of a heart attack. He also emigrated to the U.K. and published the novels *Fireflies* (1970) and *The Chip-Chip Gatherers* (1973), both set in Trinidad. Shiva Naipaul also wrote a celebrated account of the 1978 mass suicide in Guyana.

Trinidadian Samuel Selvon (1923–94) wrote more than a half-dozen novels and collections of short stories that deal with Trinidadian life and the East Indian experience there, as well as works that explore the lives of Caribbean expatriates in Britain. Among his works, the novels *A Brighter Sun* (1952) and *An Island is a World* (1955) are set in the Caribbean.

Jamaica Kincaid was born in Antigua in 1949. She emigrated to the U.S. in 1966 and eventually became a novelist, short story writer and staff writer for The *New Yorker*. Her writing is deeply evocative of Caribbean life, focusing on the bonds between mothers and daughters. Kincaid has published several works, including the story collection *At the Bottom of the River* (1983) and the novel *Annie John* (1985). The autobiographical *Lucy* was released in 1990.

Two writers of West Indian origin have become Nobel Laureates in literature. The 1992 winner, Derek Walcott, deservedly ranks among the illustrious writers of this century. Walcott, who was born in St Lucia, is recognized for his passionate affection for and delivery of the English language. The 1990 epic *Omeros* mixes Homeric legend with West Indian themes. The collections *Selected Poems 1964* and *Selected Poems 1977* are good introductions to his greater body of work. Walcott is also a prolific playwright; in 1959 he established the Trinidad Theater Workshop in Port of Spain. In Boston, where he currently lives and teaches, Walcott has founded the Boston Playwrights' Theater. And on his native St Lucia he has created an international writer's retreat called the Rat Island Foundation.

Guadeloupe-born poet/diplomat Alexis Saint-Leger Leger (1887-1975), who wrote under the pen name Saint-John Perse, won the Nobel in 1960. Perse spent much of his life in the French diplomatic service, but was forced to flee to the U.S. during World War II after voicing opposition to the policies of the Vichy government. He remained in exile until 1959. Although not widely translated, Perse's work is well-known in European literary circles. Among his works: *Anabase* (1924) and *Song for an Equinox* (1971).

Several island-based literary magazines continue to publish work by contemporary Caribbean writers. Among them is the aforementioned Bim, taken from Bimshire, a nickname for Barbados. The Caribbean Writer, published by the University of the Virgin Islands, has featured the work of Derek Walcott, and poets Marvin Williams and Paul Keens-Douglas, among others.

Slaves being forced to dance to keep healthy on their long voyage to the West Indies, (early 19th Century)

The Lesser Antilles: The Place

The Land

The formation of the Lesser Antilles, of the entire Caribbean, involves plate tectonics. Plates, the large, solid land slabs that compose the earth's crust, are estimated at a dozen to twenty worldwide and are affected by the roiling inner masses and pressures exerted at the earth's core. The 50-to-100-mile thick plates are in a constant state of flux, moving as much as several inches per year and have been doing so since the formation of the earth. Some correspond to continents and land masses, others to the floors of the great oceans. Plates do not move in a visible way; rather their changes are slow but constant, through entire geological periods. And when they move, they move against each other, bumping and grinding in the equivalent of a million-year slow dance.

This relentless pressure causes changes in the earth's surface, particularly along boundaries, the weakest links of moving plates. One such plate roughly corresponds to the area we know as the Caribbean Sea, with its eastern boundary along the Lesser Antilles chain. Throughout this boundary area, earthquakes and volcanoes are not uncommon.

About 70 to 50 million years ago a series of violent underwater volcanic eruptions thrust mountains from the floor of the sea, many of which broke the surface of the ocean. The peaks of these mountain chains became the islands in the Caribbean.

In geological terms, the easternmost islands of the Lesser Antilles are slightly older, having been thrust out of the ocean as part of a series of eruptions that also created the Greater Antilles and Andes mountain range of South America. Gradually, these eruptions subsided and, over the course of several million years, marine and other life forms developed, eventually leaving layers of limestone and sediment on the islands. By the time a second series of eruptions formed the inner arc of the Lesser Antilles, another several million years later, the first islands had become flattened, dead volcanoes. Today, in the inner-arc group of "younger" islands, active or semi-active volcanoes are still in evidence.

The result of all this underwater erupting and mountain-building activity yielded a mixed bag of Lesser Antilles, composed of rocky volcanic islands, limestone-based islands and smaller offshore cays.

By far the majority of the Lesser Antilles belongs to the volcanic group. These islands, roughly from the British and U.S. Virgins in the north to Grenada in the south, are characterized by jagged, dramatic rises, deep valleys and the remains of current or past volcanic activity, including volcanic vents, black-sand beaches, and primordial, steaming sulfur springs. Some volcanoes are active—the 1902 eruption of Mt. Pelee on Martinique destroyed the then-capital of Saint-Pierre, killing nearly 30,000 people. The 1977 eruption of Soufrière (from the French soufre, for sulfur) on St. Vincent forced the evacuation of part of the island. In Montserrat one can hike into the active volcanic crater of Galway's Soufriere.

The "older" islands on the outer arc of the Lesser Antilles, notably Anguilla, Antigua and Barbuda, parts of Guadeloupe and Barbados are relatively flat compared to their volcanic sisters and composed primarily of limestone. Trinidad and Tobago are geologically and climatically similar to the northeast coast of Venezuela—their mountains and the coast of Trinidad are thought to be an extension of the Andes.

Climate

The average temperature throughout the Lesser Antilles is about 78° F (26° C).

Though the islands are subject to some seasonal changes, all lie below the Tropic of Cancer, where their proximity to the equator limits seasonal temperature changes to less than 10° F (6° C). Additionally, the powerful Caribbean Current, which enters the Caribbean Sea at its southeastern extremity and flows northwest, helps to keep the islands surrounded by warm water year-round. The widest variations in temperature occur with elevation, dropping by about 1° F (0.6° C) for every 300 feet (98 metres) of ascent. Temperatures also drop by an average of 10° F (6° C) at night.

The Lesser Antilles are humid, although you may not always feel the humidity. Breezes keep the air moving, creating the famed balmy atmosphere of the tropics. Nevertheless, daily humidity ranges 65 to 85 per cent; it almost never drops below 50 per cent and sometimes reaches as high as 90 per cent.

Despite the locative monikers Windward and Leeward Islands, each island itself has a windward and leeward side. Windward is the side facing the prevailing northeasterlies, generally the eastern or northeast Atlantic Ocean side of the island. Leeward is the side opposite the prevailing winds—the Caribbean Sea side. Rainfall is heaviest on the windward side and moderate on the leeward, or rainshadow, side.

Average rainfall varies from island to island and from windward side to leeward side on each island. The Windward Islands—from Dominica south to Trinidad—are perhaps the wettest, with averages of 40 to 65 inches (1,016-1,651 millimetres) each year and up to 200 inches (5,000 millimetres) recorded in the mountains.

Rainfall is most common during the North American summer, roughly from May to October; the drier season lasts from February to April.

Hurricanes greatly affect the Lesser Antilles. Hurricane Gilbert, estimated to be the strongest hurricane to hit the western hemisphere in the 20th century, whipped through the Caribbean, devastating Jamaica in particular, with winds gusting up to 200 mph (320 kph). 1989's Hugo laid waste to the Leeward Islands and the east coast of the U.S., while 1995 saw Marilyn pummel the U.S. Virgin Islands. The Caribbean hurricane season lasts July through October, though June and November have been visited in the past.

Flora and Fauna

The face of the Lesser Antilles has changed a great deal since the days of pre-Columbian settlement. Since the arrival of Spanish colonials in the 15th century, forays into wide-scale agriculture, foresting, industry and tourism have altered the landscape—reducing large rainforests, partially replenishing others, and introducing new, in cases life-sustaining, plant and animal species. There are few places on any island in the Lesser Antilles that have not been touched by the hand of man.

Generalizations about the flora and fauna of the Lesser Antilles are not easy to make. The area stretches some 900 miles (1,450 km), from the eastern coast of Puerto Rico to the Venezuelan coast. Since many of the islands are separated by great bodies of ocean, each has had ample opportunity to evolve its own unique ecosystem and wallow in it for millennia. As such, endemic plant and animal species exist on certain islands. This is particularly true of the larger islands, such as Guadeloupe, Dominica, Martinique, St. Lucia and Trinidad, and less true of the smaller islands, such as British Virgin Islands or the Grenadines.

PLANT LIFE

On the coasts one is most likely to find sparse woodlands, marshes and mangrove swamps. Mangroves are the trees that give that "jungle" look to movies and travel videos shot in the tropics. Several species of mangrove have the ability to drop vertical roots from the branches of the main tree into the mucky swamp, giving it the appearance of bars on a jail cell.

Drier environments, such as on the leeward sides of several islands and large parts of the outer "flatter" islands, support sparse forests, thorny scrub bushes (such as acacia) and several cactus species.

Rainforests are characterized by towering *ceiba* (cotton), *lignum vitae* and other hardy trees. At elevations of 1,000 feet (305 m) or so, trees are covered with tree ferns, bromeliads, wild orchids, vines and a variety of epiphytes. This wet and warm environment is self-sustaining and seasonless.

Much of the region's flora has been introduced over the years by various settlers and conquerors. The first direct imports were maize, cassava, sweet potato, cocoa and tobacco, introduced by Amerindian Arawaks. The Spanish brought with them several crops that would become the basis for island economies: the banana, sugarcane (originally from the Far East) and pineapple. The islands of St. Kitts, Guadeloupe, Dominica, Martinique, St. Lucia, St. Vincent and Grenada are still reliant on these crops for much of their export income. Bananas and sugarcane, in particular, are found throughout the archipelago, covering the islands' coastal areas with a lush cloth of familiarity.

The Spanish were also responsible for the introduction of ginger, turmeric, tamarind, oranges, limes and lemons. East Indian laborers brought marijuana, or "ganja," and the British and others contributed flowering plants, garden vegetables and the ubiquitous breadfruit tree, brought originally to Jamaica and St. Vincent in 1793 by Captain William Bligh.

Bligh's first excursion to India and the South Pacific to retrieve the plant, where it is indigenous, was a notorious failure. During the 1789 voyage his crew mutinied, under the leadership of master's mate Fletcher Christian, reportedly in part because they were denied the very water that was used to nourish the breadfruit seedlings. They captured Bligh's ship, the HMS *Bounty,* and cast Bligh and 18 others adrift in a longboat. Bligh survived and went on to successfully transport breadfruit to the West Indies.

Thousands of flowering plants grow throughout the Lesser Antilles, each known by dozens of different local names. They include several hundred species of orchids, as well as angel's trumpet, monkey tail, bird of paradise, ginger, hyacinth and lobster claw. Bougainvillea, the ostentatious flowering vine of the tropics, blooms everywhere. Its delicate white, rich purple and orange flowers snake along trees, fences and other bushes. Added to the scenery are the multicolored hibiscus, frangipani allamanda and oleander bushes.

Common trees include the famous poinciana, named after an 18th century governor of the French Antilles. Its flower is bright red, hence its other popular name, the flamboyant. Also found are the tropical almond tree, soursop and sweetsop trees (the pulpy, edible fruits are not sour and sweet, but sweet and sweeter) and the huge banyan tree. Banyans are easily recognized by their roots, which drop from horizontal branches to take root at the base of the tree, giving them the appearance of dreadlocked evergreens. Calabash trees bear a large round fruit which, when ripe, can be hollowed out to make containers. The mahogany tree, native to the West Indies, produces a dark, hard wood. The papaya tree, sometimes called pawpaw, bears a soft fruit rich in vitamin C.

Mango trees yield a sweet fruit, a Caribbean favourite, from March to October. Date palms, queen palms, royal palms and, of course, coconut palms, are found throughout the region. The coconut palm is the most useful. The coconut itself produces food and drink and oil for cosmetics. The fronds have long been used to weave mats, hats and even walls for huts.

MAMMALS

Most mammal life in the Lesser Antilles is not indigenous but introduced. Early European settlers brought to the West Indies an assortment of domestic animals, including dogs, cattle, sheep, goats, horses, donkeys, fowl and pigs. In some areas pigs escaped and are now found wild in uplands and rainforests. Rats found their way to the islands, perhaps as stowaways on ships. Vervet monkeys, probably introduced from West Africa, are found on St. Kitts, Barbados and Grenada.

The mongoose, a ferret-like animal introduced by sugarcane farmers in the 18th century to help control the destructive cane rat, became notorious soon after its arrival. The prolific rodent turned to hunting chickens, fish, crab, insects and other harmless island creatures and is still the bane of small farmers.

The agouti and the opossum (also called manicou) are harmless rodents that feed on fruits and roots and are found in the forests of larger islands such as Guadeloupe, Dominica, Martinique and St. Lucia. The agouti, in looks similar to a guinea pig's bad date, was once hunted for its meat and its numbers have been reduced over the last century. A species of raccoon is found in Guadeloupe and Trinidad, again following patterns similar to South America, hosts red howler monkeys, sloths and armadillos.

Of indigenous mammals, bats are the most widespread. More than a dozen species inhabit the islands' caves and the cool shade of mangrove swamps, feeding on fruit, fish and insects.

BIRDS

Ornithologists are likely aware that the Lesser Antilles host a staggering number of bird species. Casual bird watchers will soon become aware of a small portion of the thousands of local species, from the large and multicolored parrots to the lanky pink flamingos and nattering gulls that make their homes in the rainforests, flatlands and shorelines of the islands. A difficulty in identifying birds lies with the custom of using different names for them throughout the islands, but local guidebooks will help identify the more popular species by local and scientific names.

Several islands are host to endemic species, some of which have become rare due to rainforest reduction and the international trade in exotic pets. Perhaps no other birds symbolize the tropics as succinctly as parrots and parrots are the ones that have suffered the most in international trade. St. Lucia and St. Vincent host several species, such as the richly hued St. Vincent parrot. The sisserou, or imperial parrot, Dominica's national bird, has seen its numbers decline and is now a protected species. The Grenada dove, another endemic species, is protected as well.

Multi-shaded and shimmering hummingbirds of the Lesser Antilles are frequently seen flitting over banana blossoms and other nectar-producing flowers. The tiny bananaquit, yellow-breasted with dark plumage, may be an uninvited guest, feeding at the sugar bowl of your cafe table.

The birds of Trinidad and Tobago are related more to birds of South America than to the common birds of the Lesser Antilles. The soaring flight of the scarlet ibis can be viewed at the Caroni Bird Sanctuary on Trinidad. Rare birds, such as the New Zealand shelduck and the marble teal, are also found on the island.

Seagoing boobies, or terns, recognized by their forked tails, live the better part of the year at sea and return to land or small outlying cays to lay eggs. An important breeding ground is Little Tobago Island, off the coast of Tobago, which also hosts the Audubon's shearwater and the sooty tern.

Other Antillean birds include the snowy and cattle egrets. Herons frequent swampy areas throughout the islands. Starlings and house sparrows are plentiful. As well, the islands are stopover points for migratory birds, the proverbial North American birds that go south for the winter. They include thrushes, warblers and orioles.

AMPHIBIANS AND REPTILES

The snakes, lizards and frogs of the Lesser Antilles figure into a plethora of local folktales, legends and recipes. The famous "mountain chicken" (crapaud) of Dominica and Montserrat is a large forest frog with tasty legs. Crapaud legs are the national dish of Dominica.

Other frogs inhabit the forests. Several varieties of toads have been introduced to the islands to control insects and cane rats.

The iguana (some theorize that the word may have Arawak origins) is a large, seemingly prehistoric lizard indigenous to the Caribbean. Iguanas, which can grow to lengths of five feet or more, are considered a delicacy by some and have been hunted for centuries. Many have fallen victim to the miscreant mongoose and their numbers have been greatly reduced.

Other lizards, like the gecko, are much more abundant. Geckos live around houses and feed on insects. You'll recognize them by their bobbing heads as they run down window screens or across walls, heading for electric lights and moths or other insects. Geckos are harmless, so don't hurt them. In fact, they're helpful—they eat mosquitoes.

Most snakes of the Lesser Antilles are harmless. One of the largest is the boa constrictor, which can be dangerous to small animals but will flee from humans. The venomous fer de lance is found on Martinique, St. Lucia and Trinidad.

Several species of sea turtle are common to the Lesser Antilles. Some grow to lengths of more than five feet and weigh as much as 1,500 pounds (nearly 700 kilograms). The females use isolated beaches to lay as many as 125 eggs from March to August. Though protected, it is on the beach where they are vulnerable to hunters and poachers. The most common sea turtle is the green turtle, which is actually brown. Other indigenous species are the leatherback, the loggerhead, the olive ridley and the hawksbill.

INSECTS

The Lesser Antilles has a lively array of insects, some of which consider you to be one big meal. Mosquitoes, blackflies and sand fleas make sleeping nets and repellent a necessity when hiking or spending time outdoors.

The Lesser Antilles' most notable insects are its butterflies, nearly 300 recorded species. The large orange and black monarch butterfly is found throughout the region. The hercules beetle, which lives in the rainforests of Dominica and other islands, sports an odd claw at the top of its head. One of the world's largest beetles, it grows to a length of five inches (13 centimetres).

MARINE LIFE

Ocean life originates in and around coral reefs with the smaller, microscopic inhabitants that rank low on the food chain. Coral reefs are actually colonies of living creatures called polyps that exist with the corallite or skeletal remains of past polyps, creating a life and death cycle that uses past skeletal remains as building blocks. When snorkelling or diving a reef, the brilliant colors you see on coral are provided by zooxanthellae, tiny plant cells that live within the coral structure itself. The polyps also provide color, but their skeletons are usually white. (The topsoil of some coral atolls is formed, in part, from broken corallite remains.) The organism itself is generally hollow and tubular, with an anterior mouth surrounded by tentacles for gathering tiny food particles. Polyps range in size from microscopic to several inches across. The coral polyp life-form has been in existence for over 100 million years.

The abundance of life in a coral reef is astonishing, if not always evident, and includes algae, various forms of sea sponge and sea fans. Small and exotic fish, shrimp and the spiny lobster make their homes in and among certain coral limbs, taking advantage of the rich fare that passes their way.

Coral grows in warm, clear salt water, generally no deeper than 100 feet (30 m) below the surface, its growth aided by the sun. Reef in the Lesser Antilles is often within sight of shore or a few minutes by boat from shore.

Some coral formations brush the water's surface at low tide. Coral is easily threatened by changes in ocean current and weather, particularly hurricanes, and by careless divers. Today the biggest threat to coral reefs is from fishermen and divers (both locals and tourists).

Staghorn and elkhorn corals, so named for their resemblance to the antlers of those animals, are found in local waters.

Cathedral (also called majestic) coral generally thrives in isolated colonies, away from the main reef. Finger corals and brain coral are common.

Soft corals (those with flexible skeletal remains) mesmerize as they wave back and forth with the ocean's undulation. Gorgonian coral, named after the snake-haired sisters in Greek mythology, includes sea whips and sea feathers. Gorgonian coral is among the prettiest, commonly in shades of green, purple and orange.

Black coral is also abundant and, in its natural state, quite striking. Black coral, as well as white coral, is protected by law on most islands and its sale is illegal.

FISH AND OTHER OCEAN DWELLERS

The fish along the reefs of the Lesser Antilles are plentiful and every bit as colorful as their host coral and sponge colonies. About 700 or so species are associated with the coral reef and while you may not see every one, it'll seem like you have.

Many types of groupers, snappers and the red squirrel fish (all good eating) feed on the reef. Flounders, including the common peacock flounder, are plentiful. The multicolored parrot fishes, tiny butterfly fish, hamlets and wrasses fill in the spectrum. Angelfish are among the more recognizable reef fish. In addition, a variety of nocturnal fish, including the cardinal fish, ply the waters.

Game and larger fish found in deeper waters include the blue marlin, a favourite of deep-sea fishermen for its fighting prowess and its value as a food source. Look to the British and U.S. Virgin Islands, Saint-Martin/Sint Maarten, Barbados and Trinidad and Tobago for well-organized deep-sea fishing charters.

Other large fish, many protected by fishing regulations, include the white marlin, wahoo, tuna, barracuda and the blunt-nosed dolphin fish (not the mammal). Bonito and kingfish also run in the deep waters.

Eels, rays and the aforementioned turtles are also common among Antillean ocean fauna. The most common eel is the spotted moray, a creature that seems to be all mouth and teeth. They are generally harmless and tend to feed at night. Still, it's best to stay an arm's length away. Morays should not be eaten—they're known to carry toxins that cause food poisoning. The snake eel resembles a snake and may be handled—but gently. Giant manta rays, also known as devilfish, have been known to give divers a hitch. Mantas are slow-motion ocean fish, their pectoral fins propelling them with elegant, wavy swells.

Sharks are not common in Antillean waters, but occasionally a nurse shark, as long as 14 feet (four metres), can be observed lying motionless on the ocean floor. They are not aggressive but they are, after all, sharks. If agitated or cornered they will strike. A word to the wise: do not corner nurse sharks.

Other reef dwellers are a variety of starfish, sea worms, snails and shellfish. The conch (rhymes with "honk") is prized for its meat and shell, available by the hundreds at roadside stands throughout the islands. Avoid the porcupine-like sea urchins, especially the black, long-spined urchin. The strong barbs will pierce the skin and break off, resulting in painful swelling. Remove the fragments as soon as possible, soak the affected area in vinegar or a strong ammonia solution (urine will do at a pinch) and treat with antiseptic as soon as possible. Then see a doctor. Urchin meat is a table delicacy for some.

Likewise avoid the green or orange bristle worm, found on coral and rocks, which can also make for a very bad day when its brittle, white whiskers are touched. They detach and become imbedded in the skin. Again, vinegar and medical treatment should follow.

The red fire sponge is also nice to look at, but causes swelling and discomfort if touched. Try to stay clear of all forms of jellyfish, which are not fish at all, but primordial globs of membrane and primitive intelligence. Their tentacles contain small, stinging organisms that detach if brushed. Splash the affected area with alcohol, but avoid rubbing it or you may activate detached stingers. Talcum powder and other drying agents, such as sand, are useful for jellyfish encounters.

Accommodation and Seasons

The busy tourist season in the Lesser Antilles lasts from mid-December through March to mid-April, or roughly the Northern Hemisphere's winter. The summer is off-season and, as such, priced accordingly. You can count on room rates being less expensive then, as much as a 40 per cent reduction. In addition, you'll have the added luxury of travelling in uncrowded areas. Some hotels retain the same rate all year, while others have three or more different rates, depending on the season. During the summer many hotels are short of guests and substantial rate reductions can often be negotiated, no matter what your length of stay. This is particularly true of smaller hotels.

Local government taxes may be added to hotel and restaurant bills. Check to see if the tax is included in the rate or will be added later. This tax, variable throughout the islands, ranges from five to ten per cent.

An additional charge you might see on a hotel bill is a ten to 15 per cent service charge, which is meant to be a tip for services rendered at the hotel. Ostensibly this tip is divided among the hotel staff, but if you feel like giving your chambermaid or porter something more, feel free to do so.

Most hotels and restaurants in the Lesser Antilles will accept all major North American and European credit cards. American Express, Diner's Club, MasterCard and Visa are the most common; Discover Card is gaining acceptance. Smaller hotels will accept traveler's checks, but cash is definitely the norm for most small guesthouses.

The categories used for accommodation throughout this book are based on a per person, per night rack rate during the 15 December-15 April high season: luxury US$100 or more, moderate US$50-100, budget $50 or less.

VILLA RENTALS

Villa rentals are a good bet for families or groups because of the autonomy they afford. You can cook, eat, see the sights and sleep at your leisure. Most come with cooks and household help, which gives you the chance to relax a bit and let someone else do the work. For a large family, or for two families, villas can be cost-effective. The accommodation vary widely, from apartments to quasi-mansions. Rates, which are based on size, amenities offered and location, range from US$900 per week to as much as US$12,000 in the high season.

Hundreds of companies and private individuals market their villas through publications such as *Caribbean Travel and Life, Islands, Travel and Leisure* and the U.K.-based *Caribbean World*, as well as other magazines. Major newspapers (in

their Sunday travel sections) list dozens of Caribbean villa rental possibilities.
Here are some rental companies with large inventories:

❑ Villas and Apartments Abroad, 420 Madison Ave., Suite 1105,
New York, NY 10017; 212-759-1025.
❑ Villas Caribe, 800-645-7498, fax 303-741-2520.
❑ Villas of Distinction, P.O. Box 55, Armonk, New York, NY 10504;
800-289-0900 or 914-273-3331, fax 914-273-3387.
❑ Villas International, 605 Market St., Suite 510, San Francisco,
CA 94105; 800-221-2260 or 415-281-0910.
❑ West Indies Management Company (WIMCO), P.O. Box 1461, Newport,
RI 02840; 800-932-3222 or 401-849-8012, fax 401-847-6290;
U.K. 800-89-8318.

Food and Drink

There is an old saying among hoteliers in the Lesser Antilles: "Your stay in the
Caribbean is only as good as your last meal."

Such is the power of food. Your stay in the Lesser Antilles will certainly be
enhanced by trying the local cuisine, a combination of imported recipes and
ingredients coupled with West Indian spices, fruits, vegetables, exotic meats,
seafood... and sensibilities. The end result is one of the most tangible cultural
exports from the Caribbean—one can find West Indian restaurants and food items
in many of the major cities of the world.

West Indian cuisine involves a variety of imports and native crops. Bananas
and plantains, carried over by the Spaniards from the Canary Islands, are today
both dietary staples and export crops. Sugar and pineapple were also introduced
by the Spanish and are part of island folklore and diet (sugar is the main ingredi-
ent of rum). African slaves brought, literally, the seeds of future vegetable and
fruit crops. Okra, several types of yams, the ackee of Jamaica and pigeon peas are
African imports. Pigeon peas (also called red peas and gungo peas) play a enormous part in the West Indian diet. When combined with rice, the dish is both a
staple and side dish in most homes and creole restaurants, called rice and beans
or rice and peas.

Meat dishes, such as goat stew, goat water, mutton (goat or sheep) stew, pork,
the famous curries of Trinidad and the exotic crapaud, or frogs' legs, of Dominica,
are island favourites. Pepperpot stew, which is claimed by several islands, may

originally have been an Arawak dish. A meat stock is combined with added spices, vegetables and callaloo, the leafy stalk of the eddoe (or dasheen) plant. Eddoe—the word and plant are native to West Africa—is a starchy tuber that grows throughout the Lesser Antilles.

Seafood dishes are specialties of the islands. Large game fish, such as mahi mahi, marlin and tuna, are common, as are the smaller yet no less tasty grouper and red snapper. Flying fish is considered a delicacy on Barbados. On the French islands expect rich sauces and delicate grilling. Coconut cream, called "run-down" or variations on the phrase, is a favourite sauce on fish. Other sea animals find themselves on West Indian plates no less frequently. Conch is grilled, deep fried to make fritters or steeped in chowder. Boiled crabs, stuffed crabs and even sea urchins, which yield a rich meat, are favourite West Indian snacks. Lobster (the clawless variety), as well as shrimp and crayfish (freshwater shrimp), may be served simply grilled with butter and garlic.

Spices perhaps distinguish West Indian cuisine more than anything else. Red pepper, hot sauces and curries are frequently featured either in the recipe or on the table along with the salt and pepper—just a little something to remind you that you've got a tongue. Ginger and pimento (called allspice elsewhere) are common seasonings. Nutmeg is often used; Grenada grows 40 per cent of the world's crop.

Various international cuisines also exist throughout the Lesser Antilles. Chinese, East Indian, Italian and even Vietnamese cooking is popular on several of the larger islands. Pizza is universal. On several islands local fast food restaurants serve fried chicken, hamburgers and meat patties. Several American fast-food chains have found their way to the Lesser Antilles and are popular with locals. Among them are Kentucky Fried Chicken, Pizza Hut and Burger King.

Caribbean drinks are a treat—and a surprise. The native mauby (rhymes with "Toby"), made from tree bark, tastes a bit like sarsaparilla. Said to be healthful for pregnant women and tired men, mauby may be an acquired taste. Much the same can be said about sea moss (also called Irish moss), a drink made from gelatin extracted from seaweed, which is then sweetened and combined with milk or ginger. Sea moss is used as a restorative tonic, particularly in matters of sexual potency. Coconut water, the clear, potassium-rich liquid from the center of a green nut, is found on virtually every corner and in every market throughout the islands. Coconuts are inexpensive, germ-free and can be fun to drink. Coconut water is not to be confused with coconut cream or coconut milk, which is derived from the meat of the nut.

Dozens of small soft-drink producers exist throughout the islands and the drinks range from the thick ginger beers of Trinidad to the ubiquitous Ting, a grapefruit-based carbonated sweet drink produced on several islands.

All sorts of alcoholic drinks are available in the resorts and pubs of the Lesser Antilles, many of them oddly colored with tiny umbrellas that poke your nose. But only two are universally available: beer and rum. Several of the islands produce their own beer, some of it quite good. Hairoun Lager of St. Vincent stands out, as does the Carib brand, which is brewed on several islands. Banks is an excellent beer produced on Barbados. Red Stripe is brewed in Jamaica, but has found its place in the Lesser Antilles; so have several other foreign brands, such as Heineken and Miller.

Rum, however, is the beverage of the islands. Made from sugarcane, the drink originated in Barbados and was first called rumbullion, presumably for the escapades it induced. Today's rums can be dark, amber, white (overproof and extremely strong) and spiced. Every major island in the Lesser Antilles hosts one or more rum distilleries.

In the destinations of this book, restaurant prices will described using the following categories, per person, per entree: expensive US$25 or more, moderate US$10-25, inexpensive US$10 or less.

Health and Personal Safety

In the Lesser Antilles the problems most visitors encounter are overexposure to sun, rum and spicy foods, all preventable by common sense. It's always wise to increase your intake of nonalcoholic fluids in a tropical environment— you'll lose quite a bit through sweat. Doctors recommend at least eight large glasses (about eight pints) of water per day.

SKIN CARE

It's hot, the water is inviting and you'd like to get out of doors as soon as possible. But remember, the tropical sun is extremely strong, even when the sky is overcast. If you've got sensitive skin, a wide-brimmed hat and strong sunscreen are musts. Sunscreen is universally available; however, it is not always the best brand and prices may be more than you'd pay at home. It's best to bring your own brand and to go easy on the tanning process for the first few days. Aloe vera is good for a sunburn, but it doesn't replace the best preventative: shade. If you are light-skinned and snorkelling for any length of time, you might want to wear a T-shirt to guard against overexposing your back.

Mosquitoes carry the protozoan infections malaria and dengue fever. While malaria is problematic in areas of Haiti, the Dominican Republic and parts of Venezuela, it has not been reported as frequently occurring in the Lesser Antilles since the 1960s. Dengue fever (symptoms: fever, joint and muscle pains, severe headaches) has been reported in all the Lesser Antilles islands, but is more prevalent in the Greater Antilles. The only prevention for dengue fever is to avoid mosquitoes. In mosquito-dense areas use a good repellent and wear clothes that cover your arms and legs. Mosquito nets and screened bedrooms will provide protection. If the smoke doesn't bother you, mosquito coils are helpful.

ISLAND WATER
Drinking water is generally safe throughout the Lesser Antilles and most is filtered and/or chlorinated. After hurricanes, floods and other high-water situations, however, contaminants may mix with the drinking water supply. Infectious hepatitis, called jaundice or hepatitis A, can be carried by contaminated water. If you are in a situation where you are unsure, drink bottled water, which is available in most situations, or coconut water, which is naturally sterilized. Washing or peeling fruit and paying strict attention to personal hygiene will reduce the likelihood of contracting hepatitis. A commonly available inoculation, gamma globulin, has a good rate of effectiveness against hepatitis A. Doctors can prescribe it and it should be administered as close as possible to your departure date.

VACCINATIONS, PRESCRIPTION DRUGS AND INSURANCE
Smallpox and yellow fever vaccinations are no longer required of North Americans and Europeans when travelling to the Lesser Antilles. Travelers originating from other Caribbean countries and from other parts of the world should check regulations before departure.

Don't count on prescription drugs being readily available—bring enough to last your trip. An extra pair of prescription glasses or contacts is advisable.

Check your health insurance to see if you're covered overseas and what the coverage entails. If you want to purchase more, the following companies offer treatment and evacuation coverage, as well as hard-to-find protection for scuba-diving injuries. Payment is determined by the length of travel time and by the amount of coverage you need, which may include medical, evacuation, accident, loss of life and even trip cancellation coverage. In the U.S., try American Express Travel Protection Plan, P.O. Box 919010, San Diego, CA 92191-9010, tel: 800–234–0375; or Access America International, 600 Third Ave., New York, NY 10163, 800–284–8300.

PERSONAL SAFETY

Women who travel alone are taking the chance, not unlike in many other parts of the world, of incurring verbal harassment. Staring, whistling and getting approached are not uncommon—remember, tourists often represent people out for a good time. That may not apply to you, but it is true for some people and you'll have to put up with the behavioral flotsam left in their wake. Women travelling in groups or with a companion are better able to avoid it.

The people of the Lesser Antilles are more conservative than not, but the proximity of tourist activity lends a looseness to the social atmosphere that may be misinterpreted. Beachwear, for instance, is just that and wearing bathing suits or revealing clothing in other public places may send the wrong signals. Avoid walking along deserted beach stretches at night, or getting into unmarked cars declaring themselves to be taxis. Areas in and around large towns may be dangerous, particularly at night, for locals as well as for visitors. If you are unsure, ask the hotel staff or a taxi driver whom you trust.

Be street smart as you would in any major city worldwide. Lock your rental car. Carry your wallet or purse in a pouch or front pocket. Avoid basket-type or open handbags; they're easy targets for pickpockets. Pulling out large wads of cash to buy things sends a signal as bright as a lighthouse beacon. Don't leave bags unattended at the beach.

DRUGS

Parts of the Lesser Antilles have reputations as party centers, with some justification. Marijuana, cocaine, hallucinogens—the usual suspects—are available throughout. They are also illegal. Local authorities are very sensitive to the drug problem and the police are sophisticated in detecting drug use and trafficking. Possession and use are punishable by heavy fines, deportation and jail sentences. The penalties for smuggling are worse and the bottom line is this: you do not want to spend time in jail in the Caribbean.

Essential Information

TIME ZONES

The Lesser Antilles lie in the Atlantic Standard Time zone, which is four hours behind Greenwich Mean Time (e.g., 16.00 in London is 12.00 in Barbados). The Atlantic Standard Time zone is directly east of the US Eastern Standard Time zone and does not make seasonal adjustments; this makes it one hour ahead of Eastern

Standard Time during the winter months and the same as daylight savings time during the spring and summer months. (In the U.S. daylight savings time begins at 2.00 on the first Sunday of April and ends at 2.00 on the last Sunday of October). For example, if it's 12.00 in New York on Christmas Day, then it's 13.00 in Antigua. But when it's 12.00 in New York on a hot day in July, it's also 12.00 in Antigua. The Greater Antilles islands, from the Dominican Republic to the west, operate on a combination of Eastern Standard and daylight savings time.

ELECTRICITY

One wonders who dreamed up the confusing business of 110-120 volts alternating current (AC), which powers most North American households and appliances, and the 220-240 volts direct current (DC) that is Europe's mainstay. Despite the merits of one system or another, it surely has made international travel a challenge.

In the Lesser Antilles you will be similarly voltage-challenged. A 220-240 volt, 50-60 cycles AC system dominates the region. There are exceptions. Anguilla, Barbados, Saba, St. Eustatius, Trinidad and Tobago, the British and U.S. Virgin Islands use 110-120 volts. Antigua and Barbuda uses 110-120 volt systems in some locations, 220-240 volts in others.

The island of Saint-Martin/Sint Maarten, in keeping with its separate currencies, languages and cultures, is no different where electricity is concerned. The French side operates on 220-240 volts, while the Dutch side uses 110-120.

The rest of the Lesser Antilles (Saint-Barthélémy, St. Kitts and Nevis, Montserrat, Guadeloupe, Dominica, Martinique, St. Lucia, St. Vincent and the Grenadines and Grenada) use the 220-240 volts system, although, again, exceptions can be found.

When booking ahead, check to see if the hotel will have the proper current to run your appliance. These days many travel appliances such as hair dryers, shavers and even computers, have built-in voltage converters. The French islands, as well as certain hotels throughout the islands, use European-style round plugs. Plug and voltage adapters are available at electrical stores in the U.S. and Europe.

Travelling

Getting to the Lesser Antilles is easier than you might think and flying is the fastest way to do it. Many major North American and European airlines operate regular routes (see destination chapters for specifics). Airline routes may change with the seasons and some, Northwest Airlines for example, only operate Caribbean routes during the high season.

Getting around the islands presents some interesting logistical puzzles. It's best to plan well ahead, confirm ongoing flights and have patience. Several of the smaller islands cannot land large aircraft and rely on small, internal airline companies for their transport. Others have no facilities for night landings or erratic ones, so plan your trip around them. Ferries and cargo transports are an option when travelling from island to island, but tend to take more time and are more affected by weather conditions than are aeroplanes.

IMMIGRATION AND CUSTOMS

Island regulations vary, but as a general rule most will proffer a two- or three-month visitor's visa for those with proper identification and proof of an onward ticket. That can be a driver's license with photo, a voter registration card or other proof of citizenship. A notable exception is Trinidad and Tobago, which requires a valid passport from everyone for entry. In general, as a life choice, it's better to travel with a passport than to rely on driver's licenses and other identification. This is particularly true for Americans—when returning home, U.S. customs officials require documentation of your identity and U.S. citizenship. Several countries, among them Barbados and Grenada, have been known to refuse to board Americans who do not have sufficient proof of U.S. citizenship.

In general, advance entry visas are not necessary for citizens of the U.S., Canada, Britain and most European countries. Citizens of other countries, including Australia, New Zealand, India, certain African states and others should inquire well ahead before travelling to the Lesser Antilles.

Customs regulations vary throughout the islands, but as a rule you will be allowed to bring in one carton of cigarettes and one quart of liquor duty-free to most islands.

Upon returning home you will, of course, encounter your own country's customs policies. These are too involved to detail here, but will almost always involve the amount of time you've spent in the Lesser Antilles and what you've purchased there, with special provisions for fruit, animal and other agricultural products you may want to bring home. The first place to go for information is a reputable travel agent. In the U.S. current information is available, for a dollar, in the pamphlet Tips for Travelers to the Caribbean, U.S. Government Printing Office, Washington, DC 20402, 202-783-3238.

A note for all visitors: The phrase "duty-free" applies to the vendor from whom you've bought your perfume, jewelry, trinkets and other goods. It means that the vendor was not required to pay duty on these items and, ostensibly, has passed on these savings to you. It has nothing to do with your own country's duty requirements.

AIRLINES

Following is a list of major international airlines servicing the Lesser Antilles from Europe and North America, with North American contact numbers: American (800-433-7300), Air Canada (800-776-3000), Air France (800-237-2747), British Airways (800-247-9297), British West Indies Air International (800-327-7401 or 538-2942), Continental (800-231-0856), KLM (800-374-7747), Lufthansa (800-645-3880) and United (800-241-6522).

Major airlines servicing San Juan, Puerto Rico, a gateway to the Lesser Antilles, include: Delta (800-241-4141), US Air (800-428-4322), Northwest (800-447-4747), Trans World Airlines (800-892-4141), Kiwi International (800-538-5494) and Carnival Airlines (800-437-2110).

Major inter-island airlines and their contact numbers follow: Leeward Islands Air Transport (LIAT), New York (212-251-1717, fax 212-545-8474); Alken Tours, Brooklyn, NY, (718-856-7711); Edenbridge Travel, Toronto, Ontario (416-249-8489); EC World Wide Travel, Miami, FL, (305-653-7264/5); Transatlantic Wings, Kensington, London (171-602-4021); and V.C. Bird International Airport, Box 819, St. John's, Antigua, West Indies, (809-462-0700, fax 809-462-2682).

British West Indies Airlines International (BWIA), U.S. (800-538-2942 or 327-7401); Canada (800-283-2942); and BWIA International Airways, Box 604, Port of Spain, Trinidad, West Indies; (809-669-3000, fax 809-669-1865).

Windward Islands Airways (Winair), Princess Juliana Airport, Sint Maarten, Netherlands Antilles, (599-522313).

In addition, a dozen or so smaller, island-based airlines, such as Air Saint-Barthélémy, Air Martinique, Air Guadeloupe, St. Vincent Airways and others, operate regular, though limited, services to various nearby islands.

Keep in mind that virtually all Lesser Antilles islands charge a airport departure tax (if you've stayed for 24 hours or more), often payable in the local currency. Make sure to put that money aside when checking in for your departure flight.

CRUISE SHIPS

A cruise is a wonderful, relaxing experience and makes for a great vacation. A cruise recalls the days of elegance and grandeur, when travelling was a major and costly undertaking. Today cruises are within the reach of middle-class incomes and we know that cruising on these floating hotels is a wildly popular way of visiting the Caribbean. Overall, 8.8 million cruise ship passengers visited the region in 1992 (up from 8.2 million in 1991), compared to 12 million stay-over visitors. If you plan to cruise, it's best to find a travel agent that specializes in cruise packages. For further information on the ins and outs of cruising, send a self-addressed, stamped envelope requesting the pamphlet "Cruising Answers to Your Questions" to the Cruise Lines International Association, 500 Fifth Ave., Suite 1407, New York, NY 10110.

Here are several of the dozens of cruise lines that ply the Lesser Antilles:

❑ Carnival Cruise Lines, 3655 NW 87th Ave., Miami, FL 33178 (305-599-2600 or 800-327-9501).
❑ Celebrity Cruise Lines, 5200 Blue Lagoon Dr., Miami, FL 33126 (305-262-8322 or 800-437-3111).
❑ Commodore Cruise Lines, 800 Douglas Road, Suite 700, Coral Gables, FL 33134 (305-529-3000 or 800-832-1122).
❑ Costa Cruise Lines, World Trade Center, 80 SW Eighth St., Miami, FL 33130 (305-358-7352 or 800-462-6782).
❑ Cunard Line, 555 Fifth Ave., New York, NY 10017 (800-221-4770).
❑ Dolphin Cruise Line, 901 South America Way, Miami, FL 33132 (305-358-2111 or 800-222-1003).
❑ Fantasy Cruises, 5200 Blue Lagoon Dr., Miami, FL (305-262-5411 or 800-423-2100).
❑ Princess Cruises, 10100 Santa Monica Blvd., Los Angeles, CA 90067 (310-553-1770).
❑ Royal Caribbean Cruise Line, 1050 Caribbean Way, Miami, FL 33132 (305-539-6000).
❑ Royal Viking Line, 95 Merrick Way, Coral Gables, FL 33134 (305-447-9660 or 800-422-8000).

BOAT CHARTERS

In many ways the sea defines the Caribbean. Sailing is a fascinating way to get to know a large part of island living, and options are available for those with a yen to travel on the water. You can either charter boats on the mainland of the U.S., on Puerto Rico or in the Virgin Islands, or from just about any island in the Lesser Antilles. Your options when chartering, which is really nothing more than renting, range from day charters to long-term charters, either with crew or bareboat, with a group or by yourself.

Sailors tend to enjoy the Virgin Islands and the Grenadines because of the relative closeness of the islands—you'll never leave one without seeing the next—and the hundreds of small harbors, inlets and coves, perfect for dropping anchor for a day. Throughout the Lesser Antilles, however, sailing is very popular. Crewed boats come with a professional crew and options of meals, fishing and sporting equipment, perhaps a bar and other choices. The cost varies depending on options and season, and they can be expensive, from US$2,000 per week, without provisions. Bareboat charters start at about US$1,500 and require the renters to have sufficient sailing and anchoring experience to handle the boat. One option is to charter a bareboat and work as crew, but hire a skipper who knows the ins and outs of local waters.

The following companies are good places to start:

❑ The Moorings, 1305 U.S. 19S, Clearwater, FL 33546 (800-535-7289).

❑ Nicholson Yacht Charters, 9 Chauncy St., Cambridge, MA 02138 (617-661-8174 or 800-662-6606).

❑ Virgin Islands Sailing, Ltd., Box 146, Road Town, Tortola, B.V.I. (800-233-7936, fax 809-494-6774, Florida 800-382-9666).

UNITED STATES VIRGIN ISLANDS

ST. THOMAS
ST. JOHN
ST. CROIX

BRITISH VIRGIN ISLANDS

TORTOLA
VIRGIN GORDA
JOST VAN DYKE
ANEGADA
OTHER ISLANDS

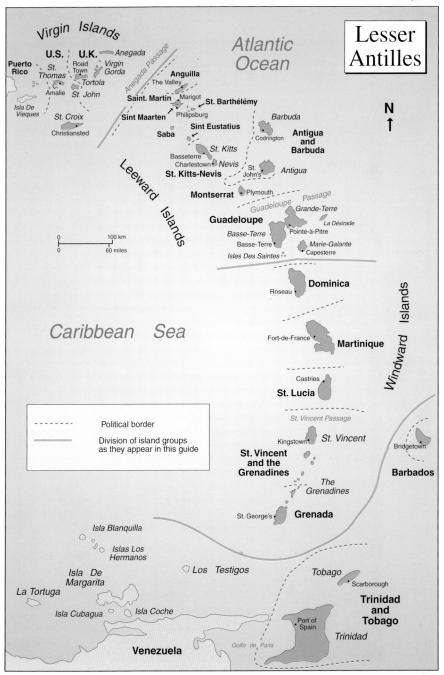

Lesser Antilles

N ↑

Atlantic Ocean

Virgin Islands

U.S. | U.K. Anegada
Puerto Rico | St. Thomas | Road Town | Virgin Gorda | Anguilla
C. Amalie | St. John | Tortola | The Valley
Isla De Vieques | St. Croix | Saint Martin | Marigot | St. Barthélémy
Christiansted | Sint Maarten | Philipsburg | Barbuda
Saba | Sint Eustatius | Codrington | Antigua and Barbuda
St. Kitts | Basseterre | Charlestown Nevis | St. John's | Antigua
St. Kitts-Nevis
Montserrat | Plymouth | Guadeloupe Passage
Guadeloupe | Grande-Terre | La Désirade
Basse-Terre | Pointe-à-Pitre
Basse-Terre | Marie-Galante
Isles Des Saintes | Capesterre
Leeward Islands

Dominica
Roseau

Caribbean Sea

Fort-de-France | Martinique

Castries
St. Lucia

Political border
Division of island groups as they appear in this guide

St. Vincent Passage
St. Vincent
Kingstown
St. Vincent and the Grenadines | Bridgetown
Barbados
The Grenadines
St. George's | Grenada

Windward Islands

Isla Blanquilla
Islas Los Hermanos
Isla De Margarita | Los Testigos | Tobago | Scarborough
La Tortuga
Isla Cubagua | Isla Coche | Port of Spain | Trinidad and Tobago
Venezuela | Golfo de Paria | Trinidad

0 — 100 km
0 — 60 miles

Pirates pretending to be harmless passengers, unnamed artist (1883)

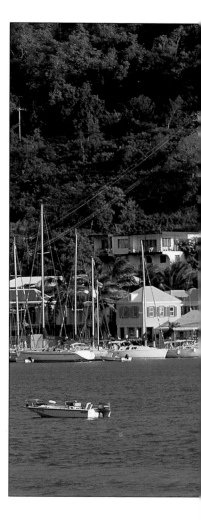

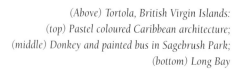

(Above) Tortola, British Virgin Islands:
(top) Pastel coloured Caribbean architecture;
(middle) Donkey and painted bus in Sagebrush Park;
(bottom) Long Bay

Sailing boats at Soper's Hole, Tortola, British Virgin Islands

'Pirates extorting tributes from citizens, West Indies' by Howard Pile,
from Harper's Monthly

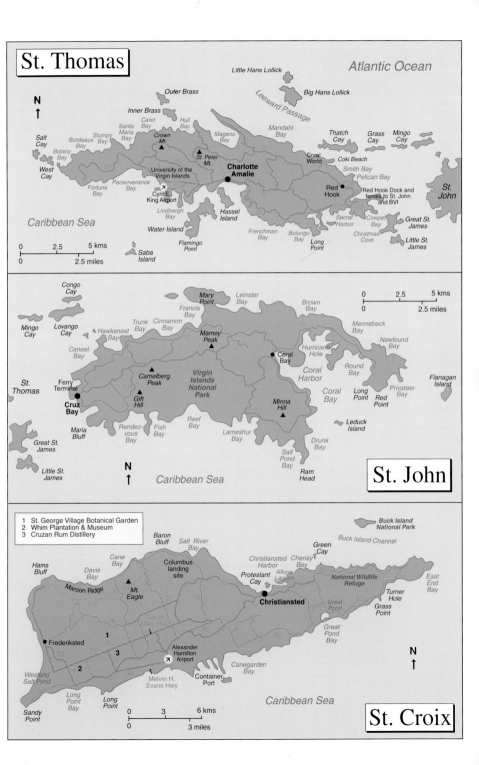

St. Thomas

Atlantic Ocean

N ↑

Little Hans Lollick

Outer Brass
Big Hans Lollick

Leeward Passage

Inner Brass

Caret Bay
Hull Bay
Mandahl Bay
Thatch Cay
Grass Cay
Mingo Cay

Santa Maria Bay
Magens Bay

Salt Cay
Bordeaux Bay
Stumpy Bay
▲ Crown Mt.
St. Peter Mt. ▲

Botany Bay
Coral World
Coki Beach

West Cay
University of the Virgin Islands
● Charlotte Amalie
Smith Bay
Pelican Bay

Fortuna Bay
Perserverance Bay
Red Hook ●
Red Hook Dock and ferries to St. John and BVI

Cyril E. King Airport ✈
Lindbergh Bay
Hassel Island
Frenchman Bay
Secret Harbor
Cowpet Bay
Great St. James

St. John

Caribbean Sea
Water Island
Flamingo Point
Bolongo Bay
Long Point
Christmas Cove
Little St. James

0 — 2.5 — 5 kms
0 — 2.5 miles
Saba Island

Congo Cay
Mary Point
Leinster Bay
Brown Bay
0 — 2.5 — 5 kms
0 — 2.5 miles

Mingo Cay
Lovango Cay
Francis Bay
Mennebeck Bay

Hawksnest Bay
Trunk Bay
Cinnamon Bay
▲ Mamey Peak
Newfound Bay

Caneel Bay
Hurricane Hole
Round Bay

St. Thomas
Ferry Terminal ●
Cruz Bay
▲ Camelberg Peak
Virgin Islands National Park
● Coral Bay
Coral Harbor
Long Point
Red Point
Privateer Bay
Flanagan Island

▲ Gift Hill
▲ Minna Hill

Maria Bluff
Rendez-vous Bay
Fish Bay
Reef Bay
Lameshur Bay
Leduck Island
Drunk Bay

Great St. James
Salt Pond Bay

Little St. James
N ↑
Caribbean Sea
Ram Head

St. John

---

1 St. George Village Botanical Garden
2 Whim Plantation & Museum
3 Cruzan Rum Distillery

Buck Island National Park

Buck Island Channel

Baron Bluff
Salt River Bay
Green Cay

Hams Bluff
Cane Bay
Davis Bay
Columbus landing site
Christiansted Harbor
Chenay Bay
National Wildlife Refuge
East End Bay

Maroon Ridge
▲ Mt. Eagle
Protestant Cay
Altona Lagoon
Turner Hole

● Frederiksted
1
● Christiansted
Great Pond
Grass Point

3
Alexander Hamilton Airport ✈
Great Pond Bay
N ↑

2
Melvin H. Evans Hwy
Canegarden Bay

Westend Salt Pond
Container Port

Long Point Bay
Long Point
Caribbean Sea

Sandy Point
0 — 3 — 6 kms
0 — 3 miles

St. Croix

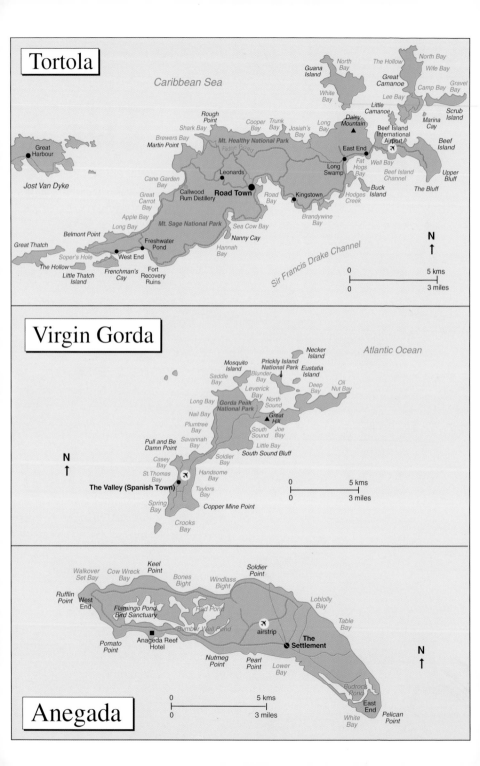

The United States Virgin Islands

Introduction

Early on in a trip to the U.S. Virgin Islands it is hard to overcome the sense that St. Thomas is little more than a large, albeit exotic, sidestreet off the North American vacation boulevard. From the ubiquitous McDonald's to the Hard Rock Cafe to the Surgeon General's warning on cigarette packs, it seems as if the U.S. has come to stay.

Yet the island, for all the trappings of familiarity for those coming from North America, is distinctly West Indian as well, reflected in the people, their language and their history. Of course, the magnificent beaches also count for something. All are reminders that the mainland has, indeed, been left behind. This is truer the farther one gets from Charlotte Amalie in St. Thomas and truer still as one leaves St. Thomas for its sister islands, St. Croix and St. John.

There is much to recommend here. The distinctions between the major islands, as well as possibilities for exploring the nearby British Virgin Islands, make for a wide array of choices.

The Land

The U.S. Virgin Islands comprises an estimated 70 islands, islets and cays, of which three, St. Thomas, St. John, and St. Croix, are significantly large and inhabited. The islands are located just 40-70 miles (64-112 km) east of Puerto Rico and 1,100 miles (1,760 km) southeast of the southern tip of Florida. Geologically, the U.S. Virgin Islands are related to the British Virgin Islands to the east and to Puerto Rico and the Greater Antilles, as part of the extensive underwater shelf called the Virgin Bank.

St. Thomas is the hub of the three islands, separated from the Puerto Rican islands of Culebra and Vieques by the Virgin Passage. The island measures 13 miles (21 km) by three miles (five km) at its widest point and is 32 square miles (83 sq km) in area. It is, as are the rest of the U.S. Virgin Islands, a volcanic island, hilly, rugged and dramatic, with a jagged, irregular coast. Both St. Thomas and St. John are touched by the Atlantic on their north coasts and by the Caribbean Sea on the south. St. Croix sits squarely in the Caribbean Sea.

Crown Mountain on the western end of St. Thomas is the island's highest point at 1,556 feet (467 m). The rest of the thickly populated (60,000) island is characterized by lesser hills, lowlands to the south and southeast and a dented coastline of small bays and inlets. Dozens of cays and islets surround the coast and include the National Park of Hassell Island in St. Thomas Harbor, across from the south coast's capital of Charlotte Amalie (pronounced A-MAHL-yah). Charlotte Amalie is busy, the largest town on St. Thomas, the cruise-ship center and the capital and administrative center of the territory. The passage of Hurricane Marilyn in 1995 caused widespread damage to the island.

St. John, some four miles (six km) east of St. Thomas and seven miles (11 km) west of Tortola in the British Virgin Islands, is, at 20 square miles (52 sq km) in area, the smallest of the U.S. Virgin Islands. It is also the least populated (2,900) and unique in that nearly 70 per cent, or more than 10,000 land and off-shore acres, is managed by the Virgin Islands National Park system. The land, donated by the millionaire Laurance Rockefeller in 1956, is one of the oldest U.S. national parks. St. John is hilly and lush, with its highest point the central Camelberg Peak, at 1,193 feet (358 m). The coast is lined with quiet bays and long beaches, some of the most compelling in the islands. The far western portion of St. John is home to Cruz Bay, the island's main center.

St. Croix, located some 40 miles (64 km) south of St. Thomas, is the largest of the U.S. Virgin Islands at 84 square miles (217 sq km), measuring 28 miles (45 km) long by seven miles (11 km) wide. It is less dramatic than its sister islands, characterized by gently sloping hills, some semi-rainforest topography to the west and dry areas featuring cacti and scrub brush, in the southern and eastern sections of the island. Christiansted, on the central north coast, and Frederiksted, on the west coast, are home to the majority of the island's 60,000 population.

History

The U.S. Virgin Islands were settled by pre-historic Stone Age groups and later Amerindian groups, long before Columbus and his crew made their heroic, if erroneous, discoveries and assumptions about the New World. The first groups that made their way from the Orinoco regions of South America were the Arawaks (also called Taino), who settled islands from Trinidad and Tobago in the south Lesser Antilles to the northern Greater Antilles and arrived in the U.S. Virgin Islands about AD 500. They were followed by the aggressive Caribs, who arrived not too long before Columbus charted the islands. Important archaeological discoveries at Salt River Bay in St. Croix that show the area was a major cultural center for various Amerindian groups.

By the time Columbus sailed upon St. Croix, during his second voyage in November 1493, the Caribs had taken control of the island. They called it Cibuquiera, or "Stony Land." Columbus sent a landing party—the first and only documented landing Columbus was to accomplish on what is now a U.S. territory—which took several Arawak slaves from the Caribs. Hours later a Carib vessel approached Columbus' flagship, the *Nina,* and a fight ensued in which one Spaniard and one Carib were killed. This, in turn, was the first documented resistance of native peoples to the Old World explorers.

Columbus then thought it prudent to sail off, first to chart San Tomas and then on to the larger Greater Antilles, driven by the quest for the gold of El Dorado and for a meeting with the ever-elusive Great Khan. On his departure he dubbed the island Santa Cruz ("Holy Cross") and dubbed the entire Virgin Islands archipelago Las Once Mil Virgenes, or "The 11,000 Virgins" (some say the name was Las Islas Virgenes), in honour of the British 4th-century Saint Ursula and her 11,000 virgins, murdered at the hands of the Huns at Cologne.

While Columbus claimed the islands for Spain, the Spanish did little to colonize them over the next century. Instead they used the islands as stopover points and as ready sources for Indian slave labor, whom they exported to their mines and plantations in Puerto Rico and the larger islands. By the late 16th century the Caribs were virtually eliminated in the U.S. Virgin Islands.

Over the next century, the U.S. Virgin Islands were settled by the Dutch, the English and the French, often simultaneously. St. Croix proved to be the touchstone, as it was profitable agriculturally and simply one of the largest islands in the vicinity. By 1645 the Dutch had left St. Croix and by 1650 the Spanish had reclaimed the island and driven off the English. The Spaniards were, in turn, disposed of by the French, who in 1653 invited the Knights of Malta to settle and manage the island. The Knights in turn sold the island back to the French. Thus continued the schizophrenic history and cultural and linguistic paths that today define the entire Caribbean region.

During this period the tobacco, cotton, sugar, and indigo plantations of St. Croix begged for labor. The importation of African slaves commenced in 1673 and thereafter accelerated.

Also during this period, in 1666, the Danes, under the Danish West India and Guinea Company, claimed St. Thomas. Charlotte Amalie, first named Taphaus (Tap House), was founded in 1691. The name was later changed to honour the Danish queen. In 1694 the Danes claimed St. John, but continuing hostilities with the British on nearby Tortola prevented them from actually inhabiting the island until 1717. In 1733 two important events took place. The French sold St. Croix to the Danish West India and Guinea Company. A massive slave rebellion on St. John, a result of harsh working conditions coupled with that year's devastating drought and a hurricane, put the island in the hands of Africans for six months. The rebellion was put down by the Danes, who were reinforced by French warships and troops. But it would be more than one century later, in 1848, before slavery was finally abolished in the Danish islands.

With the addition of St. Croix, the Danish formed the Danish West Indies colony and the islands prospered. St. Thomas (named a free port in 1724) had flourished as a center of trade and commerce—and as a center of pirate activities, including those of Edward "Blackbeard" Teach and Captain William Kidd. St. John hosted massive sugarcane and cotton plantations, before and after the slave rebellion, and St. Croix, then host to the Danish West Indies capital of Christiansted, also had an agricultural economic base.

The end of the 18th century was a time of great upheaval in Europe and, in due course, the Caribbean. Denmark made the unfortunate, but historically inevitable, choice of siding with Napoleon against the English during the Napoleonic Wars. The British in the Caribbean saw this as an opportunity to expand their territory and they attacked and occupied St. John in 1801 and again in 1807, holding it (respectively) for a year and seven years.

When the Danes regained St. John in 1815, the demise of the sugarcane industry and the great plantocracies of the Lesser Antilles was imminent. Sugar extracted from beets rather than the more expensive sugarcane found its way into the marketplace. Additionally, the great sailing cargo ships of the 18th and early 19th centuries were soon obsolete, due to the innovation of steam ships. This rendered St. Thomas and other major Caribbean ports less important as stopover points. Agitation from abolition groups continued to abate the slave trade. In fact, Denmark had already stopped its slave trade in 1802, but the subsequent British occupations had revived it. Still, it was the beginning of the period of economic decline for the Danish islands, as it was for the rest of the Caribbean.

After the final emancipation of slaves in 1848, the Danish West Indies, along with most of the Caribbean, entered a period of economic slump and massive migrations that saw freed slaves leave for plantation and construction work in Central America and elsewhere. By the 1870s the Danes had entered a period of protracted negotiations with the U.S., seeking to unload their unprofitable and weighty Caribbean possessions. In 1917 the U.S., fearful of the sort of massive destruction wrought by the World War I and seeking a base from which to guard their new canal in Panama, bought the islands for US$25 million in gold.

The U.S. ruled the islands as a naval base until 1927, when citizenship was given to the islanders. The Navy and Army remained on the islands through World War II (and the U.S. Marine Corps still maintains airfields on St. Thomas and St. Croix). Soon after, universal suffrage was granted, roads and infrastructure were built, a university was established and a national park was created on St. John. In 1932 the Organic Act introduced self-government to the U.S. Virgin Islands and, in 1968, the U.S. Congress passed an act allowing for greater internal rule, with a governor elected by popular vote. Four years later the U.S. Virgin Islands sent their first elected delegate to Congress.

People and Culture

The blend of European and African cultures in the U.S. Virgin Islands is strong and evident in the language, food, place names and culture of the islands. While some trappings of "Americanism" are evident on the islands, in most ways this certainly isn't Kansas, Dorothy.

English is the language of the U.S. Virgin Islands, spoken with a Creole, sometimes called Calypso, twist. In St. Croix pockets of expatriate Puerto Ricans (technically, since both Puerto Rico and the U.S. Virgin Islands are U.S. territories, "expatriate" is a stretch of the word) speak Spanish. Spanish influences also affect the English of St. Croix to produce a Creole and creolized culture, called Cruzan. Cruzan is also the name of St. Croix's famous rum.

Place names such as Christiansted, Bonne Esperance, Vluck Point, Cruz Bay and America Point testify to the wide range of nationalities that have left their marks on the islands. Likewise, island religions include Roman Catholic, Anglican, Moravian, Episcopal, Jewish and Lutheran, among others. A small but significant group of Palestinians, primarily businessmen, live and work on St. Croix.

West Indian culture, which is to say predominantly African blended with various European customs, is evident in the local foods such as fungi (pasty cornmeal), goat water (goat soup), souse (pig's head soup with lime juice), johnny cakes (fried bread) and maubi (tonic made from maubi tree bark with other herbs). Local vegetables include callaloo and okra. Fruits such as soursop, mango, genip and papaya are used as they are throughout the Caribbean. Seafood is, of course, important to the U.S. Virgin Islands cuisine. Preparations of conch (conch fritters are a favourite), lobster, whelk, grouper, snapper, tuna and others are island delicacies. Other cultures in the modern U.S. Virgin Islands are represented through their cuisine. One can find world-class French, Italian, Chinese, East

Indian and more represented. U.S. fast-food culture is represented with the presence of KFC, McDonald's and others.

Holidays that keep cultural traditions strong include St. Thomas' annual post-Easter Carnival, held in late April. The Carnival utilizes African customs such as drumming, dancing the baboula and the exhibition of devils, jumbies (spirits or ghosts) and other figures through masquerades. The mocko jumbi, a stock character likely to be found on stilts and wearing a mirror, appears at many an island festival. Carnival also features masquerade parades, feasts, calypso contests, German quadrille dancing and steel bands.

Emancipation Day is celebrated in July. Organic Act Day, in June, honours the granting of internal government in the U.S. Virgin Islands. Transfer Day in March celebrates the 1917 transfer of the island from Danish to U.S. possession. St. Croix hosts the two-week Crucian Christmas Festival, from Christmas Week through the first week in January, featuring feasts, parades, contests, French quadrille dancing and Christmas festivities. Fourth of July (U.S. Independence Day) is St. John's version of carnival, complete with a week of fireworks and all the trappings of the St. Thomas Carnival.

Also celebrated are U.S. federal and religious holidays, such as Thanksgiving Day (in November, as well as an additional day in October celebrating the end of hurricane season), Christmas, New Year's, Martin Luther King Jr. Day and more, plus boating and sports festivals. Check local newspapers for schedules.

The Caribbean Dance Company performs locally at the Reichhold Center (809-774-4482) at the University of the Virgin Islands in St. Thomas, as well as around the islands. The St. Thomas Arts Council (call tourist office, 809-774-8784) can be contacted for a full schedule of local folk art companies.

Government and Economy

The Virgin Islands of the United States is an unincorporated territory of the United States. The head of state is the U.S. President and the islands combine to elect a non-voting representative to the U.S. House of Representatives. Within the internal government structure of the U.S. Virgin Islands the chief executive is a governor, elected every four years, supported by a 15 member legislature of senators. The 122,900 citizens of the U.S. Virgin Islands are also citizens of the United States. The Democratic, Independent Citizens Movement and Republican parties are the dominant political parties. There has been agitation in the past regarding the political status of the U.S. Virgin Islands. Some citizens would like to see full independence, some would like greater affiliation, even statehood, while others are happy with the present system. Ongoing debates and referendums, however, are not likely to change the islands' status in the near future.

The economy of the U.S. Virgin Islands is reliant on remittances from U.S. aid and from U.S. Virgin Islanders abroad, as well as from tourism. A Hess Oil refinery and an aluminum plant, both on St. Croix, provide some employment, but government and the tourism industry are the main employers. The average minimum wage of the islanders is the same as on the U.S. mainland, about US$5 per hour, and the standard of living is higher than on most of the neighbouring islands of the Lesser Antilles. Unemployment is low, about three per cent in 1991, against a labor force of approximately 50,000.

Tourism accounted for 60 per cent of the U.S. Virgin Islands' gross domestic product in 1993, from a total of 1,935,800 visitors. Of this number a third were bona-fide stayovers, while two-thirds were day visitors on cruise ships or yachts. St. Thomas is considered to be the number one cruise ship stop in the Caribbean—indeed, an average of nearly two ships per day dock at Charlotte Amalie, while others also stop at St. Croix. The islands offer approximately 5,000 hotel rooms and this figure is rising. In fact, the government and private sector invested some $250 million in 1988 to upgrade tourist facilities and infrastructure to meet the growing tourism demand.

In 1989 Hurricane Hugo damaged the islands, especially St. Croix. Losses were estimated at US$1 billion and the islands were declared a disaster area. U.S. troops were sent in to control looting and unrest. With US$272 million in government disaster relief, the islands have now recovered.

Practical Information

GETTING THERE

There are two airports in the U.S. Virgin Islands; the Cyril E. King Airport is located a few miles west of Charlotte Amalie on St. Thomas and the smaller Alexander Hamilton Airport, on St. Croix, is located on the southwest coast. St. Thomas is the entry point for most flights, as well as a stopover for flights heading on to other Caribbean destinations. St. Croix is a stopover for island-hoppers, particularly for flights from Puerto Rico, St. Thomas and the British Virgin Islands. St. John is reached by ferry or private boat. There is no departure tax when leaving the U.S. Virgin Islands.

St. Thomas is connected to Puerto Rico and the U.S. mainland by American Airlines (800 474-4884), American Eagle (809-776-2560), Continental (809-777-

8190), Delta (809-777-4177), Sunaire Express (809-778-9300) and Virgin Islands Paradise Airways (800-299-USVI).

For connections to nearby islands use Aero Virgin Islands (809-776-8366), Air Anguilla (809-776-5789), BWIA (809-778-9372), LIAT (809-774-2313), or Sint Maarten's Winair (809-775-0183).

GETTING AROUND

■ TAXIS AND BUSES

Taxis and buses are widely available on St. Thomas and St. Croix and to a lesser extent on St. John. Cars can be rented on all three islands.

Island taxi tours cost about US$30 for one or two persons, with US$12 extra per additional rider. Taxi rates increase between midnight and 6.00 by US$1.50 per trip and the charge for suitcases is about US$0.50 per bag.

Your hotel will be able to arrange a taxi for you, but for pickups in St. Thomas, call East End (809-775-6974), Independent (809-776-1006) or VI Taxi Association (809-774-4550). On St. Croix, call St. Croix Taxi (809-778-1088), Caribbean Taxi (809-773-9799) in Christiansted or Combine Taxi (809-772-2828) in Frederiksted.

■ RENTAL CARS

Rental cars are widely available for those 18 years or older. Some companies require that the driver is at least 25. U.S. drivers will need a valid license and others will need to obtain a temporary license through the rental company. Credit cards are almost universally accepted and the rates start at about US$30 per day.

❑ ON ST. THOMAS: ABC Auto (809-776-1222 or 800-524-2080), Budget Rent-A-Car (809-776-5774 or 800-626-4516), Cowpet Auto Rental (809-775-7376 or 800-524-2072).

❑ ON ST. JOHN: St. John Car Rental (809-776-6103), Spencer's Jeep Rental (809-776-6628 or 776-7784) or Sutton Car Rental (809-776-6479).

❑ ON ST. CROIX: Budget Rent-A-Car (809-778-9636 or 778-4663), Hertz (809-778-1402 or 773-2100), Midwest Auto Rental (809-772-0438) or Thrifty Car Rental (809-773-7200).

■ FERRY SERVICE

Ferries depart St. Thomas from Charlotte Amalie or from the National Park Dock at Red Hook, with destinations to Cruz Bay in St. John, or Tortola or Virgin Gorda in the British Virgin Islands.

Red Hook to Cruz Bay departs about every hour from 6.30 until midnight; the 15-minute trip costs US$3. Call Transportation Services (809-776-6282). The Native Son (809-774-8685) departs from Red Hook to Tortola three times daily, cost US$31 for the round trip, about 30 minutes one-way.

A ferry from Charlotte Amalie to St. John departs every two hours; the 45-minute trip costs US$7. Other ferry runs include Charlotte Amalie to Tortola, Cruz Bay to Tortola, Red Hook to Jost Van Dyke (British Virgin Islands) and Charlotte Amalie to Virgin Gorda. A number of private ferry companies, including Dohm's (809-775-6501), will take you "anywhere, anytime." There are no direct scheduled ferry services to St. Croix.

ACCOMMODATION

A government room tax of 7.5 per cent is charged.

More information regarding general accommodation can be obtained through the St. Thomas-St. John Hotel Association (809-774-6835) and the St. Croix Hotel and Tourism Association (800-524-2026 or 809-773-7117).

■ VILLAS

Private villas, cottages, condos or apartments:

❏ ON ST. THOMAS: Byrne Brown Realty, P.O. Box 7967, Charlotte Amalie, St. Thomas, U.S.V.I. 00801 (809-774-3300, fax 774-1556) and McLaughlin Anderson Vacations, 100 Blackbeard's Hill, Charlotte Amalie, St. Thomas, U.S.V.I. 00802 (800-537-6246 or 809-776-0635, fax 777-4737).

❏ ON ST. JOHN: Caribbean Villas, P.O. Box 458, Cruz Bay, St. John, U.S.V.I. 00831 (800-338-0987 or 776-6152, fax 779-4044) and St. John Properties, P.O. Box 700, Cruz Bay, St. John, U.S.V.I. 00831 (800-848-4397, fax 809-776-6192).

❏ ON ST. CROIX: American Rentals and Sales, 2001 Old Hospital St., Christiansted, St. Croix, U.S.V.I. 00820 (809-773-8470, fax 773-8472) and Island Villas, 14-A Caravelle Arcade, Christiansted, St. Croix, U.S.V.I. 00820 (800-626-4512 or 809-773-8821, fax 773-8823).

■ CAMPING

It could be argued that the campgrounds on Cinnamon Bay and Maho Bay are among the finest in the Lesser Antilles. The beaches are long and fine and the setting tranquil. The campgrounds themselves offer anything from inexpensive bare sites to luxury tents or cottages with kitchenettes. Cinnamon Bay Campground, P.O. Box 720, Cruz Bay, St. John, U.S.V.I. 00831 (800-539-9998 or 809-776-6330, fax 776-6458) is a 125-site National Park campground on a half-mile white sand beach. The range is from bare sites (US$15 in off-season) to tented sites (US$44, off-season) to cottages (US$56-60), plus watersports, some handicapped facilities and an open-air restaurant. Next door is the privately owned Maho Bay Camps, P.O. Box 310, Cruz Bay, St. John, U.S.V.I. 00831 (800-392-9004 or 809-776-6240, fax 776-6504). The camp features 114 "tent-cottages," the type you might see in a Lawrence of Arabia film, each with separate rooms (screened), wood floors, kitchenettes, furniture, a porch and electricity. Toilets and showers are communal. Watersports and a restaurant are on the grounds. Cost is US$90 per double in the winter season, US$60 off-season, more for each extra person; no credit cards.

Both campsites are extremely popular, particularly in the winter months, so call well ahead for reservations.

WATERSPORTS

❏ ST. THOMAS: Aqua Action Watersports (809-775-6285) Coki Beach Dive Club (809-775-4220) and Underwater Safaris (809-774-1350).

❏ ST. JOHN: Cruz Bay Watersports (809-776-6234) and Low Key Watersports (809-776-7048).

❏ ST. CROIX: Dive St. Croix (809-773-3434) and VI Divers (809-773-6045).

❏ DEEP SEA FISHERMEN, call St. Thomas Sportfishing Center (809-775-7990) or Sapphire Marina (809-775-3690). On St. Croix, call St. Croix Marine (809-773-0289).

Any number of sailing charter companies will rent bareboat charters, crewed charters, day sails and monthly rentals. Start with Avery's Boathouse (809-776-0113) in Charlotte Amalie (see Chapter Two for more information about charter companies).

MONEY, HOURS AND COMMUNICATION
The currency of the U.S. Virgin Islands is the U.S. dollar. If you'd like to change traveler's checks, you may do so at your hotel or at the bank. Banks give better rates and are generally open 9.00–15.00 Monday through Thursday and 9.00–17.00 Friday.

Government offices and many businesses are open 9.00–17.00 and shops, particularly in Charlotte Amalie and Christiansted, may stay open late for cruise ships. The area code for the U.S. Virgin Islands is 809, followed by a seven-digit number. Toll-free 800 numbers are also utilized. The U.S. Virgin Islands postal system is no different to that of the mainland. U.S. postal rates apply for letters, packages and foreign destinations.

SHOPPING

St. Thomas, more so than the other two islands, offers a wide range of duty-free shopping, art galleries and so on. An estimated 400 shops carry jewelry, electronic goods, crystal, linens and liquor. With no sales tax on the islands, good deals can get even better.

Charlotte Amalie is the main shopping district, particularly the area bordered by Main Street and the Waterfront Highway. At Emancipation Gardens you'll find Vendor's Plaza. Near the cruise ship dock is Havensight Mall and on the outskirts of town are a half dozen smaller malls and strip malls.

On St. John shopping is at the Wharfside Village in Cruz Bay, near the ferry dock. A short walk from the National Park Visitor Center is Mongoose Junction, with several artisan shops and studios.

On St. Croix Christiansted's Market Square on Company Street and Strand Street offer dozens of shops.

St. Thomas

BEACHES

Beaches in the U.S. Virgin Islands are open to the public, although some are fronted by hotels and resorts which have facilities for guests only. Fees for parking or use of the beach are charged on certain beaches, usually no more than US$4.

On St. Thomas there are an estimated 44 talcum-white sand beaches. Among the best: Coki Beach in the northeast hosts watersports facilities and is often crowded with cruise ship passengers.

Next door on the same beach is Coral World (809-775-1555), a marine park with nature trails, turtle pools, a baby shark pool, a Touch Pond for kids, an aviary and changing facilities. Admission is US$14 for adults, US$9 for children.

Magens Bay on the north shore is one of the island's nicer beaches: wide and roomy, with lifeguards, watersports, changing facilities, picnic area, beach bars and shops. Small fee per person and per car. Sapphire Beach at the east end faces the British Virgin Islands. This is a popular windsurfing spot. Stumpy Bay at the west end requires a short walk from the parking lot. This is more isolated, but quiet and uncrowded. Lindberg Bay, near the airport, is a popular and sometimes crowded beach, plenty of watersports.

SIGHTS

Charlotte Amalie is neatly laid out in grids and, though somewhat hilly, it's an enjoyable and easily navigated town. The Waterfront is bustling with vendors and historic architecture, including the 1874 Legislature Building. Much of the town was destroyed—not once, but twice—in the devastating fires of 1802 and 1804. The architecture today reflects Danish, French and English influences, most built after the fires. Main Street has several examples of this architecture, including Market Square, an iron-roofed structure once used as a slave market, now a produce and trinkets market, and the public library. At the eastern end of Main Street is an extension street named Norre Gade, with the cream-colored Frederick Lutheran Church. The church was lost to fires in 1750 and 1789. The present structure was completed in 1826.

North of the church is Government Hill and Government House, built in 1867 and now the residence of the islands' governor. The first floor, with its large reception area, and second floor are open to the public. Down from Government Hill to Lille Tarne Gade is the "99 Steps" staircase, built in the 1700s by the apparently ironic Danes—there are more than 99 steps. On Crystal Gade is the 1833 St. Thomas Synagogue, one of the oldest in continuous use in this hemisphere.

South from Norre Gade on Fort Plasden is Emancipation Park, where the official proclamation was made in 1848. Note the bust of the Danish King Christian and a small replica of the Liberty Bell. Nearby is the rust-red Fort Christian Museum (809-776-4566), the oldest standing structure in St. Thomas, reputedly completed in 1680 (although, confusingly, a frontpiece indicates 1671). The fort was once used as an administrative center and, more recently, a jail. Now it holds historical displays and is open 9.00-17.00 Monday through Saturday and from 12.00-16.00 on Sunday.

Offshore in the harbor is Hassell Island, a National Park. The park includes military ruins and an old, defunct shipyard. A ferry (809-774-9652) takes you from the waterfront to the island.

Accommodation

- ❏ **Bolongo Club Everything Beach Resort**, P.O. Box 7337, Charlotte Amalie, St. Thomas, U.S.V.I. 00801 (800-524-4746 or 809-775-1800, fax 775-3208), is on the south coast, great beach, amenities, sports, both all-inclusive and European Plan available. Luxury. (Bolongo's other resorts on the island are at Bolongo Bay and Red Hook).
- ❏ **Frenchman's Reef Beach Resort**, P.O. Box 7100, Charlotte Amalie, St. Thomas, U.S.V.I. 00801 (800-524-2000 or 809-776-8500, fax 776-3054), also on the south coast, is a large Marriott resort, two dozen shops, restaurants, sports. Luxury.
- ❏ **Blackbeard's Castle**, P.O. Box 6041, Charlotte Amalie, St. Thomas, U.S.V.I. 00804 (800-344-5771 or 809-776-1234, fax 776-4321), is near town, small, with a pool and reputed to be a former lair of the eponymous pirate. Moderate.
- ❏ **Calico Jack's Courtyard Inne**, P.O. Box 460, Charlotte Amalie, St. Thomas, U.S.V.I. 00804, is a 17th century building downtown in the historic district, recently renovated and small, only six rooms. The downstairs pub is popular. One room is handicapped accessible. Moderate.

Eating

Hotel restaurants are generally fine and some provide entertainment. Most accept credit cards, but it's best to call ahead to confirm and, in Charlotte Amalie, to make reservations.

- ❏ **Fiddle Leaf** (809-775-2810) on Government Hill in Charlotte Amalie, offers elegant Euro-West Indian cuisine. Expensive.
- ❏ **Romanos** (809-775-0045) at Smith Bay is one of the finest Italian restaurants in the area. Expensive.
- ❏ **Alexander's Cafe** (809-776-4211) in Frenchtown is chic and where the hip crowds are hip. Moderate.
- ❏ **Hard Rock Cafe** (809-777-5555) on the Waterfront, same as Hard Rock Cafes you have come to know and love and open until 2.00. Moderate-expensive.

St. John

Beaches

Caneel Bay, on the northwest shore, sports a series of pretty and isolated beaches, some only accessible by boat. The beaches at Hawks Nest Bay and Trunk Bay, just north of Caneel Bay, are part of the National Park system. Snack bars, picnic tables and changing facilities are available. Cinnamon Bay and Maho Bay are both wide and popular. Cinnamon Bay, bordered by the National Park, offers full facilities. Salt Pond Bay, on the south shore, is a also National Park beach and a ten minute walk from the parking lot.

SIGHTS

Nearly 70 per cent of the island of St. John, as well as hundreds of offshore acres, is devoted to the Virgin Islands National Park. Contact the National Park Visitor Center (809-776-6201) at the dock in Cruz Bay. Rangers can help you plan hikes, walks and excursions. Each of the 22 trails is self-guided, except for the Reef Bay Trail, which starts at the center of the island and heads south to the sea. Along the way you'll see rainforest-like flora, Amerindian petroglyphs and old buildings from the Reef Bay Plantation. The visitor center offers trail pamphlets.

ACCOMMODATION

❏ CANEEL BAY, P.O. Box 720, Cruz Bay, St. John, U.S.V.I. 00831 (800-929-8889 or 809-776-6111, fax 693-8280), 171 rooms with no phones or television and fans rather than air conditioning, on some of the nicest beaches on the island. Sports, watersports, pool. Luxury.

❏ HYATT REGENCY ST. JOHN, P.O. Box 8310, Cruz Bay, St. John, U.S.V.I. 00831 (800-233-1234 or 809-693-8000, fax 693-8888), south of Cruz Bay, is the largest hotel on the island, with nearly 300 rooms and suites, amenities and a pool that could swallow a small country. Luxury.

❏ CRUZ INN, P.O. Box 566, Cruz Bay, St. John, U.S.V.I. 00831 (800-666-7688 or 809-693-8688, fax 693-8590), wins the clever names award. Small and comfortable, downtown. Moderate.

EATING

❏ THE FISH TRAP (809-776-9817) in downtown Cruz Bay does seafood and does it well. Moderate.

❏ JOE'S DINER, uptown from the dock—you have to love a place called Joe's Diner. Inexpensive.

❏ LIME INN (809-776-6425) downtown is open-air, popular. Moderate.

❏ JJ'S TEXAS COAST CAFE (809-776-6908) is the place for Tex-Mex. Inexpensive.

St. Croix

BEACHES

On the northwest shore, Cane Bay is a popular snorkelling spot with plenty of shade and watersports facilities. The beach is rarely crowded and the reef is close to shore. Sandy Point is a long and pretty beach on the island's west end. North and south of Frederiksted, on the west end, are several long beaches including Sprat Hall and West End Beach Club. Columbus Beach (Salt River) on the north shore is the reputed site of Columbus' 1493 landing on St. Croix. There are few facilities here, but the historical value is a draw. Off the northeast shore, visit Buck Island, part of the National Park system and designated a national monument. The island is protected and the snorkelling features underwater trails. Boats leave from Christiansted or from the Green Cay Marina on the north shore. Call the National Park Service (809-773-1460) for information.

SIGHTS

Christiansted is St. Croix's hub and commercial center. The town is compact and busy and features architecture with a heavy Danish influence. The historic sights and buildings in town and in the equally historic Frederiksted are explained on guided walking tours sponsored by a group called Take-A-Hike (809-778-6997). The tour of Christiansted takes two hours and costs US$5.50 per person. An extended tour is also available. Call ahead for times and days of departure; meet at the visitor center, near the post office at the Old Scale House on the harbor. The tour of Frederiksted is US$6.50. The visitor center (809-772-0357) in Frederiksted is on the pier.

On your own a good first stop would be the National Park's Christiansted National Historic Site, comprising the Old Scale House, the Old Customs House, the Danish West India and Guinea Company Warehouse and Fort Christiansvaern, one of five Danish forts in the U.S. Virgin Islands built between 1730 and 1780, during the Danish heyday in the islands. All are located on or near the harbor and all have historical exhibits and displays. Admission to sites is US$2 for those 16 to 62 years of age.

Elsewhere on the island there are several sites worth visiting. On the Centerline Road, the western end's St. George Village Botanical Garden is a small park built on the ruins of an old sugarcane plantation. Trails, a cactus garden, a working blacksmith's forge, displays and a gift shop are on site. Admission is US$4 for adults, US$2 for children. Nearby, the Whim Plantation and Museum features a historic greathouse, a mill, various plantation structures and, of course, a gift shop. Admission is US$5 for adults, US$1 for children. Guided tours are conducted through the Cruzan Rum Factory (809-772-2080) and you'll get a nip after the 20 minute walk. A small admission is charged.

The north shore's Salt River historic area is marked as the site of Columbus' landing. Tours of the site are conducted by the St. Croix Environmental Association (809-773-1989). The association also conducts a number of weekly nature hikes to important environmental and wildlife sites throughout the island.

ACCOMMODATION

❑ HOTEL ON THE CAY, P.O. Box 4020, Christiansted, St. Croix, U.S.V.I. 00821 (800-524-2035 or 809-773-2035, fax 773-7046), is a small resort on an off-shore cay in the harbor, great beach, pool, tennis, restaurants, regular ferry service to town. Luxury.

❑ CARAMBOLA BEACH RESORT, P.O. Box 3031, Kingshill, St. Croix, U.S.V.I. 00851 (800-333-3333 or 809-778-3800, fax 778-1682), is just west of town on Davis Bay, large, two restaurants, good beach. Luxury.

❑ THE FREDERIKSTED HOTEL, 20 Strand St., Frederiksted, St. Croix, U.S.V.I. 00841 (800-524-2025 or 809-773-9150, fax 778-4009), is a clean 40-room hotel downtown, a few blocks from the pier and a block from the water. Moderate.

EATING

❑ ANTOINE'S (809-773-0263) on the wharf in Christiansted serves fine seafood. Moderate.

❑ STIXX ON THE WATERFRONT (809-773-5157) has a raw bar, pizza, sandwiches, great place to relax and eat light. Inexpensive-moderate.

❑ THE CHART HOUSE (809-773-7718), also on the wharf, features good steaks and seafood. Moderate-expensive.

Useful Addresses

■ TOURISM INFORMATION

In the U.S. call 800-USVI-INFO; in Canada 800-465-USVI. Otherwise, write or call the U.S. Virgin Islands Division of Tourism at the following addresses:

❑ P.O. Box 6400, Charlotte Amalie, St. Thomas, U.S.V.I. 00804 (809-774-8784, fax 774-4390).

❑ P.O. Box 200, Cruz Bay, St. John, U.S.V.I. 00830 (809-776-6450).

❑ P.O. Box 4538, Christiansted, St. Croix, U.S.V.I. 00822 (809-773-0495, fax 778-9259).

❏ 225 Peachtree St. NE, Suite 760, Atlanta, GA 30303 (404-688-0906).
❏ 500 North Michigan Ave., Suite 2030, Chicago, IL 60611
   (312- 670-8784, fax 670-8788).
❏ 3460 Wilshire Blvd., Suite 412, Los Angeles, CA 90010
   (213-739-0138, fax 739-2005).
❏ 2655 Le June Road, Suite 907, Coral Gables, FL 33134
   (305-442-7200, fax 445-9044).
❏ 1270 Avenue of the Americas, New York, NY
   (212-332-2222, fax 332-2223).
❏ 900 17th St. NW, Suite 500, Washington, D.C. 20006
   (202-293-3707, fax 785-2542).
❏ 33 Niagara St., Toronto, M5V 1C2 (416-362-8784, fax 362-9841).
❏ 2 Cinnamon Row, Plantation Wharf, York Place, London SW11 3TW
   (171-978-5262, fax 924-3171).

■ OTHER
❏ Ambulance, 922; fire, 921; police, 915.
❏ Hospital, St. Thomas; 776-8311.
❏ Myrah Keating Smith Clinic, St. John; 776-6400.
❏ Hospital, St. Croix; 776-6311.
❏ American Express representative, St. Thomas; 774-1855.
❏ American Express representative, St. Croix; 773-9500.
❏ Federal Express, St. Thomas; 776-8887.
❏ Virgin Islands National Park Service; 775-6238.

The British Virgin Islands

Introduction

The British Virgin Islands remain happily unencumbered by what often appears to be a Caribbean-wide scramble for the tourism dollar. This does not mean visitors are unwelcome—the B.V.I. gets thousands per year, most of whom are on yachts or wishing they were. This doesn't mean this is the only group of islands in the region that has maintained a quiet serenity in the face of rapid regional growth; they just do it well. It is the expressed policy of the tourism authorities to maintain the integrity of the natural environment, which has everything to do with the sea around the 60 or so islands, cays, rocks and volcanic blips that make up the archipelago. The sea, the sailing, the diving and the uncanny beauty of the beaches attract visitors to the islands. No hotels reach higher than two stories, about the height of the tallest palm tree; the islands host no casinos, no large nightclubs and, for that matter, no large towns.

The Islands

One could write an entire chapter on the origins of the names of the British Virgin Islands. Various explorers, from the Amerindian Arawaks and Columbus to the 17th and 18th-century European settlers, came up with monikers such as Tortola, Virgin Gorda, Jost Van Dyke and Anegada, for the four main and populated islands, as well as the names for Norman Island, Peter Island, Ginger Island, Fallen Jerusalem, The Dogs, Beef Island, Great Camanoe and more. Many names and their meanings have been obscured by history, while others reflect the vagaries of European colonization and whimsy.

The British Virgin Islands lie in a horizontal chain, beginning 50 miles (80 km) east of Puerto Rico and just west of their sister islands, the U.S. Virgin Islands. A larger, "parent" archipelago, comprising the U.S. and British Virgin Islands and the Puerto Rican islands of Culebra and Vieques, lies on the Virgin Bank, a huge underwater shelf that encompasses the islands and waters stretching east of, and geologically related to, Puerto Rico and the Greater Antilles.

The Sir Francis Drake Channel separates the Jost Van Dyke-Tortola group in the north from the Virgin Gorda string to the south. Virtually the entire group is of volcanic origin, save for Anegada, a flat coral formation at the northeastern end of the chain.

Of the four main islands the largest is Tortola, measuring 21 square miles (54 sq km). This is the main entry point for visitors and the economic and administrative center of the islands, with a population of 13,000, about 80 per cent of the entire group. Tortola is mountainous with an irregular coastline and fine white-sand beaches. The central spine of mountains culminates at Mt. Sage, a national park in the southwest, which is the island's highest point at 1,780 feet (534 m). The natural harbor and Road Bay at the south is host to Road Town, population 2,500, the capital and business center of the B.V.I. Tortola is connected by a toll bridge to Beef Island, site of the Beef Island International Airport.

Virgin Gorda is an irregularly shaped island; actually, it's three islands connected by isthmuses, a total of eight square miles (21 sq km). The middle section is hilly, rugged and dominated by Gorda Peak, another national park and the island's highest point at 1,359 feet (408 m). The southern section is flat and relatively arid and its beaches and attractions include The Baths, a popular rock and cave formation. The population of the island is 1,500, most of whom live in The Valley, which incorporates Spanish Town, in the south.

Jost Van Dyke, named after a reputed pirate, is a mere four square miles (ten sq km) of hills, the highest at just over 1,000 feet (300 m). The settlement at Great Harbor is home to most of the 200 residents, who are engaged primarily in tourism and related services.

Anegada, flat and 15 square miles (39 sq km), is composed of coral limestone and sandy hillocks that rise no higher than 27 feet (eight m) above sea level. The coast is smooth and natural reefs, particularly along the western, leeward side, protect the beaches. The reef is not only beautiful, but dangerous: nearly 300 shipwrecks, more than anywhere else in the Caribbean, lie offshore. In fact, the name Anegada may have come from the Spanish anegar, meaning "to drown." The attraction here is diving. Much of the island, through National Parks Trust (809-494-3904) regulations, has been set aside as a reserve for birds and other wildlife. Several large salt ponds stretch inland on the northern part of the island. Twenty miles (32 km) northeast of Virgin Gorda, Anegada is somewhat isolated from the main group. Most of the 300 residents live in The Settlement, on the west side.

Another dozen or so islands of the group, some privately owned, are inhabited, bringing the total B.V.I. population to more than 16,000. The majority are of African descent. The rest are European, North American and Caribbean expatriates, most of whom have been attracted by the islands' growing tourism and related industries.

History

Columbus sailed past the Virgin Islands archipelago during his second voyage in 1493. One imagines his dismay when confronted with a literal sea of rocks, islets and islands, which he was enjoined to name and chart. One imagines him throwing up his hands in panic and calling the entire lot Las Once Mil Virgenes, or "The 11,000 Virgins" (others contend his name for the islands was Las Islas Virgenes). Either way, the name was meant to honour the martyred fourth-century St. Ursula and her 11,000 virgins, murdered at the hands of the Huns at Cologne.

Columbus beat a hasty retreat after this christening, off to greener and golden shores, in search of the Great Khan of the Indies. Columbus' name, Virgin Gorda, literally "The Fat Virgin," stuck to that island.

Over the years, the Spanish, the Dutch and various pirates used the islands for stopovers and as bases for raiding passing ships. In 1595 Sir Francis Drake, the mercenary explorer, passed through the channel that now bears his name. One legend claims that the infamous Edward Teach (Blackbeard) once anchored off Deadman's Bay while splitting the spoils of a successful raid with his crew. An argument erupted and Blackbeard set 15 pirates on the island called Dead Chest, providing one bottle of rum to each with their sea chests to serve out their last days. Hence—and this is where legends always become suspect—the old salt's song with the line "fifteen men on dead men's chest, yo ho ho and a bottle of rum."

By the mid-1600s the British had established claims on some of the islands, yet remained in a continuous state of altercation with the Dutch and Spanish over territorial claims. In 1672 the British governor of the Leeward Islands claimed Tortola (Spanish for "turtledove") for England and sent settlers from Anguilla. By 1680 the British had established settlements on Anegada and Virgin Gorda. The peripatetic pirates and buccaneers, whose reign in the Caribbean and Americas would soon be over, dispersed for safer shores throughout the Caribbean.

Throughout the years the British fought back attempts to oust them from the islands. Most were feeble and shortlived attacks and the British Virgin Islands have remained a British entity throughout modern history. They were administered as a colony and part of the Leeward Islands Administration until 1956, when the nascent Federation of the West Indies was being formed. The federation, which administered the British West Indies, collapsed in 1962 after internecine bickering between Jamaica and Trinidad and Tobago led to Jamaica's withdrawal. The British Virgin Islands declined to join the federation, opting instead for a form of internal control over their affairs and economic links with the U.S. Virgin Islands. It was the best of both worlds for them and today that economic link is still seen—the U.S. dollar is the official currency.

During the 1960s and 1970s, constitutions were drawn that allowed for greater internal government, including the formation of political parties and local elections of a legislative council.

People and Culture

The British Virgin Islands is still a British Crown Colony and, therefore, a dependent territory. The cultural norms are British and African—with, of course, a West Indian twist. English is used by everyone, although West Indian colloquialisms and the lilting lyricism of islands' language is heard throughout. British Virgin Islands cuisine reflects the West Indian sensibility, using local fruits, vegetables, seafood and spices. Rum is the beverage of choice and still produced locally.

Among the locals, traditions of covering up remains strong. British Virgin Islanders pride themselves on neatness and appearance. Long skirts, uniformed school children and modesty are the norm; bathing attire or skimpy shorts and shirts will be offensive if worn off the beach.

Festivals and local events attest to the blending of the cultures. Virtually no month goes by where a sailing race or regatta is not held. These include the Sweet Hearts of the Caribbean Classic Yacht and Schooner Regatta in February, the British Virgin Islands Spring Regatta in April and Around Tortola Sailing Race in November. The Queen's Birthday is celebrated (July 11), as is the birthday of the Heir to the Throne (November 14). The islands' nod to West Indian and African influences, which amounts to a mid-summer carnival, is the B.V.I. Summer Festival. The festival, held in late July, features two weeks of nightly music, steelbands, calypso competitions, Prince and Princess shows, feasts and arts and crafts exhibitions and sales.

Government and Economy

The Queen is represented on the island by an appointed governor, who presides over an executive council comprising the chief minister, an attorney general and several ministers of government. The legislative council includes elected members, a governor-appointed member and a speaker of the council.

The B.V.I. economy is reliant on British and Commonwealth aid and on the tourism industry, in which yachting, boating and chartering play a large role. Between 150,000 and 200,000 visitors fly in or sail through each year and more than half go yachting during their vacations.

Another source of local income comes from the recently established BVI Film Commission (809-494-4119), which promotes island locations for motion picture and television shoots.

General Practical Information

GETTING THERE

■ BY AIR

Tortola's Beef Island Airport is the main entry point. Virgin Gorda also has an airport, which is serviced by light aircraft. St. Thomas, in the U.S. Virgin Islands, and San Juan are the main connectors from North America—there are no nonstop flights to the British Virgin Islands from North America. Several airlines connect to San Juan or St. Thomas, including Air Canada, American, Continental, Carnival, Delta and Northwest.

From San Juan, the U.S. Virgin Islands and northern Lesser Antilles: American Eagle (local tel. 809-495-2559), Sunaire Express (809-495-2480) and LIAT (809-494-3888).

■ BY SEA

Various ferry services operate between St. Thomas and Tortola, St. John and Tortola and St. Thomas and Virgin Gorda. The port at Road Town on Tortola is the entry point for cruise ships, some yachts and ferries in the British Virgin Islands. The Government Jetty is the ferry departure point. Tortola's West End is also a ferry stop.

Ferry services: Native Son, Inc. (809-495-4617), Smith's Ferry Services (809-494-4430, 494-2355, and 495-4495) and Inter-Island Boat Services (809-776-6597). The departure tax on leaving the British Virgin Islands is US$5 by air, US$3 by sea.

GETTING AROUND

■ FERRIES AND FLIGHTS

Travel among the British Virgin Islands is accomplished by ferries or airplanes. Daily flights are available between Beef Island and Virgin Gorda or Anegada on several small airlines, including Sunaire Express (see above), Aero Gorda (809-495-2271) and Atlantic Air BVI (809-495-2000).

Ferries makes regular runs from West End, Road Town or Beef Island on Tortola to The Valley and North Sound on Virgin Gorda and Great Harbor on Jost Van Dyke. From Tortola to Virgin Gorda and Jost Van Dyke: Speedy's Fantasy (809-495-5420), North Sound Express (809-494-2746), Beef Island to Virgin Gorda Service (809-495-5240), Reel World (809-495-9277) and Jost Van Dyke Ferry Service (809-495-2775 or 494-2997).

The Peter Island Boat (809-494-2561) operates between Road Town and Peter Island at least seven times daily.

■ YACHT CHARTERS
Of course, many visitors will elect to charter a boat and sail their way around. Not only is it a wonderful way to see the islands, but it is, in some ways, the most convenient.

Dozens of charter outfits in the British Virgin Islands offer everything from organized sailing, snorkelling and diving excursions to bareboat charters or crewed charters. You'll find 15 or so marinas scattered around the island group, most providing water, electricity and shopping for boat visitors, as well as anchorages scattered throughout the bays and inlets. Rates depend on the number of passengers, size and make of the boat, size of the crew and amenities.

Figure US$1,500 per week minimum for a bareboat in high season to as much as US$14,000 per week for a crewed charter for ten people. Rates are significantly reduced, by as much as half, during the off-season. Just a few of the many reputable charter outfits include:

❑ THE MOORINGS, Mariner Inn, Road Harbor, Tortola, B.V.I. (809-494-2331; U.S. tel. 800-535-7289).

❑ VIRGIN ISLANDS SAILING, Mill Mall, Road Town, Tortola, B.V.I.. (809-494-2774, fax 494-6774; U.S. Virgin Islands 800-233-7936 or 800-272-2566).

❑ DISCOVERY YACHT CHARTERS, P.O. Box 281, Road Town, Tortola, B.V.I.; (809-494-6026, fax 494-6035; Canada tel. 416-891-1999, fax 891-3623).

❑ MARINE ENTERPRISES BOAT RENTALS, P.O. Box 3069, Road Town, Tortola, B.V.I. (809-494-2786, fax 494-4744).

■ CAR RENTALS
Driving on Tortola or Virgin Gorda is not difficult, but remember to stay to the left. You'll need produce your valid license to purchase a temporary B.V.I. driving license, US$10, which can be organized by the rental company. Rates start at US$35 per day.

❏ ON TORTOLA: Alphonso Car Rentals (809-494-3137), Avis (809-494-3322), Budget (809-494-2531).

❏ ON VIRGIN GORDA: Potter's Car Rental (809-495-5329) or Speedy's Car Rental (809-495-5235).

❏ ON ANEGADA: Anegada Reef Hotel (809-495-8002).

■ PUBLIC TRANSPORTATION AND TOURS

You'll find taxis on Tortola at the airport and at the ferry docks in Road Town and West End. Taxis rates are set by the government and most will offer island tours as well as regular fares. On Tortola island tours start at US$12 per person, on Virgin Gorda US$10 per person. If you need to call a taxi, let your hotel recommend one or call BVI Taxi Association (809-494-2875) or Style's Taxi Service (809-494-2260) on Tortola, or Mahogany Taxi Service (809-495-5542) in The Valley.

Buses on Tortola are inexpensive—fares are no more than US$3 anywhere—but the schedules are confusing. Nevertheless, Scato's Bus Service (809-494-2365) in Road Town is the most reliable. They offer island tours as well.

ACCOMMODATION

All accommodation add a seven per cent government tax and a 10–12 per cent service charge. Most are located on Tortola and Virgin Gorda and, to a lesser extent, on Anegada and Jost Van Dyke, as well as several of the small private islands. Accommodation range from slick resorts, although not necessarily large ones, to hotels, guesthouses, apartments and several approved campsites.

■ VILLAS

Villas are available throughout the islands. The British Virgin Islands Tourist Board will assist in making contacts and reservations with dozens of property management companies throughout the islands. Or contact the following: Property Management Plus, P.O. Box 1072, The Valley, Virgin Gorda, B.V.I. (809-495-5867) and Kanaka Property Management P.O. Box 25, The Valley, Virgin Gorda, B.V.I. (809-495-5201).

Rates range from US$600–2,400 per week during the mid-December through mid-April high season.

■ CAMPING

Campsites offer both prepared sites with tents at US$20-35 per double or bare sites at US$10–15, during the high season. Call: Anegada Beach Campground, The Settlement, Anegada, B.V.I. (809-495-8038), Brewers Bay Campground, P.O.

Box 185, Road Town, Tortola, B.V.I. (809-494-3463 in St. John) and Tula's N&N
Campground, Little Harbor, Jost Van Dyke, B.V.I. (809-495-9302).

WATERSPORTS

❏ TORTOLA: BASKIN IN THE SUN (809-494-2858, U.S. tel. 800-233-7938), Blue
   Waters Divers (809-494-2847), Island Diver (809-494-3878), and Underwater
   Safaris (809-494-3235, U.S. tel. 800-537-7032).
❏ DIVE BVI (809-495-5513, U.S. tel. 800-848-7078) offers locations at the Virgin
   Gorda Yacht Harbor, Leverick Bay, and Peter Island.
❏ FOR DEEP-SEA FISHING, call Charter Fishing (Road Town, Tortola,
   809-495-3311), or Classic (Biras Creek, Virgin Gorda, 809-494-3555).

MONEY, HOURS AND COMMUNICATION

The currency of the B.V.I. is the U.S. dollar. U.S. travelers checks are widely
accepted; credit cards are accepted in many businesses, but not all, particularly at
smaller hotels, guesthouses and restaurants. Currencies can be changed at banks,
located in Road Town and Virgin Gorda. Bank hours may vary, but are generally
9.00-14.00 Monday through Friday, with extra hours on Friday 15.00-17.00.

Shops and other businesses are open 9.00–17.00 Monday through Saturday
and most are closed on Sunday.

The B.V.I. area code is 809, followed by a seven-digit number. Phone cards
for public phones can be purchased at the offices of Cable and Wireless in Road
Town (809-494-4444) or The Yacht Harbor in The Valley (809-495-5444). Cable
and Wireless can be used to send faxes, telexes and cables. Hours are 7.00–19.00
weekdays, 7.00–16.00 on Saturday and 9.00–14.00 on Sunday.

Tortola

Tortola is theB.V.I.'s population and administrative center and the largest island of
the group at 21 square miles (54 sq km). The island is also a center of activity,
restaurants and accommodation and one could happily spend a vacation on
Tortola alone.

BEACHES

Tortola's best beaches are found along its north and northwestern shores. Some
are accessible by car, others by boat or short hikes. Some have facilities and yacht
moorings in secluded bays, while others have few facilities. All, however, are open

to everyone. One of the best is Smuggler's Cove at the far west end, accessible by dirt road, a small beach with good snorkelling. Heading east you'll find Long Bay. The rougher Apple Bay, lined with palm trees, is frequented by surfers. This is the site of Bomba's Surfside Shack (809-895-2148) and Bomba's popular monthly "Full Moon Party." Several other small restaurants and bistros are located on this beach. Cane Garden Bay is wide and long and popular with both yachties and swimmers.

Brewers Bay was once the site of several sugar mills and distilleries and now features beach bars and a campground. Elizabeth Bay, on the eastern end, is small and secluded. Just north of the airport on Beef Island you'll find another Long Bay. The nearby salt pond is home to nesting terns and other sea birds.

SIGHTS

Road Town, a small, functional center, features a busy Main Street, government offices and waterfront. Here you'll find a post office, banks, churches, a prison, the tourist board, Cable and Wireless offices, police station, a museum, shops, the ferry dock, several hotels and, of course, the marinas. The town's style is quaint and modern West Indian; brightly painted wooden and stone buildings, particularly along the old Main Street, are attractions themselves.

The Sir Olva George's Plaza, across from the post office and near the ferry dock on Main Street, sits beneath several large ficus trees and is lined with government offices and shops. Nearby is the small, picket-fenced Virgin Islands Folk Museum, with stone artifacts from the early Amerindian presence on the islands and displays from the plantation slavery days, as well as bits and pieces salvaged from the wreck of the RMS Rhone, a British mail ship that sank off the coast of Peter Island in the 1800s. The free museum features a small gift shop here, with several good books about island history and lore. The museum is open (varies with season) 9.00-16.00 weekdays except Wednesday, when it is closed, and 9.00-12.00 on Saturday. The museum is closed Sunday.

Near the center of town and the police station you'll find the JR O'Neal Botanic Gardens (809-494-4557), four acres of local and imported tropical plants, with a hothouse, pond and self-guided walks. The gardens are open daily and admission is free, although, as with the museum, donations are accepted.

Several forts and historic ruins dot the countryside near Road Town. Fort Burt is now a hotel, one of the islands' first, built by the Dutch and later rebuilt by the British. The foundation is all that remains of the original structure. The ruins of Fort George and Fort Charlotte, both built in 1794, can be found on strategic hills overlooking the harbor.

You'll find Sage Mountain National Park at the island's west end. At 1,780 feet (534 m) it's Tortola's highest point and the views are stunning. Trails lead from the parking area through the park's 92 acres and up to the peak, an easy walk. The rainforest hosts a variety of flora and fauna, including a wide array of birds. Free.

At the far west end of the island is Sopers Hole, believed to be the site of the first Dutch landing on the island in 1648. The harbor has a ferry landing with customs and immigration facilities, as well as a marina, restaurants and shops. Nearby is Fort Recovery, in the Fort Recovery Villas complex. The remains of the fort consist of a tower and a few crumbled remains. There are no tours, but you can clamber around.

At Cane Garden Bay, along the North Coast Road, you'll find the Callwood Rum Distillery in an old stone plantation building. It's not a big distillery, but rum is still produced in copper vats and a still, much the same as it was during the plantation era. You can buy bottles of rum here. At Mt. Healthy, another small national park, you'll find an old stone windmill, once part of a sugar plantation.

ACCOMMODATION

❏ FRENCHMAN'S CAY RESORT HOTEL, P.O. Box 1054, West End, Tortola, B.V.I. (809-495-4844, fax 495-4056, U.S. tel. 800-223-9832) features self-contained villas on the beach at the southwestern tip of the island. Luxury.

❏ TAMARIND COUNTRY CLUB HOTEL, P.O. Box 509, East End, Tortola, B.V.I. (809-495-2477), mainly villas, short walk to beach. Luxury.

❏ SEBASTIAN'S ON THE BEACH, P.O. Box 441, Tortola, B.V.I. (809-495-4212, fax 495-4466, U.S. tel. 800-336-4870), is medium-size, 26 rooms, on the surfing beach at Little Apple Bay, clean, comfortable. Moderate.

❏ TURTLE DOVE LODGE, P.O. Box 11, West End, Tortola, B.V.I. (809-495-4430, fax 495-4070, U.S. tel. 800-223-4483) overlooks Long Bay, cabins with twelve beds, spartan but clean, no credit cards. Budget.

EATING

❏ BRANDYWINE BAY (809-495-2301) near Road Town features elegant seaside dining, continental and Florentine cuisine, dinner only. Moderate.

❏ FORT BURT HOTEL (809-494-2587) in Road Town serves a wide array of West Indian and traditional English dishes. Moderate-expensive.

❏ PUSSER'S CO. STORE AND PUB (809-494-2467) in Road Town is actually two restaurants, one serving sandwiches and meat pies, the other with a more formal fare. Inexpensive-moderate.

❏ SUGAR MILL (809-495-4335) at Apple Bay is one of the island's best and serves an eclectic range of creative West Indian and continental dishes. Moderate-expensive.

Virgin Gorda

Virgin Gorda is strung out over seven miles (11 km) from east to west, comprising a hilly middle section and the flatter east end and populated southwest end. There you'll find the island's center, The Valley, which incorporates the island's original settlement, Spanish Town. Virgin Gorda was once a major commercial center, but today is better known as an excellent anchorage for yachts and for its secluded beaches. A road connects the west end of the island with North Sound, a large bay separating the east end of the island with the offshore islets of Prickly Pear Island, Necker Island and Eustatia Island. Prickly Pear Island has been declared a protected national park.

Transport to Virgin Gorda is by ferry or by shuttle flight from Tortola. The airstrip is located in The Valley.

BEACHES

The British Virgin Islands' best-known beach is The Baths, south of The Valley, a natural formation of colossal boulders that form pools, caves and oddly lit, shimmering grottos. Walking trails—slogging trails, actually—are marked through the boulders and pools. This is an enormously popular attraction and is likely to be swamped with visitors, especially during cruise ship stopovers. Still, The Baths are unlike most beaches you've seen. Go early or later in the day to avoid crowds.

Other popular beaches on Virgin Gorda include Spring Bay, nearby The Baths, and Trunk Bay, a series of secluded beaches north of Spring Bay, accessible by boat or by a hike from Spring Bay. There is a path linking the bays. Savannah Bay, on the narrow isthmus between the west and central sections of the island, is wide and expansive. In total Virgin Gorda has nearly 20 beaches, many secluded, some easily accessible by shuttle boats.

SIGHTS

South of the Yacht Harbor in The Valley is Little Fort National Park, once a Spanish fort. The fort is in ruins and you can see part of the old Powder House. The park is now a 36-acre wildlife sanctuary. On the eastern shore of the western tip of the island is Copper Mine Point, worked by English miners from 1838–67 and probably by Spanish miners 300 years before that. Remains of stone buildings, a cistern and mine shafts can be seen.

Gorda Peak National Park is located on the central section of Virgin Gorda and encompasses 265 acres, all land starting 1,000 feet (300 m) above sea level. The peak, at 1,359 feet (408 m), is the island's highest point. There is a small observation platform at the top and the surrounding forest is heavy with mahogany and semi-rainforest flora.

South and west of the island are strings of small cays, including Fallen Jerusalem and Dog Island. Several of the islands are available for mooring and are frequently visited by nesting sea birds. Fallen Jerusalem and Dog Island are protected by National Park Trust regulations.

ACCOMMODATION

❑ BIRAS CREEK ESTATE, P.O. Box 54, Virgin Gorda, B.V.I. (809-494-3555, fax 494-3557, U.S. tel. 800-223-1108) in North Sound can be reached by boat only; the resort sits on 150 acres, with individual villas. Luxury.

❑ BITTER END YACHT CLUB, P.O. Box 46, Virgin Gorda, B.V.I. (809-494-2746, U.S. tel. 312-944-5855) is also on North Sound, a retreat reached by boat only, featuring 95 rooms and some villas. Luxury.

❑ LITTLE DIX BAY HOTEL, P.O. Box 70, Virgin Gorda, B.V.I. (809-495-5555, fax 495-5661, U.S. tel. 800-223-7637), one of the island's first hotels, features tennis, water sports and a marina. Luxury.

❑ OCEAN VIEW HOTEL, P.O. Box 66, Virgin Gorda, B.V.I. (809-495-5230, U.S. tel. 800-621-1270) is small, conveniently located near the ferry, simple and clean. Budget-moderate.

EATING

❑ OLDE YARD INN (809-495-5544) in The Valley is large on country charm and French continental cuisine. Expensive.

❑ THE BATH AND TURTLE (809-495-5239) at the Yacht Harbor is a relaxed and informal pub with light fare, on the harbor. Moderate.

❑ CHEZ MICHELLE (809-495-5510) in town serves French and continental. Moderate.

❑ THE CRAB HOLE (809-495-5307) in The Valley serves West Indian creole and features live entertainment. Moderate.

Jost Van Dyke

Great Harbor on Jost Van Dyke is the island's center of activity and the place to start your exploration. There you will find shops, a harbor, customs and immigration facilities and several small beach bars and bistros. This tiny island, population about 200, received electricity in 1991 and features just a few miles of paved road.

ACCOMMODATION

❏ SANDCASTLE, P.O. Box 540, White Bay, Jost Van Dyke, B.V.I. (809-777-1611) consists of four beach cottages; some watersports are available. Luxury.

❏ RUDY'S MARINER INN, Great Harbor, Jost Van Dyke, B.V.I. (809-495-9282), a small inn, features rooms with kitchenettes, no credit cards. Moderate-luxury.

❏ HARRIS' PLACE, Little Harbor, Jost Van Dyke, B.V.I. (809-495-9302, fax 9296) is a small guesthouse in Little Harbor, just two rooms, on the beach. Budget.

EATING

❏ ABE'S BY THE SEA is a bar and restaurant in Great Harbor, featuring frequent barbecues. Moderate.

❏ ALI BABA'S in Great Harbor serves West Indian. Inexpensive-moderate.

❏ RUDY'S MARINER'S RENDEZVOUS has live music and pig roasts. As a matter of fact, pig roasts seem to be the thing on Jost Van Dyke—keep your eye out for roasts on specialty nights.

Anegada

The island's low-lying coral limestone formation and miles of white-sand coastline make it unique in the British Virgin Islands group. The atoll's reef is considerable, relatively untouched and the diving, snorkelling and fishing here are big attractions. An estimated 300 wrecks lie offshore and provide wide opportunities for divers searching for treasure (doubtful) or pristine fish and coral colonies (likely).

In 1992 the government released flamingos on the island, with the aim of creating a preserve. Turtles can be seen nesting on the beaches along the north shore during their nesting season. The entire north shore and west end is an uninterrupted beach, with little shade and few facilities, so bring along hats and sunscreen. Beach bars are found at Lloblolly Bay, on the north shore.

Most of the island's population of 300 live in the appropriately named The Settlement, which is near the airstrip in the south-central section of the island.

ACCOMMODATION

❏ ANEGADA REEF HOTEL, Anegada, B.V.I. (809-495-8002, fax 495-9362) is the only hotel on the island and the center for activity, watersports and rentals. Luxury.

EATING

❏ Choices are limited here, but you won't starve. On Anegada it's best to make reservations for dinner. The popular POMATO POINT (809-495-9466) serves local seafood and drinks on the beach. DEL'S (809-495-8014) in The Settlement is good for lunch and local dishes. NEPTUNE'S Treasure serves seafood and continental. The ANEGADA REEF HOTEL serves breakfast, lunch and dinner. The above are inexpensive-moderate.

Other Islands

❏ GUANA ISLAND, a private 125-acre island with a nature preserve and several fine beaches, is located off the north coast of Tortola. Stay at the Guana Island Club, P.O. Box 32, Road Town, Tortola, B.V.I. (809-494-2354, U.S. tel. 800-544-8262). Luxury.

❏ MOSQUITO ISLAND, just off the Virgin Gorda coast, is privately owned, with walking trails, watersports and beaches. Accommodation are at Drake's Anchorage, P.O. Box 2510, North Sound, Virgin Gorda, B.V.I. (809-494-2254, U.S. tel. 800-624-6651), consisting of villas, rooms and suites, a French restaurant and lots of privacy. Luxury.

❏ NECKER ISLAND, north of Virgin Gorda, is owned by Richard Branson, of Virgin Air and other Virgin ventures. The island features an exclusive rental villahouse that sleeps up to 20. Call 800-926-0636 for details.

❏ NORMAN ISLAND, south of Peter Island, sits uninhabited and is widely believed to be the setting for Robert Louis Stevenson's Treasure Island. Day trips are available for snorkelling and lolling about its beaches and the floating restaurant, The William Thorton, converted from a 1910 Baltic Trading ship, is moored off The Bight.

❏ PETER ISLAND, a 1,000-acre island south of Tortola, features beaches, watersports, anchorages and the Palm Island Resort, P.O. Box 211, Road Town, Tortola, B.V.I. (809-494-2561, fax 494-2313, U.S. tel. 800-562-0268), a 50-room resort with villas. Luxury.

USEFUL ADDRESSES

■ BRITISH VIRGIN ISLANDS TOURIST BOARD:
- ❑ P.O. Box 134, Road Town, Tortola, B.V.I.; 809-494-3134, fax 494-3866.
- ❑ 370 Lexington Ave., New York, NY 10017; 800-835-8530 or 212-696-0400, fax 949-8254.
- ❑ 1686 Union St., San Francisco, CA 94123; 800-232-7770 or 415-775-0344, fax 775-2554.
- ❑ 110 St. Martin's Lane, London WC2N 4DY; 44-171-240-4259, fax 240-4270.
- ❑ Sophienstrasse 4, D-65189 Wiesbaden, Germany; 49-611-300262, fax 300766.

■ OTHER
- ❑ Emergencies, tel. 999.
- ❑ Peebles Hospital, Tortola; 494-3497.
- ❑ Chief Immigration Officer, Tortola; 494-3701.
- ❑ National Parks Trust; tel. 494-3904.

THE LEEWARD ISLANDS

ANGUILLA
SAINT-MARTIN/SINT MAARTEN
SAINT-BARTHELEMY
SABA
SINT EUSTATIUS
ST. KITTS AND NEVIS
ANTIGUA AND BARBUDA
MONTSERRAT
GUADELOUPE

North Friar's Bay, Southeast Penin, towards North St Kitts

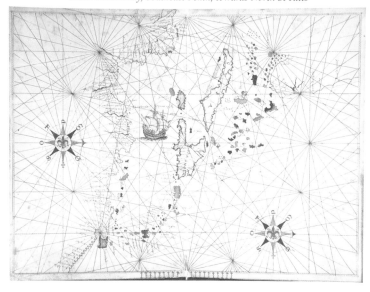

Chart by Angel de Conte Fraducci, 1555

A giant Yucca flower, North Friar's Bay, St Kitts

Rawlins Plantation Hotel, Old Sugar Mill, St Kitts

(Left and top) Sugar land train, Northwest Coast, St Kitts;
(above) Sugar cane harvest, St Kitts.

Sunday churchgoing, Christchurch, St Kitts

View of St Eustacian sunset, St Kitts

Palm trees and sunset on the west coast of St Kitts

Edgar Challenger, historian at the St Kitts Museum

Antigua Cricket Club, 1913

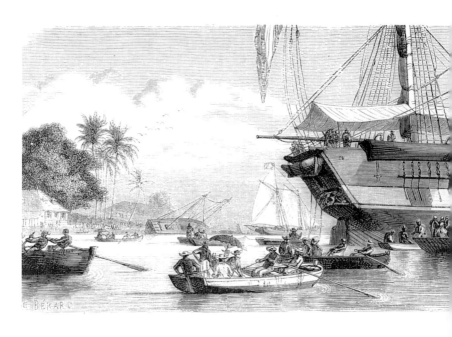

'French importing non-slave labour to
Guadeloupe',
from The Illustrated London News, *1858*

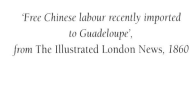

*'Free Chinese labour recently imported
to Guadeloupe',
from* The Illustrated London News, *1860*

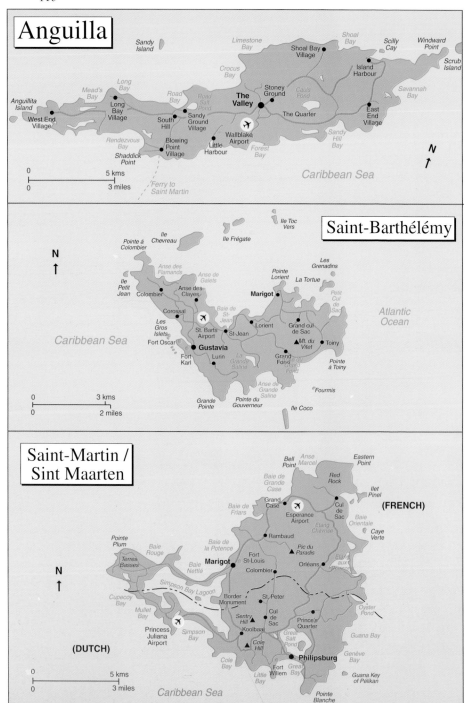

Anguilla

Sandy Island
Limestone Bay
Shoal Bay
Scilly Cay
Windward Point
Shoal Bay Village
Scrub Island
Crocus Bay
Island Harbour
Savannah Bay
Mead's Bay
Long Bay
Road Bay
Road Salt Pond
Stoney Ground
The Valley
Cauls Pond
Anguillita Island
Long Bay Village
South Hill
Sandy Ground Village
The Quarter
Sandy Hill Bay
East End Village
West End Village
Rendezvous Bay
Blowing Point Village
Little Harbour
Wallblake Airport
Forest Bay
N
Shaddick Point

0   5 kms
0   3 miles

Caribbean Sea

Ferry to Saint Martin

Saint-Barthélémy

Ile Toc Vers
Ile Chevreau
Ile Frégate
Pointe á Colombier
Les Grenadins
N
Pointe Lorient
La Tortue
Anse des Flamands
Anse de Galets
Marigot
Petit Cul de Sac
Ile Petit Jean
Colombier
Anse des Clayes
Baie de St-Jean
Corossal
Lorient
Grand cul de Sac
Atlantic Ocean
Les Gros Islets
St. Barts Airport
St-Jean
Mt. du Vitet
Toiny
Caribbean Sea
Fort Oscar
Gustavia
Lurin
La Grande Saline
Grand Fond
Pointe á Toiny
Fort Karl
Fourmis
0   3 kms
0   2 miles
Grande Pointe
Pointe du Gouverneur
Anse de Grande Saline
Ile Coco

Saint-Martin /
Sint Maarten

Bell Point
Anse Marcel
Eastern Point
Baie de Grande Case
Red Rock
Ilet Pinel
Baie de Friars
Grand Case
Esperance Airport
Cul de Sac
(FRENCH)
Baie Orientale
Caye Verte
Pointe Plum
Baie Rouge
Baie de la Potence
Rambaud
Etang Chevrise
Pic du Paradis
Terres Basses
Marigot
Fort St-Louis
Etang aux Poissons
N
Baie Nettlé
Colombier
Orléans
Cupecoy Bay
Simpson Bay Lagoon
Border Monument
St. Peter
Oyster Pond
Mullet Bay
Sentry Hill
Cul de Sac
Prince's Quarter
Princess Juliana Airport
Simpson Bay
Koolbaai
Great Salt Pond
Guana Bay
Cole Hill
Genève Bay
(DUTCH)
Cole Bay
Fort Willem
Philipsburg
Guana Key of Pélikan
0   5 kms
0   3 miles
Little Bay
Great Bay
Caribbean Sea
Pointe Blanche

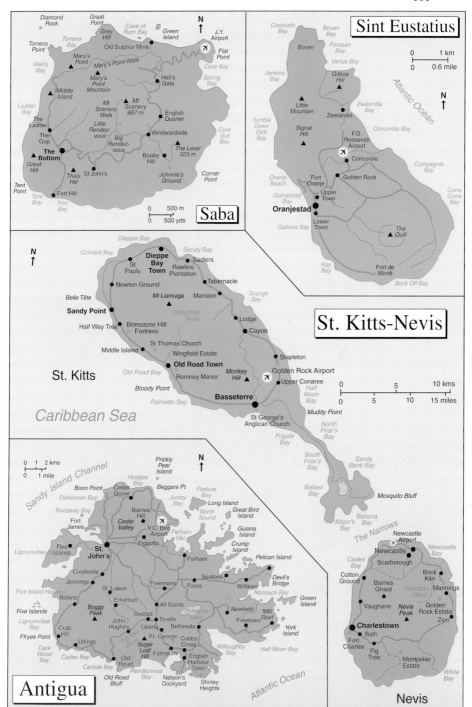

Saba

Diamond Rock · Great Point · Grey Hill · Cave of Rum Bay · Green Island · J.Y. Airport · Torrens Point · Torrens Bay · Old Sulphur Mine · Flat Point · Well's Bay · Mary's Point · Mary's Point Walk · Cove Bay · Spring Bay · Mary's Point Mountain · Hell's Gate · Ladder Bay · Middle Island · Mt Scenery Walk · Mt Scenery 887 m · English Quarter · Core Gut Bay · The Ladder · Little Rendez-vous · Big Rendez-vous · Windwardside · The Gap · The Bottom · Booby Hill · The Level 523 m · Great Hill · Thais Hill · St John's · Johnnie's Ground · Corner Point · Tent Point · Fort Hill · Tent Bay · Fort Bay

0   500 m
0   500 yds

Sint Eustatius

Cocoluch Bay · Boven Bay · Boven · Fontaan Bay · Venus Bay · Gilboa Hill · Jenkins Bay · Little Mountain · Zeelandia · Zeelandia Bay · Concordia Bay · Tumble Down Dick Bay · Signal Hill · F.D. Roosevelt Airport · Concordia · Oranje Beach · Fort Oranje · Golden Rock · Compagnie Bay · Upper Town · Corre Corre Bay · Oranjestad Bay · **Oranjestad** · Lower Town · Gallows Bay · The Quill · Kay Bay · Fort de Windt · Back Off Bay

0   1 km
0   0.6 mile

St. Kitts-Nevis

Dieppe Bay · Sandy Bay · Convent Bay · **Dieppe Bay Town** · Sadlers · St Pauls · Rawlins Plantation · Newton Ground · Tabernacle · Mt Liamuiga · Mansion · Belle Tête · Grange Bay · **Sandy Point** · Wingfield River · Lodge · Half Way Tree · Brimstone Hill Fortress · Cayon · Middle Island · St Thomas Church · Wingfield Estate · Stapleton · Old Road Bay · **Old Road Town** · Monkey Hill · Golden Rock Airport · Romney Manor · Upper Conaree · Bloody Point · **Basseterre** · Half Moon Bay · Palmetto Bay · Muddy Point · St George's Anglican Church · North Friar's Bay · Frigate Bay

St. Kitts

Caribbean Sea

South Friar's Bay · Sandy Bank Bay · Ballast Bay · Mosquito Bluff

0   5   10 kms
0   5   10   15 miles

Antigua

0   1   2 kms
0   1 mile · Sandy Island Channel · Prickly Pear Island · Hodges Bay · Beggars Pt · Pasture Bay · Boon Point · Cedar Grove · Jumby Bay · Long Island · Dickenson Bay · Barnes Hill · North Sound · Great Bird Island · Runaway Bay · Cedar Valley · V.C. Bird Airport · Parham Hbr. · Guiana Island · Fort James · Piggotts · Crump Island · **St. John's** · Parham · Pelican Island · Lignumvitae Islands · Creekside · Freemans · Seatons · Devil's Bridge · Jennings · St Lukes · Pares · Willikies · Nonsuch Bay · Bolans · Emanuel · All Saints · Newfield · Green Island · Five Islands · **Boggy Peak** · Swetes · Tyrells · Bethesda · Mill Reef · Lignumvitae Bay · John Hughes · Liberta · Freetown · York Island · Ffryes Point · Crab Hill · Ft. George · Cobbs Cross · Urlings · Sugar Loaf Hill · Falmouth · English Harbour Town · Willoughby Bay · Half Moon Bay · Dark Wood Bay · Cades Bay · Old Road · Carlisle Bay · Old Road Bluff · Rendezvous Bay · Nelson's Dockyard · Shirley Heights · Atlantic Ocean

Nevis

The Narrows · Major's Bay · Banana Bay · Newcastle Airport · Cades Bay · Newcastle · Newcastle Bay · Cotton Ground · Scarborough · Brick Kiln · Barnes Ghaut · Mannings · Fountain Ghut · Vaughans · Nevis Peak · Golden Rock Estate · Zion · **Charlestown** · Fort Charles · Bath · Fig Tree · Montpelier Estate · White Bay

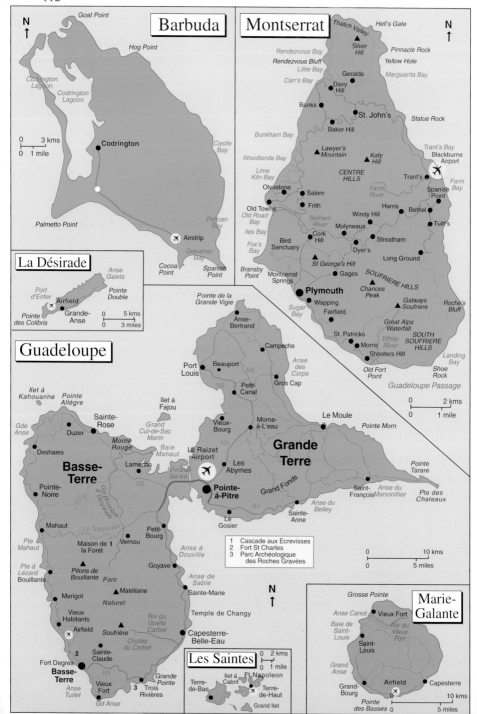

Barbuda

N ↑

Goat Point
Hog Point
Codrington Lagoon
Codrington Lagoon
Castle Bay
Codrington
0 3 kms
0 1 mile
Palmetto Point
Pelican Bay
Cocoa Point
Spanish Point
Gravener Bay
Airstrip

La Désirade

Anse Galets
Port d'Enfer
Airfield
Pointe Double
Pointe des Colibris
Grande-Anse
0 5 kms
0 3 miles

Guadeloupe

Ilet á Kahouanne
Pointe Allégre
Gde Anse
Sainte-Rose
Duzer
Morne Rouge
Ilet á Fajou
Grand Cul-de-Sac Marin
Deshaies
Basse-Terre
Lamentin
Baie Mahault
Pointe-Noire
Riviére Salée
Mahaut
La Traversée
Gd Rivière à Goyave
Maison de la Forêt
Vernou
N2
Pte Mahaut
Pte á Lézard
Bouillante
Pitons de Bouillante
Parc
Petit-Bourg
Matéliane
Naturel
Goyave
Riv du Grand Carbet
Marigot
Vieux Habitants
Airfield
Soufrière
Chutes du Carbet
2
Fort Degres
Basse-Terre
Sainte-Claude
Vieux Fort
3 Trois Rivières
Grande Pointe
Anse Turlet
Gd Anse

Pointe de la Grande Vigie
Anse-Bertrand
Campeche
Port Louis
Beauport
N8
Anse des Corps
N6
Petit-Canal
Gros Cap
Vieux-Bourg
Morne-á-L'eau
Le Moule
Pointe Morn
Grande Terre
Le Raizet Airport
Les Abymes
N5
Pointe Tarare
Pointe-á-Pitre
Grand Fonds
N1
Saint-François
Anse du Mancinillier
Pte des Chateaux
Le Gosier
Sainte-Anne
Anse du Belley
Anse á Douville
Anse de Sable
Sainte-Marie
Temple de Changy
Capesterre-Belle-Eau

1 Cascade aux Ecrevisses
2 Fort St Charles
3 Parc Archéologique des Roches Gravées

0 10 kms
0 5 miles

N ↑

Montserrat

N ↑

Thatch Valley
Hell's Gate
Silver Hill
Pinnacle Rock
Rendezvous Bay
Rendezvous Bluff
Little Bay
Carr's Bay
Geralds
Yellow Hole
Marguerita Bay
Davy Hill
Banks
St. John's
Baker Hill
Statue Rock
Bunkham Bay
Lawyer's Mountain
Katy Hill
Trant's Bay
Blackburne Airport
Woodlands Bay
CENTRE HILLS
Trant's
Farm Bay
Lime Kiln Bay
Olveston
Salem
Farm River
Spanish Point
Old Towne
Old Road Bay
Frith
Harris
Bethel
Windy Hill
Iles Bay
Beiham River
Molyneaux
Tuitt's
Fox's Bay
Cork Hill
Streatham
Bird Sanctuary
Dyer's
Bransby Point
St George's Hill
Long Ground
Montserrat Springs
Gages
SOUFRIERE HILLS
Plymouth
Chances Peak
Galways Soufriere
Roche's Bluff
Wapping
Fairfield
Great Alps Waterfall
SOUTH SOUFRIERE HILLS
Sugar Bay
St. Patricks
White River
Morris
Shooters Hill
Old Fort Point
Shoe Rock
Landing Bay
Guadeloupe Passage
0 2 kms
0 1 mile

Marie-Galante

Grosse Pointe
Anse Canot
Vieux Fort
Riv du Vieux Fort
Baie de Saint-Louis
Saint-Louis
Grand Anse
Grand-Bourg
Airfield
Capesterre
Pointe des Basses
0 10 kms
0 5 miles

Les Saintes

0 2 kms
0 1 mile
Ilet á Cabrit
Ft Napoleon
Terre-de-Bas
Terre-de-Haut
Grand Ilet

Anguilla

Introduction

Anguilla, removed from the ravages of the 18th and 19th century West Indian wars for island domination, removed as well from the ravages of the plantation slave economy and today still a bit removed from the modern tourism industry, is one of two islands in the Lesser Antilles that, in this century, experienced enough political turmoil to warrant military intervention by outside forces. It amounted to a revolution and, outside Anguilla, it was ponderous. Why would a tiny island with a population smaller than a medium-sized university launch a revolution with sticks and stones and protest signs?

Who but an Anguillan can ever truly answer the question? But the observable fact is the incident portrayed something about the Anguillan character and its tenacity and about national pride. These are people not wholly given over to concepts devised by a tourism board, yet who are among the most welcoming you'll find in the islands.

The Land

Anguilla (An-GWIL-ah), the northernmost of the Leeward Islands, lies 190 miles (304 km) east of Puerto Rico and five miles (eight km) north of Saint-Martin/Sint Maarten. The Atlantic Ocean meets the island's north shore and the Caribbean touches its south coast.

The island has ancient volcanic origins, but today little reminds one of the sort of topography—sharp hills, rugged coastline, dramatic cliffs—associated with volcanic islands. Anguilla is now a flat, low-lying and coral formation, 16 miles (26 km) long and three miles (five km) wide, with inland depressions forming small salt ponds and valleys. The highest point on the 35 square mile (90 sq km) island is the central Crocus Hill, only 213 feet (64 m) above sea level. The soil is thick with clay and not arable in many places and the local flora of hardy shrubs and trees can withstand some relatively dry conditions. There are no running rivers or streams. The coastline is irregular, serrated by small coves and bays with white coral sand beaches.

Several offshore islands, used for fishing and recreation, include Dog Island, Prickly Pear Cay and Seal Island in the northwest, Anguillita Island and Blowing Rock off the southwestern shore and Scrub Island off the northeastern Windward Point.

History

The first known inhabitants of Anguilla were Amerindians, most probably Arawaks or sub-divisions of that group. Remnants of their existence, dating from 2,000 BC to 1,500 AD, are still being discovered in an archaeological excavation begun in 1988 in the Island Harbor area, on the island's northeast coast. The natives' name for the island was Malliouhana.

It is doubtful that Columbus ever charted the island. Various European explorers passed by in the late 15th and early 16th centuries and, somewhere along the way, it acquired the name Anguilla, possibly from the Spanish anguila or the French anguille, both meaning "eel," a reference to the shape of the island. The first recorded mention of Anguilla was in 1564, by the French explorer Rene Laudonniere.

The English claimed Anguilla in absentia, but it wasn't until 1650 that the first English landing party attempted a settlement. They farmed tobacco, cotton and sugarcane, cultivated salt from the ponds and raised some cattle, but the agricultural part of the island's nascent economy failed to gain a strong foothold and never, throughout the island's history, proved a major contributor.

In 1656 an Amerindian raid devastated the first settlement. The raid may have been conducted by Caribs from nearby islands, although there is little evidence of the Caribs ever having lived on Anguilla. The French also raided Anguilla, in 1666 and 1689 and later in 1745 and 1796, but weren't able to hold onto the island for any length of time. Pirate parties also took their toll. However, despite the intrusions, the island remained a British colony throughout most of its early colonial history.

In 1816 Anguilla was incorporated with St. Kitts, Nevis and the Virgin Islands for administrative purposes, a move that would have a profound influence on the island over the next 150 years. At this time the population was approximately 3,000—400 whites, 300 free blacks and 2,300 slaves.

From the mid-19th century on, Anguilla was, alternately, a free port, a minor sugar producer and a reluctant member of the Federation of the Leeward Islands (1871). In 1872 the islanders petitioned Queen Victoria to dissolve their relationship with St. Kitts and Nevis, but were rebuffed.

An officer from the colonial administrative center on St. Kitts characterized the request as "a petition from a large number of illiterates." Which was bound to produce some animosity on Anguilla. This animosity, coupled with Anguilla's status as a second-class colony associated with the successful sugarcane colonies of St. Kitts and Nevis, continued throughout the 19th and early 20th centuries.

In 1958 the British Federation of the West Indies was formed, with the colony of St. Kitts-Nevis-Anguilla represented as a single political unit. That same year, the island legislative council petitioned the colonial governor for separation from St. Kitts and Nevis, again to no avail. In 1962 the Federation collapsed under the withdrawal of wealthy Jamaica and several of the other larger states. During the next several years, political parties on the island grew in strength, as did the small tourism industry.

In 1966 talks began in London with the aim of producing a constitution for a proposed semi-autonomous state of St. Kitts-Nevis-Anguilla. Anguillans were alarmed and against the idea, supposing, with good reason, that St. Kitts and Nevis would continue to relegate the poor and relatively unproductive island to the status of an indigent country cousin.

By 1967 demonstrations to reject the state had grown into a full-fledged separatist movement. Violence flared in early February of that year and, by mid-month, the British sent an extra police attachment from St. Kitts to the island. In March, Anguillan separatists burned down Government House and attacked police headquarters. By May of that year, the movement voted to expel the Kittitian police force, which they did. In June a boatload of Anguillans sailed to St. Kitts and, with surprising naivete, attempted to overthrow the government. They were routed, captured and five men went to trial.

Throughout this period various peacekeeping initiatives from the U.K., Jamaica and Barbados were proposed and failed. By 1969 negotiations with the governments of St. Kitts and Britain had broken down. Early that year the British cut off economic aid to the island and by February Anguilla had declared itself an independent republic. The elected president of the republic was Ronald Webster and the island braced itself for reprisals after its expulsion of a British junior minister and negotiator in early March. Reprisals—perhaps a stretch of the word—came on 19 March 1969, when the British invaded the island.

"Invaded" might be an overstatement. Troopers and parachuters were brought in by offshore frigates and a contingent of the London police force was installed on the island. President Ronald Webster flew off to the United Nations to gather support for the expulsion of British troops, but was turned down. The islanders themselves were in a quandary. Many wanted independence from St. Kitts and Nevis and some form of association with Britain. Others wanted full independence. Over the next few years, resistance to the British occupying force was negligible. By 1972 Ronald Webster had formed the People's Progressive Party (PPP). That same year the British government allowed the formation of an Anguilla police force. Elections were held for a local legislative council and the majority of the seats went to the PPP, with Webster as the island's first chief minister. Power in the Legislative Assembly later shifted to Emile Gumbs of the Anguilla National Alliance (ANA), who was later named chief minister in 1977. On 19 December 1980 Anguilla was formally separated from the government of St. Kitts and Nevis. Separation Day is still celebrated as a national holiday.

In 1982, with a new constitution and mandate, the island became a British Dependent Territory.

People and Culture

Anguilla's population is 9,000. The majority are descendants of African slaves and a smaller group are descended from European settlers, the Irish of St. Kitts. English is widely spoken, with, of course, West Indian colloquialisms. Religions on the island include Methodist, Anglican, Catholic, Seventh-Day Adventist, Baptist and various Protestant offshoots.

The Mayoumba Folkloric Theater, a group that keeps alive the dance, oral traditions and costume of pre-20th century Anguilla through performances, can be found at the La Serena Hotel (809-497-6827) in Mead's Bay on Thursday evenings.

Anguilla's weeklong Carnival, celebrated in late July-early August, features calypso competitions, Prince and Princess Shows, pageants, band contests, street dancing and festivals. Daytime activities include boat racing, which is practically the national sport on Anguilla. The small wooden sloops built and used in the races are unique to the island. Activities take place all over the island, but ground zero is Landsome Bowl Center in The Valley.

Government and Economy

Anguilla is a British Crown Colony, specifically a dependent territory. The Queen is the head of state. The Crown is represented on the island by an appointed governor and deputy. A local Legislative Assembly is elected every five years and consists of 12 members, including an assembly speaker and deputy speaker. An Executive Council has four assembly members, the governor, deputy governor and an attorney general. The chief minister and his or her party are elected every five years and that post has alternated since the late 1970s between Ronald Webster, then of the Anguilla United Movement (AUM), and Emile Gumbs of the ANA.

Anguilla's economy, once based on farming and salt production, now relies on tourism as the primary foreign exchange earner. The 1992 figures show 93,180 arrivals, a staggering increase over the 1982 figure of 17,562. About 32,076 stayed overnight. More than half of the island's visitors are from the U.S. and Canada. The number of hotel rooms, more than 900, is increasing gradually.

Overseas remittances and aid from the U.K. and the Caribbean Development Bank provide Anguilla with funds for capital expenditure.

Sights

BEACHES

Beaches are certainly not the sole attractions on Anguilla, but they rank among the best in the Caribbean. The 12 mile (19 km) coast is lined with an estimated 45 white-sand beaches, set in quiet bays and inlets. Many are protected by off-shore coral reefs, which makes snorkelling excellent. Beaches are open to everyone, but most have few facilities outside those offered by hotels and beach-side restaurants. Topless and nude sunbathing are not allowed by law, but tacitly accepted in places.

Among the best beaches:

Shoal Bay, on the north coast, about two miles (three km) of white sand, features plenty of small cafes, seaside beer joints and chair and umbrella rental places. The beach is popular and may be crowded on weekends; snorkelling here is very good. Limestone Bay has a small beach, rough water at times. South of Limestone Bay is Crocus Bay, then Sandy Ground, lined with hotels and offering watersports activities; this is the place to be at night for dancing and whooping it up. Mead's Bay on the southwestern Atlantic coast is also popular and the site of several of the island's luxury resorts, including Malliouhana Hotel.

On the southern, Caribbean side of the island you'll find Shoal Bay West End, Cove Bay, Maunday's Bay and Rendezvous Bay, all with views to Saint-Martin/Sint Maarten. Several large resorts, including Covecastles, Cap Juluca, Casablanca and the Anguilla Great House, have facilities and some watersports.

These are generally quieter, although not secluded, beaches. Little Harbor is less a bay than a large inlet and is accessible either by boat or by a short walk from the end of the road. Great views and good snorkelling here.

Scrub Bay and Deadman's Bay lie on opposite ends of Scrub Island. Dog Island has a few of coves and quiet bays, plus the wide Spring and Savannah bays.

OTHER SIGHTS

Beyond Anguilla's superb beaches and the galleries and shops of The Valley, not much exists in the way of historical sites or natural attractions. A half-dozen large salt ponds recall the bygone days of the salt industry and several examples of turn-of-the-century West Indian architecture, primarily in The Valley, are reminiscent of the town's growth during that time.

At Crossroads, near The Valley, you'll find Wallblake House, a restored late-18th century plantation greathouse. St. Gerard's Catholic Church currently owns the building and uses it to house its resident priests. Across the way is the Devonish Cotton Gin Art Gallery, housed in a colonial-era ginnery and factory building. The building and grounds, parts of which are renovated and parts of which stand as they did years ago, can be toured by appointment (809-497-2405).

North of The Valley, past Stoney Ground near Shoal Bay Village, is The Fountain national park. The Fountain was once an important source of water for the indigenous Arawaks.

The nearby village of Island Harbor was a central Arawak settlement, where pottery shards and stone and shell tools have been uncovered. In a cave dubbed Big Spring, used by Arawaks for ceremonial purposes, 37 petroglyphs have been discovered and recorded. This cave and the surrounding area have been incorporated into the National Parks system, operated by the National Trust, while the excavation is underway. It isn't open to the public yet, but a museum is planned for the future. Contact the Anguilla Archaeological and Historical Society (809-497-2727) for more information. Elsewhere on the island are ruins of an old Court House at Crocus Hill and an overgrown fortification at Sandy Hill.

Island tours and offshore cays excursions are offered by MultiScenic Tours (809-497-5810, fax 497-5811), which also offers mountain bike rentals and excursions. Malliouhana Travel and Tours (809-497-2431) in The Valley (The Quarter) and Bennie's Travel and Tours (809-497-2671) in Sandy Ground are both reliable tour operators.

The Valley

The Valley is Anguilla's capital and main cultural and administrative center, located about three miles (five km) west of the airport. It is a small town, with half a dozen roads, several churches, schools, banks, a post office, police station, tourism headquarters and a few restaurants and galleries. Worth noting is Landsome Bowl, the island's sports stadium and center for cultural activities, including the August Carnival.

The Anguilla Tourist Office (809-497-2759 or 2451, fax 497-3389) is located in the Social Security Building.

Practical Information

ACCOMMODATION

Anguilla has a fairly extensive range of accommodation, from guesthouses to villas to exclusive resorts, but generally the accommodation are of medium size and medium price range.

Camping is not allowed on Anguilla.

■ VILLAS

Villas range from as little as US$100 per day for two bedrooms, to as much as US$1,000 per day for luxury cottages (less by the week).

Contact SELECT VILLAS OF ANGUILLA, George Hill Road, Anguilla, W.I. (809-497-5810, fax 497-5811), SUNSHINE VILLAS, Cul de Sac, Anguilla, W.I. (809-497-6149, fax 497-6021) and CONNER'S REAL ESTATE, South Hill, Anguilla, W.I. (809-497-6433, fax 497-6410).

■ HOTELS

Add an eight per cent room tax in all cases and a 10–15 per cent service charge in most cases.

❏ MALLIOUHANA HOTEL, P.O. Box 173, Mead's Bay, Anguilla, W.I. (809-497-6111, fax 497-6011, U.S. tel. 800-372-1323, fax 203-656-3475), is large and luxurious, possibly the island's most exclusive resort. The beach below is quiet and long. No credit cards are accepted. Luxury.

❏ CAP JULUCA, P.O. Box 240 Maunday's Bay, Anguilla, W.I. (809-497-6666, fax 497-6617, U.S. tel. 800-323-0139) is a 179-acre resort on the bay, with villas and suites, built in a strangely effective Moorish style. Luxury.

❏ ANGUILLA GREAT HOUSE, Rendezvous Bay, Anguilla, W.I. (809-497-6061, fax 497-6019, toll-free 800-241-6764) features West Indian-style rooms decorated with reproduction mahogany antiques. All face the ocean, very quaint stuff. Luxury. Less expensive accommodation:

❏ JESHAL APARTMENTS, Back Street, South Hill, Anguilla, W.I. (809-497-6517). Budget.

❏ LLOYD'S GUESTHOUSE, P.O. Box 52, Crocus Hill, Anguilla, W.I. (809-497-2351). Moderate.

❏ SYD-AN'S HOTEL AND VILLAS, Sandy Ground, Anguilla, W.I. (809-497-3180, fax 497-5381), two apartments and six suites, on the beach, small restaurant. Moderate.

EATING

Local West Indian specialties feature items such as stewed whelk, conch and curried conch, mutton, rice and peas, fungi, coconut extravaganzas, guinea corn, dumplings, fish and lobster. Other restaurants serve French creole, French, Italian, Chinese and several world-class restaurants are found in hotels. Not all restaurants take credit cards, nor are all open every day, particularly during the off-season. Call ahead to check.

❏ AQUARIUM RESTAURANT (809-497-2720), in South Hill, simple, no frills. Inexpensive.

❏ ARLO'S PLACE (809-497-6810), Lower South Hill, the best Italian on Anguilla. Moderate.

❏ FISH TRAP (809-497-4488) on the beach at Island Harbor, best seafood around, gourmet and sophisticated. Moderate.

❏ GORGEOUS SCILLY CAY (no phone), an experience not to be missed, dining and swimming on a small, private cay off the Island Harbor shore. Wait for the free transport boat every few minutes. Lunch only, closed Mondays. Moderate-expensive.

❏ MALLIOUHANA (809-497-6111), French, absolutely make reservations, a day ahead if possible, views of Mead's Bay. Expensive.

❏ PIMM'S (809-497-6779), on the water at Maunday's Bay, French. Expensive.

❏ YABBA POT (809-497-2820) in The Valley, Rasta Ital (vegetarian) specialties. Inexpensive.

GETTING THERE

Anguilla's Wallblake Airport (809-497-2384) is serviced by international airports in Sint Maarten, Antigua and San Juan. All these airports have direct and non-stop connections with major North American cities such as Toronto, New York and Miami, as well as connections with European cities.

Airlines with local numbers: American Eagle (809-497-3500/1), LIAT (809-497-5000, fax 497-5576), Air BVI (The Valley tel. 809-497-2431 or 2348, airport 809-497-2488) and Winair (809-497-2748 or 3748).

Two local air charter companies service neighbouring islands: Air Anguilla (809-497-2643 or 2725, fax 497-2982) and TA Tyden Air (809-497-2719, fax 497-3079).

Departure tax is EC$5 or US$2.

GETTING AROUND

■ TAXIS

Taxis are not metered; rates are set by the government, quoted for one or two persons, with US$3 added for each additional person.

Typical rates will not exceed US$20 for a ride from the airport to anywhere on the island.

Island tours, which last two to three hours, start at US$40 for one or two people and US$5 for each additional person. Drivers will often quote rates in U.S. dollars. Stands are located at Wallblake Airport and Blowing Point (awaiting the ferry from Saint-Martin, see below) and you can always flag down a taxi in The Valley.

■ CAR RENTALS

Rental rates start at about US$35 per day for a small car or mini-moke, which is sort of an oversized go-cart. You'll have to obtain a temporary local license for US$6, which the rental company can organize. Call Avis (809-497-6221, fax 497-5052), Budget (809-497-2217, fax 497-5871, U.S. tel. 800-527-0700), Conner's Car Rentals (809-497-6433, fax 497-6410) or Triple K Car Rental (809-497-2934, fax 497-2503).

Anguilla is relatively flat and lends itself well to travel by motorcycles and bicycles. Call R&M Cycle Rental (809-497-2430) in The Valley, MultiScenic Tours (809-497-5810) on George Hill Road or Booth's (809-497-2075) at The Swamp. Bicycle rentals start at US$10 per day.

■ FERRY SERVICE

Five miles south of Anguilla is the island of Saint-Martin/Sint Maarten, reached by a 20 minute ferry ride. Saint-Martin/Sint Maarten is lively and cosmopolitan in ways that Anguilla is not and makes for an easy day trip. Casinos, duty-free shopping, an outdoor market and fine restaurants are accessible for those who want to take advantage of the island's proximity. The ferry leaves from Blowing Point, on Anguilla's south shore, to Marigot, on the French side of Saint-Martin, every 30 minutes from 7.30 until 17.00. From Marigot back to Blowing Point, ferries depart every 30 minutes from 8.00 through 17.30. Night ferries depart Anguilla at 18.00 and 21.15. The last ferry back from Marigot is at 22.45. Check with the tourist office or Blowing Point Port (809-497-6403) for changes in the schedule. Cost is US$9 (day) or US$11 (night) one way. Remember, you'll need to bring your passport or travel documentation; a departure tax of US$2 is payable either way.

MONEY, HOURS AND COMMUNICATION

Anguilla's currency is the Eastern Caribbean dollar, currently exchanging at EC$2.70 = US$1. U.S. dollars are widely used, credit cards less so. Dollars may be changed at hotels and shops, but you will get a better rate at a bank. Look for banks in the Commercial Center in The Valley. Banking hours vary, but are generally 8.00-15.00 Monday through Thursday and 8.00–17.00 Friday.

Businesses are open 8.00–17.00 weekdays, with a noon lunch hour, although some grocery stores are open until 21.00. Some stores are open until noon or so on Saturday, grocery stores until evening and most businesses are closed on Sunday. The tourist office is open 8.00–12.00 and 13.00–16.00 weekdays.

The General Post Office (809-497-2528), which has a philatelic bureau, is in The Valley and open 8.00–12.00 and 13.00–15.30, weekdays only.

The area code for Anguilla is 809. This means North Americans dial 1-809, plus 497 and a four-digit telephone number. Dial only the last four digits for local calls. Local calls are made using telephone cards, which are purchased at Cable and Wireless (809-497-3100 or 2210), located on Wallblake Road in The Valley. Cable and Wireless has telephones for international calls, as does the airport and Blowing Point ferry building. Hours at Cable and Wireless: 8.00-18.00 weekdays, 9.00-13.00 Saturday and 10.00-14.00 Sunday.

For information about goings on, the tourist publications What We Do in Anguilla and Anguilla Life are available at the tourist office in The Valley and at most hotels.

ENTERTAINMENT
■ SPORTS

For watersports the first stop is your hotel or the facilities at Sandy Ground. Tamariain Watersports (809-497-2020, The Valley tel. 497-2798) can organize boating excursions, diving resort certification and diving excursions. Marine Watersports (809-497-2671) can do the same. For sailing trips, island cruises and trips to outlying cays on the catamaran Wildcat, call Enchanted Island Cruises (809-497-3111) at Sandy Ground. Suntastic Yacht Cruises (809-497-3400) organize cruises as well as deep sea fishing.

Tennis is available at several hotels, including Carimar Beach Club, Malliouhana, Cinnamon Reef and Sea Grapes.

■ OTHER

Anguilla has no casinos and, besides hotels and bars, little weekday nightlife, particularly during the off-season. The strip of restaurants and hotels at Sandy Ground is popular for dancing and live music and things pick up on weekends. Johno's Beach Stop (809-497-2728), Lucy's Palm Palm (809-497-2253) and Dragon's Disco (no phone, best after midnight) all have music of one form or another. Round Rock (809-497-2076), a small barbecue place at Shoal Bay, features local music on Sunday evenings. Uncle Ernie's (no phone), also at Shoal Bay, often has live music on Sunday afternoons, as does Scilly Cay (no phone).

Malliouhana Hotel (809-497-6111) features live music, often the "easy listening" type, every evening.

SHOPPING

Galleries and boutiques are located all over the island and in hotels. Among the more interesting: Anguilla Arts and Crafts Center (809-497-3200), a one-stop craft shop in The Valley; Devonish Art Gallery (809-497-4971) in The Valley, across from Wallblake House; Cheddie's Carving Studio (809-497-6027) at The Cove on the West End Road, with wood and driftwood carvings; and Caribbean Style Boutique at the Anguilla Great House.

USEFUL ADDRESSES

■ TOURISM INFORMATION

Department of Tourism
- ❏ The Valley, Anguilla, W.I.; (809) 497-2795 or 2451, fax 497-2751.
- ❏ Windotel, 3 Epirus Road, London SW6 7UJ; (0171) 937-7725, fax 938-4793.

■ OTHER

- ❏ Police, 497-2333.
- ❏ Fire, 497-2333.
- ❏ Ambulance, 497-2637.
- ❏ College Hospital, 497-2551/2.
- ❏ Anguilla Drug Store, 497-2738.
- ❏ Wallblake Airport, 497-2384.

Saint-Martin/Sint Maarten

Introduction

Saint-Martin/Sint Maarten is, unlike the sister islands of Antigua and Barbuda or Trinidad and Tobago, not two islands combined to form one nation, but rather two nations combined on one island. The situation is unique in the Lesser Antilles and that is an understatement; a 37 square mile (95 sq km) island with two names, two cultures, two governments, three currencies, at least four languages and no borders ranks high on any singularity scale.

There is much to recommend in Saint-Martin/Sint Maarten—too much, in a way. It's a place thoroughly discovered, inhabited by and reliant upon tourism. Saint-Martin/Sint Maarten is one of the Lesser Antilles' most popular cruise ship stops. Some of the Lesser Antilles' best resorts, restaurants, sports activities and shopping are found here, but at a price. It is rarely a quiet place, but rather bustling, congested, exciting. Local cultures have been nearly buried by the onslaught of tourism; even residents whom you think are locals may be from another place. The 1950 population of the island, in the pre-tourism days, was about 5,000. Today, of the 60,000 population, only a fifth was born on Saint-Martin/Sint Maarten.

The island's two dominant cultures are French and Dutch, at least in the political sense. Hence, its unwieldy name. Saint-Martin is the northern French side, and Sint Maarten is the southern Dutch side. Saint-Martin/Sint Maarten (or its reverse) is used on maps; in common usage, no one repeats the two names, which are at any rate pronounced the same way.

The Land

Saint-Martin/Sint Maarten is located in the Leeward Islands of the Lesser Antilles, about 150 miles (240 km) southeast of Puerto Rico, 20 miles (32 km) north of Saint-Barthélémy and five miles (eight km) south of its nearest neighbour, Anguilla.

Saint-Martin/Sint Maarten tends to be dry, with scrubby bush and grassy plains taking up much of the low land. Rain occasionally turns the island green, but water is in general a problem. With the enormous pressure put on the island's water supply by the tourist industry, much of it is brought in by tankers.

The center of the island features some hills, the highest being the French-side Paradise Peak at 1,260 feet (420 m), easily accessible by car. The coast, particularly to the south and west, is characterized by wide bays and long, white sand beaches. The western Terres Basses region is low-lying and marshy in places, with mangrove swamps touching the shore. The southwest Simpson Lagoon is separated from the sea by narrow strips of land. Princess Juliana International Airport is on the south end.

Philipsburg, the capital of the Dutch side, sits on a strip of land separating the island's largest deep water bay and main port from the large Great Salt Pond, once the domain of salt harvesters. Several small offshore islands, including Tintamarre and Pinel, are popular recreation spots.

History

Several disputes exist regarding the history of Saint-Martin/Sint Maarten. The first involves the Amerindian inhabitants of the island. Archaeologists agree Stone Age man inhabited the island for at least a short time circa 4,000 BC, back when Saint-Martin/Sint Maarten may have been joined as one with the islands known today as Saint-Barthélémy and Anguilla. Several waves of Arawaks and related groups arrived from South America about AD 800 and lived a peaceful existence by fishing, hunting and farming. The Arawaks were followed north by another Amerindian group with its roots in South America, the Caribs. This is where the dispute occurs: some historians believe the Caribs never made it as far north as Saint-Martin/Sint Maarten, possibly no farther north than Guadeloupe, citing a lack of evidence. Others say Columbus' sightings prove the Caribs made it as far north as Hispaniola.

At any rate, Amerindians of some variety were living on the island at the time of Columbus' second voyage, in 1493. They called the island Soualiga, meaning "Salt Island," apparently referring to the huge southern salt pond and other sources on the island. Another legend has them calling the island Oualichi, or "Island of Women," which is decidedly more appealing.

Another dispute involves Columbus' sighting of the island. Some believe he never sighted Saint-Martin/Sint Maarten at all, but rather sighted the island that we today call Nevis and named it St. Martin. History later confused the names.

Initially, the Spanish made no attempt to settle. Nor did any of the subsequent European visitors of the 16th century, including the French, Portuguese, English and Dutch.

From 1630 to 1632 the Dutch established a small settlement in the south, determining the salt reserves there were valuable. At about the same time the French established a small settlement in the area that became known as French Quarter. The two groups skirmished periodically with no lasting effects.

In 1633 the Spanish reconsidered their position in the Lesser Antilles and decided to reestablish a presence. They invaded Saint-Martin/Sint Maarten and Anguilla driving off the French and Dutch inhabitants. The French and Dutch banded together to repel the Spanish and it was during a 1644 sea battle that the Dutch commander Peter Stuyvesant lost his right leg. Soon after, the fickle Spanish simply abandoned their pursuit of islands in the eastern Caribbean and the French and Dutch moved back to Saint-Martin/Sint Maarten. There they hammered out a few treaties and, with the signing of the Mont des Accords on 23 March 1648, divided the island in near halves.

A popular folk tale has it that the two groups measured the island's division by a race. A Frenchman and Dutchman started walking from Oyster Pond, on the east coast. The Dutchman went south along the shore and the Frenchman went north, and wherever they met was to be the other end of the border. The Dutchman, who was drinking gin, walked slower than the Frenchman, who was drinking wine, and therefore the French got a better deal. One wonders about the Dutch reaction to this legend. At any rate, the one factual aspect to this tale is that the French side of the island measures 21 square miles (54 sq km) and the Dutch side is slightly smaller at 16 square miles (41 sq km).

The border was violated several times and new treaties were drawn to divide the island; it wasn't until 1772 that an actual boundary was marked.

The French and Dutch planted cotton, tobacco, sugarcane and coffee, importing slaves to farm the crops. Due to lack of rain and poor soil, however, the island was never a major plantation center.

During the next century, Saint-Martin/Sint Maarten changed flags when the French conquered the Dutch and vice versa. It was a time of mild schizophrenia for the island, with one hand slapping the other and in turn slapping British invaders and others. Saint-Martin/Sint Maarten changed hands 16 times, until the French and Dutch established a permanent boundary in 1817, the same boundary that exists today.

Slavery was abolished by the French in 1848 and by the Dutch in 1863. Small plantations died. Former slaves moved away to seek work on large plantations in Cuba, the Dominican Republic, Puerto Rico and the United States. By the turn of the century sugar and cotton farming were no more and a large-scale exodus took place. France and the Netherlands treated the island as little more than an economic annoyance and by the 1940s even the salt industry had dried up, so to speak. Subsistence fishing, farming and donations from relatives abroad were all that kept locals in food and shelter. By the 1950s the population was only 5,000— half the size it was in 1915. Princess Juliana Airport was completed in 1947 as part of a U.S. military complex. Saint-Martin/Sint Maarten's first tourist hotel was built in 1955. From that point on, the history of this tiny island has been inexorably linked to tourism. By 1978 the island's population had grown to 25,000. Thousands of illegals poured in to staff the new hotels and resorts. Development during the 1980s, particularly on the Dutch side, gave the island many large and sprawling resort complexes and high employment.

People and Culture

The island's population is 28,000 on the French side and 32,000 on the Dutch side, with an additional 25,000 illegal immigrants working in the tourist industry. About 20 per cent of the total population is indigenous. The rest are French and Dutch nationals and workers from around the Caribbean and world. Some 80 different nationalities reside on Saint-Martin/Sint Maarten.

With this diversity of cultures comes a Babylon of languages and it can sometimes be hard to distinguish which belong and which do not. English is widely spoken on the Dutch side and taught in primary school. Dutch is also spoken on the Dutch side, as is Papiamento, an amalgam of Spanish, Portuguese, English, Dutch and some African languages. Spanish is also used, mainly by those who have worked in the Dutch colonies of South America and by workers from Spanish-speaking islands. French is used on the French side. English is also used, but infrequently, particularly among the French nationals. French Creole is spoken among the African-descent locals, including those from the other French islands.

Religions in Saint-Martin/Sint Maarten reflect the many cultures found here: Catholic, Anglican, Baptist, Methodist, Jehovah's Witness, Baha'i and Seventh-Day Adventist.

Both the French and Dutch sides celebrate Carnival, but at different times. The French Carnival is the traditional pre-Lenten round-up of street parades, calypso contests, feasts and masquerades. All business stops for the five days leading up to the final celebrations on Ash Wednesday. The Dutch Carnival is celebrated during Easter week and features parades, jump-ups, Calypso King and

Queen competitions, activities at Carnival Village (in Philipsburg, near the university) and the closing ceremony, which features the burning of a major Carnival masquerade character, King Moumou. Performances by folk dance groups such as Grain d'Or are worth finding. Check the local papers or call 590-87-75-80. The Fondation Historique et Culturelle (590-87-32-24) promotes Saint-Martin cultural events.

Government and Economy

Trade and exchange between the island's two sides is congenial and efficient, although the distinctions in their infrastructures, such as differing currencies, postal and electrical systems and telephone exchanges, make logistics a bit challenging. Life for visitors has been made easy by cooperation in airport entry regulations—one entry for both sides, no customs—as well as cooperation between tourism authorities. The two border points between the French and Dutch sides are nominal; at Cole Bay, the spot is marked by flags, a monument inscribed "1648–1948" and the sign "Bienvenue en Partie Francaise." At the western border, the sign reads "Welcome to Dutch St. Maarten NA."

Dutch Sint Maarten is a member of the Netherlands Antilles, along with Curaçao, Bonaire, Statia and Saba. Aruba is a separate entity within the Kingdom of the Netherlands.

The Netherlands Antilles are ruled by parliamentary democracy with the Dutch monarch, Queen Beatrix, serving as head of state. The queen is represented in the Netherlands Antilles by a governor, who is appointed by the crown. The islands are represented in the Dutch Cabinet through a minister plenipotentiary, who is appointed by the legislative council of the five Netherlands Antilles. Each island is allowed some self-rule, with administerial responsibility for water, electricity, land, schools and harbors. The legislative council consists of a council of ministers and a 22 member parliament, which meets in Willemstad, Curaçao. Sint Maarten's capital is Philipsburg, about six miles (ten km) from the airport.

French Saint-Martin is a sub-prefecture of Guadeloupe, an overseas department of France. As such it is represented in Guadeloupe's regional council, which is in turn represented in the French parliament. The capital is Marigot, on the western coast, a 20 minute drive from the airport.

The economy of Saint-Martin/Sint Maarten is virtually given over to tourism. No substantial farming is practiced and the local fishermen provide catch for hotels and the small island markets.

By 1977 there were nearly 2,000 hotel rooms on the island and 200 cruise ship visits per year. Those numbers have now at least doubled, with half a million visitors yearly. French Saint-Martin has plans to add onto an existing landing field in Grande Case, while Sint Maarten is expanding its cruise ship facilities at Great Bay in Philipsburg.

Sights

BEACHES

Many of Saint-Martin/Sint Maarten's estimated 37 beaches have facilities for parking, eating, changing and renting chairs and sun umbrellas. A few others are remote and difficult to access.

All beaches are open to the public, but few have lifeguards. There have been instances of theft from unlocked rental cars or of valuables left alone on the beach—lock up your things. Among the best beaches: Cupecoy Beach, on the Dutch side west of the airport, is set among sandstone cliffs and caves. The waves are often full and the surf strong, but wind is minimalized by the cliffs. There are no facilities. Park near the Ocean Club. One end of the beach is clothing-optional. Just west of Cupecoy is Baie Longue, a long, white-sand beach with excellent snorkelling and no facilities.

Baie Rouge is also long and pretty; a sign points the way from the main road. Parking is a problem here, just settle for a spot along the dirt road to the entrance. A small snack and umbrella rental concession is usually set up.

Grand Case Beach, in Grand Case, is a fine place to spend the day. Stop at one of the dozen roadside barbecue shacks, which offer cheap chicken, lobster, fresh fish and West Indian delicacies.

Orient Beach (Baie Orientale) is an extremely popular—read crowded—beach on the French east coast. You'll find plenty of snack huts, gift booths, chair and umbrella rentals, watersports and parking. The snorkelling here is very good and part of the outlying reef is a marine reserve. The far end of the beach, near the nudist resort Club Orient, is clothing-optional.

Philipsburg

The Dutch Sint Maarten capital is built on a narrow strip of land between Great Bay and Great Salt Pond. The main section of the mile-long land bridge comprises two streets, Front and Back and Walter Nisbet Road, a main artery built on reclaimed pond land. Front Street fronts the bay and is the main duty-free shopping center. The cobbled street is so busy it is almost a pedestrian walkway and trying to park here is futile. Opt for a side street. The beach on the bay looks out onto the open Caribbean and is clean and fine for swimming. The bay has several marinas, where most likely a cruise ship or two will be docked. Boats to Saba, Statia and Saint-Barthélémy depart from here. Near the center of Front Street is the Town Pier and Wathey Square. On the square, in addition to street vendors and souvenir shops, is the Town Hall. The building was originally built in 1793, renovated after an 1825 hurricane and again in the 1960s. Upstairs is a courthouse and below is a post office. A taxi stand is also located on the square.

Next to the Sea Palace is the Sint Maarten Museum (599–5–24917). Two upstairs rooms are packed with artifacts, photos, old maps, Arawak zemis (spirit figures), dinner sets and historical oddities of colonial life on Sint Maarten. The building is more than 100 years old. Inquire about the museum's Walking Tour of Philipsburg. The entrance donation is US$1 and hours are 10.00-16.00 weekdays (also 19.00-21.00 Friday) and 10.00-12.00 Saturday.

At the foot of town is the West Indian Tavern, with three roofs and gingerbread fretwork, typical of late-19th century West Indian homes. Once a synagogue, it's now one of the oldest restaurants on the island. This is where the island's Guavaberry liqueur is manufactured. The Pasanggrahan Hotel is one of the island's older hotels and once hosted Dutch royalty, such as Queen Wilhelmina.

Back Street is quieter than Front Street, but still has a great number of shops and cafes. The two streets are connected by small alleys and narrow streets, called *steegjies* in Dutch.

On the outskirts of town, on a hill overlooking the bay, are the remains of Fort Willem. Not much is left of the ruins and the road to the fort, starting from the Great Bay Beach Hotel, is rough. However, the nearby 300-year-old Fort Amsterdam is in better shape and you will still be able to see several cannons on the grounds. The Dutch structure was built upon the ruins of an original Spanish fortification. Both forts are currently being excavated and under renovation.

On the reclaimed Walter Nisbet Road, running alongside the salt pond, you'll find the main post office, police station, a cinema and a government building which houses the tourism board (599–5–22337, fax 31159). The stakes in the salt pond mark the "plots" of families that still harvest salt.

Just around the corner from the University of St. Martin, at Madame Estate, is the small St. Maarten Zoo (599–5–32030). The zoo features animals from the Caribbean and South America and a petting zoo and small playground for the kids. The zoo is open 9.00-17.00 weekdays and 10.00-18.00 weekends; admission is US$4 for adults and US$2 for children.

Marigot

Quiz: how many islands in the French West Indies feature towns named Marigot? Answer: all of them. And then some. Marigots are found on Dominica and St. Lucia as well. The word is derived from a French Creole word meaning "marsh."

The capital of French Saint-Martin, Marigot, with a population of 5,500, is slightly smaller than Philipsburg. The town lies on the expansive Baie de Marigot, with the Simpson Lagoon at its south end. This is a popular yachting port and the Marina Port la Royale on the lagoon is a busy dining and shopping district. Marigot itself strains to be cosmopolitan, with dozens of cafes, bistros and galleries lining the streets and alleys. People drive from the Dutch side just to buy baguettes from the many excellent pastisseries. The duty-free shopping here is plentiful and a lot of time can be spent strolling the streets, stopping at minimalls, galleries and chi-chi clothiers.

The famous open market on the Marigot port is open daily, although Wednesday and Saturday mornings are busiest. Produce comes in from as far away as Dominica for the 6.00-13.00 market. Spices, fruit, vegetables, fresh fish, crafts and T-shirts make for a pretty lively scene. In front of the parking area are duty-free shops and the St. Martin Museum, which features Amerindian pottery, stone tools, photographs and artifacts from the colonial period. The museum is open 9.00-13.00 and 15.00-18.30 on weekdays and 9.00-13.00 on Saturday.

Also at the harbor is the tourist office (87-57-23, fax 87-56-43), a taxi stand, a ferry to Anguilla and several restaurants and outdoor cafes. The ruins of Fort St. Louis, also called Fort Marigot, sit in the hills overlooking the harbor and town. It's 91 steps to the top of the circa-1786 fort, but there's not much left of the structures, save a few walls and the foundation.

Other Islands

Excursions to Ille Tintamarre and Pinel Island can be made from Marigot, but these tend to be the all-day sailing trips with lunch, drinks and more that you possibly don't want. The best way to explore the islands, which are uninhabited and used for recreation, is to drive to Cul-de-Sac on the northeastern shore. From here, numerous small boats (ask for Vanion) make the short runs to Pinel and Tintamarre for US$5-7 per person round-trip.

Practical Information

ACCOMMODATION

Saint-Martin/Sint Maarten may have more hotels and guesthouses per square mile than anywhere else in the West Indies. The Dutch side tends to feature large resorts, some with casinos, and a few smaller hotels and guesthouses. The French side offers more intimate hotels and inns, although larger resorts are found. Gambling is illegal on the French side. Campgrounds are nonexistent, but camping is allowed with permission from a land owner.

Room tax on the Dutch side is five per cent; on the French side it varies with the hotels. Both sides will tack on a service charge, usually 10-15 per cent. The tourist offices of both sides print accommodation lists with rates.

■ VILLAS

A large number of villas are available on the island and a good source for information is WIMCO (U.S. tel. 800-932-3222). Time shares, often part of hotels, are also thriving, particularly on the Dutch side.

■ HOTELS

On the Dutch side:

❏ MULLET BAY RESORT AND CASINO, P.O. Box 309, Sint Maarten, Netherlands Antilles (599-5-52801, fax 54281) is recommended for those who want to be in the thick of it all. The sprawling resort features 600 units, a golf course, pools, tennis, beach, casino and shopping. Luxury.

❏ SHERATON PORT DE PLAISANCE, Sint Maarten, N.A. (599-5-45222, fax 22323), on Simpson Lagoon, is another large complex with watersports, shops, restaurants, pools and a fitness center. The beach here, however, is small. Luxury.

❏ PASANGGRAHAN HOTEL, P.O. Box 151, Sint Maarten, N.A. (599-5-23588, fax 22885) was once the official guesthouse for visiting Dutch royalty. The hotel, on Front Street in Philipsburg, is small and has the feel of an old-style West Indian inn. Moderate.

❏ MARY'S BOON, P.O. Box 2078, Sint Maarten, N.A. (599-5-54325, fax 53316) is located on the wide Simpson Bay Beach, behind Princess Juliana Airport. This is an intimate guesthouse, with 12 studios facing the water. The hotel's list of "no's" is comprehensive: no children under 16, no credit cards, no singles, no triples, no complaining about the airport noise. If you fit the criteria, this is a lovely place. *Moderate.*

On the French side:

❏ CAPTAIN OLIVER'S, Oyster Pond, 97150 Saint-Martin, French West Indies (590-87-40-26, fax 87-40-84) is a bayside resort with a small marina, great for watersports. The complex straddles the border between the French and Dutch sides, on the east coast. *Moderate-luxury.*

❏ LA SAMANNA, BP 159, Marigot, 97150 Saint-Martin, F.W.I. (590-87-51-22) overlooks Baie Longue from a hillside location and is one of the island's most exclusive resorts. *Luxury.*

❏ LA RESIDENCE, BP 127, Marigot, 97150 Saint-Martin, F.W.I. (590-87-70-37), a small 21 room inn on Rue du General de Gaulle, is a great location for eating, shopping and walking the streets of Marigot. *Moderate.*

EATING

❏ IN GRANDE CASE: Le Tastevin (590-87-55-45), The Fish Pot (590-87-50-88), Cha Cha Cha (590-87-53-63), Hevea (590-87-56-85). All moderate-expensive.

❏ IN MARIGOT AND SANDY GROUND: La Vie En Rose (590-87-42), expensive; Etna Ice Cream (590-87-72-72), budget; Le Palmier (590-87-50-71), moderate. In Colombier: La Rhumerie (590-87-56-98), inexpensive-moderate.

❏ ON THE DUTCH SIDE: Le Perroquet (599-5-54339), expensive; Grill & Ribs (Philipsburg and Simpson Bay), moderate.

GETTING THERE

■ BY AIR

Princess Juliana International (599-5-52161 or 54211) is serviced by several large North American and European carriers: American Airlines (local tel. 599-5-52040), Air France (599-5-54212), ALM (599-5-54230), BWIA (599-5-53304), KLM (599-5-54240) and Lufthansa (599-5-52040).

For inter-island travel the major carriers are LIAT (599-5-52403), the Sint-Maarten-based Winair (599-5-54210), Air Martinique (599-5-54212) and Air Guadeloupe (same phone).

Departure tax for Princess Juliana is US$5 to Netherlands Antilles islands, US$10 elsewhere.

The small Esperance Airport in Grand Case deals with inter-island flights from, mainly, Saint-Barthélémy. Air Guadeloupe and Air St. Barthélémy use

Esperance and departure taxes are included in airfares. This airport is due for expansion in the near future.

■ FERRY SERVICE

A ferry service operates to nearby Anguilla from the harbor in Marigot. The ferry departs daily every thirty minutes from 8.00 up to and including 17.30, as well as at 19.00 and 22.30 and returns every half-hour from 7.30 until 17.00, plus 18.15 and 22.15. The trip takes about 20 minutes. One-way fare is US$9, half price for children under 12. Departure tax from Marigot and Anguilla is US$2.

The Pearl Line Express operates a daily 45 minute service from both Philipsburg (599-5-24409) and Marigot (590-87-85-45) to Saint-Barthélemy. Call for the current schedule.

GETTING AROUND

■ TAXIS AND BUSES

Taxis are not metered and government-approved rates are posted at the airport taxi stand. Rates are also posted in the tourist newspaper *Today* and are the same for both sides of the island. Add 25 per cent to taxi rates from 22.00-24.00 and 50 per cent after midnight.

Minibuses operate 7.00–19.00 between Philipsburg, Marigot and Grand Case at a flat rate of US$1.50. They also operate to the rest of the island and their destinations are marked by signs on the windshield.

■ RENTAL CARS

Rental rates start at about US$35 per day and while there are many companies operating on the island, the supply seems to run out once in a while. Book ahead if possible. Driving is on the right and all you'll need to rent a vehicle is your valid license or international license. Remember to lock your rentals when parking at the beach. Break-ins have been reported, particularly along the sometimes isolated west coast.

A dozen rental agencies are found at the airport and just about every hotel on the island can contact a rental company.

❑ AIRPORT: Avis (599-5-54265 or 542316), Budget (599-5-54274), Cannegie (599-2-52397), National (599-5-42168).
❑ DUTCH SIDE: Caribbean Auto Rentals (599-5-45211), Roy Rogers Rentals (599-5-52701).
❑ FRENCH SIDE: Hertz (590-87-76-69), Roy Rogers (590-87-54-48), Sunny Island (590-87-80-21).

MONEY, HOURS AND COMMUNICATION

Currency in Dutch Sint Maarten is the Netherlands Antilles florin or guilder, currently trading at NAF1.80 = US$1. French Saint-Martin uses the French franc, which may fluctuate daily against the dollar (as of this writing, F5.50 = US$1). Both sides, however, widely use the U.S. dollar. Items are often priced in francs, guilders and dollars, except in supermarkets and at the petrol pump. Change is often given in U.S. dollars on the Dutch side and francs on the French side, but the fact is that you never really need to exchange your U.S. dollars for francs or guilders. In some duty-free shops U.S. dollars are the only accepted currency.

To exchange traveler's checks, banks and bureaux de change are located at several shopping malls and on the main streets of Philipsburg and Marigot. Dutch banks are open 8.00–15.00 Monday through Friday and for an extra hour, 16.00-17.00, on Friday. French banks are open 8.00–13.00 weekdays. Money can also be exchanged at post offices. Major credit cards are accepted virtually everywhere.

Businesses are open Monday through Saturday, 8.00–18.00, with an hour or two off for lunch. Some shops are open on Sundays to accommodate cruise ship traffic.

Oddly, two electrical systems exist on the island. The Dutch side uses 110 volts, 60 cycles, while the French side uses a 220 volt, 60 cycle system. There are exceptions on the French side; some large hotels offer the 110 volt system.

Telephoning Saint-Martin/Sint Maarten is often a challenge. The international exchange for the Dutch side is 599, while French Saint-Martin uses 590. From North America, for Dutch Sint Maarten, dial 011–599, followed by 5 and the five-digit number. When calling French Saint-Martin, dial 011–590 and a six-digit number. To call the French side from the Dutch, dial 06 plus the six-digit number. When calling the Dutch side from the French, dial 19–599–5 plus the five-digit number. Calling from one side to the other is, in effect, an international phone call. Post offices are located in Philipsburg (599–5–22289) and Marigot (590–87–53–17).

Several free tourist newspapers, including *Today*, are available on the island. Dutch Sint Maarten publishes *The Chronicle* and *The Guardian* six days per week, as well as the regional *The Caribbean Herald*. Airport shops carry U.S. and European newspapers, the day's edition often arriving in the late afternoon.

ENTERTAINMENT

■ SPORTS

The competition among watersports centers is fierce—any island hotel will have a connection with a facility that provides some combination of water skiing, windsurfing, sailing, boating, fishing and diving.

The Mullet Bay Resort (599–5–42081) features an 18-hole golf course. As courses go it's not bad, despite the fact that a major road cuts right through it. For horseback riding contact Crazy Acres (599–5–22061) in Cole Bay. Three dozen tennis courts are located throughout the island, most of them at hotels. Try the Tennis and Fitness Center (599–5–23685) in Dutch Cul-de-Sac for public courts.

■ OTHER

The Maho Beach Hotel features Coconuts Comedy Club, with regional and international acts, some well-known, for a US$10 cover charge. The Studio Seven disco at the Grand Casino across the street from Maho Beach Hotel is very popular and rocks until the early morning. Cherry's bar is close by, fun for sundowners and pre-disco drinks. L'Atmosphere in Marigot is popular with the young French crowd. Night Fever in Colombier is more rustic, very popular with locals.

Casinos are a big attraction on the Dutch side and are often located at resorts. Gamblers must be 18. Among the casinos: Sheraton Port de Plaisance and Pelican Resort (Simpson Bay); Grand Casino and Mullet Bay Hotel (Mullet Bay); Great Bay Beach Hotel and Seaview Hotel (Philipsburg); Casino Royale (Maho Beach) and International Casino (Little Bay Resort).

SHOPPING

Saint-Martin/Sint Maarten is a duty-free port and the estimated 500 duty-free shops won't let you down. Jewelry, perfume, handbags, leather goods, electronics and art can be found in what appears to be a mall-a-mile density of shops throughout the island. Major shopping areas are found on Front Street in Philipsburg; Rue de la Liberté, Rue de la Republique and Marina Port la Royale, all in Marigot; and shopping centers at Mullet Bay and Maho Beach. Smaller shopping malls are scattered along the airport-Marigot road and in the Philipsburg suburbs.

For grocery shopping, the large Sint Maarten Food Center has two locations, at Cole Bay (559–5–22315) and on Bush Road (599–5–23232). Mammoth is the big supermarket chain on the French side.

USEFUL ADDRESSES
■ TOURISM INFORMATION
Dutch Sint Maarten Tourist Bureau:
❑ Walter Nisbet Rd, Philipsburg, Sint Maarten, N.A.; 599–5–22337, fax 22734.
❑ 275 Seventh Ave., New York, NY 10001; 212–989–0000, fax 627–1152.
❑ 243 Ellerlie Ave., Willowdale, Toronto M2N 1Y5; 416–223–3501, fax 223–6887.

French Saint-Martin

- ❏ Office du Tourisme de Saint-Martin, 97150 Port de Marigot, Saint-Martin, F.W.I.; 590–87–57–21, fax 87–56–43.
- ❏ "France on Call," U.S. tel. (900) 990–0040, cost is fifty cents per minute.
- ❏ French West Indies Tourist Board, 610 Fifth Ave., New York, NY 10020.
- ❏ French Government Tourist Office, 1981 McGill College Ave., Suite 490, Montreal, Quebec H3A 2W9; 514–288–4264.
- ❏ French Government Tourist Office, 178 Piccadilly, London W1Z 0AL; 0171–493–6594.

■ OTHER

Dutch Sint Maarten:

- ❏ Police, 22222.
- ❏ Fire, 22222.
- ❏ Ambulance, 22111.
- ❏ St. Rose Hospital, Front Street, Philipsburg; 22300.
- ❏ Post Office, Front Street, Philipsburg; 22289.
- ❏ Princess Juliana International Airport; 52161 or 54211.
- ❏ Central Drugstore, EC Richardson Road, Philipsburg; 22321.
- ❏ American Express representative, Maduro and Sons, Emmaplein, Philipsburg; 23410.
- ❏ Federal Express, DeWeever Building, Simpson Bay; 42810.

French Saint-Martin:

- ❏ Police, 87–50–06.
- ❏ Fire, 87–72–00.
- ❏ Ambulance, 87–86–25.
- ❏ Hospital de Marigot, Marigot; 87–50–07.
- ❏ Hotel Association, BP 622, 97510 Marigot, Saint-Martin, F.W.I.; tel. and fax 87–83–88.
- ❏ Post Office, Rue de la Liberte, Marigot; 87–53–17.
- ❏ Pharmacie Choisy Rita, Rue du General de Gaulle, Marigot; 87–54–09.

Saint-Barthélémy

Introduction

Saint-Barthélémy, commonly called St. Barth's or St. Barts, has for some time been regarded as a toney enclave of the ultra-wealthy or at least the ultra-hip. This has as much to do with its dominant French culture as with the attitude of the island's hoteliers and restaurateurs—small, exquisite and tasteful, it seems, has won out over large and blustery.

So much the better. On an island only eight square miles (21 sq km) everything occurs naturally in small doses, from the compact red-roofed French country homes to the toy airstrip and the dozen streets of its capital, Gustavia. St. Barts is an island with few resources beyond the natural beauty of its billowing hills and comely beaches and this, coupled with a steady source of income from France, defines the economic picture in the island's future. That picture is tourism.

St. Barts is the sort of place that has stood out for some time, attracting luminaries such as the Rockefellers, the French Rothschilds and the King of Sweden. Tourism has boomed over the last ten years. It is not always the sort of tourism that those on a strict budget will appreciate, but that situation is improving as the market expands. What one remembers most about St. Barts is its ability to simultaneously offer solitude and controlled boisterousness—the perfect recipe for a vacation.

The Land

St. Barts, a French West Indies island in the Leeward Islands chain, is located 20 miles (32 km) southeast of Saint-Martin and 125 miles (200 km) north of Guadeloupe, of which it is a dependency.

The hilly, boomerang-shaped island is volcanic in origin, with some 20 beaches set in small coves and bays along its irregular coast. The hills often appear steep when driving the winding roadways, but they never reach higher than 900 feet (300 m). The island tends to be dry and several small lakes and salt ponds dot the valleys and coastline, particularly along the windward (eastern) and southern coasts. La Grande Saline is a large salt pond on the south coast, near

Anse de Grande Saline beach. Vegetation is low-lying and hardy, with some cactus, wild pear, manchineel and other coastal plants dominating. Several small and uninhabited outlying cays are home to nesting sea birds. Iguanas are nearly extinct on the island, but might be spotted occasionally.

History

St. Barts was first inhabited by the Stone Age Ciboney (or Siboney), about 1,000 BC. Not much is known of their lives, but evidence of their existence, primarily in the form of stone tools, has been found throughout the Lesser Antilles. They were long gone by the time of the arrival of the Amerindian Arawaks, a migratory group originating from the Orinoco region of South America. Much evidence exists of Arawak (or related groups) settlements in Hispaniola, Jamaica, Puerto Rico and Cuba, less so in the northern Lesser Antilles. Still, it is conjectured that they lived for at least some time on St. Barts or neighbouring islands and were later supplanted or conquered by the Caribs, another Amerindian group that had migrated from the same area of South America. The Caribs, however, were aggressive where the Arawaks were not and they were the sole inhabitants of the island, which they called Ouanalao, when it was sighted by Columbus in November 1493.

Columbus charted the island and named it after his brother, Bartolomeo. He did not land, apparently assuming, as he did with many of the smaller islands, that St. Barts had no gold to offer and no significant strategic value. Over the next century numerous European ships visited, but none made any serious attempt at colonization. In the meantime, the Caribs became increasingly wary of the European visitors and repelled some landings. The writing for this hapless group, however, was clearly on the wall.

In 1648 a French party of about 50, under orders from the then-French governor of St. Kitts, de Poincy, landed and founded a small settlement. Pressured by Carib attacks, the French sold the island to the powerful Order of the Knights of Malta in 1651. But the Knights failed to keep order and in 1656 the Caribs launched a massive attack against the French, massacring nearly the entire group. The survivors fled to St. Kitts and the Caribs enjoyed a brief reprieve.

Under constant encroachment by Europeans, the Caribs were compelled to sign a peace treaty in 1659 and the French once again returned to the island. By 1674 St. Barts had been incorporated within the French colony of Guadeloupe and a short period of stability followed. During this time the Caribs were killed, died off or fled to neighbouring islands and little is known of them in the 18th century. In the meantime the French islanders, many from the provinces of Brittany and Normandy, started small farms. The island's natural port, called Carenage, became strategically valuable. The island attracted, among others, the infamous buccaneers, who used the island as a base for raiding Spanish merchant ships. Legend has it that the candidly named Monbars the Exterminator hid a treasure in the coves of Anse du Gouverneur, or perhaps in the thick sands of La Grande Saline.

The farms of St. Barts were smaller than the plantations of neighbouring islands and, as a result, slaves were never imported in great numbers. At any given time the ratio of slaves to Europeans never exceeded one to one, while on islands with large sugar plantations the ratio reached as high as ten or fifteen to one.

Through the early part of the 18th century, ongoing European wars had their effect on St. Barts. The British sacked the island in 1744 and most of the inhabitants escaped to other French islands, such as Martinique and St. Lucia. By 1764 the French had returned.

In 1785 France's Louis XVI traded the island to Sweden's King Gustaf, in exchange for the right to store goods in the Swedish port town of Gothenborg. The Swedes promptly declared St. Barts a free port and renamed its harbor Gustavia, in honour of the king. The local inhabitants, who then numbered 740, went on tilling their farms, while the Swedish government made a fortune from trading in the region. They built forts around Gustavia, naming them Karl, Oscar and Gustave.

The island remained in Swedish hands until for nearly 100 years, until it was repurchased by the French. To this day the Swedish influence is seen in the architecture, street names and, of course, in names such as Gustavia. In the meantime, the 1847 abolition of slavery in the French islands virtually snuffed the small plantations. When the French took over, agriculture was limited to several small cotton and pineapple farms. The conclusion of the 19th century European wars served to widen trade agreements within the island community and the free port status of Gustavia was lessened in importance. By 1878 St. Barts was less economically viable than it had been 100 years before.

During the early part of the 20th century, many of the island's inhabitants emigrated for better economic shores. During World War I, many men were drafted into the French war effort. Emigration continued, particularly to the Virgin Islands. During this period France paid little attention to the island and, with the onset of the World War II, the mother country was forced to cut off virtually all aid and contact with its West Indies colonies. Afterwards, the nascent St. Barts tourism industry began to grow; an airstrip was built, then lengthened in 1969. That same year, the first regular airline service to the island was established. The island population in 1974 was estimated at 2,500. A small percentage at that time were wealthy North Americans and the French building villas and vacation homes. By 1990 the population had doubled to 5,043.

People and Culture

Of those 5,043 nearly 90 per cent live in or around Gustavia. The majority population in St. Barts is white, either the so-called metro French, workers and temporary residents from France or those of Breton, Norman and Poitevin descent, who first colonized the island. A smaller percentage is black, either descendants of St. Barts' slaves or of workers—also slave descendants—from other islands. On the surface the two groups live with the ease of old neighbours; the slave trade on St. Barts was neither as massive nor as brutal as was the case in much of the West Indies and few apparent animosities have been carried through the generations.

Much of the culture of St. Barts is in the hands of the French settlers' descendants. Older women still wear the nun-like, ankle-length costumes, reminiscent of French provincial dress, with wide, shoulder-brushing sunbonnets called caleches or quichenottes. The men still take to the sea and are considered excellent sailors and fishermen. Variations of the French Norman dialect are heard, as are modern French dialects. Some Creole is spoken, but differs from French Creole spoke elsewhere, primarily in its vocabulary. English is not common, but among hoteliers and shopkeepers it has become more prevalent.

Catholicism is the main religion, although an Anglican church in Gustavia recalls various English conquerings and occupations.

Carnival is celebrated in late February and is a traditional pre-Lenten festival, with street parades, music contests, feasts, Mardi Gras masquerades and partying till the wee hours. Several saints' days, including the festivals of Saint-Barthélémy and Saint-Louis (both in August), commemorate the patron saint of the island and the tradition of fishing. All Saints Day (early November) honours the souls of the dead.

As on most of the islands, people are touchy about taking unsolicited photos. This applies to the St. Barts women who, with their provincial costumes, would otherwise make wonderful subjects. At the very least, ask. They will probably refuse.

Government and Economy

St. Barts is administered through the sub-prefecture of Saint-Martin, which is in turn a dependency of Guadeloupe, which is in turn an overseas department and region of France. Island affairs are overseen by an elected mayor and a representative of the Sous-Prefect on Saint-Martin. All external affairs are handled through France.

St. Barts is reliant upon aid from France and on its tourism industry. Some subsistence farming and fishing employ the residents and you are likely to see cattle and goats grazing by the roadside. The island is still a free port and an increasingly popular tourist destination. Most visitors come from France, while recently a substantial number come from North America. The island had 158,300 visitors in 1991, with 75,000 overnight stays and nearly 83,000 cruise ship or yacht visitors. This means that, on average, the number of visitors in any given month is nearly three times the island population. About 40 hotels, with a total of 700 rooms, house the island's visitors.

Sights

BEACHES

Despite its ancient volcanic origins, St. Barts' beaches are glisteningly white and smooth, a definite attraction. The number is estimated at 22; some are easy to reach, others accessible only by small boats or via hikes through the bush. All the beaches are open to the public and free. Topless sunbathing is accepted—this is, after all, a French island—but full nudity is technically against the law.

Saint-Jean, on the north shore, is the island's most popular spot. The long, white beach is divided into two sections by the Eden Rock promontory. The proliferation of small restaurants, seaside cafes, bungalow hotels and watersports outlets attests to its popularity. This is the beach at the end of the airstrip—you can't miss it as you fly in. Anse de Lorient and Anse de Marigot, both on the north shore, are smaller and more secluded. East of Marigot is Anse de Grand Cul de Sac, on a quiet lagoon. Anse Toiny on the south shore is rough and stony and not recommended for swimming, but popular with windsurfers. Anse de Grande Saline, over a small hill from the salt lake, is rougher than leeward side beaches, but is very popular and the island's clothing-optional beach. On the leeward side, Anse de Grand Galet is popular with shell collectors—the beach is composed of washed-up shells. Anse de Public and Anse de Corossol are smaller beaches, popular with boaters. Anse de Colombier, on the extreme western tip of the island, can only be reached by the sea or by a 20 minute hike from the village of Colombier. Anse des Flamands is a long, quiet, rarely crowded beach on the northwest shore.

OTHER SIGHTS

Apart from Gustavia and the beach areas, St. Barts is dotted by modest but scenic villages and rolling hills and valleys. North of Gustavia is the small fishing village of Corossol, where you'll find the descendants of the early French settlers. The women, in their traditional sunbonnets and long skirts, sell straw hats, satchels and other products woven from lantania (sabal palms). Fishing boats line the shore and the town has the feeling of the Old World. In the village the Ingenu Magras Inter Oceans Museum (590–27–62–97) houses a private collection of some 7,000 sea shells. The museum is open 9.00–17.00 daily, admission is F20.

North of Corossol is Colombier, another traditional fishing village and site of one of the island's prettiest beaches. It's a short walk from the village to the beach or you can take one of several boats operating out of Gustavia.

The Office du Tourisme (590–27–87–27) sanctions three sightseeing tours of St. Barts, ranging from one to two hours long at a cost of F150 to F250 for a party of three. The tour vans are located outside the tourist office.

For a full range of tours, excursions and trips to neighbouring islands, contact Saint-Barth Voyages (590–27–79–79) on Rue Duquesne in Gustavia.

Gustavia

The capital of St. Barts is also the main population center and hub of activity. Surrounding the town are the ruins of the various forts built by the Swedes. Most of the original town was destroyed in an 1852 fire, but several examples of Swedish and early French architecture survive. The Marie de St. Barth, or town hall, on Rue de Roi Oscar III, is a fine example of an early 19th century West Indian building. Next to The Wall House (now a restaurant), at the harbor's mouth, is the Musée de Saint-Barthélémy (590–27–89–07). The museum houses antique furniture, costumes, historical recreations and photographs and is worth a stop. The hours, though sometimes erratic, are generally 8.00-12.00 and 13.30-17.30 Monday through Friday and 8.30-12.00 on Saturday. Admission is F10.

Gustavia's harbor is rimmed on three sides by the streets of downtown, which you can explore in a few hours or a day if you linger. Several chi-chi shops, banks and a dozen cafes line the streets. The tourism office is located on Quai General de Gaulle, at the pier, and is open 10.30-12.30 and 15.00–19.00 Monday through Thursday and 8.30–10.30 on Friday.

Practical Information

ACCOMMODATION

Most hotels on St. Barts are small, homey and relaxed. Big high-rises and sprawling resorts are not the norm and quite of few of the small places are family-owned and operated. Most, however, are not cheap. There are few guesthouses on the island and camping is not allowed.

■ VILLAS

Rental agencies include Villas St. Barth (590–27–74–29) and WIMCO/Sibarth Real Estate (590–27–62–38, fax 27–65–02; North America 800–932–3222 or 401–849–8012, fax 847–6290). Sibarth lists over 200 villas, starting in the US$1,000-2,000 (per week in high season, one bedroom) range, and offer luxury villas with weekly rates of up to US$5,000.

■ HOTELS

For hotels a good first contact is the Association des Hoteliers de Saint-Barthélémy, (Hotel El Sereno Beach, Grand Cul de Sac, 97133 Saint-Barthélémy, F.W.I. 590–27–64–80, fax 27–75–47).

❑ HOTEL CARL GUSTAF, Rue des Normands, Gustavia, 97133 Saint-Barthélémy, F.W.I. (590–27–82–83, fax 27–82–37, U.S. 800–922–0276) is located on a hill near downtown Gustavia. All of the large suites have views of the harbor and town, as well as a mini-bar, private pool, sun deck. Luxury.

❑ CHRISTOPHER HOTEL, BP 571, Gustavia, 97098 Saint-Barthélémy, F.W.I. (590–27–63–63, fax 27–92–92) is a new 40-unit Sofitel hotel at Pointe Milou, with a fitness center, spacious rooms and shuttle service to beaches. Luxury.

❑ LE TOINY, Anse de Toiny, 97133 Saint-Barthélémy, F.W.I. (590–27–88–88, fax 27–89–30) is one of the island's deluxe accommodation. On the far eastern end of the island, the 12 individual villas feature reproduction French colonial antiques, private pools, television, raised poster beds and kitchens. The beach down below is rough and not good for swimmers, but the hotel can arrange trips to others. Luxury.

❑ AUBERGE DE LA PETITE ANSE, BP 117 Anse des Flamands, 97133 Saint-Barthélémy, F.W.I. (590–27–64–60, fax 27–72–30) is in Flamands, a great location near several beaches. Small, only 16 rooms, but clean, over the beach. Moderate.

❏ LA NORMANDIE, Lorient, 97133 Saint-Barthélémy (590–27–61–66, fax 27–68–64) is small (eight rooms), with only a couple of air-conditioned rooms, a bar, pool and restaurant. Inexpensive.

EATING
The emphasis is on French, French creole and a variety of international cuisines. The restaurants mentioned below are in the moderate category, US$10-25 per entree:

❏ WALL HOUSE (590–27–71–83) on the harbor in Gustavia is elegant, with views of the boats on the harbor.

❏ LA GLORIETTE (590–27–75–66) offers beachside dining, specializing in creole, in Grand Cul de Sac, no credit cards accepted.

❏ LAFAYETTE CLUB (590–27–62–51), a relaxed bar-restaurant-boutique on the beach at Grand Cul de Sac, specializes in tasty barbecues. No credit cards are accepted.

❏ LA PELICAN (590–27–64–64), a small piano bar and restaurant on Saint-Jean Bay, features seafood and creole specialties.

GETTING THERE
The airstrip is tiny and unable to land large planes, but convenient, just minutes from Gustavia. Connections to St. Barts are made via inter-island carriers, primarily through Sint Maarten, about ten minutes away. Airlines with local numbers are: Winair (590-27-61-01), Air St. Barthélémy (590-27-61-90), Air Guadeloupe (590-27-61-90) and Virgin Air (590-27-71-76). The St. Barts airport does not yet have night landing capacity; this may be important when scheduling your connection.

Several ferries travel between Philipsburg and Marigot, in Sint Maarten/Saint-Martin, and Gustavia. Call St. Barth Express (590-27-77-24) for information. In Sint Maarten contact Bobby's Marina in Philipsburg (599-52-31-70).

The departure tax is F12 if your destination is Esperance Airport in Saint-Martin or Guadeloupe. The tax is F16 otherwise, including those travelling to Princess Juliana Airport in Sint Maarten.

GETTING AROUND
St. Barts has two taxi stands, one at the airstrip and the other on Rue de la République in Gustavia. Hotels can always arrange a taxi, or you can call 590-27-66-31 or 27-61-86 for pickups.

Taxis are not metered. Rates are set by the government, the flat rate being US$5 for the first five minutes and the same for each three minutes thereafter. Rates go up after 20.00 and on Sundays and holidays. Private island tours run about US$50 for two for three hours and one driver indicated that he charged US$200 for a day's tour. With only 25 miles (40 km) of paved road, it seems better to rent a car.

Which is not difficult, except during high season when high demand results in a paucity of rentals. It is best to reserve ahead.

Rates can be as high as US$50 per day and most rental agencies operate airport offices. Call: Aubin Car Rental (590-27-73-03), Avis (590-27-71-43, fax 27-69-32), Budget (590-27-66-30 or 27-67-43), Turbe Car Rental (590-27-60-70, fax 27-75-57).

Motor scooters and small motorcycles can be rented through Saint-Barth Motobique (590-27-67-89) and Honda Rent Some Fun (590-27-70-59), both in Gustavia.

MONEY, HOURS AND COMMUNICATION

The French franc is the official currency on St. Barts, most recently exchanging at F5.50 = US$1. U.S. dollars are widely accepted, as are credit cards. You will, however, get a better rate if you change your U.S. dollars at a bank or bureau de change, rather than at a shop or taxi stand. Banks are generally open 8.00–12.00 and 14.00–15.30 Monday through Friday.

Regular business hours vary, but figure on 8.00–12.00 and 14.00–17.00 on weekdays and 8.00–12.00 on Saturday. Many businesses are closed Wednesday afternoon as well.

To call St. Barts from North America, dial 011 plus 590 and the six-digit number. Calls to the rest of the French Antilles are direct dial. Pay phones accept phone cards, which can be purchased at post offices and businesses around town.

You'll find post offices in Gustavia (590-27-62-00), at La Savane near the airport, and in Lorient. Hours vary, but the main Gustavia office is open 8.00–12.00 and 14.00–16.00 weekdays (except Wednesday afternoon) and 8.00–12.00 Saturday.

ENTERTAINMENT

St. Barts is a popular yachting center, because of its natural port and harbors and because of its location midway between Antigua and the Virgin Islands. Diving, snorkelling, windsurfing, deep sea fishing, boating, surfing equipment and sailing charters are all available on the island. Loulou's Marine (590-27-62-74) in Gustavia is a good place to begin inquiries. La Maison de Mer (590-27-81-00) in

Gustavia provides sailing, bare-boat charters, deep sea fishing and diving services. Marine Service (590-27-70-34) offers diving, fishing, boat rentals, snorkelling rentals and excursions to neighbouring islands. Yacht Charter Agency (590-27-62-38) charters yachts and offers day outings as well as deep sea fishing excursions. All of the above offer various sunset cruises and sailing packages, plus a variety of watersports.

Scuba diving on St. Barts is considered very good, particularly around some of the offshore rocks and cays. In addition to the above, contact Rainbow Dive (590-27-91-79, fax 27-91-80), Club La Bulle (590-27-68-93) and Emeraude PADI Diving Center (590-27-64-78, fax 27-83-08). Several of these dive centers are located at the Saint-Jean beach. Resort courses and advanced certification are both offered.

Several of the hotels have tennis courts, some private and some for outside guests. Other courts can be found at Le Flamboyant Tennis Club (590-27-69-82) and the Sports Center of Colombier (590-27-61-07). A squash court is found at the Isle de France (590-27-80-72) hotel in Flamands.

Horseback riding is available at La Ranch des Flamands (590-27-80-72).

SHOPPING

Two words: downtown Gustavia. Due to the island's free port status you can find good deals here, the island's greatest single concentration of shops.

Other shops line the bay at Saint-Jean, where you'll find a small mall. The La Savane Commercial Center, located across the road from the airport, also has a dozen or so boutiques, bookstores and trinket shops. The island's largest supermarket, Match, is also located at La Savane.

USEFUL ADDRESSES

■ TOURISM INFORMATION
❑ Office Municipal du Tourisme, Quai du General de Gaulle, Gustavia, 97095 Saint-Barthélémy, F.W.I.; (590) 27-87-27, fax 27-74-47.
❑ Association des Hoteliers de Saint-Barthélémy, Hotel El Sereno Beach, Grand Cul de Sac, 97133 Saint-Barthélémy, F.W.I.; (590) 27-64-80, fax 27-75-47.
❑ "France on Call," U.S. tel. (900) 990-0040; cost is fifty cents per minute.
❑ French West Indies Tourist Board, 610 Fifth Ave., New York, NY 10020.
❑ French Government Tourist Office, 1981 McGill College Ave., Suite 490, Montreal, Quebec H3A 2W9; (514) 288-4264.
❑ French Government Tourist Office, 178 Piccadilly, London W1Z 0AL; 0171-493-6594.

■ OTHER

❑ Gendarmerie, 17 or 27-60-12.

❑ Fire, 18 or 27-62-31.

❑ Police, 27-66-66.

❑ Gustavia Clinic, Gustavia; 27-60-35.

❑ Pharmacie Saint-Barth, Quai de la République, Gustavia; 27-61-82.

❑ Pharmacie de La Savane, Saint-Jean (airport); 27-66-61.

❑ St. Barts Airport, 27-65-41 or 27-65-33.

Saba

Introduction

Saba (SAY-buh) holds few ambiguities for a visitor. The island's main road, which winds from one village to another through steep mountains, is simply called The Road. The village of Windwardside sits on the windward side of the island and the capital, The Bottom, is, well, at the bottom. The volcanic pinnacle of Saba is named Mt. Scenery, another appropriate name. In a way they sound like names straight out of a child's fairy tale. In other ways they make an unequivocal statement about the quality of life here: frills, adornments and fancy names are not part of the game.

The Land

The 2,855 foot (860 m) Mt. Scenery dominates a series of smaller hills and slopes, all part of an ancient volcanic chain in the "inner arc" of the Leeward Islands, running north from Nevis to Saba. Saba's has been extinct for 5,000 years—no one even knows where the crater is.

Sheer cliffs roll off he mountains and plop into the sea, where rugged, thrashing surf is the norm. There are no true beaches to speak of, save an almost inaccessible patch of black sand at Rum Bay.

Only five square miles (13 sq km), the rock is home to the island's population of 1,200, which lives in four settlements on the east and south sides. A seven mile (11 km) road connects the villages to the airport, a road that took 20 years to carve out of the mountainside. Few views in the Caribbean are comparable to an airplane's approach of the looming monoliths of Saba. From most any point on the island the views to the open Caribbean and the neighbouring islands of Statia, St. Barts, St. Kitts and Sint Maarten are breathtaking.

The rugged terrain around Mt. Scenery varies with altitude. Whether low woodlands, secondary tropical rainforest or clouded rainforest, the vegetation is thick and lush and features the towering mountain mahogany (not related to West Indian mahogany), mountain palm, trumpet wood, cashews, elephant ears, lilies, ferns, oleander, orchids and the national flower, the black-eyed Susan.

Lizards and tree frogs inhabit the forests. More than 180 species of birds, including the pearly thrasher, bananaquit, green-throated carib hummingbird, booby and other sea birds have been sighted on the island. The harmless racer snake lives in the hills.

Before The Road was completed in 1947, Sabans either walked or rode donkeys from one village to another, resulting in an extensive network of walking trails that crisscross hills, mountains and valleys.

History

During his second voyage to these isles, in 1493, Columbus sighted Saba, but did not land, judging there were no riches to be found and wary of the impenetrability of the coast. We don't know what Columbus called the island, but according to later reports the word Siba, thought to have meant "Rock," was used by the island's first inhabitants, the Arawaks. Other reports claim the Amerindians called the island Amonhana, meaning unknown.

The island was uninhabited when Sir Frances Drake happened upon it in 1595. He was followed by the Dutch explorers Pieter Schouten and Piet Heyn in the 1620s. An English ship was wrecked off the coast in 1632 and the survivors dallied briefly. In 1635 the French, under Pierre d'Esnambuc, made a half-hearted claim—they, too, chose not to settle Saba. In 1640 some intrepid Dutch explorers established settlements on the southwest coast, in the areas now known as Tent Bay and The Bottom. The Bottom, which sits in a low valley surrounded by hills, was derived from the Dutch word botte, meaning "bowl." The Tent Bay settlement was destroyed by a landslide in 1651.

Over the years Europeans fought over the island, although why they bothered to do so isn't clear. No significant minerals were found, the coast was rugged and dangerous. No flat land existed for any sort of extensive farming. A good defensive position was Saba's only real asset, yet no substantial forts were ever built.

What is clear is that the European powers did fight constantly over the island—a favourite military tactic was to bury opponents in landslides—probably due more to momentum from their other European and West Indian battles than to any real desire to possess Saba. The island changed hands 12 times before reverting to the Dutch in a treaty signed in 1816.

During the early 20th century Saba existed as a lonely outpost of the Netherlands empire. Local citizens fished and hired out as seamen. A small shoemaking business flourished for a while, in the village of Crispeen, which was named after St. Crispin, the patron saint of shoemakers.

Construction of The Road, an astonishing feat of engineering and pure physical labor, began in the 1940s. The designer was a local carpenter named Josephus

Lambertus Hassell. After professional Dutch engineers said the road was an impossibility, Hassell proceeded to study engineering through correspondence school and then built the road. It took 20 years.

The island's first automobile did not appear until 1947; it was a jeep, lashed to two rowboats, which was floated to the pier and then lifted onto dry land by some 50 men. The tiny airstrip, one of the world's shortest at 1,312 feet (394 m) was completed in 1959 and a regular air service to Sint Maarten began in 1963. Around-the-clock electricity was not available on Saba until the 1970s.

People and Culture

Saba's population of 1,200 is split between descendants of European settlers and slaves, who were brought in to work small farms and to help in construction. Dutch names such as Hassell, Peterson and van den Berg are common.

The island's architecture today is a mix of modern West Indian and colonial Dutch. Clean white homes with red tile roofs, stone or picket fences and small country gardens are the norm—you'd almost expect to see tulips, but you won't. The official language is Dutch, but everybody speaks English. Saba's dominant religion is Catholicism, a European legacy. Old customs are still practiced. Women, even young women, still hand-embroider the famous Saban Lace, also called Spanish Work, imported to the island from Venezuela in the 1870s. A drink called Saban Spice, made with 151-proof rum, anise, cinnamon, orange peel, cloves and nutmeg, is a local favourite. These items are sold in several shops around the towns or out of people's homes. Ask a taxi driver.

Stop at the Saba Artisan Foundation (599-4-63260) in The Bottom for local silk-screened items, dolls, books and other handmade gifts.

In early December Saba celebrates Saba Days, a weekend of parties, dances and donkey races. The July Saba Summer Festival is the island's answer to carnival, a week of street dances, hill races, calypso and talent shows and the Grand Festival Parade.

Government and Economy

Saba is a semi-autonomous member of the Netherlands Antilles, which also includes the islands of Curaçao, Bonaire, Statia and Sint Maarten. Aruba is a separate entity within the Kingdom of the Netherlands.

Queen Beatrix, the head of state, is represented in the Netherlands Antilles by a governor, who is appointed by the Crown. The islands have representation in the Dutch Cabinet by way of a minister plenipotentiary, who is appointed by a legislative council of the five Netherlands Antilles. Each island has a modicum of self-rule, responsible for water, electricity, land, schools and harbors; the legislative council is responsible for police, defense, taxation, foreign exchange, health and some foreign affairs.

The economy of Saba relies on remittances from the Crown and on tourism. Two-thirds of its 25,000 visitors in 1992 stayed overnight and about 4,000 visited primarily to scuba dive. About 440 yachts visit Saba each year.

Sights

Beaches are not a concern on Saba; there are none. The closest one gets to ocean bathing involves using the ramp at the Leo Chance Pier at Fort Bay. Otherwise, boats are the way to get out on the water.

From Juancho Yrausquin Airport, the small field on the island's only accessible flat spot—not surprisingly named Flat Point—a road winds up to the village of Hell's Gate. Given the Sabans' penchant for truth in advertising, don't worry: this is not an ominous sign. Hell's Gate (Upper and Lower) is a quiet village, full of sparkling white and pastel Saban cottages. Farther on are several small banana farms, after which the road winds to Windwardside, Saba's commercial center. On the narrow streets you'll find several hotels and guesthouses, a supermarket, post office and the tourist board (599-4-62231). The tourist board can provide maps, brochures, information and is a contact point for many of the islands villa and cottage rentals. Contact Wilma Hassell or Glenn Holm.

Windwardside also hosts a few restaurants, art galleries, two banks and a dive center. The small Harry L. Johnson Memorial Museum, the former home of a sea captain, features antique furniture, a safe, a four-poster bed and a bust of Simon Bolivar, a 1983 gift from the Government of Venezuela. The museum is under renovation and has been closed for long periods in the past; otherwise it is open 10.00–12.00 and 13.00–17.00 weekdays and admission is US$1. On Sunday afternoons Sabans and visitors alike gather on the grounds of the museum for a few rounds of croquet, an island tradition. The fun and games are spiked with mimosas and everyone is invited to wear their whites and make some new friends.

At Windwardside a path leads to the summit of Mt. Scenery. This climb is difficult in only a few places and well worth the 90 minutes to the top.

From Windwardside the road passes over several hills, with spectacular views all around, until it reaches the village of St. John's, where Statia is visible to the south. Here the road drops down to The Bottom, Saba's capital. The Bottom, population 400, is situated in a valley nestled among several large hills and is considered to be the "warm" town of Saba. Everything is relative, but the indication here is that the breeze factor is diminished in the valley. Here you'll find a small inn, a guesthouse, villas, a few car rental agencies, bank and post office.

The Road continues from The Bottom, descending 800 feet (240 m) to Fort Bay, where a small pier serves as the base for dive operations. Cruise ships, small ones such as Windjammer Cruises, and private yachts can moor in the area. Also here are a small pub, a gift shop and Saba's petrol station.

Hiking is one of Saba's more popular activities and trails are maintained by the Saba Conservation Foundation (The Bottom, Saba, N.A.; 599-4-63348, fax 63299). The foundation has placed rest stops and informational signs along the trails and has detailed them in a publication called Saba Nature Trails. A tour guide is not necessary for most of the trails, which vary in difficulty. Among the named trails are Tent Point, The Boiling House, Booby Hill, Mary's Point and Mt. Scenery.

The 2,855 foot (860 m) Mt. Scenery is accessed from Windwardside by a steep trail of 1,064 steps. The walk takes an hour and a half, with rest stops and trail signs along the way to keep you informed. Climbing, you pass through several layers of rainforest, palm forests and elfin woodlands. The trail can be slippery and wet and near the summit you'll hear the constant patter of small raindrops. It is not raining, necessarily; the dew, clouds really, condense and fall at this altitude. Bring a sweater, it can get cool. From the summit, which has been cleared of trees, Windwardside appears as a series of small specks below. On a clear day you can see Saint-Martin/Sint Maarten, Statia, St. Kitts and Nevis. As one local puts it: "It's like going to heaven without having to die."

The foundation also maintains and regulates the Saba Marine Park (599-4-63295). The marine park was established in 1987 to preserve and manage Saba's reefs and marine resources. The underwater park encircles the island, plus two outlying sections, and includes waters and seabeds up to 200 feet (60 m) in depth. The park maintains 26 dive sites plus zones for diving, fishing, anchoring or combinations of all three. Visibility in place can reach up to 100 feet (30 m). The park, which is funded in part by the Netherlands World Wildlife Fund and the Saban government, charges a nominal fee for upkeep.

Park authorities also administer a hyperbaric (depressurizing) facility, which was donated by the Royal Netherlands Navy, at Fort Bay.

Practical Information

ACCOMMODATION

Saba is well-developed for the small number of visitors it takes in yearly. You'll find no large resorts, just a dozen hotels, inns and guesthouses, all spic and span, comfortable and quaint—remember, this is an island where a bad hotel will stick out like a sore thumb. Don't worry about air-conditioning, or fans for that matter. The cool breezes and higher altitudes will let nature take care of the heat. If you are a diver, inquire about hotel/diving package discounts.

All rates are subject to a five per cent government tax and 10–15 per cent service charge. Camping is not allowed on Saba.

■ VILLAS

Dozens of cottages and small villas are available for rent, ranging from US$50-100 per day. Call Wilma Hassell at the tourist board (see below) or Ruth Hassell at Saba Real Estate (P.O. Box 17, Windwardside, Saba, N.A.; 599-4-62299, fax 62415). Renting one's own home is a cottage industry here.

■ HOTELS AND GUESTHOUSES

❏ THE GATE HOUSE, Hell's Gate, Saba, N.A. (599-4-62416, fax 62415, U.S. tel. 708-354-9641), features six rooms, two with kitchenettes and a small cafe. Moderate.

❏ JULIANA'S, Windwardside, Saba, N.A. (599-4-62269, fax 62389), offers clean and simple cottages and rooms. Moderate.

❏ CAPTAIN'S QUARTERS, Windwardside, Saba, N.A. (599-4-62201, fax 62377), is a hotel with a pool and outdoor patio restaurant; this is a popular island gathering place. Moderate.

❏ SCOUT'S PLACE, Windwardside, Saba, N.A. (599-4-62205, fax 62388), is small, 15 room bed and breakfast, with great views, a pool and restaurant. Budget-moderate.

❏ WILLARD'S OF SABA, P.O. Box 515, Windwardside, Saba, N.A. (599-4-62498, fax 62482, North America 800-223-9615), is the island's sole luxury resort, although it has only five rooms. Located high on the side of Booby Hill, the hotel offers VIP, luxury or bungalow rooms with hot tubs, as well as a tennis court, pool and restaurant. No children or pets are allowed. Luxury.

❏ CRANSTON'S ANTIQUE INN, The Bottom, Saba, N.A. (599-4-63203), is fitted with antiques, unsurprisingly, a restaurant and pool. Budget-moderate.

❏ CARIBE GUESTHOUSE, The Bottom, Saba, N.A. (599-4-63259), offers five rooms and a kitchen for guests. Budget.

EATING

The hotel restaurants are all good, with special kudos to Captain's Quarters, specializing in some interesting Dutch-Indonesian creole dishes and Scout's Place, which offers a highly recommended goat curry. The choices, otherwise, are limited, but you'll find plenty to eat. Since visitor business on Saba is often at a lull, all restaurants may not be open every day. Some won't take credit cards. Call ahead to check.

❏ BRIGADOON RESTAURANT (599-4-62380) in Windwardside serves fresh fish and island and continental specialties. Moderate.

❏ SABA CHINESE RESTAURANT (599-4-62268) in Windwardside has 100 choices of inexpensive Cantonese. Budget.

❏ GUIDO'S PIZZERIA in Windwardside serves pizzas and sandwiches and is also a disco. Budget.

❏ TROPICS CAFE (599-4-62469), a part of Juliana's, serves breakfast and lunch snacks.

In The Bottom stop at QUEENIE SIMMON'S SERVING SPOON (599-4-63225), up on the mountainside, for her famous peanut chicken. In Fort Bay POP'S PLACE, next to the dive shop, is popular for lunches and drinks.

GETTING THERE

Saba's Juancho Yrausquin Airport is, at 1,312 feet (394 m), one of the shortest in the world. The approach is inspiring, to say the least; if there is one place in the world you might want to leave your safety belt buckled until the plane has completely stopped, this is it.

Winair (agent F. Johnson, Windwardside, 599-4-62255) operates at least six flights daily from Sint Maarten, which is serviced by major North American and European airlines. The flight from Sint Maarten takes 15 minutes and costs US$66 round-trip. Winair often posts special rates for day trips.

Winair also flies to and from Statia.

GETTING AROUND

Walk, hitchhike, rent a car or take a taxi—these are your choices. Taxi drivers charge about US$40 per vehicle (four people) for a two-hour tour of the island. Several will be at the airport when you arrive and you can make touring arrangements with them then. Otherwise, your hotel or guesthouse can call a taxi for you.

Rental car rates start at US$40 per day. You'll need a valid license or an international license. Contact Hardiana NV Car Rental (c/o Scout's Place, 599-4-

62205), Doc's Car Rentals (599-4-62271), Johnson Rent A Car (599-4-62269) or Steve's Scooter Rentals (599-4-62507).

Driving is on the right. For the most part, The Road is in good shape, but full of twists and winds. Drive slowly. Here's a fun fact: Saba has no traffic lights.

Hitchhiking is usually not recommended in the Lesser Antilles, but on Saba it is safe and common among both locals and tourists. The island is one of the area's safest, no doubt in part due to its small population.

The departure tax from Saba is US$2 to other islands of the Netherlands Antilles and US$5 elsewhere.

MONEY, HOURS AND COMMUNICATION

Saba's currency is the Netherlands Antilles florin, or guilder, pegged at NAF1.80 = US$1. However, U.S. dollars are widely used. Two banks operate on the island, Barclays and Commercial Bank. Barclays is in Windwardside and open 8.30-13.30 weekdays. Most businesses are open 8.00–12.00 and 13.00–17.00 weekdays and 8.00–12.00 on Saturdays.

To call Saba from North America dial the international access code 011, the country code 599, then 4 and the five-digit number.

ENTERTAINMENT

Several hotels have pools (see above) and the Youth Center in The Bottom has a tennis court. Beyond that, look to the ocean for sports and recreation.

Three dive shops operate on Saba. Sea Saba P.O. Box 530, Windwardside, Saba, N.A.; (599-4-62246, fax 62362), Wilson's Dive Shop P.O. Box 50, Windwardside, Saba, N.A.; (599-4-63410, fax 63334) and Saba Deep P.O. Box 22, Fort Bay, Saba, N.A.; (599-4-63347, fax 63397) offer a full range of equipment rentals and excursions to the Marine Park dive sites. Their boats are equipped to handle large or small groups and they offer deep, shallow and night dives. All three collaborate with island hotels and cottages for hotel/dive packages and all offer resort certification. They can also customize dives, snorkelling trips, photography trips, fishing trips and sunset cruises.

USEFUL ADDRESSES
■ TOURISM INFORMATION
Saba Tourist Board:
❏ P.O. Box 527, Windwardside, Saba, N.A.; 599-4-62231, fax 62350.

Sint Eustatius

Introduction

The Lesser Antilles tourist boards are fond of using sobriquets: "The Island of Spice" for Grenada and "The Nature Isle" for Dominica, for example. For Sint Eustatius one wonders what would be appropriate. In earlier days "The Ghost Town Isle" might have fitted, but it is perhaps too strong and not entirely true today. The island was once bustling—enviably called "The Golden Rock"—and its streets and pubs swelled with as many as four times the current population.

It was, in its heyday, one of the Caribbean's most important free ports and transfer points, profiting from trade and the smuggling of goods from the French, English and Spanish islands. As many as 200 ships on any given day were stacked outside its harbor, waiting to load or discharge cargo. So strategic was the island that it changed hands 22 times, as European powers vied for control of the Caribbean trade routes. And then it all went bust. Why? Well, things happen.

First, a bit about the island itself.

The Land

Sint Eustatius, called Statia (STAY-shuh) by just about everyone, is a tiny pinch of a volcanic island situated in the Lesser Antilles inner arc, stretching from Saba south to Montserrat. Each of these islands is believed to be a pinnacle of the same volcanic ridge. Saba lies 17 miles (27 km) to the northwest of Statia; Sint Maarten, the best gateway for getting to the island, lies 38 miles (61 km) to the north; to the south is St. Kitts.

Encompassing eight square miles (21 sq km), Statia is dominated by a southern volcanic peak called The Quill, a long-extinct crater rising 1,980 feet (600 m). The slopes and inner crater are covered by lush, tropical rainforest, which hosts a wide array of flora and fauna, including assorted hummingbirds, lizards, hanging vines, mosses and towering mahogany trees. Accessible by trails, The Quill is one of the island's more popular excursions.

Conversely, the central part of the island is blanketed by low-lying plains and grassy scrubland. The land here was never particularly fertile and Statian plantations never achieved the output and status of those on neighbouring islands.

Several small beaches are found on the western, leeward side of the island, near the capital of Oranjestad. The island, shaped like a lumpy pillow, measures roughly five miles by two miles (eight km by three km), and is crisscrossed by several roads and walking trails.

History

Statia was inhabited by Amerindian Caribs and the Arawaks before them, as shown by artifacts displayed in the local museum. It is not clear that the warlike Caribs ever protected the island with any vigor; it certainly was not the sort of island that provided strategic hiding places for its defense.

Columbus sighted Statia on his second voyage in 1493. He charted it and named it, then left it alone. Columbus' name for the island, reputedly St. Anastatia, was later changed to Sint Eustatius by the Dutch.

The Spanish decided to pass on Statia. The first attempted colonization occurred in 1625, when then-rivals France and Britain landed and established settlements. The colonies fell prey to pestilence, Carib opposition and, finally, Dutch invasion. In 1636 the Dutch built Fort Oranje, which became the first permanent European settlement on the island.

The Dutch West India Company bankrolled development on Statia and plantations—numbering 76 in their heyday—sprung up on the land. Slaves were imported from Africa and mercantilism grew. Goods found their way from the French, Spanish and British islands—some smuggled, some stolen, some under legitimate trade conditions—to a growing number of warehouses in the Dutch port. Fine silver, pewter, silk, cloth, crystal, cotton, tobacco, sugar, rum and, importantly, slaves helped Statia become the primary mercantile port in the Lesser Antilles. Sensing profit, and a somewhat easy mark, the British, French and Spanish invaded the island 22 times over the years, until it became Dutch for good in 1816.

In the meantime the port continued to prosper. By 1790 the population had reached 8,124, consisting of 5,140 whites, 2,341 slaves and 43 freed slaves. This, compared to today's population of 1,860, attests to the former affluence of the island.

A not-insignificant footnote to Statia's mercantile history occurred just after the War for Independence in the soon-to-be United States had ended. During the 1700s Statian merchants had made a good profit dealing arms and supplies to the rebellious colonies. On 16 November 1776 (a day still celebrated on Statia) the brig *Andrew Doria*, flying the Grand Union flag of the Continental Navy, approached the harbor. She saluted and the Dutch commander Johannes de Graaff returned the a 13-gun salute of recognition. This was a customary thing to do at the time and was probably not intended as a formal recognition of the newly formed state. In fact there is every indication that the salute was intended to welcome the *Andrew Doria* as a merchant vessel and nothing more. Nevertheless, it was the first recorded recognition of the colonies' sovereignty and, understandably, provoked the British. De Graaff was forced to resign and the British, in order to save face, took more drastic action.

A fleet under the British commander Admiral Sir George Brydges Rodney sailed into the harbor in December 1781 and took the island. Not a shot was fired from Fort Oranje. Rodney confiscated 130 ships that sailed into the harbor over the next month. He sacked the town and island and reputedly made off with five million pounds sterling (which was in turn recaptured by the French and Dutch while in transit to Britain). Yet he left the Oranjestad infrastructure intact, taking only timbers from a warehouse to refurbish his ships.

This non-destruction of Oranjestad allowed for Statia's quick recovery, which soon was, once again, a thriving mercantile port under the British and French. Then several events curtailed trade throughout the islands. The French Revolutions and subsequent Napoleonic Wars disrupted Europe on a massive scale. In the early 19th century the slave trade and sugar boom had begun to wind down. Europe began to ignore the islands. The forts of Statia, no longer needed to protect the islands' trade routes, fell into disrepair. The British almost eagerly turned Statia back over to the Dutch in 1816, but by then the days of trade and plantocracy in the Caribbean were over. The sugar industry virtually collapsed after the abolition of slavery on the British, French and Dutch islands, between 1834 and 1863, and thereafter Statia's economy all but died. Merchants and former slaves left in droves. Statia has never recovered any of that former glory.

Six territories were remitted to the Dutch in 1816: Statia, Saba, Sint Maarten, Aruba, Bonaire and Curaçao. All became Dutch colonies. In 1954 the Dutch government made the islands autonomous and consolidated them as a single entity called the Netherlands Antilles, a member of the Kingdom of the Netherlands. Aruba separated from the Netherlands Antilles in 1986 and became an autonomous member of the Kingdom in and of itself.

Today Statia is in effect supported by the Dutch government. Recent efforts by the government and historical society have concentrated on restoring many of the buildings in Oranjestad and around the island. The chief industry, albeit a small one, is tourism. Local government employs the most workers.

People and Culture

The population of Statia is only 1,860. Statian workers have traditionally found better employment opportunities elsewhere, a trend that has only recently abated and only somewhat at that. The population is almost wholly the descendants of slaves. Some whites, mostly Dutch and some North American retirees, make their homes on the island. Oranjestad, which is the island's sole town, hosts the majority of the population.

Statia's official language is Dutch, but most everyone speaks English. Dutch is taught in schools and is found on most government documents, as well as street signs. Dutch influence is also shown in the Dutch Reformed Church. Other, mostly Protestant, religions exist.

Statians have a historical and curious affinity for the U.S. This perhaps started with the arms and supplies smuggling business of the 1770s. An official state holiday, the 16 November Sint Eustatius Day (often called "Statia-America Day"), is celebrated on the anniversary of the day the Dutch commander, de Graaf, saluted an American brig. That this act brought down the wrath of the British government and the subsequent sacking of the island is not a fact lost on Statians, who seem to have taken it in their stride. A verse of the Statia national anthem declares: "Statia's past you are admired/ though Rodney filled his bag./ The first salute fired/ to the American flag." Apparently Statians are nothing if not ironic and they celebrate the day by dressing in colonial garb and staging a reenactment of the event. Parades, feasts and contests are also part of the celebration. Another result of the *Andrew Doria* incident is the additional nickname for the island, "America's Childhood Friend."

The Franklin Delano Roosevelt Airport was named in honour of the U.S. president, who in 1939 presented the island with a plaque inscribed: "Here the sovereignty of the United States of America was first formally acknowledged to a national vessel by a foreign official." Later, in 1976, Statia honoured the U.S. bicentennial by restoring the island's first bastion, Fort Oranje.

Government and Economy

Statia is an semi-autonomous member of the Netherlands Antilles, which also include the islands of Curaçao, Bonaire, Sint Maarten and Saba.

The Netherlands Antilles are ruled by parliamentary democracy, with the Dutch monarch, Queen Beatrix, as head of state. The queen is represented in the Netherlands Antilles by a governor, who is appointed by the crown. Each island is responsible for water, electricity, land, schools and harbors. The legislative council comprises a Council of Ministers and a 22-member elected parliament. The council is responsible for police, defense, taxation, foreign exchange, health and major foreign affairs decisions. Statia's major political party is the Democratic Party (DP).

The economy of Statia is reliant on remittances from the Crown and from overseas relatives. Government on the island employs about 20 per cent of the working population. Some subsistence farming and fishing feeds the local economy, but is no longer significant. An oil storage facility employs several dozen Statians.

So tourism has emerged as the bright light on the island's economic dashboard. Nearly 18,000 visited in 1992 and the island currently hosts more than 90 guest rooms. In an effort to attract more tourists the Dutch government has pledged US$5 million, in a ten year project to restore historical buildings and sites around the island. The cruise ship dock at Gallows Bay will also be expanded.

In 1989 Hurricane Hugo swept through the island, destroying a third of all the houses and damaging just about every building standing. The island has recovered, through large input from the Dutch government and relief agencies.

Sights

Keep in mind that euphemistic tourism terms, like "unspoiled" and "natural," often draw a thin line between reality and enticement. "Natural" can mean "tattered," "in ruins" or "barely visible," which is true in some cases on Statia. Of the dozen small forts built around the perimeter of the island during its defensible days, many are in a "natural" state. Granted, the island is still a tourism destination in progress and that ought not to limit its true qualities: large doses of nature, history and relaxation, but not much else.

The capital, Oranjestad, is located on the southwest leeward side of the island. The town is built partially on a 130 foot (39 m) cliff overlooking the sea. Upper Town sits on the cliff and Lower Town on the water. The town's Fort Oranje is one of the island's major attractions. The fort, built in 1636 by the Dutch, was partially restored in 1976 in honour of the U.S. bicentennial. It now houses some government offices, a post office (currently closed) and a tourist office (599-3-82433), where you can pick the historical foundation's Walking Tour Guide to Oranjestad, a guide to the island's 12 hiking trails and a number of other brochures.

Tourist information booths are also located at Lower Town and the airport. In the center of Upper Town you'll find the Sint Eustatius Historical Foundation Museum (599-3-82288). The restored red-roofed building, called the Doncker-de Graaff House even though the ill-fated Dutch commander never lived there, did, however, house Admiral Rodney during his profitable looting of Statia in 1781. The museum displays Amerindian artifacts, as well as furniture, old currency and other artifacts from the island's heyday. Note the strings of blue glass beads, still occasionally found around the island by amateur historians and beachcombers. The beads were manufactured by the Dutch West India Company and once used in the trade of various goods, including rum, tobacco, land and slaves. Some speculate that these were the same type of beads used in 1625 by the Dutchman Peter Minuit to purchase Manhattan island from the natives. The museum is open 9.00-16.00 weekdays and closes at noon on weekends. Admission is US$1.

Also in Upper Town is the Dutch Reformed Church, built in 1775. The building, with a square tower housing a historical society information center, is partially restored and you can climb it for a good view of town. Nearby is the ruin of the Honen Dalim Synagogue. During the 16th and 17th centuries Statia, as well as other Caribbean islands, became a refuge for Jews experiencing persecution in South America and Europe. This synagogue, built in 1738, is the second-oldest in the Western Hemisphere. Both churches were abandoned during the general exodus after Rodney's pillage of the island in 1781.

Elsewhere in Upper Town is 4 Fort Oranjestraat, a house built earlier this century and typical of the architecture of the time. Nearby, an 18th century complex called Three Widows Corner, features a cookhouse and garden.

Lower Town was home to the docks, warehouses, taverns and slave quarters during Statia's glory days. Much of it has been restored and now hosts several hotels and shops.

Elsewhere on Statia you'll find the remnants of the 16 or so small forts built during the island's 22 flag changes. Many are so completely ruined and buried by sand, scrub and time that they are practically no longer discernible. Statia is an archaeologist's dream and several organized digs are ongoing, including student visits sponsored by William and Mary College and the University of Leiden.

Statia's 12 nature trails range from difficult to easy. The trails are old slave paths, later goat and donkey paths, and are marked. Tour guides, available through the tourist office, can be hired starting at US$20 per hike.

Hiking to the summit of The Quill is the island's most popular excursion. The Quill, a corruption of the Dutch word kuil, for "pit," is the crater of an extinct volcano. Damage from Hurricane Hugo rendered parts of the hike around the rim impossible, but experienced guides can take you to the best spots, including the highest point, the Mazinga. The path to the inside of the crater is accessible. Allow two to three hours for the hike.

Oranje Beach, also called Smoke Alley Beach, features dark sand in places and stretches north along the coast from Lower Town.

Several beaches on the windward side of the island, including those at Corre Corre and Zeelandia bays, are rough, with strong undertows. These are better for wading and beachcombing than for swimming.

Practical Information

ACCOMMODATION

Statia's dozen small hotels and guesthouses/apartments provide adequately for the island's small tourism and business needs.

Add a seven per cent government tax and a 10–15 per cent service charge to rooms. Credit cards are accepted in most hotels, but several are closed in the slow September-October season. Call ahead to confirm.

❑ THE OLD GIN HOUSE, P.O. Box 172, Oranjestad, Sint Eustatius, N.A. (599-3-82319), in Lower Town, is a reconstructed 18th-century cotton ginnery and warehouse, built using the ballast bricks of Dutch ships. The hotel is small, only 20 rooms, but finely decorated with period antiques and furniture. Luxury.

❑ LA MAISON SUR LA PLAGE, P.O. Box 157, Zeelandia Bay, Sint Eustatius, N.A. (599-3-82256, U.S. 800-845-9405), is located on the eastern, windward side of the island on a small, sometimes frothy, but pretty beach. The 20 rooms are in cottages and the restaurant serves fine French cuisine. Moderate.

❑ TALK OF THE TOWN (599-3-82236), just outside of Upper Town on the way to the airport, somewhat spartan, but clean. Moderate.

❑ HENRIQUEZ APARTMENTS (599-3-82299) features two locations, one near the airport and the other in Upper Town. The simple apartments have kitchenettes and private baths. Budget.

EATING

Hotels host some fine restaurants, including the Mooshay Bay Publik House of the Old Gin House and the French cuisine of La Maison Sur la Plage. Hotel restaurants are also convenient, in that they are open on Sunday.

- FRANKY'S (599-3-82575) in Upper Town serves West Indian (bullfoot soup, grapefruit soup, whelk stew), sandwiches and features occasional entertainment. No credit cards. Inexpensive.
- STONE OVEN (599-3-82543) serves West Indian and is a popular bar and gathering spot, with occasional entertainment. No credit cards. Moderate.
- CHINESE RESTAURANT (599-3-82389) serves, well, you know. No credit cards. Inexpensive.

GETTING THERE

Winair (599-3-82362 or 82381) operates daily connections from nearby Sint Maarten, a 20 minute flight, US$31 one way. Sint Maarten is a major entry point from North America and Europe. Winair also makes the ten minute connection to and from St. Kitts.

The departure tax for destinations other than the Netherlands Antilles, is US$5; to other Netherlands Antilles islands, US$2.

GETTING AROUND

Any one of Statia's dozen taxis will provide an island tour for about US$40.

Renting a car is the best way to see the island. This can be done in a day or two, depending on your degree of inquisitiveness. The roads are fair, although you will discover potholes and various debris. Cow and goats roam with impunity and it's better to refrain from a lot of high-speed, cross-island night driving. Drive slowly. With a valid license from home, you can rent a car for US$35-40 per day; driving is on the right.

Rental cars available at FDR Airport include Avis (599-3-8-2421 or U.S. 800-331-1084), the island's largest rental agency. Lady Ama's (599-3-82451) rents Jeeps and cars.

MONEY, HOURS AND COMMUNICATION

Statia's currency is the Netherlands Antilles florin or guilder (NAF1.80 = US$1). However, U.S. dollars are widely used. The one bank on the island, Barclays, is open Monday through Friday 8.30–13.00 and with extra afternoon hours on Friday 16.00–17.00.

Businesses are open 8.00–12.00 and 13.00–17.00 weekdays and 8.00–12.00 on Saturdays. Most businesses close on Sunday and some are not open at all on weekends. A shop or two may remain open odd hours to accommodate cruise ship schedules.

To call Statia from North America dial the international access code 011, plus the country code 599, then 3 and the five-digit number.

ENTERTAINMENT

Statia is not a big sports center. Tennis and basketball courts are found at the Oranjestad Community Center and, other than that, diving is the thing. The surrounding reef may soon be converted into an protected marine area; beyond that, some 200 shipwrecks sit on the floor of the surrounding waters. Of the 16 charted sites, one, The Supermarket, features two downed ships about 60 feet (18 m) underwater and 150 feet (45 m) apart off the shore of Lower Town. The area in general is replete with coral, sponges and exotic fish.

The one dive operation on the island, Dive Statia (599-3-82435, fax 82539), will organize open water certification, snorkelling and boat charters, as well as deep sea fishing excursions.

USEFUL ADDRESSES

■ TOURISM
❑ Sint Eustatius Department of Tourism, 3 Fort Oranjestraat, Oranjestad, Sint Eustatius, N.A., 599-3-82433.

■ OTHER
❑ Police, 82333.
❑ Queen Beatrix Medical Center, 82211.

St. Kitts and Nevis

Introduction

For more than a century St. Kitts and Nevis have been linked as an entity—first as a colony, then as part of a three-island protectorate in association with Great Britain and finally as an independent federated state. St. Kitts is where the history of English colonization in the Lesser Antilles begins. The first settlement was established in 1623 and was then used as the base for further island colonization. The island was called the "Mother Colony of the West Indies." Yet even at that St. Kitts and Nevis have not emerged as highly developed tourist hot spots. All the better, in most ways.

The land has changed over the years, but only slightly. There are few hotels, mostly guesthouses and old plantation greathouses, and little in the way of trendy, organized entertainment. These are islands on which to be quietly diverted and amused and to enjoy several outstanding natural and historical sites. St. Kitts and Nevis retain a Lesser Antilles sensibility that some islands can only wish they could recapture.

The Land

St. Kitts is the larger of the two islands, at 68 square miles (175 sq km). Nevis is about half the size, 36 square miles (93 sq km). While St. Kitts is long and thin (23 miles or 37 km), Nevis is nearly circular, like a dollop of green floating in the sea. The two are often likened to a cricket bat and ball, although one wonders how Nevisians feel about getting the short end of the stick in the comparison.

St. Kitts, Nevis and St. Eustatius to the north are really three summits of an underwater volcanic chain. These islands, in addition to Montserrat to the south and Saba farther north, lie in an inner arc of Lesser Antilles islands, all surrounded by the Caribbean Sea. The calmer Caribbean waters have wrought less havoc on the windward sides of St. Kitts and Nevis, compared to nearby islands which face the open Atlantic.

The central mountainous spine of St. Kitts, towering and vivid when viewed flying over the island, came about as a result of the ancient underwater volcanic activity. The highest point, Mt. Liamuiga (Lee-a-MWEE-gah), is a dormant volcanic crater in the northwest some 3,792 feet (1,138 m) above sea level. The volcano was called Mt. Misery, apparently an unhappy place, by Kittitians until the 1983 independence. It then reverted to "Liamuiga," the Carib name for St. Kitts, reputedly meaning "Fertile Land." The volcano has been dormant for years, although it did rumble and growl in the 1980s.

Heading southeast, the central spine's altitude gradually tapers. The mountains are surrounded by rainforest and mountain woodlands near the summits, low-lying and fertile plains along the coast. This is the center of the island's still-viable sugarcane industry.

The oddly-shaped Southeast Peninsula is characterized by scrub and acacia trees and some of the island's best bays and beaches. The peninsula was virtually inaccessible for years, until it was "connected" to the rest of the island with the opening of the Dr. Kennedy Simmonds Highway in 1990. The peninsula is relatively low, very different from the rest of the island, only reaching heights of 150 feet (45 m) or so. Several large salt ponds, including the Great Salt Pond, are located at its tip.

The windward coast of St. Kitts does have some rough waters and dramatic, though not very high, cliffs. The Black Rocks near Belle Vue, on the northeast coast, are solidified lava that "froze" upon reaching the sea. Past volcanic activity has also produced beaches of gray volcanic sand to the north. To the south and on the Southeast Peninsula the beaches are honey-colored.

Nevis (NEE-vis) was originally called Oualie by the Caribs, thought to mean "Land of Beautiful Waters." The island is dominated by the central Nevis Peak, some 3,232 feet (970 m) above sea level. Mountain rainforests and low mountain woodlands surround the peak, which tapers to low-lying plains along the shore.

In 1989 Hurricane Hugo swept through the St. Kitts and Nevis, laying waste to much of the agricultural, tourism and fishing industries and causing an estimated US$40 million in damage.

Both islands are home to the vervet, or green monkey, introduced by the French in the 1600s. The estimated monkey population exceeds 50,000 (some estimates put it at 125,000—which proves either that some humans tend to exaggerate or that monkeys tend to hide), greater than the combined human population of the two islands. The Southeast Peninsula is also home to a dwindling number of wild deer. The famous royal poinciana tree, often called the flamboyant, was developed on St. Kitts by an 18th century French governor, de Poinci.

History

Stone Age people, and later Amerindian Arawaks, arrived on St. Kitts and Nevis several thousand years before Christ. They left evidence of their settlements in stone tools, pottery and ceremonial artifacts. The Arawaks were displaced, killed or absorbed (or perhaps a combination of all three) by the warrior Caribs, who were living on St. Kitts and Nevis at the time Columbus visited in the late 15th century. Examples of Carib petroglyphs can be viewed on St. Kitts, near Old Road town.

During his second voyage, in 1493, Columbus charted the islands, but apparently did not land. He called Nevis Nuestra Senora de las Nieves, or "Our Lady of the Snows." This reference was to the wispy white clouds that constantly encircled the summit of the island's highest peak, now Nevis Peak. Columbus then named the larger island Saint Christopher after, apparently, himself, although the patron saint of travelers is also Saint Christopher. Today the official name of the island remains St. Christopher. No one seems to know when St. Kitts was coined as the island's name, but today virtually all government documents and references use the shorter version.

The Spaniards paid little attention to St. Kitts and Nevis. Columbus no doubt had bigger islands and the search for gold on his mind. Plus he had encountered the Caribs elsewhere and they seemed like the right sort of people to leave alone.

The Caribs flourished for another hundred years after Columbus, with virtually no European contact. A party led by Captain John Smith, of the Virginia Colony, landed on Nevis in 1607, but the visit was short-lived: Smith used the island merely to gather water, wood and supplies.

In 1623 England's first expedition to the New World, under Sir Thomas Warner, put down anchor on the west coast of St. Kitts, in the area known as Old Road. The arrival of the first French party in 1625, a small group escaping a sea battle with the Spanish, complicated the situation. Now the British, the French and the Caribs, all mutual enemies, lived on a piece of land no larger than Brooklyn.

When in doubt, however, the Europeans stuck together. The French and British became uneasy allies with a common purpose: elimination of the Caribs. This they accomplished, culminating in the massacre of an estimated 2,000 Caribs at Bloody Point in 1626. They promptly turned to fighting among themselves, then reunited to repel a Spanish attack in 1629.

For the next century the British and French fought for control of St. Kitts and Nevis. Under several minor treaties, the north and south sections of St. Kitts were awarded to the French and the middle section to the British. The French managed to expel the English in 1664, but the English were back 15 years later. In 1713 the Treaty of Utrecht ended one of a series of ongoing European wars and St. Kitts and Nevis were ceded to the British. However, this did little to stop the fighting in the Lesser Antilles. In 1782 the French fought and won on St. Kitts at the British stronghold Brimstone Hill, known as the "Gibraltar of the West Indies." This fort is one of the Caribbean's largest restored garrisons.

Finally, in 1783, the Treaty of Versailles ended the major British-French conflicts. St. Kitts and Nevis became colonies of Great Britain and the local sugarcane industry grew from that point on. St. Kitts, and often to a greater extent Nevis, became profitable cotton, sugar and rum producing islands. Slavery was the backbone of the industry and their importation also accelerated during the late 18th century.

During the zenith of the plantation days Nevis attained the reputation and status of a wealthy island. One of the first hotels in the Lesser Antilles, the Bath Hotel, was built in 1778 near the island's capital of Charlestown. American statesman Alexander Hamilton was born on Nevis in 1757; his family home is now a landmark and museum. Britain's Lord Admiral Horatio Nelson, the famous admiral who was, for a time, based in Antigua, married on Nevis in 1787.

After slaves were freed in 1834, St. Kitts and Nevis entered an age of uncertainty. As on many of the British sugarcane-producing islands, indentured laborers were imported from East India and other parts of the U.K. Still, the sugar industry declined and never reached its former eminence. During the second half of the 19th century and the early 20th century St. Kitts and Nevis became little more than economic dependents, poor relations of England with little hope for economic viability. During that period the political makeup of the modern Lesser Antilles took shape. Anguilla, another British colony some 50 miles (80 km) north of St. Kitts, was added as a dependency to the St. Kitts colonial administration. Later, in 1882, Nevis was added as well. Both moves were met with understandable consternation and alarm by locals on all three islands, who had not been consulted. They resented the move. This feeling would simmer for about one hundred years.

The islands, and the entire Caribbean, entered this century with anxiety and frustration over fragile economies and racial injustice. World War I changed the face of Europe and the world and the innocent days of isolated, tranquil Caribbean island life were over. The industrial revolutions had engendered the growth of trade unions and democracies in Europe; with advanced post-war communication, these concepts found rapt audiences in the Caribbean.

Then the worldwide Depression brought increased labor and economic crises to the feet of Caribbean islanders. Local economies suffered extreme unemployment and shortages. By the 1930s labor conditions brought about strikes and riots in many of the British islands. Nominal representative government was granted to the St. Kitts-Nevis-Anguilla colony in 1937 and by 1952 universal adult suffrage was granted. The St. Kitts and Nevis Labor Party dominated Executive Council elections and by 1960 the council was headed by a chief minister. Agitation for independence intensified and, in 1967, Great Britain granted the status of associated state to the St. Kitts-Nevis-Anguilla government.

This turned out to be a bad move. Anguilla had had enough. The small island to the north, lumped with St. Kitts and Nevis purely for administrative purposes, had little in common with the two other islands save their common status as former British colonies. It was separated from the two larger islands by miles of ocean and the four French and Dutch islands of the Leewards. Further, Anguilla had never been a sugarcane island and had different economic and social concerns. The island felt, in effect, that it would become the economic backwater of the St. Kitts-Nevis-Anguilla federation.

So it rebelled.

Soon after the 1967 referendum protest movements coalesced into armed revolution, which was, in fact, never a threat to the greater populace. The St. Kitts police force was tossed off the island. By 1969 the situation became untenable and British police and army paratroopers were called in. They squashed armed resistance and the rebellion evolved into a constitutional quagmire that took years to resolve. The upshot was that Anguilla finally pulled out of the federation and St. Kitts and Nevis became the Federated State of St. Kitts and Nevis.

Nevis, which was never wholly comfortable with its status as half of the federation, nevertheless has accepted that certain aspects of association with St. Kitts are beneficial. The uneasy strain between the two was exacerbated in 1970, when a dangerously overloaded inter-island ferry sank and left some 240 dead. The majority of the passengers on the Christena were Nevisians. In a population of only 10,000, the loss was devastating.

St. Kitts and Nevis quietly achieved independence on 19 September 1983. The current party in power is the People's Action Movement (PAM), headed by the Prime Minister, Dr. Kennedy Simmonds, who has held office since 1980. The PAM has formed something of a coalition with the Nevis Reform Party (NRP). Other parties include the opposition St. Kitts-Nevis Labor Party and the Concerned Citizens Movement (CCM).

St. Kitts and Nevis were brought to world attention in early 1994 when riots broke out in the St. Kitts capital, Basseterre. Labor Party rallies turned ugly, as demonstrators threw rocks and looted downtown shops in protest over their exclusion from the ruling parliamentary coalition, which had been formed after the general elections. The government declared a three week state of emergency and restored order—fortunately, no one was seriously injured—but it is clear that the PAM's long-term rule faces serious opposition.

People and Culture

The population of St. Kitts is 35,000, Nevis about 10,000. The majority population of the two islands is of African descent; in addition there are small groups of European, East Indian and mixed-race citizens. Culturally the islands take their cue from Britain, with a West Indian twist. English is spoken, though with a dialect not unlike a rapid Patois. The predominant religion is Anglican, although Methodist, Seventh-Day Adventist, Catholic, Moravian, Baha'i, Jehovah's Witnesses and several evangelical sects are also found.

French influence, despite the years of French occupation, is hardly in evidence. Several place names such as Basseterre ("low land") and Molineux remind Kittitians of that aspect of their heritage.

Caribbean cultural traditions are strong during the annual St. Kitts Carnival. The Carnival takes place during late December and early January and is a week-long extravaganza of masquerades, calypso and steel band competitions, food festivals, parades, street dancing and private parties. The equivalent celebration in Nevis is called Culturama, held in late July and early August. For more information on these events and others, contact the tourist offices (St. Kitts 809-465-2620, Nevis 469-5521).

Government and Economy

The Federated State of St. Kitts and Nevis is a member of the Commonwealth, with the Queen the official head of state. The monarch is represented on the St. Kitts by a governor general and a deputy governor general represents the Queen on Nevis. Power is vested in the ruling party, headed by the prime minister. The legislature consists of an elected National Assembly and an appointed Senate. Nevis is represented in Parliament, but also has its own internal government, comprising a premier and a House of Assembly. Under provisions of the federation, Nevis may elect to secede.

The economy of St. Kitts and Nevis is based largely on agriculture and tourism. Sugar represents about 55 per cent of the state's export revenue and employs about 12 per cent of the working population. The industry increased its output from 1991 to 1992 by 27 per cent and, indeed, the low-lying plains of the two islands are covered by acres of pastel green sugarcane. St. Kitts produces a sugarcane spirit, Baron's CSR, the quality of which is exceptional, due, according to locals, to the clarity of the water. Over the years the government has encouraged agricultural diversification and more small farmers are growing yams, potatoes and other vegetables.

Tourism is gathering strength as an industry and has recently overtaken agriculture as the main foreign exchange earner. Nearly 140,000 visitors arrived in 1992, about 24,500 of them bound for Nevis. Most come from North America and the U.K.

Currently there are 1,371 rooms in 29 hotels, plantation inns, guesthouses and cottages on the islands. This number is expected to increase dramatically in the next few years. The 1990 opening of the Dr. Kennedy Simmonds Highway on St. Kitts, which provides access to the Southeast Peninsula, has put into motion several large hotel and resort development projects for that area. Included among them are plans for a large Sandals Resort and a Casablanca Resort. Expansion of facilities and the airstrip at Newcastle Airport in Nevis is planned.

More than 400 cruise ships, representing 80,000 passengers, visited the two islands in the 1993-94 season (100 to Nevis, 318 to St. Kitts).

Sights

A modern coastal road loops around St. Kitts, making travel around the countryside easy and pleasant. As you drive the generally unhurried roads, note the stone ruins of dozens of sugar mills, relics from 18th and 19th century plantation estates. In the main sections of the small towns and fishing villages you'll see small bathhouses and public taps, also relics of a time when running water was not available in households. The bathhouses were used by sugarcane plantation workers to wash up after a long day's toil in the fields.

North of Basseterre is the village of Challengers and the nearby Bloody Point, site of the conclusive massacre of the Carib population, some 2,000 people, in 1626. Farther along is Old Road Bay, site of the first European settlement in the British Lesser Antilles. It was here, in 1623, that Thomas Warner and a small group landed to establish a colony. A river runs through the town and is no doubt one of the reasons Warner and his party settled here. Inland is Wingfield Estate, site of an old Carib settlement; several petroglyphs are carved into the rocks. Past the rocks and through section of rainforest is Romney Manor, an old plantation greathouse and gardens. The picturesque greathouse is now home to Caribelle

Batik (809-465-6253), a fabric and clothing shop utilizing original designs executed on the property—you may watch the artisans in action. On the property note the huge, 350-year-old saman tree, also called a rain tree for its capacity to hold water in its leaves and continue to "rain" long after an actual downpour.

Farther inland is the village of Middle Island and the St. Thomas Church. The church is the burial place of, among others, Sir Thomas Warner, who died in 1648. He is in the tomb under the canopy. The inscription identifies Warner as "...Generall of Ye Caribbee Ieland W Goverr of Ye Ieland of St. Chris...."

Back on the coastal road, head north to Brimstone Hill Fortress National Park. The imposing fortress has the distinction of being the second-largest pre-20th century fort in the Caribbean (The Citadel in Haiti is larger). The Brimstone Hill complex covers nearly 40 acres and rises 800 feet (240 m) above the sea.

Construction was begun by the British in 1690 and completed more than 100 years later, most of it by slave labor. The British fought several important battles with the French before the fort was captured in 1782. It was later returned the British after the 1783 Treaty of Versailles. The British continued to build upon existing structures until the fortress comprised five bastions, including officers' quarters, a hospital, water storage tanks and Fort George, the highest point, or citadel, of the complex.

On a clear day the views are stunning. Saba and Statia are visible to the north and a nearly 360-degree view shows off the rest of St. Kitts, including scars of areas where rock was mined for construction, as well as Nevis and Montserrat to the south. From the citadel it is not difficult to understand the strategic advantage of the fort.

Over the years hurricane damage and apathy took their toll on the buildings. The fortress was abandoned in 1851 and fell into further disrepair. It became a national park in 1965 and restoration is ongoing. A snack bar, gift shop and small museum are on the grounds. Admission is EC$13, open 9.00-17.00 daily.

The coast road will bring you to Sandy Point, a small fishing and port town that seems to have more churches per square foot than the Vatican.

To the far north is Dieppe Bay, a black-sand beach and small fishing town. Along the coast road is Belle Vue, where you'll see the black volcanic deposits looming like monoliths from the foaming surf. This is the site of the Caribbean Museum of Gems and Rocks, which seems like an good idea. Trouble is, there is no museum. Just a sign.

Heading south on the coastal road you'll come to the Southeast Peninsula, currently untouched save for a few small beach bars and unfinished hotels. If the tourism industry grows as planned, this area will someday host several hotels and resorts. The peninsula features some of the island's best beaches, which are the honey-colored type, rather than the black sand of the north. Frigate Bay and Friar's Bay, on the peninsula's "skinny" section, are two of the island's best known beaches; Frigate Bay is the quieter of the two. In the extreme south are several good bays and beaches, although some are hard to get to by car and you'll need to walk. They include Cockleshell Bay, Major's Bay and Green Point. The Turtle Beach Bar and Grill, operated by the Ocean Terrace Inn in Basseterre, sits on the south end facing Nevis. The best swimming, snorkelling and diving on the peninsula is right here, as well as live entertainment on some evenings.

Nature excursionists will want to hike around the Great Salt Pond, where you might see vervet monkeys or wild deer. Several hikes to the crater of Mt. Liamuiga, through rainforests, or to a mountain lake on Mt. Verchild can be arranged through Kriss Tours (809-465-4042), Greg's Safaris (809-465-4121) or Kantours (809-465-2098), all in Basseterre.

Basseterre

Basseterre, the capital and chief port of St. Kitts and Nevis, was not the original capital of the islands. That would have been Old Road, the site of the first British landing in 1623. Basseterre was founded by the French after their arrival in 1625 and served as a base and small port town for more than 40 years. The town was damaged several times by earthquakes, most notably in 1689. During one of the many repossessions of the island the British moved their administrative center from Old Road to Basseterre and there it has since remained. The year was 1727.

An 1867 fire destroyed much of the town. It was again rebuilt, but the architectural styles of the city reflect layers of disaster and repair accumulated over more than two centuries. A primary style is Victorian-West Indian-Colonial, with plenty of gingerbread fretwork and wide verandahs and balconies. It is a large and sprawling town, population about 17,000, and comfortable. Independence Square is central and in an old section of the city. The square, once called Pall Mall Square, was built in 1790 to hold slave auctions and public gatherings. It is now a gathering place and small park, where schoolchildren lounge and goats graze. The Immaculate Conception Catholic Church sits on the east side of the square, dating from the early part of this century. On Cayon Street is St. George's, the Anglican church. The original structure on the site was Notre Dame, a Catholic church built by the French. This was leveled by the British in 1706, who rebuilt it as St. George's. Fires and earthquakes destroyed it three more times. It was last restored in 1869.

The center of Basseterre today is The Circus, a roundabout at Bank, Fort and Liverpool streets. The Circus, apparently modeled after Piccadilly of the same name, features the most photographed landmark in Basseterre and possibly St. Kitts. It is the Berkeley Memorial, a gaudy cement structure with a clock and drinking fountains. It was named after Thomas Berkeley, a former colonial council president. On The Circus you'll find banks, taxi stands, bus stands, a hotel, a restaurant and many businesses. Near The Circus is the General Post Office, Treasury Building, several piers, Tourist Office and Pelican Mall, the town's only shopping plaza.

Good shopping, including numerous book stores (try Walls Deluxe, 809-465-2159), pharmacies and gift shops are found on Fort and Central streets.

Bay Road, north of The Circus and town, runs along the fisherman's beach. Here you'll find small markets, rum shops, grocery stores and the public market. Farther north is a War Memorial, dedicated to those who served in the world wars.

Practical Information

ACCOMMODATION

The St. Kitts and Nevis Hotel Association (P.O. Box 438, Basseterre, St. Kitts, W.I.; tel. and fax 809-465-5304) publishes a complete list of island hotels and guest-houses; those listed below are recommended.

Many hotels will accept credit cards, but it's best to check first. Hotels charge a seven per cent tax and often a ten per cent service charge, which is tacked on to the bill. There are no camping facilities on St. Kitts and Nevis.

❑ THE GOLDEN LEMON INN AND VILLAS, P.O. Box 17, Dieppe Bay, St. Kitts, W.I. (809-465-7260, fax 465-4019, U.S. tel. 800-223-5581), features rooms and comfortable villas individually decorated with antiques gathered from the West Indies and around the world. Luxury.

❑ OTI OCEAN TERRACE INN, P.O. Box 65, Basseterre, St. Kitts, W.I. (809-465-2754, fax 465-1057, U.S. tel. 800-524-0512 or 800-74-CHARMS), is one of the island's best buys, located a short walk from The Circus in Basseterre. Moderate-luxury.

❑ OTTLEY'S PLANTATION INN, P.O. Box 345, Basseterre, St. Kitts, W.I. (809-465-7234), is an old plantation greathouse at the foot of Mt. Liamuiga. Luxury.

❑ ON THE SQUARE, 14 Independence Square, Basseterre, St. Kitts, W.I. (809-465-2485), is located, not surprisingly, on the square in Basseterre. The small guesthouse is clean and convenient, some rooms with private baths, most with air conditioning. Budget.

EATING

❑ FISHERMAN'S WHARF (809-465-2754) serves West Indian and seafood in an open air bistro on the wharf across the street from the OTI. Very good deal, good service. Open for dinner only. Inexpensive-moderate.

❑ THE BALLAHOO (809-465-4197), on The Circus in Basseterre, is upstairs in an open verandah, a great place to watch the town walk by. Inexpensive-moderate.

❑ FRIGATE BAY BEACH HOTEL (809-465-8935) serves elegant West Indian and Continental. Moderate-expensive.

❑ THE GEORGIAN HOUSE (809-465-4049) is on Independence Square and features West Indian and some barbecues. Moderate.

GETTING THERE

Golden Rock Airport is located minutes from Basseterre in St. Kitts and Newcastle Airport is minutes from Charlestown in Nevis. Neither airport is large, but Golden Rock can land international flights.

From North American and Europe to St. Kitts, use BWIA (809-465-8644), American (809-465-2273) or charter company Liberty Airlines (809-465-5000).

Inter-island connections are made by LIAT (809-465-2286), Winair (809-465-2186 or 465-8010) or Air St. Kitts Nevis (809-465-8571).

Nevis: LIAT (Newcastle Airport tel. 809-469-5302), Air St. Kitts-Nevis (809-469-9241 or 465-8751) and Winair (809-469-9583) make connections to Nevis from St. Kitts.

Departure tax from St. Kitts and Nevis is EC$20 or US$8. There is no departure tax between St. Kitts and Nevis.

GETTING AROUND

■ TAXIS

Taxi and minibus rates are set by the government. Taxis are available at Golden Rock Airport and The Circus in Basseterre, while minibuses are found on Bay Road. On Nevis taxis and minibuses are found at the airport, the public market and the town pier. Bus stops line the roads, but the vans can be hailed at any point.

Fares are posted at both airports and in the tourist board publication called The St. Kitts and Nevis Traveler. On St. Kitts a three hour island tour will cost US$80 for up to four per vehicle; on Nevis an island tour runs US$45.

For taxis call Riley's Taxi Service (809-465-2444). Mr. Pat Riley is very knowledgeable, efficient and the best man for an island tour. Also try The St. Kitts Taxi Association (The Circus 809-465-4253). On Nevis call Airport Taxi (Newcastle Airport 809-469-9402) or Fitzroy "Teach" Teacher (809-469-1140). On both islands add 25–50 per cent to the fare after 22.00.

■ CAR RENTALS

Rental cars are available, starting at about US$30 per day plus a five per cent tax. The driving is easy, just remember to stay on the left. You'll need to get a temporary local license, at a cost of EC$30 or US$12, which can be arranged by the rental company. Rental companies include: on St. Kitts: Avis (809-465-6507, fax 465-1042), Caines Rent-a-Car (809-465-2366, fax 465-6172), Delisle Walwyn Rentals (809-465-8449); on Nevis: Avis (809-469-1240, fax 469-5604), Nevisian Rentals (809-469-5423 or 469-9583, fax 469-0487) or Skeete's Car Rental (809-469-9458).

■ FERRY SERVICE

A regular passenger ferry service operates between Basseterre and Charlestown. The two boats are the Carib Queen and the Spirit of Mount Nevis, the latter operated by the Mt. Nevis Hotel and Beach Club. One way fare on the Carib Queen is EC$10 or US$4; on the Spirit of Mount Nevis the fare is EC$15 or US$6 and the crossing takes 30 to 45 minutes. The schedule changes often, but the Basseterre to Charlestown ferries leave daily, sometimes three times a day, starting at 8.00. Call the tourist board for current schedules.

Additionally, the Four Seasons Hotel on Nevis runs a ferry service from and to St. Kitts, for guests only.

MONEY, HOURS AND COMMUNICATION

St. Kitts and Nevis use the Eastern Caribbean dollar (EC$2.70 = US$1). Many businesses will accept U.S. dollars and often Canadian dollars, but your change will probably be in EC dollars. Do yourself a favour: exchange your money. Banks give better rates than hotels and they are located on the main streets and malls of Basseterre and Charlestown. Banking hours are generally 8.00–15.00 Monday through Thursday and 8.00–17.00 on Friday.

Commercial business hours are 8.00–12.00 and 13.00–16.00 Monday through Friday and 8.00-12.00 on Saturday. Many shops close for the entire afternoon on Thursdays and others stay open through Saturday or for cruise ship business. The General Post Office (St. Kitts tel. 809-465-2521, Nevis 469-5221) on both islands is open 8.00-15.00 Monday through Saturday, except Thursday, when it is open 8.00–11.00. Branch hours vary slightly.

The telephone area code on St. Kitts and Nevis in 809. Dialing is direct and public phones accept coins or phone calling cards. The St. Kitts and Nevis Telecommunications (SKANTEL) offices are located on Main Street in Nevis (809-469-5000) and at Fort and Cayon streets in Basseterre (809-465-1000); hours are 8.00–18.00 weekdays, 8.00–13.00 Saturdays. In Basseterre the offices keep Sunday evening hours, 18.00–20.00.

ENTERTAINMENT

Golf, tennis and horseback riding can be arranged through your hotel. Watersports are also available through hotels, but several dive shops are worth exploring, too. An estimated 400 ships went down in the St. Kitts and Nevis waters between 1492 and 1815, some due to storms and natural calamities, others sunk by cannonballs. Only a dozen or so wrecks have been located.

Other attractions include coral reefs and underwater caves. Call Kenneth's Dive Center (809-465-2670) or OTI Dive Center (OTI Ocean Terrace Inn, 809-465-2754) in Basseterre for St. Kitts dives. On Nevis, call Scuba Safaris (809-469-9518) at the Oualie Beach Club.

USEFUL ADDRESSES

■ TOURIST INFORMATION

St. Kitts and Nevis Tourist Board:

❑ Pelican Mall, Basseterre, St. Kitts, W.I.; 809-465-2620 or 465-4040, airport 465-8970, fax 465-8794.

❑ 414 East 75th St., New York, NY 10021; 800-562-6208 or 212-535-1234, fax 879-4789.

❑ 11 Yorkville Ave., Suite 508, Toronto, Ontario M4W IL3; 416-921-7717, fax 921-7997.

❑ 10 Kensington Court, London W8 5DL; 0171-376-0881, fax 937-3611.

❑ St. Kitts and Nevis Hotel Association, P.O. Box 438, Basseterre, St. Kitts, W.I.; tel. and fax, 809-465-5304.

❑ Nevis Tourist Office, Main Street, Charlestown; 809-469-5521.

■ OTHER
- ❑ Emergency, 465-5391.
- ❑ Police, 465-2241.
- ❑ Joseph N. France General Hospital, Basseterre; 465-2551.
- ❑ Immigration, 465-8470.
- ❑ City Drug Store, Basseterre; 465-2156.
- ❑ American Express representative, Kantours, Palms Arcade, The Circus, Basseterre; 465-2098.
- ❑ Alexandra Hospital, Government Road, Charlestown, Nevis; 469-5473.

Nevis

Nevis has much to recommend, not the least being its fine beaches and unencumbered lifestyle. There isn't much to do here, but one can do it in style. The administrative center is Charlestown, population 1,500, a rickety and tarnished town, steeped in history and disaster. Earthquakes and tidal waves have taken their toll over the years and the town has been rebuilt in and around some of the oldest buildings in the Caribbean.

Charlestown was established in 1660 on the southwest shore of the circular island. It became a port town and its principal activity was the export of cotton, once the main crop on Nevis. Adjacent to the pier is the old Cotton Ginnery, which is still used during the harvest season in March and April. The ginnery is adjacent to the public market, busiest on Saturdays. Along the pier are several shops and cafes, some located in renovated buildings. The Rookery Nook, for instance, was built in an 1850 livery stable.

Main Street is as busy as it gets on Nevis and here you'll find banks, the post office, shops, taxis and businesses. The tourist board is located at DR Walwyn Plaza, open daily (and on Saturdays during the high season). Nearby is the War Memorial Square, which features a cannon captured from German forces in World War I.

Nearby, the Court House, circa 1825, once served as government and Assembly headquarters. It burned in an 1873 fire and was restored. A public library (open 9.00–18.00 Monday through Saturday) is located on the second floor. On Main Street, The Museum of Nevis History at the Alexander Hamilton House is a mouthful. The original birthplace of Hamilton was built in 1680 but burned in a mid-19th century fire. The present structure was rebuilt at independence. The museum features memorabilia and artifacts from Nevis history; the Nevis House of Assembly meets upstairs. The requested donation is US$1 and the hours are 8.00-16.00 weekdays and 10.00-12.00 on Saturday. Turn in (east) from the museum and you'll see the Charlestown Methodist Church, built in 1844. On Government Road is the old Jewish Cemetery, believed to date to 1679. A small but intrepid group of Jews settled on Nevis after a forced exile from Brazil in the early 17th century. An archaeological dig is being conducted at a site near the government offices to determine if a crumbled stone building is the site of an old synagogue. If so, it would be the oldest known synagogue in the Caribbean.

On the southern outskirts of town is the Bath Hotel, built in 1778 and reputedly the oldest standing hotel building in the Caribbean. That may or may not be true, but it is old and solid, built of stone and mortar that have withstood hurricanes. A 1950 earthquake did extensive damage, but the building has been restored. Now used as a police barracks, it is no longer open to the public. A bathhouse has been constructed around a hot mineral spring, courtesy of underground volcanic activity. The spring is said to have been used by the Caribs for restorative purposes and the temperature of the water, 108° F (41° C), is said to have remained constant since the 16th century. The bath is open to the public, 8.00–17.00 weekdays and until noon on Saturday. Admission is US$2 for a recommended 20 minutes maximum; towels are EC$0.50. Nearby is the Nelson Museum, containing over 600 pieces of the great admiral's memorabilia. Admission is US$2, open 9.00–16.00 weekdays, 10.00–13.00 Saturday.

Elsewhere on the island are several historical sites. Most prominent as you drive around the island (the road is circular, with the central Nevis Peak often obscured beneath its cloud cover) are the plantation houses and ruins, many of which have been converted into small guesthouses and inns.

East from Charlestown is St. John's Fig Tree Anglican Church, the church that posted the banns of the marriage of Lord Nelson to his bride, Fanny Nisbet. The church no longer displays the marriage certificate. The Hermitage, now a hotel, features a well-preserved wooden greathouse on the grounds of an old plantation. The main structure was built in 1740 and is one of the Caribbean's oldest.

The northeast side of the island is curiously barren, except for a few small settlements and ancient churches. The land is dry and the flora scrubby and desert-like in places, which is curious because this side of the island is the windward side, where prevailing rains should fall. Nearby is the small fishing village of Newcastle, which features some old buildings built in the West Indian colonial style.

On the leeward east coast are the island's hotels and better beaches. Note the St. Thomas Anglican Church and graveyard. This is the oldest church on Nevis, built in 1643. The present structure is an amalgam of repairs and refurbishments and is still used by parishioners.

For touring the island, a specialized group is Eco-Tours Nevis P.O. Box 493, Charlestown, Nevis, W.I.; (809-469-2091, fax 469-2113). One of its hikes is the three-hour "Eco-Ramble."

NEVIS ACCOMMODATION

❏ THE MT. NEVIS HOTEL AND BEACH CLUB, P.O. Box 494, Nevis, W.I. (809-469-9373/4, fax 469-9375, North America 800-75-NEVIS or tel. and fax 212-874-4276), sits at the north of the island, facing St. Kitts and the two-mile (three km) Narrows Channel. The hotel's 16 acres of gardens are elevated 275 feet (83 m) up the slopes of Mt. Nevis. The restaurant is one of the island's best, and the view almost certainly is. Good deal. Moderate-luxury.

❏ THE FOUR SEASONS, P.O. Box 565, Charlestown, Nevis, W.I. (809-469-1111, U.S. 800-332-3442, Canada 800-268-6282), is huge, sprawling and everything you would expect in a Four Seasons hotel, including 196 rooms built along the famous west coast Pinney's Beach, 18 holes of golf, ten tennis courts, three restaurants, pools and a health club. Luxury.

❏ THE HERMITAGE, 129 Kelmar Ave., Malvern, PA 19355 (800-682-4025, or Nevis tel. 809-469-3477, fax 469-2481), sits on plantation land, with Old World style. Luxury.

❏ SEA SPAWN GUESTHOUSE, Old Hospital Road, Charlestown, Nevis, W.I. (809-469-5239, fax 469-5706), features 18 rooms, all with fans, on Pinney's Beach on the outskirts of Charlestown. Budget.

Antigua and Barbuda

Introduction

The State of Antigua and Barbuda comprises the islands of Antigua (An-TEE-gah) and its sister island Barbuda (Bar-BEW-dah), which lies 27 miles (43 km) north of Antigua, and speck-like Redonda, an uninhabited half square mile (1.3 sq km) cay some 30 miles to the west.

The three islands are located at the heart of the Leewards and nearly at the midpoint of the Lesser Antilles archipelago—generally east and south of St. Kitts and Nevis and northeast of Montserrat. Antigua's airport, V.C. Bird International, is the home base of LIAT, the regional airline. As such, Antigua has become something of a hub for inter-island travelers and is a popular destination in itself. Tourist numbers have grown in leaps over the past dozen years, a 16 per cent increase in 1993, and the island is one of the most tourism-conscious, and developed, of the Leewards. There are, at last count, 103 hotels and guest houses on the island. Yet, for most visitors, Antigua and Barbuda retain an ease and simplicity of life and remain a relaxed Caribbean experience.

The Land

Antigua is, at 108 square miles (281 sq km), the second largest, behind Guadeloupe, of the Leeward Islands. The island's formation resulted from volcanic activity that thrust the outer islands of the Lesser Antilles through the surface of the sea. The island's highest point is Boggy Peak, located at the southwest corner of the island, 1,319 feet (396 m) above sea level. The area around Boggy Peak, in the parish of St. Mary, is the mountainous part of Antigua, where small sections of rainforest can be found. The interior of the island is essentially unassuming and is by and large flat and scrubby, with some forest cover and gentle, rolling hills. Because of infrequent and sporadic rainfall—about 45 inches per year—Antigua is one of the Lesser Antilles' drier islands, actually prone to drought. September through November are the wettest months, but daily showers last no longer than 20 minutes or so. There are no permanent streams or rivers and water conservation is of great concern to the government.

Antigua's irregular coastline has formed numerous small bays and outlying cays, considered by many to be the island's primary attraction. Tourism lore has placed the number of Antigua's beaches at 365—one for every day of the year. Whether true or not, you'll certainly find an abundance of stunning white and salmon-colored sand beaches throughout the island. A barrier reef off the north coast, as well as numerous other reefs and shoals, provide excellent diving opportunities.

If Antigua is relatively flat, then Barbuda is definitively flat. The highest point on the 68 square mile (177 sq km) island is 145 feet (44 m) above sea level, in the eastern coastal area known, without apparent irony, as The Highlands. The island of Barbuda, a ten minute flight from Antigua, was, in the 17th century, the private estate of the Codrington family. Hence the main town of Codrington, where most of the island's population of 1,500 live, and Codrington Lagoon, a large body of water and mangrove swamp on the western side of the island. The lagoon is home to hundreds of frigate and other birds, which migrate here to breed from August to December. Much of Barbuda is still overgrown and untamed and domestic animals gone wild roam about. Sheep, fallow deer, pigs, ducks and guinea fowl have all found a place on the island and are hunted for sport. (Game hunting is allowed on Barbuda, with proper licenses and game limits administered by the Secretary of the Barbuda Council).

Barbuda is coral-based, with some of the finest and least populated beaches in the Caribbean. The diving is spectacular. At least 73 charted shipwrecks provide ample opportunities for exploration and an estimated 200 wrecks lie twisted and gouged on the shoals and reefs surrounding the island. Divers can also explore several sinkholes and underwater caves.

Redonda is a dependency of Antigua, although today that means little in real terms. Redonda was first sighted by Columbus on his second voyage in 1493 and named after the Spanish church Santa Maria de Redonda. He did not land, however, and the island remained unexplored for years. The island was annexed by Britain and came under the jurisdiction of Antigua in 1869. Migrating and breeding birds had dumped several tons of guano, rich in phosphate, on the island and mining was profitable until 1914, when the guano ran out. Today Redonda is home to gulls, goats and the infrequent intrepid explorer.

History

The original inhabitants of Antigua and Barbuda were the Stone Age Ciboney, so-called for the stone implements they used for hunting and farming. The Ciboney may have inhabited Antigua at about 2,000 BC, but moved on due to the lack of a consistent supply of fresh water. The Arawaks arrived on the scene some 2,000 years later, around the time of Christ. Archaeological evidence shows that they stayed on the island until about AD 1,200, when they were driven off by marauding Caribs. This was the Arawaks' lot throughout the Caribbean, always one step ahead of the Caribs and one step behind in their capacity to defend themselves. The Caribs used the islands as bases for raiding nearby islands and were on the scene when Columbus sighted Antigua on his second voyage, in 1493.

Columbus never set foot on the island, but named it Santa Maria de la Antigua, after a painting of the Virgin Mary in the Seville chapel. Having christened the islands, Columbus and the Spanish, as well as the Dutch, French, English and other colonizers, left them in the hands of the Caribs, who defended them with characteristic aplomb.

By 1632 settlement of the Caribbean was well underway, when a group of British colonizers from nearby St. Kitts landed on Antigua to claim it for the crown. Despite attacks from the Caribs, the colonizers managed to establish several tobacco and ginger plantations. Antigua has since remained in British hands, except for a few months in 1666 when the French claimed the island, during one of the many skirmishes played out for Caribbean (and European) sovereignty and possessions.

In 1674 Sir Christopher Codrington arrived from the then-famed Barbados sugar plantations and established the Antigua and Barbuda sugar industry at Betty's Hope, on Antigua. So successful were Codrington's plantations that in 1685 he leased the entire island of Barbuda and turned it into a profitable 300-acre estate, used primarily to grow food for the burgeoning slave population. Entire sections of Antigua's then-forested interior were razed for plantations and today many Antiguans believe that the island's continuing water problems were exacerbated by this deforestation.

The growth of the sugar industry engendered the growth of slavery and it is estimated that by 1834, the year Britain abolished slavery, there were some 30,000 Africans working on the Antigua and Barbuda plantations, managed by 2,000 white planters and overseers. Sugar remained an important industry until the early 1970s and today the remains of an estimated 140 sugar mills dot the Antiguan countryside.

After the abolition of slavery sugar became less profitable and Antigua and Barbuda entered into a long period of economic decline. This situation existed in many of the Caribbean islands that relied on sugar and other plantation crops as their economic bedrock. The decline in turn accentuated the already extant racial, and resulting social and class, fissures in Antiguan society that existed well into the 20th century.

Regional discontent in the 1930s centered around unacceptable working conditions, low pay and a distinctly poor quality of life. Throughout the islands, labor strikes and some violence broke out, crippling local production. The British astutely allowed the formation of labor and trade unions, the first step toward organized political parties. The first on Antiguan was the Antigua Trades and Labor Union, established in 1939.

World War II interrupted the natural growth of politics in the islands and diverted the world's attention for some time. By 1943 Vere Cornwall (V.C.) Bird was elected president of the union and used it as a base to merge with other unions to form the Antigua Labor Party (ALP). In 1946 Bird was elected to the colonial legislative council. In 1951 universal suffrage was granted and, in 1956, the island was granted a ministerial form of government. Antigua and Barbuda were governed as part of a Leeward Islands association until 1959. Full self-government as an associated state, with foreign affairs and defense under the auspices of Britain, was granted in 1967. Finally, independence was granted on 1 November 1981. Except for a brief period in the early 1970s, when general elections were won by the Progressive Labor Movement, the ruling party has been the ALP.

An arms smuggling and narcotics scandal shook up the government in 1990 and nearly brought it down. The Communications and Works Minister, Vere Bird Jr., a son of V.C. Bird, was implicated in the scandal, in which Antigua allegedly helped smuggle Israeli arms to Colombian drug cartels. The junior Bird resigned his post, but remained a member of parliament.

In 1994 V.C. Bird Jr. ascended to the head of the ALP and was appointed prime minister after an ALP victory in general elections.

People and Culture

A 1991 census estimated the population of Antigua and Barbuda at 66,000. Some estimate the combined population is closer to 75,000, of which only 1,500 live on Barbuda. A more significant figure, perhaps, is the racial breakdown. Descendants of African slaves account for about 95 per cent of the population and the remainder is white, Asian and mixed-race.

Culturally Antiguans celebrate their African heritage—with a distinctly British hue. You're as likely to hear lively steel bands and bawdy calypso singers as you are to catch a good cricket game. Cricket is played far and wide in the Caribbean, particularly on the British-influenced islands. The West Indian cricket team has played in test matches since 1928 and since the 1970s has been considered one of the best in the world. Antiguans Viv Richards, who retired in 1992 as one of the most celebrated batsmen of all time, and Richie Richardson, currently the West Indies' captain, rank among the world's best players. World-class matches, such as the 1993 West Indies/Pakistan Test Match, are part and parcel of Antiguan life and watched with fervor.

Religions, as well, reflect the British influence. There are more than 100 churches on the island, with the Anglican church the most prevalent. Others include Roman Catholic, Methodist and Seventh-Day Adventist.

At the same time the food, carnivals, music and language of Antigua and Barbuda are clearly creole. While English is the official language, the lingua franca is a lyrical English-based Patois.

Antigua sponsors a Jazz Festival, featuring international musicians, held for three days in late May. The Antigua Carnival, considered by many to be second only to Trinidad's in style and energy, is held for ten days from late July to the first Tuesday in August. Carnival activities include dancing, reggae bands, pan and calypso bands, contests, beauty pageants, food, costumes and "jump-ups" (street marching). The grand finale, on the first Monday night in August, is J'Overt, a huge jump-up, where bands and crowds pour into the streets at 4.00, dancing and letting loose. Most carnival activity takes place in St. John's, at the open-air Carnival City. For information call the Carnival Office (809-462-0194 or 462-4707). Barbuda's smaller carnival, held in June, is called Caribana.

Antigua-born Jamaica Kincaid writes novels, short stories and essays which describe Caribbean life, especially the strong bonds between mothers and daughters. Kincaid has published several works, including the story collection *At the Bottom of the River* (1983) and the novel *Annie John* (1985). The autobiographical *Lucy* was released in 1990.

Government and Economy

The State of Antigua and Barbuda is a democratic republic and a member of the British Commonwealth. The sovereign is represented on the island by a governor general and the government is legislated by two bodies: an elected, 17 member Parliament, or House of Representatives, and an Upper House, or Senate, which is appointed by the governor general on the advice of the prime minister and opposition leader. Representatives come from the six parishes of Antigua, plus Barbuda.

Antigua's economy has changed radically since sugar's heyday. Today tourism earns more than half of the gross national product, accounting for more than 60 per cent of all economic activity. The tourism infrastructure has grown further with the 1994 expansion of V.C. Bird International Airport, as well as the current development of several large resort properties. LIAT, the regional airline based at V.C. Bird International, has experienced mounting losses over the years. It is rumored, in fact, that LIAT has never had a profitable year. Its board of directors, drawn from 11 member governments, has recently elected to privatize the airline and this may mean some loss of jobs and revenue for Antigua. Other economic activity takes place in the offshore banking and insurance industries, but the corruption scandals of 1990 apparently have slowed down private sector investment.

A small amount of farming takes place, primarily cotton, bananas, coconuts and pineapples. Antigua exports some petroleum products, but imports most of its food, fuel and large machinery.

Sights

BEACHES

The rallying cry of the sun and fun crowd, "life is a beach," has found its proper place in Antigua and Barbuda. Beaches are a large attraction and, if there is a modicum of truth to the tourism department's claim that a year's worth of beaches—365—dot the coast of Antigua, this may be the place to start exploring.

Antigua's beaches are open to the public. In theory, this means that one should be able to go to any beach at any time. In practice, however, this means that beaches fronting exclusive hotels, particularly some of the all-inclusives, can be difficult to get to if one must pass through hotel property to access the beach. Hotels may reserve the right to limit entry. On the other hand, many of Antigua's beaches are isolated and secluded and some are deserted. Keep in mind that most have no lifeguards, changing rooms or other facilities.

The east and northeast coast is on Antigua's windward side, facing the Atlantic, and has a more irregular and somewhat rougher coastline than the leeward side. Still, there are several bays and protected harbors that offer excellent, quiet beaches. Beachcombing is excellent all along the coast. Head east from St. John's toward the town of Willikies, where you'll find Long Bay Beach and the Pineapple Beach Club. South of Long Bay is Nonsuch Bay, also the sight of several secluded spots. Half Moon Bay is considered by many to be one of the top beaches on the island. To the north, near the village of Parham, is Fitches Creek

Bay and the lagoon-like beaches of Crabbs Peninsula (on the Parham Harbor side), naturally protected from the winds of the Atlantic.

On the west coast, where the water is calmer, try Dickenson Bay, which is lined with hotels, restaurants and watersports facilities. The public beach is popular with locals. South of Dickenson Bay and west of St. John's is Five Islands Village, which has half a dozen good beaches. Hawksbill Beach Resort features four beaches, one of which is clothing-optional. The farther you get away from the hotel, the more secluded the beaches. Deep Bay, on which the Ramada Renaissance is located, is long enough to get out of the hotel's way. The beach at Galley Bay is also long and quiet, with secluded spots.

Darkwood Beach, south of Fryers Point, is a popular local hangout. On a clear day you can see Montserrat to the west.

On the south shore, another resort area, try Rendezvous Bay for secluded and calm beaches. The beach at Falmouth Harbor, Pigeon Point, is a popular white-sand beach.

Barbuda's beaches are superb. As a matter of fact, Barbuda is just about all beach. Long Bay, to the west of the lagoon, is a seven mile (11 km) beach with some of the best whitish-pink coral sand you'll find anywhere. The beach at Coco Point, near one of the island's two airstrips, is also popular—which, on Barbuda, still means uncrowded.

OTHER SIGHTS

Antigua's rich history of colonization and development has left the country with a visible legacy. Abandoned and decrepit sugar mills poke up from the countryside, while the remains of ancient fortifications and other defense facilities can be found along the coast. As many as 40 defense positions were manned during the 17th and 18th centuries, one of the main reasons that Antigua, with its strategic location, remained in British hands throughout most of its history.

Falmouth Harbor, on the south coast, was once heavily fortified and the home of Nelson's Dockyard, one of Britain's main ship restoration facilities of the day. Admiral Horatio Nelson took charge of the Leeward Islands' fleet at age 26 and the dockyard, built around 1745, was named after him. Nelson, however, had nothing to do with its construction. Operational until it closed in 1889, the dockyard remained unchanged until restoration began in 1951. Now a national park (parks commissioner, 809-460-1053), the dockyard is in the surprisingly large town of English Harbor. You'll find a museum; the Admiral's Inn (809-460-1027), located inside the historic pitch and tar building; the Copper and Lumber Store Hotel (809-460-1058), featuring a bar and restaurant; and a working masthouse, marina, several T-shirt and trinket vendors, restaurants and gift shops. Admission to the complex is EC$4 (US$1.60), free for children under 12, open 9.00-17.00 daily.

Visible from the dockyard is Clarence House, an official residence of the Governor General, also used by Britain's royal family on visits to the island. The house was built in 1787 and is open to the public only in the Governor General's absence.

In the hills overlooking English Harbor is Shirley Heights, a fortification named after General Sir Thomas Shirley, an early governor of the Leeward Islands. The view is one of the best on the island. Up on the bluff you'll find the remains of Fort Shirley, built in the late 1700s. The fortifications are spread over the hill and consist of barracks, magazines, cannon platforms and an ancient water cistern. On Shirley Heights the Lookout Restaurant is a popular place for barbecues and dancing on Thursdays and Sundays.

A fork off the road to Shirley Heights leads to the Dow's Hill Interpretation Center (809-460-2777), another National Park facility, established in 1984. The center offers fortification ruins, an intriguing multimedia presentation on Antigua's history and a gift shop. On a good day you can see Guadeloupe to the south. The center is open Monday through Saturday 9.00-17.00 and Sunday 10.00-18.00; admission is EC$10.

Elsewhere on the island forts and sugar estate ruins are plentiful. The road north from English Harbor leads to the village of Table Gordon Hill, east of Liberta. From the village, a mile's walk or ride in a 4WD vehicle brings you to Fort George, on Monk's Hill. The fort was completed in 1669 to defend Falmouth Harbor. The ruins, on about seven acres, are overgrown with weeds and vines.

Take the road east from St. John's to the village of Pares and turn south to find Betty's Hope, the ruins of the first sugar plantation in Antigua, established by Christopher Codrington in 1674 (Betty was his daughter). Two windmill towers and a boiling house stand out among the ruins. The site, which was the seat of the Leeward Islands government while Codrington was governor, is being restored by the Antigua Historical and Archaeological Society. A visitor's center is open Tuesday through Saturday.

In the village of Parham, north of Pares, is Parham Harbor, Antigua's first port, once used to export sugar from the island's first plantations. With the decline of the sugar industry, economic activity moved to the capital of St. John's and Parham Harbor declined. A restoration project is currently underway, funded by the government and the Organization of American States. In Parham you'll find the striking St. Peter's Church, an Anglican parish church originally completed in

1755. The first structure was gutted by fire and a second shaken by an earthquake; the present one dates to the 1840s.

As for quasi-natural attractions, the manmade Potworks Dam and Reservoir, which has a capacity of one billion gallons, is located north of Bethesda, a town on Willoughby Bay. Fig Tree Drive stretches from the village of Old Road, on Carlisle Bay on the south coast, to Swetes, near the center of the island. The drive, through the lush vegetation of a small rainforest, is rough but navigable.

Boggy Peak, the island's highest point, can be reached by car from the village of Urlings. The road is maintained by Cable and Wireless, which also maintains a complex of buildings at the peak.

Devil's Bridge National Park, at Indian Town Point east of Willikies, features a natural bridge and several blowholes created in the limestone rocks by thousands of years of thundering surf.

St. John's

St. John's is Antigua's capital, its largest town and the economic center. A third of the population lives here, engaged in light manufacturing, shipping and government work. Tourism is important in St. John's and dozens of cruise ships stop here each week. The shopping centers at Redcliffe Quay and the relatively new Heritage Quay add a sleek sheen to the downtown area. Still, it's an old town, with structures dating back to the 17th century, and a rambling town with as much traffic as Antigua can muster. Which isn't much.

The Cathedral of St. John, between Long and Newgate streets, is Antigua's largest church. A wooden cathedral was built in 1681 on the orders of Governor Codrington, and later replaced by a stone structure, which was destroyed in a 1843 earthquake and rebuilt two years later. The interior is cool and quiet, except on Sundays, and lined with strong pitch pine to ensure its safety in the event of an earthquake.

The Museum of Antigua and Barbuda (809-462-1469) is located on Long Street, across from the police station. The circa 1750 building was once the colonial courthouse and now houses Arawak artifacts, a children's section with games and hands-on displays, a gramophone and hand-cranked telephone and cricketer Viv Richards' bat. A gift shop can be found inside and on the second floor is a library and the national archives office. The museum is open Monday through Friday 8.30-16.00, Saturday 10.00-14.00 and closed Sundays and holidays. The suggested donation is EC$5.

The Antigua and Barbuda Botanical Gardens (809-462-1007) cover eight acres on Independence Avenue, overlooking the parliament building. Established in 1893, the gardens had deteriorated by the 1950s, due to a lack of interest. A botanical society began the task of renovation in 1987 and now the garden is back in operation. Projects under development include an aviary, aquarium, orchid collection and playground.

Fort James, northwest of town on Fort Road, was built in the early 18th century to protect St. John's Harbor. The ruins of the buildings date to 1739 and ten of the 36 two-ton cannon originally in place are still there. On the south side of the harbor you'll find the ruins of Fort Barrington, overlooking St. John's and Deep Bay. This fort saw more action than any other in Antigua's defense.

Barbuda

Barbuda is uncomplicated. This is the island's attraction. The big thing to do? Walk the miles of beach or maybe view the teeming bird life on the tiny Man of War Island or in the mangrove swamps of Codrington Lagoon. An estimated 400 species of birds migrate to the lagoon yearly. Diving is spectacular, with several reefs offering a plethora of exotic corals and reef fish for observation. Serious divers can explore some of the 73 charted wrecks along the reefs.

The 56 foot (17 m) Martello Tower and fort, on the south shore, once hosted nine cannon. The tower was also used as a signal station. In the Highlands, Barbuda's highest point, you'll see the ruins of Highland House, a complex once occupied by the Codrington family. Ruins of slave quarters, the main house and a cistern are visible.

The three-road village of Codrington is where most everyone on Barbuda lives. The 1743 government house and the Old Church are attractions and you can see the entire village in a few unhurried hours. At the wharf, catch a boat for a tour of the lagoon.

Practical Information

ACCOMMODATION

Antigua and Barbuda accommodation ranges from small guesthouses, of which there are a few, to luxury hotels, of which there are many. At last count there were 103 hotels and dozens of villa rentals available on the islands. Camping is not allowed on the islands.

Hotels generally add a ten per cent service charge to the bill, which may be regarded as a tip for the hotel staff, and a seven per cent government tax. Resort hotels tend to cluster around the northwest coast, where you'll find a concentration of fine beaches, and the quiet south coast.

❏ BLUE WATERS BEACH HOTEL, P.O. Box 256, St. John's, Antigua, W.I. (809-462-0290, fax 462-0293; U.S. 800-372-1323, Canada 800-338-8782, U.K. 081-367-5175, fax 081-367-9949), a family hotel featuring rooms and villa-suites, sits on the north coast on a quiet bay. Luxury.

❏ RUNAWAY BEACH CLUB, P.O. Box 874, St. John's, Antigua, W.I. (809-462-3280, fax 462-4172; U.S. 800-74-CHARMS or 212-251-1800), is located on the Runaway Bay strip of hotels, with a great beach and plenty to do in the area. Moderate-luxury.

❏ ST. JAMES'S CLUB, P.O. Box 63, St. John's, Antigua, W.I. (809-460-5000, fax 460-3015; U.S. 800-274-0008, fax 212-308-6392, Canada 800-268-9051, U.K. 01-589-700), on Mamora Bay, is one of the most exclusive resorts in the Caribbean. The 100-acre property features four pools, four restaurants, a half-dozen bars, a casino, health club, all sports and luxury villas and suites. Luxury.

❏ SANDALS ANTIGUA, P.O. Box 147, St. John's, Antigua, W.I. (809-462-0267, fax 809-462-4135; U.S. and Canada 800-SANDALS, U.K. 071-581-9895), on Dickenson Bay, is everything you'd expect in a Sandals, one of the Caribbean's premier all-inclusive chains, meaning three bars, a pool, fine dining, sports, entertainment and great beach. Sandals allows couples only. Luxury.

❏ JOE MIKE'S DOWNTOWN, P.O. Box 136, St. John's, Antigua, W.I. (809-462-1142, fax 462-6056 or 462-1187; U.S. 212-541-4117, Canada 416-961-3085, U.K. 144-148-67073), sits downtown on the corner of Corn Alley and Nevis Street; clean and basic and you'll find a small restaurant, ice cream shop and lounge, and a casino downstairs. Budget.

❏ On Barbuda, the K CLUB (809-460-0300, fax 460-0305) and COCO POINT LODGE (809-462-3816) are the two luxury resorts, both quiet and exclusive, located on the south coast of the island. NEDDS GUEST HOUSE (809-460-0059) is small and homey, located above a small supermarket in Codrington. Budget.

EATING

Hotel restaurants are generally excellent and recommended, but keep in mind you won't be able to eat at the all-inclusives. Most restaurants add a ten per cent service charge and seven per cent tax to the check and many accept major credit cards, but call ahead to confirm.

❏ ALBERTO'S (809-460-3007), at Willoughby Bay, serves Italian and West Indian and is noted for its extensive wine list. The restaurant is open for dinner only and closed July through October. Expensive.

❏ CALYPSO RESTAURANT (809-462-1965) on Redcliffe Street is one of the island's best local restaurants, open for lunch and drinks Monday through Saturday. In the open-air patio, try curried goat with rice and peas and top it off with homemade coconut ice cream. Inexpensive-moderate.

❏ CHEZ PASCAL (809-462-3232) on Tanner Street is set in an rustic, tin-roofed Caribbean home and serves some of the best French and West Indian in town. Open for lunch and dinner, dinner only on Saturday and closed Sunday. Expensive.

❏ HEMINGWAY'S (809-462-2763) is upstairs in a 19th century building on Jardine Court, over the Sugarmill Boutique. The cuisine is solid West Indian. The open veranda overlooks St. Mary's Street and Heritage Quay. Inexpensive-moderate.

❏ COMMISSIONER GRILL (809-462-1883) is located on lower Redcliffe Street and Commissioner Alley. The cuisine is West Indian and the open kitchen gives it the ambiance of a busy city diner. Open daily for breakfast, until midnight. Inexpensive-moderate.

GETTING THERE

V.C. Bird International Airport is located in northeastern Antigua, about five miles (eight km) east of St. John's. The airport is the main entry point on Antigua and is serviced by several international and regional airlines: Air Canada (809-462-1147), American Airlines (809-462-0950/1/2), British Airways (809-462-0876 or 462-3219), BWIA (809-462-0262/3 or 462-0934), Continental Airlines (809-462-0323/4 or 462-3195), Lufthansa (809-462-0987) and LIAT (809-462-0700 or 462-3142/3).

V.C. Bird gets fairly crowded when international flights are boarding. Give yourself two hours to get through the checkout and remember to have money for your departure tax on hand, currently EC$25 (US$10) per person.

GETTING AROUND

■ PUBLIC TRANSPORTATION

Taxis and other public transport vehicles are unmetered. Rates are regulated by a taxi association and posted at the customs exit from V.C. Bird. Every driver is supposed to carry a copy of applicable rates in their vehicle, but don't count on it. Negotiate before you get into the cab. Hotels often subcontract taxis for their guests and you can be sure their rates are a couple of dollars higher than street taxis. If you want to call a taxi in St. John's, try Daylight Taxi (809-462-3015) or Twenty Four Hour Taxi Service (809-462-5190/1). In Dickenson Bay call Incorporate Taxi Service (809-462-4325). Taxis can be hailed most anywhere in St. John's, particularly at the West Bus Station and Heritage Quay.

If you've got time to figure out the system, buses and vans can be inexpensive. Look for destinations posted on the front windshield. In St. John's catch buses at the Public Market for points south and east. Buses are, apparently and amazingly, banned from areas north of St. John's and V.C. Bird. A typical fare from St. John's to English Harbor is about EC$3.

■ CAR RENTALS

Car rentals are probably your best bet. Most agencies are located in St. John's or at the airport and a temporary local license, good for 90 days, is needed to operate a rental vehicle. They can be obtained at a local police station, but a reputable rental agency will do it for you. The cost is EC$30 (US$12). Lowest daily rates for car rentals start at US$35-50 daily. Try: Carib Car Rental (809-462-2062), Jonas Rent-A-Car (809-462-3760), Avis (809-462-AVIS or 462-2840, fax 462-2848), Budget (809-462-3009 or 462-3007, fax 462-3057) or National (809-462-2113).

A good selection of bicycles, including mountain bikes, are found at Sun Cycles (809-461-0324) in Hodges Bay, or Take 1 Video and Bicycle Rentals (809-460-2604, fax 460-1871) in English Harbor. Cost ranges from US$10-20 per day.

■ INTER-ISLAND TRAVEL

For inter-island travel, flying is the best way to go. LIAT serves the most destinations and sets the standard in fares, but air charters can be cost-effective, provided there are enough travelers to split the fare. Try Antigua and Barbuda Airlines (809-462-1124) or Carib Aviation (809-462-3147, fax 462-3125). LIAT's current round-trip fare to Barbuda is US$44 and the schedule easily accommodates a day trip.

MONEY, HOURS AND COMMUNICATION

The Eastern Caribbean dollar is official, but the U.S. dollar is widely used in Antigua and Barbuda. The official exchange rate is EC$2.70 = US$1, but when shopping or using taxis, the rate of EC$2.50 is commonly used. This makes it worthwhile to exchange your money. Hotels will change money, but banks give better rates. Some, such as Barclays, charge a small commission. Several banks are found on St. Mary's Street and High Street in St. John's and at English Harbor. The Antigua Barbuda Investment Bank (809-462-1652, fax 462-0804) on High Street operates a branch on Barbuda (809-460-0162). Bank hours vary, but most are open Monday through Thursday 8.00-15.00 and Friday 8.00-17.00.

As a general rule shops are open weekdays and Saturdays 9.00-17.00, with an hour off for midday lunch. Grocery stores may stay open later on Fridays and some are open Sundays as well. Tourist shops often remain open into the evening and on Sundays to accommodate cruise ships. On Sunday virtually everything is closed, save a few curio shops and Kentucky Fried Chicken.

The general post office (809-462-0023) is located on Long and High streets in St. John's. There is a branch at the airport and a branch in Codrington, Barbuda (809-460-0075). Hours are 8.15-12.00 and 13.00-16.00 Monday through Thursday and until 17.00 on Friday.

Telephone cards may be purchased at some tourist shops, bookstores and small superettes. Your best bet, however, is to go to Cable and Wireless (809-462-0840) on St. Mary's Street. Cards are available in EC$10, EC$20, EC$40 and EC$60 denominations. C&W is also the place to send faxes and cables and make calls. Coin phones are available as well. The area code for Antigua is 809.

ENTERTAINMENT

Water sports facilities are mainly operated from hotels and your hotel will be able to provide equipment or point you in the right direction. Prices for equipment rented at hotel facilities do not vary wildly. Halcyon Cove Watersports (809-462-0256) operates out of the Halcyon Cove Hotel on Dickenson Bay. Wadadli Watersports (809-462-2980 or 462-4792) conducts cruises on its three catamarans and rents charter boats as well. Cruises visit Bird Island, a small cay off the north shore. Wadadli also offers a circumnavigation cruise and snorkelling cruises and will pick up at certain hotels on the north and west coasts. At the Jolly

Harbor marina and complex, at Lignumvitae Bay on the west coast, contact Caribbean Water Sports (809-460-3550)

Scuba divers should contact Jolly Dive (809-462-2824, fax 462-3496) at Jolly Harbor marina. Dive Runaway (809-462-2626), at the Runaway Beach Club, will pick up at certain hotels. Aquanaut diving centers are located at the St. James Club (809-460-5000), the Galleon Beach Club (809-460-1024) and the Ramada (809-462-3733).

Fishing charters are available through Obsession Deep Sea Fishing (809-462-2824). Game fishing off Antiguan shores is excellent. Yacht and pleasure boat charters are available through Kokomo Catamaran Day Sails (809-462-7245, fax 462-7725) at Jolly Harbor or Nicholson Yacht Charters (809-460-1530, fax 460-1531) at English Harbor. If you've got a desire to go on one of those fun day-cruises where you limbo and drink too much rum, then the Jolly Roger (809-462-2064) is for you. Docked at Heritage Quay in St. John's, the ship is one of the largest in Antiguan waters. You'll get to "walk the plank," pirate-style.

Golfers will find three courses on Antigua and one on Barbuda. (Barbuda's nine-hole, double tee course is located at the K Club, but can only be used by guests of the hotel.) On Antigua try the 18-hole, par 70 public course at Cedar Valley (809-462-0161), home of the annual Antigua Open; or the 9-hole course at the Half Moon Bay resort (809-460-4300). At the Jolly Harbor complex (809-462-6166) you can play a short 18-hole golf course.

Riding stables are found in Dickenson Bay or at the Spring Hill Riding Club (809-460-1333) at Rendezvous Bay in the south.

Most hotels feature tennis courts and fitness clubs, but a public court can be found at Temo Sports (809-460-1781) in English Harbor, where squash courts are also available. Temo is open Monday through Saturday, 7.00-22.00.

If you don't have a health center at your hotel, try the National Fitness Center (809-462-3681) on Old Parham Road in St. John's. It has a workout room, weights and aerobics classes. Open 6.00-10.00 and 12.00-20.00, Monday through Friday and 9.00-14.00 on Saturday. The cost is US$10 per day.

For sports events look to the Annual Antigua Sailing Week. The 1994 tournament, held 25 April through 1 May, was the 27th race held, featuring three classes of competition yachts and nearly 200 competitors. This is a world-class regatta and the week is filled with special events, music and, of course, the races.

For music, dancing and nightlife, hotels are generally the best bet. The larger ones often offer scheduled entertainment, from bands to limbo contests, virtually every day. Shirley Heights Lookout Restaurant (809-460-1785) offers a packed Sunday afternoon barbecue, with a steel band 15.00-18.00 and a reggae band

18.00-21.00. The Lime Disco at Redcliffe Quay is small but popular. Several casinos operate on Antigua, the newest and possibly largest being King's Casino (809-462-1727) at Heritage Quay in St. John's, open every day until the early morning.

SHOPPING

St. John's is the shopping center and the modern Heritage Quay and more funky Redcliffe Quay are its shopping meccas. The two mini-malls are located on parallel streets down by the harbor's cruise ship dock and contain all manner of duty-free shops, including jewelry, leather, liquor, curio, art and "beach" stores. Name brands such as Benetton, Gucci, even Radio Shack and others are represented. The Toy Shop at Redcliffe Quay is very good and the West Indies Ice Co. in Heritage Quay is recommended for its decor as well as (relatively) inexpensive jewelry. There are public toilets at Heritage Quay.

Elsewhere in town, try The Map Shop (809-462-3993) for books and maps. The Jolly Harbor marina complex also features a handful of duty-free shops.

Art galleries include Islands Arts Galleries (809-462-2787), one of the island's best, at Heritage Quay. This gallery has a large branch and studio at the Le Gourmet Restaurant (809-462-2977) on Fort Road. Harmony Hall (809-460-4120) in Freetown is also quite large and has a restaurant.

If you're renting a villa or apartment or otherwise have a need to cook for yourself, a good place to shop is the open St. John's Public Market (809-462-1216) located on, not surprisingly, Market Street. The market is open every day, but it's busiest Thursday through Saturday. Here's where you can buy fresh fruit, vegetables and even meat (lots of flies, maybe not so fresh). Try the famous "black pineapple," which is grown near Urlings and reputed to be the sweetest in the world. The market is bustling and loud and provides an Antiguan experience you're not likely to find at your resort hotel. It's conveniently located next to the West Bus Station, which services the southern section of the island.

USEFUL ADDRESSES

■ TOURISM INFORMATION

Antigua and Barbuda Department of Tourism:
- ❏ P.O. Box 363, St. John's, Antigua, W.I.; (809) 462-0480, fax 462-2483.
- ❏ 610 Fifth Ave., Suite 311, New York, NY 10020; 212-541-4117, fax 757-1607.
- ❏ 121 SE First St., Suite 1001, Miami, FL 33131; 305-381-6762, fax 381-7908.
- ❏ 60 St. Clair Ave., Suite 205, Toronto, Ontario MT4 IN5; 416-961-3805, fax 961-7218.
- ❏ Antigua House, 15 Thayer St., London W1M 5DL; 071-486-7073, fax 486-9970.

❑ Postfach 1331, Minnholzweg 2, 6242 Kronberg 1, Germany; 06173-5011.
❑ Antigua Hotel and Tourist Association, P.O. Box 454, Lower Redcliffe St., St. John's, Antigua, W.I.; 809-462-0374, fax 462-3702.

■ OTHER
❑ Emergencies, 999 or 911.
❑ Fire, 462-0044.
❑ Police, 462-0215.
❑ Ambulance, 462-0251.
❑ Holbertson Hospital, Hospital Road, St. John's; 462-0251.
❑ American Express representative, Antours, Long Street, St. John's, 462-4788, (lost cards, 800-528-2121; lost checks, 800-828-0366).
❑ Customs Antigua, 462-0028.
❑ Customs Barbuda, 460-0085.
❑ Immigration Antigua, 460-0050.
❑ Federal Express, Church Street, St. John's; 462-4854/8.
❑ The City Pharmacy, St. Mary's Street, St. John's; 462-1363.

Montserrat

Introduction

Montserrat is a nation where the Irish shamrock adorns Government House; it's also featured on the country's immigration stamp and is the national airline's logo. The local phone book lists names such as Cadogan, Galloway, Hogan and O'Brien. St. Patrick's Day is a national holiday. The land is tall and rugged with rolling green hills and deep, lush valleys and the island is often referred to as the Emerald Isle. The island's Irish roots are historical and deep and the physical parallels are striking, yet Montserrat is today a land of people rooted in the West Indies, with a distant and somewhat wistful attachment to the old country.

The Land

The teardrop-shaped island, some 39 square miles (100 sq km) and roughly 25 miles (40 km) southwest of Antigua in the Leeward Islands group, is dominated by dramatic mountain ranges and active volcanic peaks. The towering southern range is home of the towering Galway's Soufriere (from the French word for sulfur), part of a 13-acre National Landmark site. Located just below the 3,002-foot (901 m) Chance's Peak, Galway's is not a true volcano, but rather located along a fault line in the Lesser Antilles' volcanic chain; it emits heated streams and sulphurous gases, but no lava. More fascinating, however, is its access. Hikers can walk directly into the crater, enveloped by its thick, pungent gases and steaming vents. In the late summer of 1995 the eruption of Chance's Peak led to the temporary evacuation of the entire southern half of the island.

Vegetation in the Soufriere hills is a mix of lush rainforest, high-altitude elfin woodland and fumarole vegetation. Areas along the coast and in the lowlands are scruffy, covered by grasses, acacia bushes and cacti.

Montserrat's beaches are not the striking powdery white sand of nearby islands. Due to the island's volcanic activity, beach sand is composed mostly of crushed pumice and other volcanic jetsam, giving it a gray sheen or dark brown hue. Volcanic residue has also enriched the soil and many Montserratans take advantage of this by cultivating substantial home gardens.

The island's coast is rugged, irregular and there are no deep natural harbors.

History

The Irish connection on Montserrat evolved some time after Columbus encountered the island on his second voyage in 1493. Called Alliouagana ("Land of the Prickly Bush") by the native Caribs, who'd displaced the Arawaks, the terrain of the island reminded Columbus of the countryside surrounding the Barcelona abbey Santa Maria de Montserrate. Beyond that, the Spanish connection ends. Columbus bestowed the name, but bypassed the island, prudently avoiding confrontation with the bellicose Caribs. Soon after, however, most of the Caribs also abandoned the island, presumably to continue their northern push toward unconquered land.

In the early 17th century nearby St. Kitts was colonized by British Protestants and some Irish and British Catholics, a historical recipe for difficulties. Freedom of religion was not tolerated by the Protestants, even legislated against, and the Irish Catholics were proffered no political rights in the British colonies. In 1632 dissident Irish were ordered off St. Kitts by the governor Sir Thomas Warren and sent to colonize Montserrat for Britain. Soon after Montserrat became a haven of religious freedom for Catholics, who arrived from nearby islands and from Europe—their numbers would later include those conquered and exiled by the lord protector, Oliver Cromwell. The island quickly became an outpost of thriving indigo and tobacco plantations and by 1650 African slaves were imported to work the growing sugarcane plantations. In its heyday Montserrat hosted about 100 large sugarcane estates.

During the European wars of the 17th and 18th centuries Montserrat was twice occupied by the French. The 1783 Treaty of Versailles ultimately returned the island to the British, who have retained control to this day. Meanwhile, as the plantations grew, so did the slave population and discontent. A 1768 slave rebellion, staged on St. Patrick's Day (hence today's national holiday, which commemorates both St. Patrick and the heroes of the uprising), was suppressed and its leaders executed. Slavery was abolished in 1834, signaling the end of Montserrat's boom days. Today the majority population of Montserrat comprises descendants of slaves.

People and Culture

The island's population center is the capital of Plymouth, on the southwest leeward coast, population 3,500. The rest of the island's population of 12,000 is scattered throughout the three parishes (St. Anthony's, St. George's and St. Peter's), none of which lies more than 12 miles (16 km) from the capital. Catholicism dominates the religious life, but other, mainly Protestant, sects are also represented.

Culturally, Montserrat borrows from its African and Irish-British heritage. English, the official language, is spoken with a subtle and anomalous hybrid Irish brogue, the result of years of Irish settlement combined with African-West Indian influences and vocabulary. St. Patrick's Day is an important holiday, particularly in the village of St. Patrick's, where a three day celebration is held. Masquerades, street theater, calypso and soca marches, and a Freedom Run honour the Irish patron saint and the March 17th slave rebellion of 1768. A popular folk dance, the "heel and toe," has Irish roots, as does one of the country's national dishes, "goatwater," derived from Irish stew.

Numerous festivals take place from mid-December through New Year's Day, Montserrat's carnival season. Calypso competitions, including the naming of the Calypso King, concerts, parades, street music, jump-ups and food festivals culminate on Festival Day, or New Year's Eve day, continuing all night into the new year.

August Monday, the first Monday of the month, commemorates the emancipation of slaves.

Literature and the arts are promoted on Montserrat through the efforts of several organizations. The Montserrat Writers' Maroon (on Montserrat "maroon" means the gathering of people for a common cause) was founded by, among others, the poet and prominent historian Dr. Howard Fergus, whose latest work is the poetry collection Calabash of Gold. The group is a writers' collective attached to the University of the West Indies School of Continuing Studies (809-491-2344). Look for announcements of poetry recitals and dramatizations in the local papers or call for information.

Government and Economy

Montserrat is a British Crown Colony with a representative, ministerial form of government. A governor represents the Queen, who is the official head of state. A two body legislature, consisting of legislative and executive councils, is elected by popular vote and a chief minister is appointed head of the government. The crown, in the form of the governor, is responsible for external affairs, the police and defence.

Movements for independence have occasionally surfaced, but complete independence is recognized by most Montserratans to be dicey at best. The reason is economics.

Montserrat's economy is based on foreign aid, primarily from Britain and Canada, and on tourism, light manufacturing, offshore banking and some subsistence farming. None of these industries, tourism included, is substantial, yet the infrastructure of the country is solid and extremes of poverty and wealth are not directly evident. The offshore banking industry was introduced in 1978, but after ten years of relatively unchecked growth, fraud and money laundering schemes were discovered. Strict regulations have since been instituted and investment confidence remains somewhat shaken, yet Montserrat remains the third-largest offshore banking facility in the English-speaking Caribbean. Still, if not for British and other overseas aid, Montserrat would be severely limited in developing internal resources for generating income.

In 1989 Hurricane Hugo wreaked havoc on the island, destroying or damaging an estimated 95 per cent of housing, as well as much of the public infrastructure, and killing 12 people. Tourism and small farmers were also hard hit. Residual evidence of that devastation exists today and it wasn't until late 1993 that the government and private sector claimed full recovery. Today more than 400 refurbished rooms in hotels and villas service the tourism industry.

Sights

It doesn't take long to drive around Montserrat and see the sights. Even if you stop and linger, climb and hike, it still won't take more than a few days. This is a small island, one on which you are likely to run into the same people several times as you make the rounds.

BEACHES

The best beaches are found on the west coast of the island. Toward the south the beaches are of dark volcanic sand, but clean and comfortable. Long Sugar Bay is south of Plymouth, within walking distance of town, and you'll find a small yacht club here. The beach at the Montserrat Springs Hotel is also nice and a bar and hot water springs bath (open seasonally) are available for public use. The hot water springs come courtesy of the volcano, which emits the water at 165 F° (28° C). The water is carried down from the mountainside in an aqueduct system and cooled in tanks. Fox's Bay, Isles Bay and Old Road Bay, just north of the Fox's Bay Bird Sanctuary, are all good beaches, with dark sand. Old Road Bay, by the Vue

Point Hotel, features a beach bar, telephones and Shamrock Watersports (snorkelling, sailing dinghies, windsurfing and water skiing). Woodland's Bay offers small huts and caves for exploring. On the breathtaking northwestern coast Carr's Bay and Little Bay are both popular. Some consider the island's best beach to be at Rendezvous Bay, the island's only light sand. It can be reached by a long hike from Little Bay, but the popular way to go is by boat. Trips can be arranged at the Vue Point Hotel, at a cost of US$20 per person.

OTHER SIGHTS

Good roads, though at times winding and dipping through the hills and valleys, make driving a easy task in Montserrat. Many of the island's hikes and climbs may be easier with a guide, but this has become an unfortunate situation for would-be explorers. "Official" guides, who can almost always be found at the entrance and parking areas of certain sites or in Plymouth, are in it for a quick buck and are apparently unencumbered by the phrase, "No, thank you." Avoid these guys. By and large you do not need a guide if you are fit and in possession of an adventurous spirit. A good map helps. The Department of Tourism (P.O. Box 7, Plymouth, Montserrat, W.I.; 809-491-2230, fax 491-7430) is in the process of compiling standard rates for qualified guides and can recommend the right person for the job. Write or call ahead if you have a planned itinerary.

The road south to St. Patrick's is a good place to start. Galway's Soufriere is located east of the town. The drive up to the volcano passes Galways Plantation, the hillside ruins of a 1750 sugarcane plantation, mill and slave village. The plantation, first established in the 17th century, originally encompassed 1,300 acres and is now the site of archaeological activity. It was owned by the dynastic Blake family of Galway, which also controlled plantations on other islands.

The hike to Galway's Soufriere is short and not very strenuous (about 20 minutes). Lock your car. Along the path you'll note the pungent stink of sulfur and what seems to be rotten onions. At the Soufriere a rocky path leads down to the boiling springs, yellow and blue mineral-stained rocks and bubbling vents. It gets hot down there. A round-trip taxi ride from Plymouth to the Soufriere costs EC$60 and the driver will wait for you.

Chance's Peak is accessible by an estimated 2,000-step path. The steps don't help much and disappear in places, but there are ropes to help you along. The arduous climb will take two or three hours, depending on your comfort level. A legend has it that a mermaid resides in the shallow pond near the summit of the peak. She and her friend, a snake, sit by the pond while she combs her hair and he who can grab the comb and run with it down to the sea, without being caught by the snake, is said to be in for good fortune. And the views from the top are astonishing. The best time for viewing is early morning.

Great Alps Waterfall, also near St. Patrick's, is a 70 foot (23 m) waterfall, about a 45 minute walk from the parking area. You may want a guide for this one, although the hike through the rainforest generally follows the White River. You can swim at the falls. Guides can be found at the carpark and the recommended rate is EC$15 for a lone hiker or EC$10 per person in a larger group. A return-trip taxi ride to the carpark is about EC$39 and the driver will wait (the driver may even be a good guide).

North of Plymouth, the Fox's Bay Bird Sanctuary is worth a free visit. The 15-acre preserve, mangrove swamp and light woodlands, is the roosting place for egrets, herons, coots and more. The beach at Fox's Bay is also one of the island's nicest. Inland from the bird sanctuary are the overgrown ruins of Fort St. George, on St. George's Hill. Two cannon and a magazine, part of a French fortification built in 1782, overlook Plymouth and the ocean. You won't find much else here, but the view alone is worth the drive. Note the nearby flamboyant tree, planted by the non-flamboyant Queen Elizabeth in 1967. A refreshment stand is open in high season.

In ritzy Richmond, a suburb of Plymouth, you'll find the tiny Montserrat Museum (809-491-5443) in a restored sugar mill tower. Open for the blink of an eye, only Sunday and Wednesday 14.30-17.00. Donations are accepted.

Air Studios, a recording studio built by former Beatles' manager George Martin, has hosted Sting, Jimmy Buffet, Elton John and The Rolling Stones, as well as local artists. The studio was battered during Hurricane Hugo and has not been in full operation since.

Plymouth

Plymouth is the small and compact, even slightly busy, hub of the island. The architecture is Georgian, the streets are clean and the waterfront pleasant. The public market, on Strand Street next to the prison, bustles on Fridays and Saturdays. The gardens of the 18th century Government House are open to the public weekdays from 10.00-12.00. The General Post Office (open 8.15-15.55 Monday, Tuesday and Friday and 8.15-11.25 Wednesday and Saturday) on Marine Drive operates a philatelic bureau. Next to the post office are the clock tower and War Memorial, honoring soldiers of both world wars. On Marine Drive you'll find Arrow's Manshop, a clothing store owned by the famous Montserratan calypso and soca singer Arrow, whose hit "Hot, Hot, Hot" is heard throughout the islands.

Plymouth is the island's center for shopping and several souvenir stores are found along Parliament Street and downtown. Duty-free shopping is minimal, but good bargains can be found, especially in the locally manufactured Perk's Rum Punch or Cassell's hot sauce. For local art and crafts visit Jus' Looking on George Street, The Island House Gallery on John Street and Tapestries of Montserrat on Parliament Street. Papa's Supermarket on Church Road sells groceries.

Practical Information

ACCOMMODATION

There are no mega-resorts on Montserrat, just a few hotels and a fistful of picturesque villas and guesthouses set in the hills or villages. By and large accommodation in Montserrat is a good buy compared to other Lesser Antilles islands. Large hotels charge a 7-10 per cent government tax and a ten per cent service charge, less common with guesthouses.

Camping is allowed in the countryside, with permission from the Ministry of Agriculture and Trade (contact the tourist board, 809-491-2230).

■ VILLAS

The tourist board (address below) offers a comprehensive list of agencies that rent villas, but you can begin by contacting: Montserrat Villas (P.O. Box 445, Plymouth, Montserrat, W.I.; Canada tel. 416-737-5638, fax 884-1465); Shamrock Villas (P.O. Box 221, Plymouth, Montserrat, W.I.; 809-491-2431, fax 491-4660); Villas of Montserrat (444 Castro Street, Suite 400, Mountain View, CA 94041; 415-964-3498).

■ HOTELS

❏ VUE POINT HOTEL, P.O. Box 65, Plymouth, Montserrat, W.I. (809-491-5210, fax 491-4813, U.S. 800-253-2314 or New York 800-223-9815), is one of the island's premier hotels, located in the hills above a beach, with cottages and rooms, tennis, a pool and entertainment. Luxury.

❏ MONTSERRAT SPRINGS HOTEL, P.O. Box 259, Plymouth, Montserrat, W.I. (809-491-2481, fax 491-4070; U.S. 800-223-9815, fax 212-545-8467; Canada 416-484-4864, fax 416-485-8256), features simple but comfortable suites and rooms, a large pool and a great view. Don't miss the excellent Sunday afternoon buffet (US$16), a tradition with Montserratans and guests. Luxury.

❏ LIME COURT APARTMENTS, P.O. Box 250, Plymouth, Montserrat, W.I. (809-491-6985) are downtown on Parliament Street, clean, basic, good location. Budget.

❑ NIGGY'S GUESTHOUSE, Aymers Ghaut, Kinsale, Montserrat, W.I. (809-491-7489), located south of Plymouth, has five clean rooms, shared baths and a restaurant and bar. It can be noisy at times, but at US$15 per single and US$20 per double, you'll get your money's worth. Budget.

❑ IDA MOOSE GUESTHOUSE AND SUPERMARKET, in Kinsale village, features five rooms, overlooking the water. You wouldn't want to swim there and the guesthouse place is not precisely pretty, but at US$25-30, the price is right. Budget.

EATING

The cuisine on Montserrat is a combination of West Indian creole and continental, although specialties such as Chinese and East Indian can also be found. The large frog called mountain chicken, which is indigenous to Montserrat and Dominica, provides its legs for the local dish. Goatwater, based on an Irish dish, is a thick stew of local vegetables and goat meat. Hotels offer good deals, such as the Vue Point's Wednesday evening barbecue (entertainment as well) and the Montserrat Springs' Sunday afternoon buffet. Many of the smaller restaurants are open seasonally and do not accept credit cards.

❑ BELHAM VALLEY HOTEL RESTAURANT (809-491-5553) overlooks the ocean and features a jazz band on Fridays and numerous fresh seafood dishes, including a Seafood Delight of lobster, scallops and snapper. Moderate-expensive.

❑ IGUANA CAFE (809-491-2328) is located in Wapping, just outside Plymouth. Seafood is a specialty and the pizzas are the best on the island. No credit cards are accepted. Moderate.

❑ EMERALD CAFE (809-491-3821), also in Wapping, serves seafood and steaks. Also, no credit cards. Moderate.

❑ MRS MORGAN'S (809-491-7489) located in St. John's, near Little Bay, serves the island's best goatwater. Inexpensive.

❑ BLUE DOLPHIN (809-491-3263) in Amersham specializes in mountain chicken and seafood. Inexpensive.

GETTING THERE

Blackburne Airport (809-491-6494), on Montserrat's east coast, about ten miles from Plymouth, is too short for landing large airliners. Plans are afoot to expand the airstrip, but as of yet no direct flights from North America or Europe are possible. LIAT (809-491-2533 or 491-2362) operates four non-stop flights per day from Antigua (20 minutes) and is the best connection. LIAT's offices are located on Lower George Street in Plymouth.

Montserrat Airways (809-491-5342 or airport 491-6494, fax 491-6205) is primarily a charter outfit, but now operates a shuttle service between Blackburne Airport and VC Bird. The flight departs Antigua for Montserrat every hour from 7.00-19.00 and the fare is EC$89 one-way, half fare for children. For visitors whose stay has exceeded 24 hours, the departure tax is EC$15 or US$6.

GETTING AROUND

■ PUBLIC TRANSPORTATION

Taxis and minibuses are easily recognized, if not by the large number of arms protruding from the windows and the colorful names such as "Mango" and "Terminator," then by an "H" on the license plate. Rates are set by the government; the tourist department and the driver should have rate sheets. Taxi stands are found behind the War Memorial and clock tower on Marine Drive and at the airport.

Island tours by taxi run approximately EC$30 per hour; a day tour costs EC$130. Call James "Mango" Frith (809-491-2134) for reliable island tours.

Minibuses run from Plymouth to the rest of the island, leaving from the stand on Church Road. Fares are considerably less expensive than taxis, around EC$2-4.

■ RENTALS

Care hire is easy, just remember to drive on the left. This is a pleasant way to explore the island and the approximately 120 miles (190 km) of road affords access to many of the sights. Rental rates are less than on many of the neighbouring islands, averaging US$35 per day. You'll need a valid driver's license and a temporary local license, which can be arranged by the rental company or obtained at the traffic desk at the Treasury Building in town, 8.00-14.30 on weekdays. The cost is EC$30. Call Budget Rent A Car (809-491-5778, fax 491-6066), Ethelyne's Car Rental (809-492-2885), Edith's Car Rental (809-491-6696) or Pauline's Car Rental (809-491-2345, fax 491-2434). Reliable (809-491-6990, fax 491-8070) rents the tiny, go-cart-like mini-mokes.

Biking Montserrat is a popular way to see the countryside and also good exercise. Americans Susan Goldin and Butch Miller own Island Bikes (P.O. Box 266, Harney Street, Plymouth, Montserrat, W.I.; 809-491-4696, fax 491-3599) and promote the annual "Round Montserrat Road Race." They also organize tours and excursions and rent bikes.

MONEY, HOURS AND COMMUNICATION

Montserrat's currency is the Eastern Caribbean dollar, currently pegged at EC$2.70 =US$1. U.S. and Canadian dollars, and some European currencies, are accepted, but the exchange rate on the street will drop to EC$2.50. It's best to change your money and several banks are located in downtown Plymouth. Hours vary, but most banks are open 8.00-15.00 Monday to Thursday and until 17.00 on Friday. Bank of Montserrat is open Saturday mornings as well and its airport branch is open 9.00-17.00, Monday to Friday.

Major credit cards are accepted at many hotels, restaurants and shops, but not all.

The General Post Office on Marine Drive is open 8.15-15.55 Monday, Tuesday, Thursday and Friday, and 8.15-11.25 on Wednesday and Saturday. In general, business hours, including government office hours, are 8.00-12.00 and 13.00-16.00 weekdays. Many shops close Wednesday afternoons, yet others are open Saturday mornings.

Telephone cards are obtainable and calls can be made from Cable and Wireless (809-491-2112, fax 491-3599) on Houston Street, open Monday through Saturday 7.30-18.00 and Friday until 20.00. From North America you can call Montserrat directly by using the 809 area code, plus the seven digit number. Locally you need only dial the last four digits.

ENTERTAINMENT

■ SPORTS

Tennis is available, for a fee, at the hotels Vue Point and Montserrat Springs and at the Montserrat Golf Course (809-491-5220). All feature lighted courts. Golf at the Montserrat Golf Course, in Belham Valley, is played on a sprawling and picturesque 11-hole course, generally played as two courses of nine holes each. Greens fees are EC$50 per day.

Watersports, including catamaran sailing, fishing and snorkelling, are best arranged at the Vue Point Hotel (809-491-5738). Two dive centers handle Montserrat's scuba diving business: Dive Montserrat (809-491-8812) and Seawolf Diving School (809-491-6859). Both operate Plymouth offices.

■ OTHER

Festivals (above) are a great source of entertainment in Montserrat and occur sporadically throughout the year. Local dance, drama and choir groups perform at schools and other venues.

Hotels are the other source of regular entertainment and often feature steel and reggae bands. The Vue Point and Montserrat Springs offer live music on some weekends, mostly in high season. La Cave in Plymouth and Nepcoden in Weekes are popular nightclubs and the Yacht Club in Wapping features live music on weekends.

Sturge Park hosts regular cricket and soccer matches, some at night.

The island's one cinema, The Shamrock, is located downtown.

USEFUL ADDRESSES

■ TOURISM

❑ Montserrat Department of Tourism, P.O. Box 7, Plymouth, Montserrat, W.I.; 809-491-2230, fax 491-7430.

❑ Caribbean Tourism Organization, 20 East 46th St., New York, NY 10017; 212-682-0435, fax 697-4258.

❑ TravMark, 33 Niagara St., Toronto, Ontario M5V 1C2; 416-362-3900, fax 416-362-9841.

❑ Montserrat Chamber of Commerce, P.O. Box 384, Plymouth, Montserrat, W.I.; 809-491-3640, fax 491-4660.

■ OTHER

❑ Police emergency, 999.

❑ Medical emergency, 999.

❑ Glendon Hospital, Plymouth; 491-2552.

❑ American Express, Carib-World Travel, Plymouth; 491-2713.

❑ Federal Express, Carib-World Travel, Plymouth; 491-2713.

❑ Piper's Drugs, Plymouth; 491-2084.

Guadeloupe

Introduction

Rustic and very French, Guadeloupe lies nearly dead center in the Lesser Antilles archipelago, between Montserrat to the north and Dominica to the south. It is itself, however, an archipelago and counts as its dependencies the offshore islands of Marie-Galante, Les Saintes and La Désirade, visible from Guadeloupe, as well as Saint-Barthélémy and Saint-Martin, which both lie over 120 miles (192 km) north. Combined with the island of Martinique, a separate French départment, these islands are known collectively as the French Antilles or French West Indies.

   In this chapter we will deal with Guadeloupe, Marie-Galante, Les Saintes and La Désirade, if for nothing else their proximity and convention.

The Land

To make matters more confusing, Guadeloupe itself is technically two islands. The common analogy is that the two are shaped like the wings of a butterfly. This is not only poetic but true. The islands of Grande-Terre to the east and Basse-Terre to the west are separated by a narrow saltwater strait, Rivière Salée, the backbone of the butterfly. Together the two create the second largest island, after Trinidad, in the Lesser Antilles.

   The triangular Grande-Terre, about 218 square miles (567 sq km), is generally low-lying and flat. The eastern Atlantic coast is characterized by rough surf and dramatic cliffs, with some beaches hidden in inlets and coves. The southern coast, sometimes called the "Riviera" of Guadeloupe, hosts strings of hotels and some of the island's best beaches. The soil and terrain of Grande-Terre are conducive to growing sugarcane, a major crop. The commercial center and largest town, Pointe-à-Pitre, is located on Grande-Terre's western coast, south of Rivière Salée. North of Pointe-à-Pitre is Raizet, the island's main airport.

   A mountainous north-south volcanic ridge dominates Basse-Terre, the 312 square mile (811 sq km) western half of Guadeloupe. The southern portion of the ridge is dominated by the highest point on Guadeloupe, La Soufrière, a 4,813 foot (1,444 m) dormant volcano. Basse-Terre is lush and hilly and much of it is part of the central Parc Naturel, 74,000 acres of protected rainforests, lakes and waterfalls. Other sections of the interior are given to banana plantations and the coast is characterized by small fishing villages and some hotels. The administrative center of Guadeloupe, also called Basse-Terre, sits on the southwestern corner of the island.

The outlying islands of La Désirade, Les Saintes and Marie-Galante are small, occupied mostly with fishing and agriculture, and relatively untouched by tourism. Les Saintes is a group of islands of which two, Terre-de-Bas and Terre-de-Haut, are inhabited. They are flat, somewhat barren and feature several excellent beaches and historically important French fortifications.

La Désirade is also flat and dry, known for one or two fine beaches, but perhaps better known as a place to truly get away from it all. Marie-Galante, population 16,000, is larger at 60 square miles (156 sq km) and has a history of sugar cultivation. The island is dominated by a central limestone plateau, which reaches a height of 670 feet (223 m).

History

The Arawaks were the original inhabitants of Guadeloupe, but were driven off, as they were throughout much of the Caribbean, by the Caribs. The Caribs called the island Karukera, reportedly meaning "Island of Beautiful Waters." Columbus sighted it on 4 November 1493, on his second voyage, and claimed the island for Spain, naming it Santa Maria de Guadeloupe de Estremadura in honour of the Virgin of Guadeloupe. Attempts to colonize the island were repelled by the Caribs and for nearly 200 years no Europeans were able to settle with any success.

In 1635 a group of French colonists landed on the island and embarked on a series of fierce fights with the Caribs, eventually driving them from the island. Guadeloupe was officially claimed by the King of France in 1674. The colonists established settlements and introduced crops such as sugarcane—which brought slavery to the island, setting the foundation for its present racial and economic makeup.

The European powers battled for possessions and naval domination in the Caribbean throughout the 18th century. Guadeloupe changed hands several times, most notably from 1759 to 1763, when it was occupied by the British. Wars, revolutions and turnovers continued, however, and in 1815, under the provisions of the Treaty of Paris, Guadeloupe was permanently restored to France. After several attempts, the efforts of Martiniquan Victor Schoelcher to have slavery abolished in the French colonies met with success—by 1848 slavery was illegal. Sugar production slowed and indentured laborers, mostly from East India, were imported to shore up the plantations.

Despite representation in the French legislature since 1871, by the early 20th century Guadeloupe was little more than a backwater state and enjoyed few of the fruits of French association. Labor disputes and racial disenfranchisement rocked the entire Caribbean during this period and radical elements in Guadeloupe, and to an extent Martinique, agitated for degrees of independence. In 1946 Guadeloupe was made a département of France, and, in 1974, was granted the further status of région.

People and Culture

The combined population of the département, including the northern islands of Saint-Martin and Saint-Barthélemy, is 390,000. The black majority descends from the slave families of the early years and East Indians, descendants of indentured laborers from, among other cities, Calcutta, make up about a tenth of the population. Europeans are either blanc metropolitain (the "metro" French, or temporary immigrants) or the blanc pays or creole beke, whites who are members of families long established on, or even settlers of, Guadeloupe. The so-called "coloreds," or mixed-race Guadeloupeans, have been an important social, economic and now political class on the island. Racial tension is not unheard of and some radical pro-independence movements have found strong adherents, particularly among the mixed-race and black intelligentsia and working class.

French is the official language. French Creole, the unique blend of French and African grammatical structures and vocabulary, is widely spoken. English is spoken at some of the larger hotels some of the time, but do not expect it in the countryside or at smaller hotels and restaurants.

Culturally Guadeloupe (as well as Martinique) is unique among Caribbean islands, in that its colonial culture remains somewhat intact. This is no doubt due to the fact that the island is, in fact, France and French law and customs dominate. However, some of the music and dances of Guadeloupe has a distinct flair, as seen in the beguine, which emulates the grace of ballroom dancing. Zouk, a musical form, mixes the techno-pop of France with beat of equatorial Africa. More distinct forms of Africa's influence manifest themselves at carnival time, the pre-Lenten festival of music, dancing and costume parades. The African-styled gwoka, based on drumming, has resurged in recent years. The drums were originally fashioned from tree trunks and served as a catalyst for a call-and-response musical narrative.

In food French is the influence, but creole is the result. The mix of fresh seafood, island spices, fruits and local vegetables with the traditional sauces and flair of French cooking is evident in the four-star restaurants, as well as smaller roadside stands. Ti punch, a traditional and popular drink of rum, lime and sugar, dates to colonial days. Wine is served with all meals. Due to the East Indian population, the Hindu influence in local cuisine and some ceremonies is also evident.

Guadeloupe's dominant religion is Roman Catholicism, not surprising given the French influence. However, Methodist, Jehovah's Witnesses, Seventh-Day Adventist, Jewish and other services can be found. Superstition and magic, holdovers with ancient African roots, play a large part in Guadeloupean life. The quinboiseur, a traditional doctor who can be a herbalist or spell-caster, can be found in villages and towns throughout.

Guadeloupe's festivals are important to the life and culture of its people. Carnival festivities begin with weekend activities in January and end with a Mardi Gras on Ash Wednesday—much singing, dancing, street marching.

La Fête des Cuisinières (The Festival of Women Cooks) takes place in early August, honouring Saint-Laurent, the patron saint of cooks. The festival dates to 1916 and involves traditional costumes, parades and what can only be described as a mega-banquet, a five hour Creole feast, featuring too much food, rum and dancing.

Government and Economy

Guadeloupe is represented in the French Parliament by two senators and four deputies, as well as members in the Economic Council. Locally elected legislative bodies are called the Conseil General and the Conseil Regional. A Prefet Commissaire de la République, a governor, is appointed by the French Minister of the Interior. Two Sous-Prefets, one responsible for Guadeloupe and the other for Saint-Martin and Saint-Barthélémy, help administer the islands.

Guadeloupe's economy is based on agriculture, some manufacturing and tourism. Above all, a great amount of Guadeloupe's income comes as direct aid from France, in evidence in the modern infrastructure and excellent roads on the island. The agricultural sector produces sugarcane, bananas and melons, accounting for 13 per cent of the island's working population. In 1989 Hurricane Hugo wiped out an estimated six months of sugarcane production and a year's worth of bananas. Close to 45 per cent of arable land is covered by sugarcane. Related industries, such as rum and sugar production, employ many, but in general manufacturing and light industry have seen little real growth this century. This is due to strong overseas competition, the high cost of raw materials and a modest local market for consumption. The result is a relatively high unemployment rate, estimated at more than 20 per cent.

Tourism employs 10,000 of the islands' inhabitants and this sector has grown in recent years. The number of hotel rooms increased from about 1,000 in 1970, to currently more than 9,000 (including Saint-Martin and Saint-Barthélémy). Of the average 330,000 annual visitors to the islands, about four out of five are French, with the remainder from other European countries and North America.

Sights

BEACHES

Guadeloupe's estimated 50 beaches are covered by fine, honey-colored sand and are generally easy to find. Some beaches charge parking fees and offer facilities such as changing rooms, bistros and picnic facilities. Others are just wide open and yet others front hotel property. All beaches are open to the public. Take the usual precautions and don't leave your rental car unlocked or personal items unattended

Gosier, south of Pointe-à-Pitre, sits at the western end of a string of beaches and hotels that extend across Grande-Terre's south coast. This area is perhaps the most tourist-dense of the island and many of the beaches are crowded on weekends and holidays. A beach, shared by the hotels Salako, Arawak and Callinago, offers watersports and shade. Plage de Petit-Havre is a small but popular public beach east of Gosier.

In the small but busy town of Sainte-Anne, stop at Plage du Borg or Plage de Bois Jolan, two long and calm beach areas, both very popular. Plage de Caravelle, accessed at one end through the Club Méditerranée (Club Med), is long, expansive and very popular. Saint-François, a resort town given almost completely to hotels and a marina, offers at least seven public beaches, including the clothing-optional Plage de L'Anse Tarare.

On the eastern peninsula's Pointe des Châteaux, with its Atlantic exposure, note the rocky limestone promontories and thundering surf. Swimming here can be dangerous, but it's a good place to have lunch and take some striking photographs. Hike up to the Pointe des Colibris, a cross erected in 1951. From this point you can see the islands of La Désirade, Petite Terre, Marie-Galante and even Dominica. Pointe des Châteaux is part of the National Park system. Further north at Le Moule, Guadeloupe's first capital, you'll find Plage de la Baie du Moule, a good surfing beach. At Anse Bertrand, on the northwestern coast, beaches have strong currents and can be rough, but are often uncrowded.

On Basse-Terre, beaches to the south tend to be of dark, volcanic sand, due to La Soufrière. Plage de Grande-Anse, near Deshaies on the northwestern coast, is huge and the island's most popular beach, with sports, picnic and camping facilities. Not to be confused with Plage de Grande-Anse, on the southern coast near Trois-Rivières. Divers have said that the leeward coast of Basse-Terre is excellent for scuba activities.

OTHER SIGHTS

Much of Basse-Terre and sections of Grande-Terre belong to the National Park system (Parc National de la Guadeloupe, Habitation Beausoleil, BP 13 Monteran, 97120 Saint-Claude, Guadeloupe, F.W.I.; 590-81-17-20 or 80-24-25). The park, open since 1989, is unique in that there are no gates and no admission fees to the greater park itself, although visitor centers and nature centers keep regular hours. Roads through the park areas are in good shape and hiking trails are clean and well-marked. Three visitor centers on Basse-Terre, where you can pick up copies of the Guide to the National Park, will provide details on various hiking trails. Take along good hiking shoes and bathing gear and a sweater or jacket if you intend to hike the high-altitude La Soufrière.

The Route de la Traversée, a 16 mile (26 km) road, crosses the park and midpoint of Basse-Terre from east to west. Travelling from the east you'll see the Cascade aux Ecrevisses (Crayfish Falls) and La Maison de la Forêt (open 10.00-17.00), an information center that abuts several hiking trails. Farther east is the Parc Zoologique et Botanique (590-98-83-52), a botanical garden where you can see caged animals such as a mongoose, iguanas, the big-headed crab eater (a rare bird) and "Titi the raccoon." Raccoons (raton laveur) have been protected since 1954 and serve as the park's mascot. There's a small restaurant here with great views of the mountains. Admission is F25, F15 for children, open 9.00-17.00. The Traversée ends at the western coastal town of Mahaut. A short drive south brings you to the Pigeon-Malendure Underwater Reserve (590-98-89-08). The attractions here, other than the fact that the reserve was developed by Jacques Cousteau, are the glass-bottomed boats that scoot around the marine park and end up at the tiny Illets Pigeon (Pigeon Island), where you can snorkel. Cousteau has dubbed the island one of the world's ten best diving spots. Cost is F80 for adults and F40 for children.

A turn to the north from Mahaut will bring you to another visitors center, Maison du Bois (open 9.00-18.00), at Pointe-Noire. The center is partially an arboretum and has a display of local woods and their uses. The village of Pointe-Noire is a traditional cabinet-making and artisans' village.

At the south of the park, on Route de la Soufrière, you'll find La Maison du Volcan (open 10.00-18.00), the visitor center where you can learn about volcanoes and La Soufrière. The best route to the volcano's summit is from the town of Saint-Claude to the parking area at Savane a Mulets. The dome and billows of sulfurous vapor are partially visible from here, but a 900 foot (300 m) climb on a marked path will bring you to the top, where the view is impressive if you manage to get there on a cloudless day.

East of La Soufrière, at l'Habituée and past the Grand Etang (Big Pond), you'll find the Chutes de Carbet, a series of three waterfalls reaching as high as 410 feet (123 m). The hike up the falls is marked, but the path is slippery. The second cascade features a hot water spring, great for a dip.

About 188 miles (300 km) of hiking trails, called "traces," snake throughout the park and most are well-marked. Some trails are difficult; the one to La Soufrière, for instance, takes four hours or so. Guides are available for hire through Organisation des Guides de Montaigne de la Caibe (590-80-05-79) or Emeraude Guadeloupe (590-80-16-09).

On Basse-Terre's southern coast is the Parc Archéologique des Roches Gravées (Archaelogical Park of Very Old Rocks), in the small fishing village of Trois-Rivières. A path through the park leads through a botanical garden and displays pre-Columbian rock petroglyphs from Carib days. Open 9.00-17.00 daily, admission F4.

The capital town of Guadeloupe, Basse-Terre, with a population of 16,000, was established in 1640 and today features several churches, forts, colonial buildings and a town square. Basse-Terre has been evacuated during a few eruptions of La Soufrière, the latest being a false alarm in 1976. Generally quiet and a bit run-down, the charm is there for those who look for it. Head down the central Boulevard General de Gaulle to find the town market.

On the north coast of Grande-Terre, east of Anse Bertrand, the views are extraordinary. The northernmost point is La Grand Vigie, at the crest of dramatic limestone cliffs that drop straight down into a rumbling surf. You can park your car and walk right to the edge, it seems, of the world. The drive along this road, also part of the National Park system, shows how flat and vast this side of the island actually is.

The best way to see Grande-Terre is to drive right around the island, an 85 mile (136 km) trip. You'll encounter dozens of small towns and villages, characteristically filled with red-tile-roof country homes, wooden buildings, brightly decorated cemeteries and fish markets.

La Moule, once an east coast fortification, features a neoclassical church, now a historic monument, at the town square. The nearby Distillerie Bellevue is open for tours Monday through Friday, 8.00-14.00. Just outside town, in La Rosette, is the Musée d'Archéologie Precolumbienne Edgar Clerc (590-23-57-43). The free museum features Amerindian artifacts and is open 9.00-12.30 and 14.00-17.00 every day except Tuesday; on Saturday, the museum is open in the morning only.

Pointe-à-Pitre

With a population of 80,000, Pointe-à-Pitre is Guadeloupe's main commercial and shipping center, as well as cultural center. Just south of Raizet airport (taxi about F60), the town is the place for shopping, business and some sightseeing. The outskirts, particularly toward the Rivière Salée bridge to Basse-Terre, are characterized by concrete high-rise apartment buildings and small malls. Downtown is slightly tarnished, noisy and congested, but its charms are evident as well. An 1834 earthquake destroyed some of the old colonial structures, but the remaining buildings, with iron balconies jutting out over narrow sidestreets, retain the ambiance of the old days. Hurricanes in 1979 and 1980 and 1989's Hugo further damaged the city. The Place de la Victoire, the central square, is surrounded by historic buildings, markets and cafes and once held a guillotine. At its southern end, opposite Rue Duplessis, is La Darse harbor, where ferries depart for the outlying islands. Taxis and buses cram the area. At the southwestern corner of the square, on Rue Bebian, is the office départmental du tourisme, where you can pick up a copy of Bonjour Guadeloupe (in English and French), a fairly complete practical guide. The tourism building is surrounded by stalls that sell everything from wigs to pantyhose to sandals.

Turn right out of the tourism office and you'll find several boisterous open-air (but covered) markets bordered by Saint-John Perse, Peynier, Schoelcher and Frebault streets. The vendors sell vegetables, fruits and spices and don't often speak English, but are helpful nonetheless.

The Musée Saint-John Perse (590-90-01-92), a restored 19th-century colonial house, is dedicated to the famous Guadeloupean poet and Nobel Laureate and houses a complete collection of Perse's poetry and memorabilia. The museum, on rues Norzieres and Achille Rene-Boisneuf, is open 9.00-17.00 every day except Sunday and the admission is F10. Saint-John Perse is ubiquitous in the city; a new commercial complex on the town pier, with hotel, shops, a tourism information booth and cafes, is called Center Saint-John Perse. Perse's birthplace, at 54 Rue Rene-Boisneuf, is marked with a plaque.

On Rue Peynier the Musée Schoelcher (590-82-08-04) is dedicated to the abolitionist Victor Schoelcher. Open weekdays 9.00-12.30 and 14.00-16.30 and Saturday 9.00-12.30, the entrance fee is F10. Don't miss the astounding Cathedrale de St. Pierre et St. Paul at the northern end of Place de la Victoire, a structure dating to the 1840s. Over the years it's been weakened by hurricanes, but is now propped up by huge, bolted metal columns that give it the appearance of being in jail.

Practical Information

ACCOMMODATION

■ ROUGHING IT

Accommodation on Guadeloupe and the outlying islands range from inexpensive guesthouses or apartments (gîtes) to exclusive hotels. Contact Gîtes de France (Tourism Office, 610 Fifth Ave., New York, NY 10020; 212-315-0726, Guadeloupe 590-82-09-30) for a comprehensive list. Gîtes range from small inns to apartments to rooms in homes, or other variations, and can be inexpensive, an average of F1000-2000 per week. Choose carefully and ask questions when choosing—some can leave much to be desired.

Camping is allowed in designated areas and at some beaches, usually involving rented camping vans. In general, it is not encouraged (by the tourism department) and permission from town mayors is needed to simply pitch a tent on an inviting beach.

Camping is allowed at La Grande Anse on Basse-Terre and the facilities at Les Sables d'Or (590-28-44-60), which have bungalows as well, are recommended. Tents start at F85 per night. Camping la Traversée (590-98-21-23), at Pointe-Noir on Basse-Terre, also offers facilities. Camping vans, which can accommodate four to six people, can be rented starting at F600. Call Antilles Locap Soleil (590-90-95-72) in Gosier or Vert'Bleu (590-28-51-25) in Deshaies.

■ HOTELS

Hotels will often include or add a service charge of 10-15 per cent to your bill and this can be considered your tip for the hotel staff. The majority of Guadeloupe's hotels are on Grande-Terre and sit on the beach areas between Gosier and Saint-François.

❏ LE MERIDIEN (590-88-51-00, fax 88-40-71), in the resort town of Saint-François, is a large four-story complex with more than 260 rooms, on a large beach. Luxury.

❏ HOTEL SALAKO (590-88-22-22, fax 84-38-15) is soon to become a Holiday Inn, but a very nice Holiday Inn. In Gosier, the hotel shares three beaches with nearby hotels and offers a pool, aerobics, watersports, tennis and a kid's club, all included. Moderate-luxury.

❏ LA MAISON de Marie-Galante (590-90-10-41, fax 90-22-75) on the Place de la Victoire in Pointe-à-Pitre is small, only nine rooms, but clean, with air conditioning, television and a central location. Budget-moderate.

❏ HOTEL GRAND ANSE (590-92-90-47), in the southeastern town of Trois-Rivières on Basse-Terre, is basic, with a pool, some kitchenettes, air conditioning and a beach. Moderate.

❏ ON LA DÉSIRADE
Choices are limited to the aptly named L'OASIS DU DESERT (590-20-02-12, moderate) and GÎTES DE FRANCE (590-91-64-33). The island, only eight square miles (21 sq km), can be covered fairly quickly.

❏ ON LES SAINTES
Terre-de-Haut is the place to stay. The small LA SAINTOISE (590-99-52-50) offers ten rooms, moderately priced. HOTEL KANOA (99-51-36) has 20 no-frills rooms. Moderate.

❏ ON MARIE-GALANTE
Several hotels, including HAJO (590-97-32-76, moderate) and LE SOLEIL LEVANT (590-97-31-55, fax 97-41-65, moderate), can be found in CAPESTERRE. LE TOULOULOU (590-97-32-63, fax 97-33-59) in Capesterre features bungalows and a recommended restaurant.

EATING
The cuisines of France, Italy, Vietnam, China, Germany and more can be found on the island, but the restaurants and cafes of Guadeloupe are known throughout the Caribbean for their distinctive creole cooking. The beaches and towns are lined with cafes and patisseries and open-air bistros and it would have to be a truly bad restaurant to disappoint you.

Credit cards are not accepted everywhere; it's best to call ahead. Check, too, to see if the restaurant is open evenings. Beachside bistros do a brisk lunch business, but may not be open for dinner.

❏ LA MAISON DE MARIE-GALANTE (590-90-10-41) has a great location on Pointe-à-Pitre's Place de la Victoire and serves simple creole. Inexpensive.

❏ LA CANNE A SUCRE (590-82-10-19) is Pointe-à-Pitre's renowned creole restaurant. Located on the town pier, the dining is elegant and jackets are required for upstairs seating in the evening. Expensive.

❏ LA GARGANTUA (590-90-97-32) at the marina, for its name if for nothing else. Moderate.

❏ LA PECHERIE (590-84-48-41) in Saint-François serves simple, fresh seafood. Inexpensive.

❏ LE KARACOLI (590-28-41-17), directly on the Plage de la Grande Anse in Deshaies on Basse-Terre, serves an excellent boudin creole (blood pudding) and colombo de poulet, which is hot and spicy chicken. The beach setting under the shade of almond trees is perfect. Open for lunch only, 12-17.00 daily; moderate.

GETTING THERE
Guadeloupe's main entry point is Aeroport du Raizet (590-82-80-80 or 90-32-32 or 90-34-34), about three miles (five km) north of Pointe-à-Pitre.

Airlines servicing Guadeloupe: American Airlines (local contacts at Raizet and Pointe-à-Pitre, 590-83-62-62 or 82-99-48), Air Canada (590-83-62-49), Air France (590-82-50-00 or 82-11-11), Air Guadeloupe (590-82-28-35), LIAT (590-82-12-26), Air St. Barths (590-27-71-90) and Winnair (590-83-89-06).

No departure tax is paid when leaving Guadeloupe.

GETTING AROUND
■ INTER-ISLAND FERRIES
Guadeloupe's boat service to nearby islands is extensive and fairly efficient. The ferries are high-speed, comfortable and a bit less expensive than flying—but not that much. Weigh the relative time and effort it takes to travel by ferry and make your choice. Schedules and fares, which are always subject to change, are available at the tourism office in Pointe-à-Pitre.

❏ FROM LA DARSE IN POINTE-À-PITRE TO MARIE-GALANTE: Trans Antilles Express (590-83-12-45 or 91-13-43, fax 91-11-05) and the car ferry Amanda Galante (590-83-12-45).

❏ FROM POINTE-À-PITRE TO LES SAINTES: Transports Brudey Freres (590-90-04-48, fax 82-15-62).

❏ FROM POINTE-À-PITRE TO DOMINICA, MARTINIQUE, OR ST. LUCIA: Caribbean Express or Trans Antilles Express (590-83-04-45 or 91-13-43), Caribia Ferries (590-89-42-67, fax 91-91-66).

❏ FROM BASSE-TERRE OR POINTE-À-PITRE VIA TROIS-RIVIÈRES TO LES SAINTES: Princess Caroline (590-96-95-83).

❏ FROM SAINT-FRANÇOIS TO LA DÉSIRADE: Sotromade (590-20-02-30), Socimade (590-88-47-28) and Le Mistral (590-88-48-63).

■ PUBLIC TRANSPORATION

Most taxis are unmetered and rates are set by the government. Rates are 40 per cent higher from 21.00 to 7.00 and on Sundays. You can hire a taxi for touring, but it can cost as much as US$100 for a trip around the island, or US$25 per hour. Taxis are found at the airport, at the pier in Pointe-à-Pitre and in the town of Basse-Terre. Taxi stands can also be found on the main streets of Sainte-Anne and Saint-François.

The public bus system works well, but language may be a problem. Buses operate from about 5.00 to 19.00 and traverse Grande-Terre and Basse-Terre. You can wave the driver down anywhere, or use bus stops marked "arret-bus." Pay when you get off. On Grande-Terre buses from Pointe-à-Pitre to the southern coast (as far as Saint-François, F12) depart from the La Darse station, on the pier. Buses to the northern and eastern coasts depart from Mortenol Station, located at the northern end of Rue Vatable. Buses to the airport (about F5) depart from Rue Peynier.

■ RENTALS

When all is said and done, however, car rentals are perhaps the best way to get around. The 1,200 miles (1,920 km) of roads on the islands are excellent and well-marked, in French. Some companies have certain cars that, for some odd reason, require the driver to be 25 years of age. Still, 21 is the norm and all drivers must have a valid license. Credit cards are widely accepted, otherwise substantial deposits are required.

A few of the many, with airport numbers first: Avis (590-82-33-47 or 90-46-46), Budget (590-82-95-58), Europcar (590-82-50-51 or 84-45-84), Euro Rent (590-91-42-16 or 88-48-96), Hertz (590-82-00-14 or 82-88-14).

Scooters and motorcycles are another way to see the island. In Pointe-à-Pitre call Vespa Sun (590-91-30-36). In Saint-François try Dingo Location (590-88-76-08) or Rent a Bike (590-88-51-00). Mopeds can be rented through Velo-Vert (590-83-15-74) in Pointe-à-Pitre. A scooter costs about F170 per day.

Bicycling is a major sport in Guadeloupe, especially on flat Grande-Terre, and bikes are easy to find. Try Velo-Vert or Cyclo-Tours (590-84-11-34) in Gosier. In Saint-François Rent-a-Bike (590-84-51-00) is at the Hotel Meridien. Bikes go for about F50-70 per day.

For information regarding biking tours and excursions, contact Association Guadeloupéen de VTT (590-82-82-67). The "VTT" is *velo tout terrain* or all-terrain bike.

For outer islands car and bike rentals: On Marie-Galante, Caneval (Grand Bourg, 590-97-97-76) or Le Touloulou (Capesterre, 590-97-32-63). On La Désirade try Loca 2000 (590-20-02-65). On Les Saintes call Archipel Rent Service (Terre-de-Haut, 590-99-52-63).

MONEY, HOURS AND COMMUNICATION

The French franc is Guadeloupe's currency, exchanging at F5.5 = US$1. Dollars are used fairly widely, but the franc is easiest to use in markets and with taxi drivers and small businesses. Banks and bureaux de change are located throughout Pointe-à-Pitre and major towns, open weekdays 8.00-12.00 and 14.00-16.00; some are open on Saturdays and some may open on Sunday mornings as well. Exchange booths at the airport are open during flight arrivals and often crowded.

General business hours are weekdays 8.00-12.00 and 14.30-17.00, with some variations. Many businesses are open Saturday mornings as well.

The country code for Guadeloupe is 590. This is not an area code where you dial 1 first. For Americans this means dialing 011 plus 590 and the six-digit number.

ENTERTAINMENT

■ SPORTS

Most hotels feature tennis courts and some allow non-guests to play. Clubs that allow players are the Marina Club (590-90-84-08) in Pointe-à-Pitre and the Center Lamby-Lambert (590-90-90-97) in Gosier. Squash courts can be found at Vive Forme (590-90-98-74), at the Villa Viva hotel in Bas-du-Fort.

Call Comite Guadeloupéen de Surf (590-91-77-64) for information on the islands' surfing conditions.

Sailboats, glass-bottomed boats, windsurfing, snorkelling and paddle-boats are easily arranged through a beach-front hotel, whether you are staying there or not.

Yacht charters are best arranged through the marina at Bas-du-Fort, the largest of three on the island. For advance information contact ATM Yachts (590-90-92-02, U.S. 800-634-8822). The Marina de Saint-François also offers dozens of charters and deep-sea fishing excursions; call Les Heures Saines (590-98-86-63) or the Nautilus Club (590-98-85-69).

Several companies specialize in adventure tours of the kayaking, canoeing, 4WD, biking and hiking variety. Contact Guadeloupe Decouvertes (590-84-29-32, fax 26-80-10) in Gosier and Espace Losiers (590-88-71-93, fax 88-44-01) and Parfum d'Aventure (590-88-47-62), both in Saint-François.

Golf is offered at many of the hotels, but the island's premier course is the 18-hole, 6,755-yard, Robert Trent Jones Sr.-designed Golf International de Saint-François (590-88-41-87, fax 88-42-20). Greens fees are F250.

Fitness clubs are located at the Villa Viva hotel's Viva Forme (590-90-98-74) in Bas-du-Fort and in many of the island's hotels. For horseback riding try Le Criolo (590-83-38-90) in Saint-Felix and the Poney Club (590-24-03-74) in Le Moule.

■ OTHER

For something completely different, you can see a cockfighting match during the November through April cockfighting season. Matches are flamboyant and loud and the betting is frenetic. For extra action, sometimes a mongoose is pitted against a snake. Newspapers will carry schedules.

For bloodletting of a different sort, Casinos de Gosier (590-84-18-33) stays open from 21.00 until the wee hours every day except Sunday. Casino de Saint-François (590-88-41-31) is closed on Monday. Neither offer slot machines, but you can play roulette and blackjack. An admission fee (currently F69) is charged and you'll need a photo ID to get inside. The minimum age is 21.

USEFUL ADDRESSES
■ TOURISM
❏ F.W.I. Tourist Board, 610 Fifth Ave., New York, NY 10020; 212-315-0726.
❏ Service Francais du Tourisme a Montreal, 1981 Ave. MacGill College, Suite 490, Montreal, Quebec H3A 2W9; 514-288-4264.
❏ Office Départemental du Tourisme, 5 Square de la Banque, BP 1099, 97181 Cedex Pointe-à-Pitre, Guadeloupe, F.W.I.; 590-82-09-30, fax 590-83-89-22.

■ OTHER
❏ Pointe-à-Pitre police, 17 or 82-00-17.
❏ Basse-Terre police, 81-11-55.
❏ Pointe-à-Pitre emergency medical, 89-11-20.
❏ Pointe-à-Pitre fire, 18 or 82-00-28.
❏ Center Hospitalier de Pointe-à-Pitre, 89-10-10.
❏ Weather forecast, 90-22-22.
❏ Raizet Airport, 82-80-80.
❏ Federal Express, 26-85-44.

THE WINDWARD ISLANDS

**DOMINICA
MARTINIQUE
ST. LUCIA
ST. VINCENT AND THE GRENADINES
GRENADA**

Palm trees with a sailing boat in the distance, Tobago Cays, The Grenadines

Tall-masted ships in Tobago Bay, The Grenadines

228

An uninhabited island off Harbour Island

Fishing boat in Anguilla

View of the east coast of Mustique, The Grenadines

Rawlins Plantation Hotel, Old Sugar Mill, St Kitts

(*Above*) *Harbour Isand, The Bahamas;*
(*below*) *Local primary school in Mustique, The Grenadines*

(Above) Harbour Island, The Bahamas; (below) St Barths

6age number.

*(Left) Schoolgirl in Bassterre,
St Kitts;
(below) Anguilla*

'Todd and Driller, Cedar Hill Test Well, Trinidad', by W J Dunstall

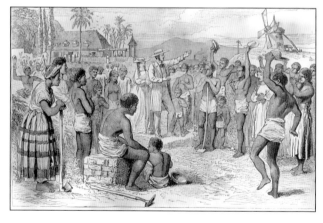

(Top) *Scene from a Sugar Mill,*
from The Illustrated London News, *1849;*
(above) Emancipation reaches the West
Indies, from Cassell's History;
(opposite) The Black Iguana *by P J Smit*

P. J. Smit.

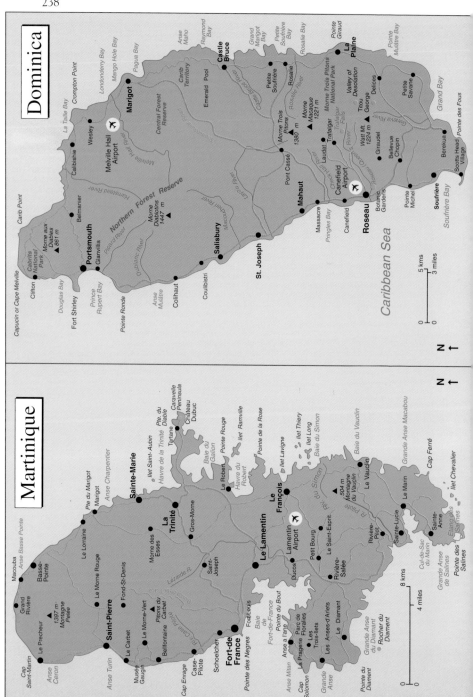

Martinique

Dominica

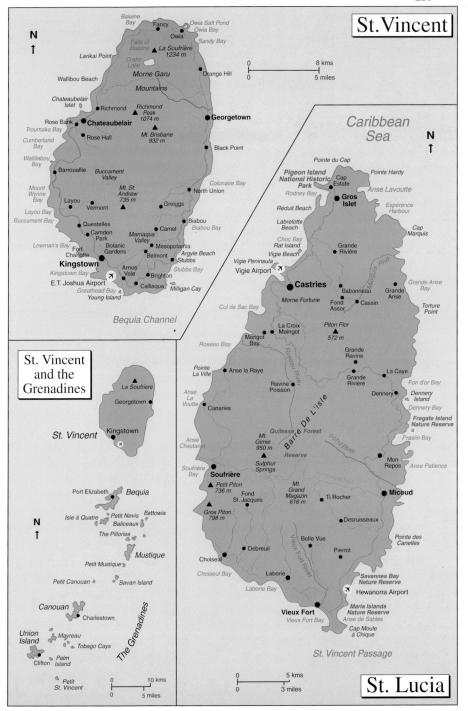

St. Vincent

N↑

Baleine Bay
Fancy
Owia Salt Pond
Owia
Owia Bay
Sandy Bay
Falls of Baleine
Larikai Point
La Soufrière 1234 m
Crater Lake
Orange Hill
Wallibou Beach
Morne Garu
Mountains
Chateaubelair Islet
Richmond
Richmond Peak 1074 m
Georgetown
Rose Bank
Chateaubelair
Troumaka Bay
Rose Hall
Mt. Brisbane 932 m
Cumberland Bay
Black Point
Wallilabou Bay
Barrouallie
Buccament Valley
Mount Wynne Bay
Mt. St. Andrew 735 m
Colonaire Bay
Layou
Vermont
North Union
Layou Bay
Greiggs
Buccament Bay
Questelles
Biabou
Camel
Biabou Bay
Camden Park
Marriaqua Valley
Mesopotamia
Lowman's Bay
Fort Charlotte
Botanic Gardens
Belmont
Argyle Beach
Stubbs
Kingstown
Arnos Vale
Brighton
Stubbs Bay
Kingstown Bay
Calliaqua
Milligan Cay
E.T. Joshua Airport
Greathead Bay
Young Island

0 ___ 8 kms
0 ___ 5 miles

Bequia Channel

Caribbean Sea

N↑

Pointe du Cap
Pointe Hardy
Pigeon Island National Historic Park
Cap Estate
Anse Lavoutte
Rodney Bay
Gros Islet
Réduit Beach
Espérance Harbour
Labrelotte Beach
Cap Marquis
Choc Bay
Rat Island
Grande Rivière
Vigie Beach
Vigie Peninsula
Vigie Airport
Castries
Babonneau
Grande Anse Bay
Morne Fortune
Fond Assor
Cassin
Grande Anse
Torture Point
Cul de Sac Bay
La Croix Maingot
Piton Flor 572 m
Marigot Bay
Roseau Bay
Grande Ravine
Pointe La Ville
Anse la Raye
Grande Rivière
La Caye
Fon d'or Bay
Anse La Voutte
Ravine Poisson
Dennery
Dennery Island
Canaries
Dennery Bay
Fregate Island Nature Reserve
Anse Chastanet
Mt. Gimie 950 m
Quilesse Forest
Fond River
Praslin Bay
Reserve
Barre De L'isle
Sulphur Springs
Mon Repos
Anse Patience
Soufrière Bay
Soufrière
Petit Piton 736 m
Fond St. Jacques
Mt. Grand Magazin 616 m
Ti Rocher
Micoud
Gros Piton 798 m
Desruisseaux
Belle Vue
Pointe des Canelles
Choiseul
Debreuil
Pierrot
Vieux Fort River
Choiseul Bay
Laborie
Savannes Bay Nature Reserve
Laborie Bay
Hewanorra Airport
Vieux Fort
Maria Islands Nature Reserve
Vieux Fort Bay
Anse de Sables
Cap Moule à Chique

St. Vincent Passage

St. Lucia

St. Vincent and the Grenadines

La Soufrière
Georgetown
St. Vincent
Kingstown

N↑

Port Elizabeth
Bequia
Isle á Quatre
Petit Nevis
Battowia
Baliceaux
The Pillories
Mustique
Petit Mustique
Petit Canouan
Savan Island
Canouan
Charlestown
Union Island
Mayreau
Tobago Cays
Clifton
Palm Island
Petit St. Vincent
The Grenadines

0 ___ 10 kms
0 ___ 5 miles

0 ___ 5 kms
0 ___ 3 miles

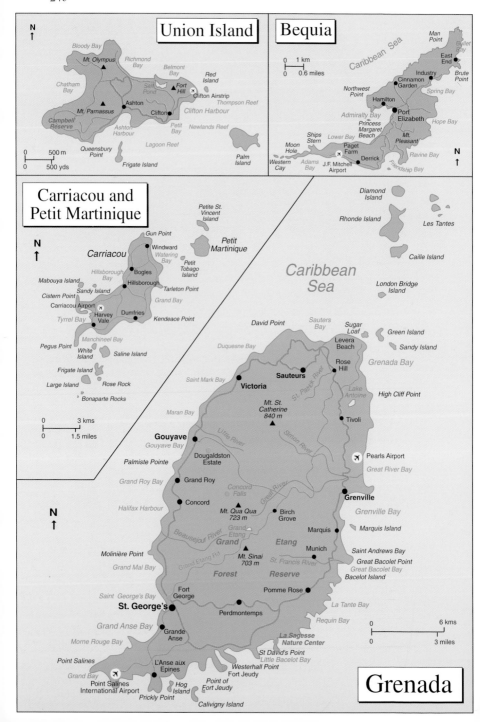

Union Island

N

Bloody Bay
Mt. Olympus ▲
Richmond Bay
Belmont Bay
Red Island
Chatham Bay
Salt Pond
Fort Hill
Clifton Airstrip
Thompson Reef
Mt. Parnassus ▲
Ashton
Clifton
Campbell Reserve
Ashton Harbour
Clifton Harbour
Petit Bay
Newlands Reef
Queensbury Point
Lagoon Reef
0 500 m
0 500 yds
Frigate Island
Palm Island

Bequia

Caribbean Sea
Man Point
Bullet Bay
East End
0 1 km
0 0.6 miles
Industry
Cinnamon Garden
Brute Point
Northwest Point
Hamilton
Spring Bay
Port Elizabeth
Admiralty Bay
Princess Margaret Beach
Hope Bay
Mt. Pleasant
Ships Stern
Lower Bay
Moon Hole
Paget Farm
Ravine Bay
Western Cay
Adams Bay
J.F. Mitchell Airport
Derrick
Friendship Bay
N

Carriacou and Petit Martinique

N

Petite St. Vincent Island

Gun Point
Carriacou
Windward
Petit Martinique
Watering Bay
Bogles
Petit Tobago Island
Hillsborough Bay
Hillsborough
Mabouya Island
Tarleton Point
Cistern Point
Sandy Island
Grand Bay
Carriacou Airport
Harvey Vale
Dumfries
Kendeace Point
Tyrrel Bay
Manchineel Bay
Pegus Point
White Island
Saline Island
Frigate Island
Large Island
Rose Rock
Bonaparte Rocks
0 3 kms
0 1.5 miles

Diamond Island
Rhonde Island
Les Tantes
Caille Island

Caribbean Sea

London Bridge Island

David Point
Sauters Bay
Sugar Loaf
Green Island
Levera Beach
Sandy Island
Duquesne Bay
Rose Hill
Grenada Bay
Saint Mark Bay
Lake Antoine
High Cliff Point
Victoria
Sauteurs
St. Patrick River
Mt. St. Catherine 840 m ▲
Tivoli
Maran Bay
Simon River
Gouyave
Little River
Gouyave Bay
Dougaldston Estate
Palmiste Pointe
Pearls Airport ✈
Great River Bay
Grand Roy
Concord Falls
Great River
Grand Roy Bay
Concord
Grenville
Halifax Harbour
Mt. Qua Qua 723 m ▲
Birch Grove
Grenville Bay
Grand Etang
Marquis
Marquis Island
N
Beausejour River
Grand Etang
Munich
Saint Andrews Bay
Molinière Point
Mt. Sinai 703 m ▲
St. Francis River
Great Bacolet Point
Grand Mal Bay
Forest
Reserve
Great Bacolet Bay
Grand Etang Rd
Bacolet Island
Fort George
Pomme Rose
La Tante Bay
Saint George's Bay
St. George's
Perdmontemps
Requin Bay
0 6 kms
0 3 miles
Grand Anse Bay
Grande Anse
La Sagesse Nature Center
Morne Rouge Bay
St David's Point
Little Bacolet Bay
Point Salines
L'Anse aux Epines
Westerhall Point
Fort Jeudy
Grand Bay
Point Salines International Airport ✈
Hog Island
Point of Fort Jeudy
Prickly Point
Calivigny Island

Grenada

Dominica

The Land

Dominica (Dahm-in-EEK-uh), officially the Commonwealth of Dominica (not the Dominican Republic, which shares the island of Hispaniola with Haiti), is the northernmost Windward Island, lying almost equidistant, 30 miles (48 km) on either side, between the French territories of Guadeloupe to the north and Martinique to the south. The rugged, mountainous island is some 29 miles (46 km) long, 15 miles (24 km) wide and 290 square miles (750 sq km) in area; about the same size as the combined Netherlands Antilles.

The descriptions rugged and mountainous hardly do the island justice. Big, lush and dramatic, Dominica's mountains, formed by ancient volcanoes, loom like monster Hershey's Kisses over valleys and small villages. The island's highest point, the 4,747-foot (1,424 m) Morne Diablotin in the Northern Forest Reserve, is also the second highest in the Lesser Antilles, behind Guadeloupe's La Soufrière.

A spine of mountain ridges snakes along the center of the island from north to south, surrounded by several national parks: the Northern Forest Reserve, Central Forest Reserve and the magnificent Morne Trois Pitons National Park (the word "morne" is a Creole combination of the Spanish morro and the French mont), which dominates the southern half of the badger-shaped island. The smaller, coastal Cabrits National Park, to the northwest, adds to the picture of a nation that takes its natural resources seriously. The national motto of Dominica, Apres Bondie C'est La Ter, is Creole for "After God, The Land."

The rest of the countryside and coast seems to drip off the mountain peaks, in cases cutting straight into the sea in sheer cliffs. The hills and mountains are blanketed by degrees of ripe and wet rainforest, including seasonal rainforest and the higher elevation mountain rainforest. Parts of this elevated primordial rainforest, found generally at altitudes higher than 1,000 feet (304 m), are not easily accessed and considered by many to be as virgin as they get in the Lesser Antilles. There are plant and animal species found here and nowhere else in the world. Among the 162 recorded bird species on the island, the large imperial parrot, known locally as the sisserou, and the red-necked parrot, or jaco, are endemic to Dominica. They are also endangered and protected by law. A variety of bats and frogs, including the often frying pan-bound "mountain chicken" or crapaud, and five species of snakes, such as the ten foot (three m) boa constrictor, or tete chien, also inhabit the rainforests and woodlands of the island.

The windward (eastern or Atlantic side) coastal region is characterized by woodlands, swamp forest and some marshland. The windward coast is somewhat more irregular than the leeward, but this is a fine point and a matter of degree—much of Dominica's coast is rough and offers little in the way of flat beaches and quiescent bays. The leeward lowlands, which are in a rainshadow for the most part, are drier and given to scrub forest, grasslands and rocky shorelines. The valleys of the central section of the country are covered by woodland, farms and plantations.

Due to the island's high altitudes, rainfall is consistent and cumulative, particularly from July to October. Rainfall is 75-80 inches per year, but the true rainfall in the mountainous areas is estimated at three times greater. The mountains hold the water, craters and lakes created by volcanic activity provide the island with plenty of fresh, clean water. So well-regarded is Dominica's water that a medium-sized industry centers around exporting bottled drinking water to neighbouring islands. Dominicans like to say that there are 365 freshwater rivers and streams throughout the country. Well, there are quite a few, at any rate, and put to good use for recreational swimming and bathing. The water and unusually rich soil of the island, created by years of volcanic deposits, makes for uniquely prolific growing conditions. The island's soil produces a large variety of tropical fruits, vegetables and cash crops, year-round. Dominica's fruits and vendors are seen in markets throughout the Lesser Antilles, as far north as the busy outdoor market in Saint-Martin.

Testament to the growing power of Dominica's combined soil and water resources followed the devastation of 1979's Hurricane David. Driving rains and winds of 150 mph (240 kph) whipped across the island, killing 37, injuring another 5,000 and destroying three quarters of the country's homes. The banana and citrus fields, mainstays of Dominica's economy, were crushed. Yet, within two years, much of the rainforest had regenerated itself and the banana and citrus farms had taken root once again. While the toll in human suffering lingered, the promise of quick economic recovery flourished on the land.

History

The confusion about the Dominica versus the Dominican Republic business is Columbus' fault. His devotion to Catholicism apparently required him to name the islands he encountered after saints, abbeys and all manner of religious icons. The Lord's Day was one of them, twice.

The Stone Age Ciboney were Dominica's first inhabitants. The hunting and gathering Amerindian Arawaks followed them, around the time of Christ, and were in turn followed by the aggressive Caribs, who had begun their northern push up the Lesser Antilles chain around 1,000 AD. The Caribs supplanted and absorbed the Arawak groups and were the native group on the island when Columbus sighted it in November 1493.

The Caribs called the land Wai'tukubuli, reputedly "Tall is Her Body." One of Columbus' caravels, in search of fresh water, landed on the western side of the island at the inlet now called Prince Rupert's Bay. The Caribs fiercely defended the island, turning back the Spanish with arrows dipped in poison. Columbus, never one to get too deeply into the fray while there was gold to be discovered elsewhere, moved on. No real further colonization was attempted by the Spaniards.

For the next century the Caribs, who were well-established in the Lesser Antilles at that point and who valued Wai'tukubuli for its fresh water and as a base for raiding neighbouring islands, continued to ward off incursions by European colonizers. The Caribs controlled the hills and rugged terrain of Dominica and were well-suited for the type of fighting that took place there. The British and French, in conjunction with their colonization of neighbouring islands, attempted to establish settlements on Dominica, but were continually repelled by the Caribs. The European wars of the 17th and 18th centuries kept the British and French busy at any rate and, in the meantime, the Caribs held their own.

In 1748 the French and British signed the Treaty of Aix-la-Chapelle, which promised mutual neutrality on Dominica and basically gave over the island to the Caribs. The French, however, in spite of the treaty, continued to expand their small settlements. This didn't seem sporting to the British, who raided and captured the island in 1761. The British were officially given possession, at least in their own eyes, by the 1763 Treaty of Paris. After this treaty was signed, the British sectioned off land parcels and left a small area of 232 acres to the Caribs, whose numbers and resources had dwindled to the point where they could offer little resistance.

The French retook Dominica in 1778. The island changed hands like this for years—nine times—through the American Revolution, the French Revolution and the Napoleonic Wars. The struggles between the British, French and Caribs finally culminated in an 1805 raid by the French, who in essence held the island hostage for several days and were finally paid a ransom by the British to disappear. Thus began the long period of British rule, although, with the French islands of Guadeloupe and Martinique to the north and south respectively, the French influence on Dominica abated little.

Constant Carib harassment inhibited Dominica's development under the British, a situation that resulted in the island's status as the least developed of the British isles. Still, the British began to import greater numbers of Africans to work their plantations and, by the time of emancipation in 1834, the majority population on Dominica was African, setting the tone for today's demographics.

By the late 19th century the once-powerful Caribs had been relegated to the status of little more than curious has-beens, living in abject poverty on poor land. Their leaders made a desperate appeal to Queen Victoria for more land and representation. The request was granted through Gov. Henry Hesketh Bell and in 1902 a total of 3,700 acres in the eastern section of the country was given to the Caribs, the area today known as Carib Territory.

By the 1930s worldwide depression had affected the fragile economy of Dominica. New crops, such as coffee, tobacco, lime and other citrus fruits and cocoa had been introduced, but the market dried up as the world hunkered down for war. Still, during this period local trade unions were founded and Dominica was granted a system of elected representation. In the 1950s the world seemed to discover bananas and the countries of the Caribbean, including Dominica, found new sources of wealth. Dominica's infrastructure and towns grew and the economy was relatively healthy.

Universal adult suffrage became law in 1951. By 1967 Dominica was granted full internal government under an associated statehood agreement with Britain. The country became independent and a republic within the Commonwealth on 3 November 1978, with the Dominica Labor Party (DLP) and Prime Minister Patrick John at its helm.

However, due to the inconsistent policies of the generally left-wing DLP, the country soon degenerated into something akin to anarchy. The opposition party quickly joined with religious and civic leaders to form what they called the Committee for National Salvation and managed to usurp the government, in conjunction with DLP insiders, in what was described as a "constitutional coup." The coalition ruled until elections were called in 1980.

The winner in this election was the opposition Dominica Freedom Party (DFP), headed by Prime Minister Mary Eugenia Charles. Born in 1919 and educated in the law in Canada, Dame Eugenia Charles became the first woman elected head of a Caribbean government. Dame Charles, citing advanced years, declined to run in an early 1995 election. The victor was the relatively young United Workers Party (UWP), headed by 51 year old biochemist Edison James.

People and Culture

The population, 86,000, is small for an island this size, the smallest in the Windwards. The Dominican majority is of African descent, although pockets of mixed-race descendants of old and nouveau settlers are found, particularly in the capital of Roseau.

The 3,000 remaining descendants of the original Caribs represent a significant portion of the population, if not in numbers, then at least culturally. Many of the Caribs have been integrated into the general population and Carib Territory, with village names such as Salybia and Sineku, exists mostly as a remnant of colonial days. The Caribs have nominal powers vested in a chief and a six member council, who draft bylaws with the approval of the central government. There are no actual borders to the territory. The Caribs have in the last few years made efforts to revive their culture—1993 was, as well as the quincentennial of Columbus' arrival, the Year of Indigenous Peoples and included a Carib Month.

A general Carib revival, however, seems unlikely. The Caribs did not have a written language and therefore did not record their more intricate cultural customs, although a 1642 Carib dictionary, compiled by a French priest, survives. The Caribs still practice some traditions, such as crafting canoes from the gommier tree and baking the staple cassava bread. They do not celebrate Independence Day, 3 November, believing that the sighting by Columbus began their slow but inexorable decline as a culture. In Dominica, as on neighbouring St. Vincent, few Caribs of pure ancestry remain.

The evolution of language on Dominica mimics the evolution of its original and colonial inhabitants. English is official and widely spoken, but a French Creole, laced with vocabulary from Carib and various African languages, dominates. A typical phrase: ti beau doudou ("pretty little girl"). Dominican Creole shares some commonalities with Creoles spoken on the French islands and on St. Lucia.

The language amalgam is evident in all aspects of Dominican life, but perhaps most evident to a visitor looking at a map. Names such as Marigot and Roseau reflect the French influence. Concord and Scotts Head recall the British rule. Some Carib words have over the years lost their meaning, but words such as agouti (a large gerbil-like rodent), waiwanao (a fish) and the endangered imperial parrot, the sisserou, have Carib origins.

Due to its early French influence, Roman Catholicism is Dominica's dominant religion. Anglican, Methodist, Pentecostal, Baptist, Seventh-Day Adventist and even Baha'i denominations are represented, as well as several smaller Protestant sects.

Island folklore and culture are captured in oral tales and occasionally in the performances of local troupes and bands. Hotels and public venues present performances by the National School of Dance, the Wai'tukubuli Dance Troupe and the Dominican Folk Singers. Check newspapers for listings.

Dominica's fine writers have produced a small but significant body of work, that offers in-depth portrayals of Dominican and other Caribbean cultures, as well as descriptions of life during and after the colonial period.

Novelist Jean Rhys is considered by some to be less Caribbean than European-influenced, yet she used a Caribbean setting for one of her most famous works, *Wide Sargasso Sea* (1966), which deals with post-emancipation West Indian life and the dwindling years of the colonial period. Other works by Rhys, particularly several short stories, use intricate West Indian speech rhythms.

The poet and novelist Phyllis Shand Allfrey left Dominica for education in the U.S. and England when she was a teenager. She returned in the early Fifties and edited several local newspapers. On Dominica she wrote her only novel, *The Orchid House* (1953), a loosely autobiographical story of the decline of colonialism, as seen through the lives of three Dominican sisters. The novel was made into a film in 1990.

Historian Lennox Honychurch has written several excellent guides to Dominica and its culture, including The Dominica Story and Our Island Culture.

FESTIVALS

Dominicans take great pride in their blend of African, European and Carib culture. The French have given the country Carnival, one of the island's larger celebrations. The pre-Lenten festival starts several weeks before Ash Wednesday, with calypso contests, feasts and shows. On the Monday and Tuesday before Ash Wednesday people take to the streets in jump-ups, masquerades and parties.

Christmas and Easter are important, as are most Christian holidays. Tou Saintes (All Saints) is celebrated on 1 November, when Dominicans honour the dead by visiting graves, lighting candles and joining in public prayer.

Creole Day is celebrated on the Friday before the 3 November Independence Day celebration. Women dress in madras costumes, the flowing jupe and la wobe douillete, a skirt with lace petticoats and a wide blouse and headpiece. Men wear the dark trousers and white shirts of the national dress. Business on Creole Day is conducted in Creole and restaurants make a point of serving crapaud, agouti and other traditional dishes. There is much dancing and singing, accompanied by traditional jing ping bands (comprising a "boom-boom" string bass instrument, accordion, a "shack shack" percussion instrument and other traditional music and noisemakers) and some organized activities that include storytelling and folk dancing. Independence Day celebrates the 3 November 1978 event and involves calypso competitions, speeches and marching.

Government and Economy

The Commonwealth of Dominica is an independent republic, nominally headed by a president, with power is vested in the elected government led by a prime minister. A 21 member House of Assembly is elected every five years from the nation's ten parishes and from the majority party of that assembly a ministerial cabinet is chosen. The Carib Territory is represented by a member in the house. A nine member Senate is appointed by the president; five members from the ruling party are selected by the prime minister and four are selected by the opposition party.

Agriculture is the basis for the island's economy. The island is, in fact, self-sufficient in fruit and vegetable production. Even though only a tenth of the land is arable, bananas, citrus fruit, coconuts and coconut by-products are grown for export. Nearly half of the gross domestic product is agricultural and that sector employs close to half of the work force. A third of the work force is employed in industry and commerce.

Most of Dominica's banana farmers operate small farms, not the type descended from massive plantations of the colonial and post-colonial period. This arrangement is a reminder of the old days: Dominica's land is so fertile that many in the slave population, who were often given small plots of land, were able to grow enough to eventually buy their freedom. In fact, slavery on Dominica was generally considered to be less harsh—a relative judgment, no doubt—than on neighbouring islands.

Through blights and competition from Central America, bananas have managed to hold their own in the economy. Dominica's principal trading partner is the U.K. and preferential trade agreements with the EEC have allowed the banana trade to flourish. This arrangement ends in 1999, whereupon Dominica, which is already in the process of negotiating to maintain price standards, will have several difficult bridges to cross.

The government has already looked to tourism to help bolster the economy. This is a delicate matter in Dominica, where the official line is that no one wants the agricultural sector contribution to be replaced by tourism. Tourist numbers, however, have steadily increased, from 24,000 in 1986 to 55,000 in 1992. Figures for 1993 showed an expected seven per cent increase. The Caribbean region contributes nearly two-thirds of all Dominica's overnight visitors. U.S. cruise ships call at the rate of about 180 per year; this number has dropped slightly over the years, even though cruise ship passenger arrivals have increased (the ships are larger).

The government is actively promoting nature-oriented tourism, not surprising given the nature of the island. Dominica's official tourism moniker is the "Nature Island of the Caribbean" and it rings true. This is not an island where you'll find long sandy beaches and large resorts. Rather, the virgin rainforests, waterfalls, mountain lakes, rivers, diving opportunities and unaffected culture of the island lends itself to exploring, hiking and getting to know Dominicans.

Most of the island's hotels are small, family-owned operations. The island's capacity is about 650 rooms, expected to double by 1997.

Sights

Beaches are not this island's main attraction. The best are in the northeast, near Portsmouth, Dominica's second largest town. The area is still undeveloped and you'll have a chance to really get away from it all if you decide to explore the small bays and inlets here. The honey-colored beach at Picard, south of Portsmouth, is about two miles (three km) long and one of the island's best, offering several small guesthouses and hotels along the water. Douglas Bay, north of Portsmouth, is also recommended.

The interior trails and sights of Dominica are perhaps the most compelling and challenging in the Caribbean. The National Parks Service Forestry Division (809-448-2401, fax 448-7999) publishes brochures, booklets dealing with the flora and fauna of the island, as well as posters and trail maps. Cost is less than EC$15 for anything they produce and the trail map is a bargain at EC$1. Find the forestry division at the Botanical Gardens in Roseau.

Guides are not always necessary, but can be helpful and are available at practically every attraction. The tourism department (at the National Development Corporation, 809-448-2351) fears that too many eager guides at the foot of every attraction will become overbearing, as is already beginning to happen. Often the guides are from local villages and very knowledgeable and if you simply show up you can negotiate a price. But if you want a recommended guide, contact the tourism department first or contact: Astaphan Tours (809-448-3221, fax 448-3124), Dominica Tours and Dive (809-448-2638, fax 448-5680) or Wilderness Tours (809-448-2198, fax 448-3600).

Trafalgar Falls is one of the island's most accessible sites. The twin falls are located about five miles (eight km) from Roseau. Park at the hydro station, where you'll find a small kiosk selling drinks and walk about ten minutes to a platform, from which you can view the falls. Another 15 minute hike and you're there, under 200 feet (61 m) of cascading water. Hot springs feed water to the cool of a natural swimming pool.

The Morne Trois Pitons National Park is accessible from various points near Roseau. The name comes from the three-peaked volcanic mountain, height 4,550 feet (1,365 m), that dominates a 17,000-acre rainforest. A half-dozen trails, some of which have shelters and picnic areas, lead to the park's sites. The Emerald Pool is found off the road to Castle Bruce. The hike is an easy ten minutes through rainforest to a small waterfall-fed pool, surrounded by tropical flowers and plants. Use the village of Laudat to hike about three miles (five km) to Freshwater Lake, a calm supply reservoir—no swimming allowed—and the source of the Roseau River. Boeri Lake, a large and deep lake 3,000 feet (900 m) above sea level, is found farther on, about 45 minutes past Freshwater Lake.

Boiling Lake can also be reached from Laudat; some claim it is the largest of its kind in the world. The steaming lake is not always at a rolling boil, but is pretty hot—the water, reaching 190° F (60° C), can boil an egg. The lake sits in a crater and is heated by escaping volcanic gases. Don't even think about swimming here. Below the lake is the attractively named Valley of Desolation, an area rendered nearly barren by sulfuric emissions. The entire hike is only about six miles (ten km) one way, but is a difficult, all-day excursion, about four hours in all. A guide is recommended for this one and costs EC$40 per person.

In the north of the country the 1,300-acre Cabrits National Park (the word comes from the Creolized Spanish cabras for "goats," which were left to run wild in the area as sources of fresh meat for passing Spanish ships) encompasses both land and sea. Part of the park is on the Cabrits Peninsula, surrounded by Prince Rupert's Bay to the south and Douglas Bay to the north. A thousand acres are dedicated to the marine environment. A large swamp, home to many bird species, lies between the peninsula and the mainland. Remains of old fortifications are scattered over the property, including Fort Shirley, an 18th century garrison, abandoned in 1854. There is a small museum on the grounds. The towering Morne Diablotin can be seen from Cabrits. It is possible to hike to the summit of Morne Diablotin. Drive south from Portsmouth to the old Syndicate Estate and the hike, along a rough and often vertical path, is about 3,000 feet (900 m) to the summit. You may want a guide here, too.

Portsmouth, population 5,000, is Dominica's second largest town. The town sits on Prince Rupert's Bay, which was used as a port of call by Spanish ships on their trips to the New World. The attraction here is beaches or maybe a trip up the quiescent Indian River. Guided boats will take you past mangrove swamps and thick rainforest. The cost should be about EC$20 per person.

A drive northeast along the Transinsular Road, which bypasses the Morne Trois Pitons National Park, will bring you past banana and sugarcane fields and small villages, the heart of rural Dominica. The road divides at Pont Casse and the Transinsular Road continues straight through the Central Forest Reserve and on to the windward coast town of Marigot. The other branch leads to Castle Bruce, also on the windward side, and the Carib Territory. There are no signs that indicate you've entered the 3,700-acre territory, but you'll know you're there by a subtle change in the look of the people sitting by the roads or at small craft stands. You can stay at the five room Carib Territory Guesthouse (809-445-7256). A few minutes from the village of Sineku, stop at L'Escalier Tete Chien, a "staircase" of hardened lava that reaches from the ocean up a hillside. The resemblance is of a frozen snake crawling up the hill and the solidified lava has formed natural footsteps in the rock, hence the name "Staircase of the Snake" (literally "dog's head," for the resemblance of a boa constrictor's head to a dog's head).

Roseau

The island's capital, population 20,000, is located on the flat delta of the Roseau River on the southwestern leeward coast and is the picture of an old Caribbean port town, struggling with modernization. The orderly and generally clean streets are lined with rambling, dilapidated buildings with rusty roofs—some are downright rickety—as well as fine examples of Victorian and post-colonial wooden structures. Parts of town, such as Bay Front, the New Market and the General Post Office, are gleaming and new, reflecting efforts to give the town a new face.

Roseau was first settled by the French in the early 1700s and takes its name from roseaux, for the "river reeds" which were plentiful in the rivulets that ran throughout the delta. The British laid out the town in the late 1700s and several structures around town date back to that period, although many older buildings have been lost to fire, military encounters and hurricanes.

The Fort Young Hotel was originally a fort, constructed in 1770. The State House dates from the mid-19th century. The Old Market Square, at the bottom of Church and King George V streets, was, during the 18th century, the site of slave auctions, executions, political rallies and other public functions. It is now a gathering place, restored in 1988, with several small craft shops and a tourism booth (open Monday through Friday 8.00-16.00 and Saturday 9.00-13.00). The promenade along the new Bay Front seawall is a pleasant area to stroll and watch fisherman out on the water. Along this road you'll see the old Post Office, which was built in 1810. The trim of this cream building is a shade of green found nowhere else on the planet. Nearby is the Court House and Registry and at the northern end of the seawall is the Roseau Pier. The new General Post Office is just a few blocks north. The New Market is also at the northern end, facing the Roseau River. The market is the best place for fresh fruit and produce and is busiest on Friday and Saturday mornings.

The 40-acre Botanical Gardens, to the east within walking distance from downtown, were originally established in 1890, but today seem curiously empty. The garden was laid low by Hurricane David, but has now recovered to an extent and features the sausage tree from Africa and the ylang-ylang from Asia. Note the bus crushed under a fallen baobab tree. Also on the grounds is a small aviary, an orchid house and the forestry division offices. At the far end of the garden are the offices of the National Development Corporation, where you'll find the tourism department headquarters.

Practical Information

ACCOMMODATION

Most of Dominica's accommodation is in small guesthouses and hotels. Large resorts are not in the plan, although more hotels are in the process of development. Larger hotels will add a ten per cent service charge and all hotels add a five per cent government tax; many retain the same basic tariffs year-round, not changing for high and low season.

❑ FORT YOUNG HOTEL, Box 519, Roseau, Commonwealth of Dominica, W.I. (809-448-5000, fax 448-5006) has been built in the remains of the old Fort Young, just above the city next to the National Library and Government House. The hotel is newly renovated and features special events on holidays and weekends. Moderate-luxury.

❑ THE GARRAWAY HOTEL, Place Heritage, Bay Front, Roseau, Commonwealth of Dominica, W.I. (809-448-3247, fax 448-3962) opened in 1993 and features 31 rooms, located downtown on Bay Front. Moderate-luxury.

❑ VENA'S GUESTHOUSE, 48 Cork St., Roseau, Commonwealth of Dominica, W.I. (809-448-3286) is as downtown as it gets, on the corner of Queen Mary and

Cork. The rooms are small and some don't have private baths, but they do have fans. The place can be noisy. This was the birthplace of Jean Rhys. Budget.

❏ CHERRY LODGE, Box 138, Roseau, Commonwealth of Dominica, W.I. (809-448-2366) is downtown, clean, historic, eight rooms, with and without bath. Budget.

❏ PICARD BEACH RESORT, Prince Rupert's Bay, Picard, Commonwealth of Dominica, W.I. (809-445-5131, fax 445-5599) features eight 18th century style cottages with kitchenettes, on one of the island's better beaches. Luxury.

EATING

The cuisine on Dominica is creole, both simple and exotic. Try the crapaud, or "mountain chicken," which is frog's legs. Tee tee rees, also titiris, are tiny fish that live in the saline environment of rivers near the sea. Fried with garlic and lime, they're a treat. Crab backs (stuffed crabshells) are an island specialty and the stewed rodents agouti and manicou are also popular.

LA ROBE CREOLE (809-448-2896), on Victoria Street across from the Fort Young Hotel, is one of the finest creole restaurants on the island. Specialties include agouti and crab backs. Moderate-expensive. Downstairs is the MOUSE HOLE CAFE, a good place to stock up on sweets, pastries and pies. EVERGREEN (809-448-3288), at the Evergreen Hotel, offers views to the sea and creole and continental cuisine. Moderate. CATHY'S PIZZERIA sits across the street from the Old Market Square and serves very simple but hefty amounts of creole-based food. Rice and peas are served with everything. Inexpensive.

GETTING THERE

Dominica's Canefield Airport is located just five minutes from Roseau and lands small aircraft. The larger Melville Hall airport is located on the northeast coast about 32 miles (51 km), a drive of an hour and fifteen minutes, from town. It is important to note which airport you will be using and plan your check-in times and taxi fares accordingly. The best way to get to Melville Hall from Roseau is to take a shared taxi, EC$42 for the seat. A private taxi costs around EC$130. For Melville Hall transport call Mally's Taxi (809-448-3114 or 448-3360).

There are no direct flights from North America or Europe to Dominica, as the airports cannot land large aircraft. Connections must be made through San Juan and neighbouring islands on LIAT (809-448-2421, Canefield Airport 449-1421, Melville Hall 445-7242), Air Guadeloupe and Air Martinique (809-448-2181), Air Caraibes (809-449-1416, Canefield Airport 449-1629) and Winair (Trois Pitons Travel, 809-448-6977).

The Madikera, a 352-passenger ferry, travels from Roseau to Guadeloupe and Martinique daily, except Tuesday and Thursday. Trois Pitons Travel (809-448-6977) is the agent. Caribia Ferries makes regular connections with Guadeloupe, Martinique and St. Lucia; contact the local agent, Whitchurch Travel (809-448-2181, fax 448-5787).

When leaving Dominica, the departure tax and airport security fees total EC$25.

GETTING AROUND

■ PUBLIC TRANSPORTATION

Taxis are fine for around town, but prohibitive for travelling the island. Touring rates start at EC$45 per hour per car. Buses, which congregate on King George V Street in Roseau, run from point to point and are inexpensive. Buses are fine, and intriguing, if you can figure out the schedules. Most do not make return runs from far points on the island on the same day. That is, if you travel from Roseau for Calibishie, you may not be able to get a return bus until the next day.

■ RENTALS

Most agencies require renters to be 25 years old and, interestingly, no older than 65. Rates start at about US$35 per day and most credit cards are accepted. You'll need a valid driver's license and you will have to purchase a temporary Dominica permit from the police/traffic department, at a cost of EC$20.

Roseau rental companies include: Antours (809-448-6460, fax 448-6780), Avis (809-448-2481, fax 448-0413), Bonus Rentals (809-448-2650) and Budget (809-449-2080).

MONEY, HOURS AND COMMUNICATION

The Eastern Caribbean dollar, currently EC$2.70 = US$1, is Dominica's currency. Several banks are located on the main streets of Roseau and are open 8.00-14.00 Monday through Thursday and 8.00-17.00 Friday.

General business hours are 8.00-13.00 and 14.00-16.00 Monday through Friday and 8.00-13.00 Saturday.

Dominica's telephones use the area code 809. To call the country from North America dial 1 and the area code, plus a seven-digit number. Cable and Wireless on Hanover Street in Roseau is open from 7.00 to 20.00 Monday through Saturday for telephoning and faxing. Local calling cards are available at Cable and Wireless, the post office or at numerous small shops in town.

ENTERTAINMENT
■ SPORTS

Diving has surfaced as one of Dominica's big draws and divers have found the clear and relatively untouched waters to be rife with exotic coral and fish. A U.S.-based magazine, Skin Diver, once declared Dominica to be among the top five dive destinations in the world. The area south of Roseau at Scott's Head and Soufriere Bay is particularly popular. The large reef at Barracuda Point starts at ten feet (three m) below the surface and drops dramatically. An area called Champagne, so named for the bubbles that rise from volcanic hot air vents on the ocean's floor, is a popular night diving spot. In the northwest, the protected areas of Cabrits National Park offer excellent diving.

Your best bet for an organized excursion is one of the oldest companies on the island, Dive Dominica (809-448-2188, fax 448-6088, U.S. 800-544-7631). The owners, Ginette and Derek Perryman, package dive trips with their hotel, Castle Comfort Lodge.

SHOPPING

Dominican crafts are good buys. Aside from the aforementioned Carib Territory kiosks and the Old Market Plaza, mats woven from a special grass called vertivert are produced at Tropicrafts Island Mats (809-448-2747, fax 448-7126). The shop is at the corner of Turkey Lane and Queen Mary Street in Roseau. You can watch the women weaving the mats (please ask permission to take photos) and order one from a chosen design. Tropicrafts is the island agent for UPS and will ship your mat. They also sell straw hats, spices, local rums, bay rum (a body lotion) and other island crafts.

Caribana Handcrafts (809-448-2761) on Cork Street has a large selection of art and local crafts.

For books, magazines and stationery go to Cee Bee's, across from Celia's Snackette on Cork Street, or Paperback Books on King George V Street.

USEFUL ADDRESSES
■ TOURISM

❏ Division of Tourism, National Development Corporation, P.O. Box 73, Roseau, Commonwealth of Dominica, W.I.; 809-448-2351/2186, fax 448-5840.
❏ Dominica Hotel Association, 27 Great Marlborough St., Roseau, Commonwealth of Dominica, W.I.; 809-448-6565, fax 448-2285.
❏ Caribbean Tourism Organization, 20 East 46th St., New York, NY 10017-2452; 212-682-0435, fax 697-4258.

❏ Caribbean Tourism Organization, Suite 3, 15 Vigilant House, 120 Wilton Road, Victoria, London SW1V 1JZ; 071-233-8382, fax 873-8551.

■ OTHER

❏ Police, fire, ambulance emergency, 999.

❏ Princess Margaret Hospital, 448-2231.

❏ American Express agent, Whitchurch Travel, 448-2181, fax 448-5787.

❏ City Drugstore, 448-3198.

❏ Forestry Division, 448-2401, fax 448-7999.

Martinique

Introduction

Large, wealthy and stylized, Martinique is sophisticated in ways unlike its
Antillean sisters. Its rich culture is immersed in the ways of modern France and
the Caribbean, yet defined by a long and harsh history of colonialization. The
Carib Indians called it Madinina, meaning "Island of Flowers." And Columbus is
said to have called it "the most beautiful thing I have ever seen."

The Land

The island's shape strikes one as that of a large-headed, dancing tadpole. Fifty
miles (80 km) long by 22 miles (35 km) wide, the 425 square mile (1,100 sq km)
island has the same area as the city of Phoenix, Arizona. Its northern central part
is characterized by a volcanic mountain range that includes the still-active volcano Mont Pelée, the highest point on the island at 4,660 feet (1,397 m). The
island's center features the low-lying Lamentin plain, also the center of agricultural activity. Smaller hills and sweeping valleys connect this to the mountainous
southern region.

Martinique's Atlantic-facing east coast is irregularly shaped, with hundreds of
small bays, coves and the large Caravelle Peninsula. The island's population of
400,000 is found mostly along the southern coast and western, leeward side of
the island, where the capital of Fort-de-France (pop. 102,000) is located. The natural harbor at Fort-de-France is large and picturesque, the center of commerce on
the island.

History

Columbus may have sighted Martinique in 1493, but it wasn't until his fourth
voyage, in 1502, that he landed at the point now known as Le Carbet, on
Martinique's northwestern coast. He named the island Martinica for St. Martin
and that was about the extent of Spanish involvement on Martinique. The Caribs,
who had already driven off the Arawaks, did not welcome the newcomers and,
after several defeats on the battlefield, the Spanish gave up on the island.

French settlers, under the leadership of Pierre Belain d'Esnambuc, founder of the St. Christopher Company, arrived in 1635 and the following year King Louis XIII authorized the introduction of slaves to France's West Indies possessions. For the next 25 years the French fought the Caribs for the island's control.

In 1660 the Caribs, defeated by superior weaponry, signed a treaty that promised them half the island. Instead the Caribs were killed, or captured and enslaved, and more slaves were imported from Africa. The heirs of d'Esnambuc sold trading rights to their king and France officially annexed the island in 1674. It then became one of the many pawns in the ongoing European battles of the 17th and 18th centuries. From 1762 to 1814 the British occupied the island. In 1815 European treaties restored Martinique to France and accelerated sugarcane production became the economic staple of the island.

While the French Revolution of 1789 diverted attention in Paris, a chain-reaction surge of unrest throughout the French colonies made planters and colonialists uneasy. Slaves outnumbered planters by the tens of thousands. Eventually the British were invited to occupy Martinique again, essentially as a strong-arm security force, from 1794 to 1802. By 1804 a slave revolt in Haiti, led by Toussaint l'Ouverture, had succeeded in turning that colony into the New World's first black republic and nearby French islands took heed. Agitation and revolts plagued the Caribbean plantocracy and calls for the abolition of slavery became louder. Slavery, which had been made illegal several times in the French West Indies' past, only to resurge again (notably with Napoleon's late-18th century rise), was officially and finally outlawed in 1848. Thereafter, thousands of indentured laborers from East India were brought in to work Martinique's declining plantations.

In 1946 Martinique became an overseas department of France and was deemed a region in 1974.

People and Culture

In the early days of slavery, a mixed-race group produced by forced miscegenation, called gens de couleur or free colored, emerged in Martiniquean society. They occupied a peripheral—and confusing—social and economic position between the slave class and the ruling whites. Their presence, in one of the ironies of racial intolerance, served to emphasize and exacerbate racial differences rather than bridge the gap. Gradations of color were defined in the infamous Code Noir of the late 18th century, which outlined nearly 130 degrees of color between white and black. Since white skin was associated with enhanced wealth and social status, this led to some scrambling among the free black population to be classified "up," while the whites endeavored to keep their population "pure." To varying extents this situation existed throughout the West Indies; its ramifications are felt even today.

The mixed-race group plays a significant part in Martinique's middle and upper-middle class economic structure and is evident throughout the population. Still, the majority of the population is black and this group has only recently, as early as the 1920s, become accustomed to political recognition and a strong societal position. Much of the emergent black pride of that era can be attributed to the Négritude movement, which was first articulated among black expatriates in Paris, including the Martiniquean scholar, politician and poet, Aimé Césaire. Négritude called for the recognition and advancement of black cultural values and black heritage worldwide—black humanism—while rejecting French colonial influences.

A smaller but not insignificant group is the whites, both descendants of settlers (bekes) and long-term residents and the so-called "metro" French or short-term workers. Whites have controlled great chunks of the economy in the French Antilles since colonial days and the situation remains, in many ways, unchanged. East Indians, descendants of post-emancipation indentured laborers, also contribute a significant presence to the population.

Martinique's culture is African-based with strong French influence. The dress, food, music and dance, as well as belief systems, are uniquely creole. The island is, in some ways, the sophisticated sister of Guadeloupe and the two islands share characteristics of culture. Religion is primarily Roman Catholic, with others represented, including the ever-pervasive belief that magic and Christianity are not mutually exclusive.

The dance of Martinique is sophisticated and is represented by Les Grands Ballets de la Martinique, one of the Caribbean's most respected dance companies. The popular beguine and zouk are denizens of Fort-de-France's nightclubs. At festivals and carnivals Martiniqueans wear the traditional checkered madras cloth and women's headdress called tete, sort of a turban, and men may be seen wearing a bakoua, a fisherman's straw hat.

Martinique's festivals are colorful, loud and rife with history. Carnival begins on the day after New Year's with weekend events and culminates in dances, marches, contests and feasts on Ash Wednesday.

Several smaller carnivals and cultural festivals take place in Fort-de-France and Sainte-Marie in July. Martinique's Catholic tradition has given each town a patron saint and towns celebrate Saint's Days, from January through July. Saint's

Days feature local sailors racing traditional gommier fishing boats. The name is taken from the word for gumtree, which was traditionally used for the oversized canoe's hollowed-out hull. Today the sleek, 30 foot (ten m) boats are fashioned from lumber and more modern materials.

An International Sailing Week, featuring competitions and exhibitions, is held in March.

Government and Economy

A Prefet, appointed by the French Minister of the Interior, administers the island and a 45 member Conseil Général and 41 member Conseil Regional are the elected legislative bodies in Martinique. The island sends four Deputies and two Senators to the French Parliament. The system is multi-party and includes established parties agitating for independence or greater measures of autonomy from France.

The primary contributor to Martinique's economy is France, by way of direct aid. France supplies more than half of the island's gross income, and the roads, hospitals and social programs of the island are modern and reflective of this input.

Tourism plays a greater part in Martinique's economy today than it did 20 years ago, but is still not the primary industry. Agriculture and agricultural products account for the largest export block, yet employ less than ten per cent of the working population. Main agricultural products are sugarcane, bananas, rum and pineapple, with bananas accounting for half of all agricultural exports. Others are spices, vanilla, some fruit and vegetables and exotic flowers.

Nearly a third of the labor force works in the service industry, which includes tourism. Tourism income is derived from cruise ships, which account for nearly 400,000 visitors per year, and from overnight visitors, numbering 345,000 annually. Most visitors are from France (68 per cent) and other European countries (13 per cent). North America accounts for less than a tenth of all visitors.

Sights

BEACHES
As on most Lesser Antilles islands, the windward Atlantic side of Martinique is irregular and rough in places, while the southern and leeward coasts are quiet and

less frothy. Excellent beaches can be found all around the island. All beaches are open to the public and many feature picnic, shower and other facilities.

On the south coast, from Trois-Ilets to Grande Anse des Salines, the famous beach south of Sainte-Anne, you'll find more than a dozen fine beaches. This is a popular strip, crowded on weekends. Anse des Salines is featured on many a postcard, with palm trees lunging over the sand of the 1.5 mile (2.4 km) crescent beach. This is the southernmost tip of the island, from which you can often see St. Lucia. There is only one road to Salines from Sainte-Anne and you may experience traffic jams on holidays and weekends. Stay on the road past Salines for Anse-Trabaud, an often deserted but lovely beach on the Atlantic coast. Sainte-Anne itself features a beach, which stretches north to the large beach at Club Med.

North of Sainte-Anne is a beach at Pointe Marin, near the town of Le Marin, site of a large marina. Le Diamant is a popular resort town, with the island's longest beach (2.5 miles; four km). The volcanic rock, Rocher du Diamant, about a mile off shore, is a landmark. West of Le Diamant, at Les Anses-d'Arlets and Grande Anse, you'll find several bays and beaches.

Martinique's busiest tourist area is the village of Trois-Ilets and the nearby Pointe du Bout, across the bay from Fort-de-France. Here you'll find large resorts, hotels, marinas, cafes, shops and several beaches. The beaches at the Meridien and Bakoua hotels are nice, but small. The beach at Anse-à-l'Ane also features the nearby Musée de Coquillages, a shellfish museum and gallery.

North of Fort-de-France the beaches are less crowded and the sand becomes darker, due to Mont Pelée, the volcano. Small fishing villages are the norm and dark mountains loom from the center of the island.

North Martinique

The modern history of Martinique starts in the north. Along the coastal road from Fort-de-France, the first town you'll encounter is Schoelcher. Originally called Case-Navire, it is now named after Victor Schoelcher, the 19th century abolitionist. Schoelcher is really a suburb of Fort-de-France and, with its congested streets, looks the part. The University of the French West Indies is located here.

Farther north is Case-Pilote, a small fishing village and one of Martinique's oldest settlements, given the (French) name of a Carib chief. Bellefontaine, another small fishing village, is notable for a boat-shaped house up on the hill. It is also notable for the roughly 11 million cubic feet of earth that slid to the road during a 1981 earthquake. A quick side-trip to Le Morne-Vert will bring you into the hills and an altitude of about 1,200 feet (360 m).

Le Carbet is purported to be the site of Columbus' 1502 landing and a marker on the pier notes the event. The fishing village is one of the oldest on the island, with a church dating to 1645. The town has a honky-tonk sort of feeling, with narrow streets and local restaurants crowded along the beach. Here you'll find the Jardin Zoologique Amazona (596-78-00-64), a small garden and zoo featuring wildcats and snakes from Africa, South America and the Caribbean. Admission is F20, open daily 9.00-18.00.

Just north of Carbet is the Musée Gauguin (596-78-22-66), which features work, letters and memorabilia of Paul Gauguin, from the five months in 1887 the artist spent with friend Charles Laval in Anse Turin. Admission is F10, open daily 10.00-17.30.

The doomed town of Saint-Pierre, destroyed by one of this century's most powerful volcanic blasts, is legendary in the annals of Caribbean history. The settlement was first established at the site of a fortification built by d'Esnambuc and company after their arrival in 1635. It soon became a flourishing town and the capital of the colony. By 1902 it was a sophisticated and bustling city, often called "Little Paris of the Antilles." Then, in late April of that year, residents began to feel the rumbling of Mont Pelée, the 4,660-foot (1,397 m) volcano to the north. Fires were spotted emitting from its dome and frightened animals vacated the area. On 5 May the volcano spewed hot mud and alarmed residents were inclined to evacuate. In a tragically ironic twist, they were encouraged by the colonial government to remain in town to participate in a forthcoming election. Big mistake. On 8 May the volcano exploded—a blast estimated at 40 times greater than that of the atomic bomb over Hiroshima—excoriating the town with hot ash and deadly, noxious steam.

The 29,000 residents were killed in 47 seconds, according to a museum guide. While one wonders how anyone would arrive at such a precise figure, death was nonetheless estimated to be absolute within three minutes. The lone survivor, a drunk named Cyparis, was in jail during the blast, saved by the thick walls of his underground cell. In later years, Cyparis met with a modicum of notoriety and success exhibiting his scars in a side show with the Barnum & Bailey Circus. The volcano erupted several more times that year and last had a major eruption in 1929.

Saint-Pierre was rebuilt but never recovered its former eminence and its residents today number only about 6,000. Remains of the old town, including a church, theater and the cell that saved Cyparis, can be seen. Two museums, both on the main Rue Victor Hugo, record the life of the time: the small Historical Musée Saint-Pierre on the road's west side houses artifacts and photos of the town, pre- and post-eruption, and is open Monday through Saturday 9.30-17.30 and on Sunday 9.00.30-13.00. Admission is F10 for adults, F3 for children. The larger Musée Franck A. Perret (596-78-15-16) is dedicated to the study of the volcano. The photographs are fascinating and on display are melted glass, porcelain, a crunched church bell and even carbonized kitchen items, such as honey and spaghetti. Tours in English are available. Open 9.00-17.00 daily, admission F10.

Mont Pelée itself is accessible if you are determined. Turn inland from Saint-Pierre to Le Mourne Rouge, known for its natural water springs. (Bottled water from Le Mourne Rouge is sold throughout the island.) The carpark here is the starting point for the climb, which will take close to three hours—a map at the carpark shows the route. From the carpark you can see the Atlantic Ocean and Saint-Pierre.

The coastal road continues north from Saint-Pierre to La Precheur, the northernmost village and, literally, the end of the road. Nearby is a hot water springs, courtesy of Mont Pelée, and the northernmost village of Grand' Rivière. There is no direct road to Grand' Rivière and the hike is about five hours, one way.

ATLANTIC COAST

The Atlantic coast is characterized by rough surf and a few picturesque fishing villages. Basse-Pointe, in the north, is notable for being the birthplace of Aimé Césaire, the poet and advocate of Négritude. The area is covered with pineapple and banana plantations and the restored Plantation de Leyritz features a hotel and museum of doll sculptures made from plant leaves. In the relatively large town of Sainte-Marie you can visit the Saint-James Rum Distillery and Musée du Rhum (596-69-30-02). You'll get a good history of the sugarcane and rum industries here. Admission is free, as is the rum-tasting. Open 9.00-13.00 and 14.00-16.30 Monday through Friday and 9.00-12.00 on weekends.

Farther south is La Trinité, a small town at the foot of the Caravelle Peninsula. Much of the peninsula's land is protected and you'll find opportunities for hiking and swimming at Anse l'Etang. Stop at Chateau Dubuc, the ruins of a 1773 castle, once inhabited by one of the island's settlers. It is now a park, open daily 8.30-12.30 and 14.30-17.30, Saturdays 8.00-12.00; admission is F5.

Farther south is the vast Lamentin plains area, where much of the island's arable land is located. Le Vauclin, the southernmost coastal town on the windward side, sits at the base of Mont Vauclin, at 1,654 feet (496 m) the highest point in the southern mountain range. This is an important fishing village and a good place to buy fresh seafood.

SOUTH MARTINIQUE

Aside from the coastal and beach attractions, the southern part of the island features several interesting historical and natural sites worth stopping for. In Trois-Ilets, the small village across the bay from Fort-de-France, you'll find the Musée de la Pagerie (596-68-34-55), where Napoleon's Empress Josephine (given name Marie-Josephe Rose Tascher de la Pagerie) was born in 1763. A garden and the main buildings, partially destroyed by fire, and the ruins of a sugar plantation comprise the museum, where you can see her bed, love letters from Napoleon and antique furnishings. The museum is open Tuesday through Friday 9.00-17.30 and weekends 9.00-13.00 and 14.30-17.30. Admission is F20 for adults, F5 for children.

Also in Trois-Ilets is the Musée de la Canne (596-68-32-04), a sugarcane museum, in the restored buildings of an old distillery. The museum is open every day except Monday from 9.00-17.30, admission is F15. Nearby, stop at The Pottery (596-68-17-12), a working artisans center.

In Rivière-Pilote, inland from the coastal town of Sainte-Luce, tour another rum museum at Le Mauny Distillery (596-62-62-08). Rivière-Pilote is also known for one of the island's more popular cockfighting "pitts," at Clery (596-62-61-69), open Sundays at 14.30.

Fort-de-France

Fort-de-France, with nearly a quarter of the island's population, is a relatively large city by Lesser Antilles standards. The downtown area, fronting the Baie des Flamands, has an Old World feel, with narrow streets, iron-balustrated buildings, and markets, cafes, banks, taxis and people competing for space. Congested suburbs are visible in the hills surrounding town and nowhere is the striking view more complete than when crossing the bay by ferry, from Pointe du Bout to the south.

Located on a large natural harbor, Fort-de-France is now the economic and cultural center of the island and became the capital after Mont Pelée's obliteration of Saint-Pierre in 1902. The town was originally called Fort Royal and was developed around the large Fort Saint-Louis, which dominates the waterfront. The fort is still used by the French Navy, but is occasionally open for tours.

Downtown is easily covered by foot and the 12-acre La Savane is a good place to start. Located across from Fort Saint-Louis, the park is filled with palms, gardens, fountains and benches and is often the site of public gatherings and concerts. A bronze statue of d'Esnambuc, leader of the island's first European settlers, and a white marble statue of native daughter Empress Josephine are located on the western side. As of this writing the Empress had suffered an unfortunate accident or dark practical joke—her head was missing. East of the park is the Baie du Carenage and the cruise ship pier. At the height of the season Fort-de-France accepts an average of three cruise ships per day, which inevitably adds a sort of frenzied quality to the town. A market, adjacent to La Savane, sells T-shirts, wraps, art and other items and is particularly busy during cruise ship stopovers. You'll find other markets in town; a walk west along Rue Lamartine will bring you to a large fruit and vegetable market; two blocks north on Rue François Arago is a fish market. Fish are unloaded straight from boats on the Rivière Madame. Markets are open daily, but Friday and Saturday are busiest.

On Rue Ernest Deproge, which runs perpendicular to the park, you can find the tourism office (596-63-79-60, fax 73-66-93). The office is very helpful and can provide brochures and information in English. The Air France building is located in the same complex.

A walk up Rue de la Liberte, along La Savane's west side, will bring you past the main post office and the telephone company. Across from the post office, facing the park, is the Musée d'Archeologie Precolombienne et de Prehistoire de la Martinique (596-71-57-05). The museum features pottery, beads, bones, maps and artifacts from Martinique's Arawak and Carib periods, as well as exhibits exploring the slavery and colonial days. Open 9.00-13.00 and 14.00-17.00 daily except Saturday afternoon, admission F15. Turn west on Rue Blenac to the central square, Place Labat, to see the Saint-Louis Cathedral. The Romanesque church, completed in 1895, was designed by Henri Pick, a contemporary of Gustave Eiffel, architect of the Eiffel Tower.

At the corner of Rue de la Liberte and Rue Victor Severe is the extravagantly baroque Bibliotheque Schoelcher (596-70-26-67), another Henri Pick creation. The Byzantine-style library, trimmed with iron and majolica tiles, was built for the 1889 Paris Exposition, then later dismantled and shipped to Martinique, where it was reassembled in 1893. Named for the abolitionist and writer Victor Schoelcher, the now-public library holds an extensive collection of his books.

Farther west along Rue Victor Severe is the ornate Hotel de Ville, once a city hall and now a municipal theater. Still farther west, just north of the fish market, is the Parc Floral et Culturel (596-71-66-25). The gardens and galleries document many of the 2,800 plant species found in Martinique. Open 9.00-12.00 and 14.00-17.00 daily, except Sunday.

Main shopping areas, which include duty-free shops, curio shops, banks and some of the Lesser Antilles' finest patisseries and cafes, are found in the city blocks bordered by Rue Victor Hugo and Rue de la Liberte. Rue Victor Schoelcher is the heart of the shopping district.

Practical Information

ACCOMMODATION

■ GENERAL

Hotel reservations can be made through Centrale de Reservation (BP 823, 97208 Fort-de-France, Martinique, F.W.I.; 596-71-56-11, fax 73-66-93).

About 50 small hotels, grouped under the umbrella name Relais Creoles, are good bets for inexpensive accommodation. Gîtes, which are small villas, apartments or studios, often located in private homes, can also be inexpensive and can put you in touch with a local family, certainly a good way to experience Martinique. Contact Gîtes de France (Tourism Office, 610 Fifth Ave., New York, NY 10020, 212-315-0726; or in Martinique, 596-73-67-92) or Centrale de Reservation for a complete list of gîtes.

Villas are also available throughout the countryside and may be prove to be inexpensive for large parties. Some accommodate as many as eight people. The tourist office operates a rental service that will help locate villas: Office Départementale du Tourism, Service de location de Villas (BP 520, 97206 Fort-de-France, Martinique, F.W.I.; 596-63-79-60, fax 73-66-93). English is spoken.

■ CAMPING

Camping facilities can be found at: Tropicamp (596-62-49-66), Vivre & Camper (596-76-72-79, fax 76-97-82), Courbaril Campsites (596-68-32-30) and Le Nid Tropical (596-68-31-20), all along the Sainte-Anne to Anse-à-l'Ane strip on the southwest coast.

For camping van rentals call West Indies Tours (596-54-50-71).

■ HOTELS

❑ LA BAKOUA (596-66-02-02, fax 66-00-41; U.S. 800-221-4542 or 212-575-2262, fax 719-6763), which takes its name from the traditional straw hat worn by fisherman, is located at Point du Boat and the view across the bay to Fort-de-France, especially at night, is worth lingering over a ti punch. This may be the most luxurious hotel on the island and located in the thick of it all. Luxury.

❑ LE MERIDIEN TROIS-ILETS (596-66-00-00, fax 66-00-74; U.S. 800-543-4300 or 212-245-2920) is located next to the Bakoua and shares beachfront. This is a big hotel, imposing, but in a great location. Luxury.

❑ LA PAGERIE (596-66-05-30, fax 66-00-99; U.S. 800-221-4542), another Point
du Bout hotel, is minutes from the water and the Fort-de-France ferry.
Moderate.

❑ HOTEL DIAMANT LES BAINS (596-76-40-14, fax 76-27-00) has 24 rooms and
bungalows set on a garden overlooking the beach at Diamant. Homey, simple
and local—you will encounter fewer tourists here than other places—and a
great restaurant. Moderate.

❑ CHEZ JULOT (596-74-40-93) in Vauclin, on the windward side, is modest (ten
rooms), inviting and secluded. Inexpensive-moderate.

EATING

❑ LE FROMAGER (596-78-19-07), in the hills overlooking Saint-Pierre and the bay,
is the place to stop while taking an island tour. The view and breeze alone are
worth it. This place is very popular on weekends with Martiniqueans and is
likely to be crowded. Give yourself some time. The feroce d'avocat, a spicy
avocado and saltfish appetizer, is very good. Lunch daily, dinner Thursday
through Saturday. Moderate-expensive.

❑ DAVIDIANA (596-66-00-54), at the Point du Bout Marina, has a pub feel to it
and serves seafood and creole dishes. Inexpensive-moderate.

In Fort-de-France, the sheer number of restaurants, sidewalk cafes and patisseries could keep you busy for a long while. Try LE LAFAYETTE (596-63-24-09) at
the hotel of the same name. The upstairs restaurant overlooks the Savane.
Expensive. LA CASE (596-63-04-00) serves French, Italian and creole, just right
for an elegant night out. Moderate-expensive.

For a comprehensive list of Martinique's restaurants consult Ti Gourmet, available at the tourist office.

GETTING THERE

Lamentin Airport (596-51-51-51) accommodates dozens of international arrivals
daily, including American Airlines (596-51-12-29), Air Canada (596-51-29-81),
Air France (596-55-33-00), Air Martinique (596-51-09-90 or 60-00-23), Air
Guadeloupe (596-51-51-51) and LIAT (596-51-10-00).

GETTING AROUND
■ ON MARTINIQUE

Taxis are not metered and set rates are determined by a regulating agency; the
driver should have a rate list and rates are often posted at taxi stands. Most taxis
offer touring excursions, for one to four persons, at about F800 for a tour of the

north, F600 for a tour of the Atlantic coast and about F700 for a tour of the south.
Taxis are found in Fort-de-France on Boulevard Alfassa and Rue Ernest Deproge, but if you need to call try Radio Taxis (63-10-10) or Radio Tele (63-63-62). Both offer 24 hour service.
Taxis collectif (collective taxis or minibuses) are identified by a "TC" on the license plate and function as buses. The main bus station is at Pointe-Simon, Fort-de-France. The inter-city bus station is located on Boulevard Général de Gaulle. Buses run until 18.00.
Ferries cross regularly from Point du Boat, Anse-à-l'Ane and Anse Mitan to Fort-de-France. The crossing takes 25 minutes and is much more pleasant than driving or hiring a taxi to go to town. In fact, it's fun. Return fare from Point du Boat is F25 for adults and F11 for children. Schedules are available at all hotels.

■ RENTALS
Rental agencies are plentiful and competitive (rates start at US$30 per day), major credit cards are accepted and drivers must be 21. Call Thrifty (596-51-03-73 or 66-09-59), Europcar (596-51-20-33 or 51-01-96), Hertz (596-60-64-64 or 51-01-01), Avis (596-51-17-70 or 51-45-62 or 70-11-60), Eurodollar (596-51-66-21 or 63-54-54) or Budget (596-63-69-00).
Rent motor scooters from Funny (Fort-de-France tel. 63-33-05 or Point du Bout tel. 66-04-57) or Sunset (596-66-04-27). Rates start at US$20 per day.

■ INTER-ISLAND FERRIES
Caribbean Express (596-63-12-11, fax 70-50-75) operates weekly connections to Guadeloupe and Dominica during the summer, when demand is low, and five weekly departures in the winter. The new and speedy Caribia Ferries (31 Rue Lamartine, no phone) carries automobiles and up to 1,200 passengers. Very comfortable and sleeping cabins are available. The basic route connects Guadeloupe, Dominica, Martinique and St. Lucia. One way fare is F150-190. Fares for children, 4 to 11 years old, are half price.

MONEY, HOURS AND COMMUNICATION
The French franc is the legal tender, but U.S. and Canadian dollars and some European currencies are widely used. Still, it's best to use francs, if only for the better exchange rate you'll get at banks or exchange centers. Currently, the rate is F5.5 = US$1.

Banks and exchange bureaus are found at the airport, throughout Fort-de-France, in Trois-Ilets and major towns. Hours vary, but banks are generally open 8.00-12.00 and 14.00-17.00 and many are closed Wednesday and Saturday afternoon. General business hours include a mid-day lunch closing and some Wednesday afternoon closings. Much of Martinique closes down on Sunday. Public telephones utilize the phone-card system, although some coin phones are available. Phone cards may be bought at cafes, some bookstores and small shops. The international country code for Martinique is 596. From the U.S. dial 011, plus 596 and the six-digit number.

ENTERTAINMENT

■ SPORTS

Watersports, including diving, snorkelling, water skiing and glass-bottomed boat excursions are almost always available at major hotels and marinas. Otherwise, the Point du Bout Marina and the marina at the Meridien hotel in Trois-Ilets are good places to start. Bathy's Club (596-66-00-00) at the Meridien organizes scuba diving and deep-sea fishing excursions. The scuba-diving outfit Planete Bleue (596-66-08-79) is located at Point du Bout.

Sailing charters: Caraibe Evasion (596-66-02-85) and Soleil et Voile (596-66-09-14) at the Point du Bout Marina.

Horseback riding: Ranch Jack (596-68-63-97) at Anses d'Arlets and Black Horse Ranch (596-66-03-46) in Trois-Ilets.

Tennis: try hotels first. The Meridien, Bakoua, Plantation Leyritz and others all have courts. Many private clubs allow day players. For information call La Ligue Regionale de Tennis (596-51-08-00) in Lamentin.

Golf: Golf de l'Imperatrice Josephine (596-68-32-81, fax 68-38-97), also called the Empress Josephine Golf Course, is an 18-hole course, designed by Robert Trent Jones Sr., in Trois-Ilets. Fully equipped pro shop and lighted tennis courts as well.

Hiking and biking: contact the Parc Naturel Regional (596-73-19-30). The park department publishes a guide, Guide de la Randondee, which outlines the island's trails and hikes. Cost is about F30. Biking tours can be organized by VT Tilt (596-66-01-01) in Point du Bout.

■ OTHER

Nightlife is the domain of hotels and activities run the gamut from mellow jazz bars to steel band and limbo-fueled rev-ups. The bands are often very good.

In Fort-de-France the New Hippo, on Boulevard Allegre, is the happening place for disco-driven dancing. Swing Club, on Rue François Arago, and Le Coco

Loco, on Rue Ernest Deproge, with a piano bar, are less hectic. The Hotel
Meridien hosts the island's big casino, which is open from 21.00 until about 3.00
(a picture ID is needed to enter, and admission is F70).

Several hotels (Bakoua and Meridien, among others) feature regular performances by Les Grands Ballets de la Martinique, thought by many to be one of the
Caribbean's finest folk-dance troupes. A very polished and professional group,
their repertoire includes singing, drumming, storytelling and traditional dancing.
Not to be missed.

USEFUL ADDRESSES

■ TOURISM

❏ Office Départementale Du Tourisme de la Martinique, Blvd. Alfassa, 97206
Fort-de-France, Martinique, F.W.I.; 596-63-79-60, fax 73-66-93.

❏ French West Indies Tourist Board, 610 Fifth Ave., New York, NY 10020; 212-
315-0726, fax 247-6468.

❏ Martinique Tourist Office, 1981 Ave. McGill College, Montreal, Quebec H3A
2W9; 514-844-8566, fax 844-8906.

■ OTHER

❏ Police emergency, 17.

❏ Police, Fort-de-France, 55-30-00.

❏ Fire emergency, 18.

❏ Ambulance, 71-59-48.

❏ Lamentin Airport, 51-51-51.

❏ Federal Express, 75-56-56.

St. Lucia

The Land

Lush St. Lucia (LOO-sha), thrust up from the ocean floor eons ago by underwater volcanic activity, exhibits many of the same physical characteristics of the neighbouring islands of St. Vincent, Martinique and Dominica. Sharp, dramatic peaks loom over the middle of the island, where high altitudes create rain and nourishing mist, generating woodlands and mountain primordial rainforests. The volcanic peaks culminate in the southwestern part of the island with the 3,118-foot (936 m) Mt. Gimie, the landmarks Petit Piton and Gros Piton and the semi-active volcano at Soufriere.

The windward, Atlantic side of the island features shorter volcanic peaks and an irregular, pounded coastline. Small bays and inlets provide shelter for villages, fishermen and beach-goers, but the population is, compared to the leeward side, less dense.

Mangrove wetlands and woodlands are found inland from the sea and flat plains spread out near the base of the central mountains, where many of St. Lucia's large banana plantations are located.

The variety of the land supports a disparate array of localized plants and animals, including the endemic St. Lucia tree lizard and the pygmy gecko. The fer-de-lance, a poisonous snake, is found in isolated sections of the countryside. The large and colorful St. Lucian parrot was revered by the Caribs. Also seen, though less frequently these days, are turtles and the agouti and manicou. Migratory and indigenous birds make their homes in the rainforests, mangrove swamps (St. Lucian oriole and black finch, among others) and outlying islets of the country. At the Fregate Islands Nature Reserve, off the central eastern coast, you can see nesting frigate birds and many other species.

The Forestry Division (809-450-2231) and National Trust (809-452-5005) organize lectures, guided tours and cross-island hikes for those interested in viewing the natural environment. St. Lucia's protected reserves include the Edmond Forest Reserve, Quilesse Forest Reserve, Marine National Park, Pigeon Island National Historic Park, Savannes Bay Nature Reserve and Maria Islands Nature Reserve.

The triangular island measures roughly 27 miles (43 km) long, 14 miles (22 km) at its widest point and is 238 square miles (616 sq km) in area, which makes it slightly smaller than Dominica. St. Lucia lies in the Windward Islands chain, separated from Martinique by the 25 mile (40 km) St. Lucia Channel to the north and from St. Vincent by the 20 mile (32 km) St. Vincent Channel to the south.

History

St. Lucia's early history follows a pattern similar to most of the southern Lesser Antilles islands. The Stone Age Ciboney are assumed to have existed, but left few artifacts. The Amerindian Arawaks and related tribes arrived in several waves from regions of South America, from 500 BC until the time of Christ. Remnants of their villages have been found at Pigeon Island, to the north. Nearly 800 years later they were followed, or chased, by the Caribs, a fierce and warlike tribe. The Caribs either eliminated, assimilated or drove out the Arawaks, or perhaps a combination of all three, but the recorded fact is that at the time of Columbus' late 15th-century journeys to the New World, Caribs inhabited St. Lucia, the land they called Iouanalao, meaning "Land of Iguanas." The word was later modified to Hiwanarau, then to Hewanorra, which is still used on the island today.

At one time historians believed that Columbus sighted St. Lucia during his fourth and last voyage, in 1502. It is now believed that Columbus never landed and probably never even sighted the island. No references to it exist in his logs and the name itself refers to St. Lucie, an Italian saint whose feast day is 13 December—a day when Columbus was nowhere near the island. According to one theory, a Spaniard named Juan de la Cosa, who sailed with Columbus on his first two voyages, took up exploring himself and sighted the island, naming it El Falcon. The island appears on Vatican maps around 1520, named St. Lucia.

Over the next 100 years several attempts were made by French and Dutch explorers to settle the island, but all were repelled by the Caribs. In 1600 the Dutch managed to set up a small defense position, Vieux-Fort, in the south of the island, but that, too, met with calamity at the hands of the indignant indigenes. In 1605 a shipload of 67 British settlers on their way to Guiana was blown off course and landed on St. Lucia. After purchasing huts from the Caribs, they apparently made a grave mistake and several weeks later the surviving 19 settlers escaped in Carib canoes. Fifty years later the French, due to their burgeoning strength on neighbouring islands, claimed St. Lucia for France.

In a 1651 transaction the French monarch sold St. Lucia to a governor of neighbouring Martinique, M. du Parquet, who, along with a partner, proceeded to settle the island. Nine years later the British returned to establish sovereignty.

Hostilities broke out between the two and, over the next 150 years, St. Lucia changed hands 14 times—score seven for France and seven for the British. So titanic and prolonged was this struggle that St. Lucia is often referred to as "Helen of the West Indies," after the Helen of Trojan War fame.

During this lengthy conflict each group in turn used the Caribs as either bait or mercenaries. The continual position of being the battered middlemen, coupled with the colonists' stringent efforts to convert them from their heathen ritualistic behavior to the apparently non-heathen non-ritualistic behavior of Christianity, gradually reduced Carib population. Finally they could offer little resistance, whereupon the British, while they were in power, gathered up the remaining Caribs and shipped them off to Dominica's Carib reservation (now called Carib Territory).

Soufriere was the first town, and capital, of the island, established by the French in 1746. The French introduced sugarcane and, ultimately, the first African slaves. Continued hostilities between the British and French, however, prevented the sugarcane industry from becoming the major enterprise it was on other islands.

The 1814 Treaty of Paris finally ceded St. Lucia to the British, who held onto it from then on. Here again, the pattern is familiar. A period of prosperity, for the plantation owners at any rate, followed, until the abolition of slavery in 1834. In 1838, after a period of indentured servitude by former slaves, St. Lucia became part of the British Windward Islands, with its seat of government in Barbados, but by then the economy was adrift and the plantations in disarray.

In the 1860s coal warehousing became a major island industry and laborers were imported from East India to shore up the shrinking labor force. But widespread use of oil and diesel in the 1930s and 1940s weakened that industry and, with sugarcane on the decline, St. Lucia entered the 1950s as an economic backwater. This hastened the formation of trade and labor unions, and later political parties, as the country agitated for more say in its governance.

Universal adult suffrage was granted in 1951. St. Lucia joined the West Indies Federation in 1958, until fours years later the withdrawal of Jamaica and Trinidad and Tobago dissolved the entity. A new constitution was approved in 1960 and in 1967 self-government was granted. Political parties such as the St. Lucia Labor Party (SLP) and the United Workers Party (UWP) vied for power over that period.

Independence came on 22 February 1979 and St. Lucia became an independent state within the British Commonwealth, under the official name of the State of St. Lucia.

People and Culture

St. Lucia's population is 151,000, of which 57,000 live in the capital of Castries. The majority is of African descent, but East Indians, Chinese, Europeans and variations on those themes complete the mosaic of modern St. Lucia.

The legacy of Britain and France's 200 year tug of war with St. Lucia has endowed the island with a mild schizophrenia of identity. Is it "Mount" Gimie or "Morne" Gimie? Not that St. Lucians worry much about it, but travelers from the cold north may wonder just where they are. The government is based on a British system, but the official language is English; the Queen is highly regarded, but the culture is distinctly French creole.

The first indicator is language. Schools, newspapers, government and some maps conduct their business in very proper English. But at home and on the streets and in the rum shops, St. Lucians speak Patois, a Creole laced with French and West African grammar and vocabulary, as well as some English and Spanish. Some St. Lucians speak only Patois and public forums, such as certain court cases, are conducted in Patois.

Place names are French. The country is 90 per cent Roman Catholic and saints' days are honoured. Carnival, the pre-Lenten round of debauchery, song and dance, is French in origin. Even the local music, heavily dosed with calypso and reggae, features the zouk and beguine that are popular in the French departments.

Traditional music, much of it springing from the harsh days of slavery, includes work and game songs and festival tunes. Those interested in traditional St. Lucian music might want to search local record stores for "Musical Traditions of St. Lucia," compiled by an academic group, Folk Research Center of St. Lucia, and recorded at the Smithsonian Institution in Washington, D.C.

It would be an understatement to say that poet and playwright Derek Walcott put St. Lucia on the map for quite a few people when he won the 1992 Nobel Prize in Literature. Born on St. Lucia in 1930, Walcott is recognized for his compelling and lyrical use of the English language. His works include the 1990 epic Omeros, a broad narrative that mixes Homeric legend with West Indian themes. Selected Poems 1964 and Selected Poems 1977 are good introductions to his greater body of work. In 1959 Walcott, who lives and teaches in Boston, established the Trinidad Theater Workshop in Port of Spain. On his native St. Lucia he has created an international writers' retreat called the Rat Island Foundation, located off the coast of Castries.

Walcott was not the first St. Lucian to win a Nobel Prize. The economist Sir Arthur Lewis (1915-91) shared the 1979 prize in economics with American Theodore Shultz. Lewis, a vice-chancellor of the regional University of the West Indies. They helped develop the Caribbean Development Bank and co-founded the United Nations Development Project.

FESTIVALS

St. Lucia's Carnival, Jounen Kweyol in Patois, gains momentum and energy during the two days preceding Ash Wednesday. While not as large or as infamous as Trinidad's Carnival, the St. Lucia bash, centered in Castries, is a frenetic marathon of dancing, street masquerading, calypsoing (including the Calypso King contests), feasting and wild partying—it's an experience you'll remember.

Other festivals include the 22 February Independence Day celebrations and the saints days La Rose (Feast of the Rose of Lima, 30 August) and La Marguerite (Feast of St. Margaret Mary Alacoque, 17 October).

The St. Lucia International Jazz Festival, first held in 1992, has already attracted some of the jazz world's biggest names, including Herbie Hancock, Nancy Wilson, Earl Klugh, Wayne Shorter, George Benson and Trinidadian pan artist Len "Boogsie" Sharpe. In mid-May look for the four-day event at the Cultural Center on the outskirts of Castries, at Pigeon Island and various other venues around the country.

Government and Economy

St. Lucia's economy, historically agriculture-based, at first relied on sugarcane but, due to the French-British conflicts, the island's early plantations never achieved the output of neighbouring islands, such as Barbados.

During the late 19th and early 20th centuries, a time when the world's shipping lines were converting from sail-driven ships to steam, coal was an important commodity. The ships needed good harbors within established shipping lanes for loading coal and the Port of Castries was one of them. By 1911 three major coal companies had opened their fuel operations in St. Lucia. When the world converted to petroleum products in the Thirties, a once-rich source of income for St. Lucians was lost.

About that time bananas began to attract worldwide attention and St. Lucia, along with its neighbours, stepped up production. Bananas continue to be the main crop, along with coffee, cocoa, citrus fruit and coconut. Four-fifths of the island's economic activity centres around the banana industry, which accounted for US$66 million in 1992.

St. Lucia's main trading partner is the U.K. Preferential prices for bananas have been given to Commonwealth countries of the Caribbean, but, with the formation of the European Economic Community, that is due to change within the decade. The banana crop will be forced to compete on a wider, open market. In 1993 a conflict over prices between the St. Lucia Banana Growers Association and farmers resulted in riots, in which two farmers died. The prime minister disbanded the SLBGA, but the problem appears to looming for future resolve.

Tourism may be an answer, of sorts, to the country's economic future. Tourist arrivals grew threefold in the decade since 1982, a trend St. Lucia hopes will continue. In 1992 353,671 visitors spent at least one night in the country; the majority were from other Caribbean islands, followed by the U.K., U.S. and Canada. Cruise ships arrivals average 320 per year, up from 88 in 1982. The number of hotel rooms has doubled to 2,660 over the same period. Tourism growth has been steady, yet opposition from groups such as the National Trust, who have agitated for environmental impact studies, has also been steady.

St. Lucia is an independent member of the Commonwealth, which makes the British monarch the titular head of state. The Queen is represented on the island by the governor general and power is vested in the prime minister. The island's bicameral legislature comprises an 17 member House of Assembly, elected from the nation's electoral districts, and an 11 member Senate.

Sights

The island's most popular beaches and bays lie along its leeward coast, which is also where, not incidentally, the majority of the resorts, hotels and towns are found as well. The coast on the windward side of the island tends to be rough and offers few beach opportunities.

Several of the best beaches are Pigeon Point in the north, Reduit Beach at Rodney Bay, Vigie Beach near the airstrip, Choc Bay just north of Vigie and La Toc Bay south of Castries.

The drive south from Castries passes through rolling hills and dramatic valleys and the ocean is almost always in sight.

On the south side of Castries is the elevated Morne Fortune, with striking views of the harbor and of Vigie Peninsula and the north coast beyond. You can see Martinique and, to the south, the Pitons, from a viewing platform crowded with craft and snack vendors. This hill's strategic position was the site of several battles between the French and British. Farther up the road note the Victorian Government House, official residence of the governor general. Beyond are remnants of Fort Charlotte, which now houses Ministry of Education offices and the Sir Arthur Lewis Community College. A great battle was fought here in 1776 and a monument commemorates the victorious Royal Inniskilling Fusiliers, who deserve a monument just for carrying that name around. The views alone are worth the drive up.

Farther south is Marigot, a small resort and fishing village and a favourite docking spot for yachties. Anse La Raye is another small fishing village, dominated by the impressive Church of the Nativity of Our Blessed Virgin. The town green fronts a small beach, chock full of fishing boats and drying nets, a colorful scene.

Just south of Marigot is Soufriere, the oldest town on the island, dating back to 1746, and once the French capital. The town's small bay is picturesque and the looming half-mile high Pitons, thrusting straight out of the sea, dominate the setting. Soufriere was used for scenes in the 1984 movie *Water*, starring Michael Caine. The surrounding area features nutrient-rich soil, due to past volcanic activity, and is still known for its many small farms and plantations.

Nearby is the semi-active volcano and the Sulphur Springs. Billed as the world's only drive-in volcano, the crater features seven acres filled with bubbling, stinking pools of hot, sulfurous water. A guide from the tourist board can escort you. Admission is EC$5.

The nearby Soufriere Estate was given to the Devaux family by Louis IV in 1713. The family, which was responsible for much of the development in the area, still owns the estate and allows tours. The Diamond Botanical Gardens, Waterfalls and Mineral Bath (809-452-4759), adjoining the estate, are also worth a stop. The mineral baths, believed to have curative powers, were built by Louis XVI for his soldiers, but destroyed during the French Revolution. They were restored in the 1960s. The entrance fee is EC$5.

Farther south you'll find a Carib crafts center at Choiseul. Vieux-Fort, the island's second-largest town and location of Hewanorra International Airport, is located at the southernmost point on the island. On a clear day you can see St. Vincent to the south. The two Maria Islands (Major and Minor) comprise a nature reserve and are home to several rare species of lizards and snakes, including the couresse, reputedly the world's rarest snake. The Maria Island Interpretive Center charges a small fee and is open Wednesday through Sunday, 9.00-17.00. The nearby Savannes Bay is noted for a large mangrove swamp and nature reserve.

On the east coast of the island you'll find the Fregate Island Nature Reserve, which is closed during the breeding season of the frigate birds, from May to July. Call the National Trust (see below) for information. From Dennery the main road cuts northwest across the island to Castries, past the giant national Forest Reserve.

North of Castries the coastal sand lightens in color and resorts start to pop out like cats on mice. This is beach country and the coast is dense with tourist activity. The northwestern town of Gros Islet is set on the large natural harbor of Rodney Bay, from which, in 1782, Admiral Lord George Rodney launched his famous attack on the French forces of Admiral de Grasse at the Battle of the Saints. The victory virtually assured the British of a continued presence in the Caribbean from then on. Gros Islet is known for its 1,000 boat capacity marina and for a popular Friday night street party, a jump-up complete with music, dancing, fast food and late-night goings-on.

North of Gros Ilet is Pigeon Point and the Pigeon Island National Historic Park. A manmade causeway now connects the island to the mainland and the beach there is long and inviting. The island, administered by the National Trust, opened as a park in 1979, after having been the site of a fort, a World War II U.S. military base and a privately leased island. Arawak artifacts were found here and Pigeon Island is believed to have been a stronghold for the pirate François Leclerc, also known as Jambe de Bois (Wooden Leg). The 40-acre park features remains of an officers' mess and Fort Rodney, the British armament. The National Trust has opened a small museum; entrance is EC$3. A guided 90 minute tour costs EC$10 and the park is open daily, 9.00-17.00.

The northern road ends at Pointe du Cap, but further exploration is possible with a 4WD vehicle. The island you see from Pointe du Cap is Martinique.

St. Lucians believe that, in the area called Paix Bouche in the northeast, the girl who would grow up to be Empress Josephine was born. Martiniqueans would dispute that. The dates are unclear and proof is more a matter of national pride than fact, but St. Lucians contend, based on the memories of priests of the late 18th century, that Josephine was conceived in Martinique, born in St. Lucia and, after living here for seven years, returned to Martinique with her family.

Castries

The capital city of St. Lucia burned to the ground in spectacular fires in 1796 and in 1948. Reconstruction after the 1948 fire gave the town its modern look, which features concrete as the dominant medium. The area of Brazil Street, at the south side of downtown, contains striking examples of older buildings that managed to escape the fires.

The town, population 57,000, was relocated from the nearby northern peninsula of Vigie in 1768 and named Castries after a French colonial official. The centerpiece is Derek Walcott Square, formerly Columbus Square, bordered by Brazil, Micoud, Bourbon and Laborie streets. Here you'll find some of the town's older buildings, a monument to St. Lucia's war dead and a huge 400-year-old saman tree, also known as a rain tree (its leaves are so thick and plentiful that, after a downpour, the tree continues to "rain" for a time).

At the eastern end of the square is the remarkable Cathedral of the Immaculate Conception. Construction began in the mid-1800s, but was not finished until the late 19th century. The church is large and plain on the outside, but step inside the cavernous interior for a study in diffused yellow light from ceiling portals and detailed mahogany inlay and woodwork. The church became a cathedral in 1957 and was visited by Pope John Paul II in 1986. The ceiling paintings of various saints feature Saint Lucie in the center.

A few blocks north from the square, across Jeremie Street, is the iron-framed public market, constructed in 1894. The nearby New Castries Market, at Jeremie and High, features a large selection of fruits, vegetables and crafts. The markets are busiest on Saturday morning.

The Pointe Seraphine shopping and duty-free center, built on the cruise ship dock north of the port, features the types of shops you'd expect cruise ships passengers to be directed to. The Sunshine Bookshop (809-452-3222) sells a wide range of British and U.S. newspapers, including the Miami Herald and the New York Times.

Practical Information

ACCOMMODATION

■ GENERAL

Villas are often the best sort of accommodation for families and can include a maid, a cook and a car. For villa and apartment rentals call Tropical Villas (P.O. Box 189, Castries, St. Lucia, W.I.; 809-452-8240, fax 452-8089, Canada 800-387-1201, Florida and California 800-387-2726, New York 800-387-2715, U.S. 800-387-2720) or Preferred Properties (Rodney Bay, St. Lucia, W.I.; 809-452-0732, fax 452-0401).

No facilities exist for campers and security cannot be guaranteed if you simply pitch a tent on a beach. No one is precisely sure whether camping is illegal, but it is definitely not encouraged. For a complete list of island hotels and guesthouses contact the St. Lucia Hotel and Tourism Association, P.O. Box 545, Castries, St. Lucia, W.I. (809-452-5978, fax 452-7967) or the tourist board (below).

All rooms are subject to an eight per cent tax and many add a ten per cent service charge.

■ HOTELS

❏ WINDJAMMER LANDING, P.O. Box 1504, Castries, St. Lucia, W.I. (809-452-0913, fax 452-0907, U.S. 800-743-9609, Canada 416-484-4864, U.K. 044-453-83-5801) sits on a 55-acre hill overlooking Labrelotte Bay, midway between Castries and Gros Ilet. The accommodation is white stucco, self-contained villas of up to four bedrooms. With stunning views, three restaurants, several pools (including villa plunge pools), a fine beach and programs for children, this is one of the island's best resorts, almost reason enough to go. Luxury.

❏ JALOUSIE PLANTATION, P.O. Box 251, Soufriere, St. Lucia, W.I. (809-459-7666, fax 459-7667, North America 800-877-3643, fax 305-858-4667), is an all-inclusive resort set between the Pitons, near Soufriere. The accommodation is in luxury cottages and suites and the resort provides a spa-type atmosphere, featuring saunas, hot tubs, private pools, massage and more. Luxury.

❏ THE ROYAL ST. LUCIAN, P.O. Box 977, Castries, St. Lucia, W.I. (809-452-0999, fax 452-6939, U.S. 800-668-1775, UK 081-741-5333) overlooks Reduit Beach in Gros Ilet and offers 98 luxury suites and fine restaurants. Luxury.

❏ HUMMINGBIRD BEACH RESORT, Soufriere, St. Lucia, W.I. (809-454-7232, fax 459-7033, North America 800-456-3984) offers colonial charm, with poster beds and dark mahogany decorating the rooms. The ten room hotel offers a pool, fine creole restaurant and an eclectic variety of accommodation, from spartan shared-bath rooms to luxury suites. Budget-luxury.

❏ ALL-INCLUSIVE RESORTS: Sandals Halcyon and Sandals St. Lucia (North America 800-SANDALS, U.K. 071-581-9895), for couples only, are both located north of Castries. The all-inclusive Super Club hotel Couples (809-452-4211, fax 452-7419, North America 800-544-2883), also for couples, located on Vigie Beach near Vigie Airport. Club Med (809-455-6001, North America 800-CLUBMED) sits on the southern coast, about five minutes from Hewanorra International.

EATING

- ❑ NATURAL CAFE (809-452-6241), on Chausee Road in Castries, serves vegetarian and local dishes. Inexpensive.
- ❑ RAIN (809-452-3022), a Castries landmark, is located on historic Derek Walcott Square. Moderate-expensive.
- ❑ CAPONE'S (809-452-0284), in Rodney Bay, Italian. Moderate.
- ❑ LA FLAMBE (809-452-0321), also in Rodney Bay, for a French/Creole touch. Moderate.
- ❑ CHARTHOUSE (809-452-8115) barbecues, steaks, ribs and seafood like no one else on the island, at the waterfront at Rodney Bay. Moderate-expensive.

GETTING THERE

Two airports service St. Lucia. Vigie Airport, just north of downtown Castries, lands small charters and inter-island flights and Hewanorra International Airport, at the southern town of Vieux-Fort, takes international flights.

International airlines flying to Hewanorra include American Airlines (809-454-6777), Air Canada (809-452-3051/2/3), BWIA (809-452-3778 or 452-3789) and British Airways (809-452-3951) connects from Europe.

LIAT (809-452-3051), the inter-island connection, uses Vigie Airport as its base, as does Air Martinique (809-452-2463) and the local charter operation Helenair (809-452-7196).

St. Lucia Helicopters (809-453-6950), located at Pointe Seraphine, operates a shuttle service between airports, at a cost of US$85 per person for the ten minute flight.

Caribia Ferries operates a passenger and car service between Castries and Fort-de-France in Martinique, with connections on to Guadeloupe. One way fare is FF150-190 (US$27-35).

Departure tax is EC$27, plus a security tax of EC$10.

GETTING AROUND

■ PUBLIC TRANSPORTATION

Taxis, which are identified by an "H" on the license plate, are unmetered; a governing body sets rates and all drivers are supposed to carry rate cards in the vehicle. At the airport pick up a copy of the tourist publication *Visions*, which lists rates. If you need to call a taxi in the Castries area try Courtesy Taxi (809-452-1733 or 451-6737) or Vigie Taxi (809-452-1599).

Taxis also offer tours of the island. A tour of the northern section costs EC$120 (US$48) and a full island tour starts at EC$300 (US$120), or US$20 per hour. Contact the always reliable and informative John Jeremie (809-450-5347).

If your budget is limited, or you'd like to experience travel the way St. Lucians experience it, then local bus services are the way to go. Buses, often minivans, are also identified by an "H" on the plate. Few destinations on the island will cost more than EC$10. The system, however, takes some time to master. Buses leave from points in Castries—the market area, Jeremie Street and others—to island points, which may or may not be marked on the bus. Ask a St. Lucian which bus you need. Outside of Castries you'll see bus stops along the roads and you can also flag them down.

■ TOURS

For nature walks, first contact the government Forestry Division (809-450-2231); they conduct a seven mile (11 km) hike across the Rainforest Trail in the central 19,000-acre forest reserve, as well as other excursions.

Barnard Travel (809-452-2214/5/7/8) on Bridge Street will organize island tours and excursions to neighbouring islands.

St. Lucia Helicopters conducts sightseeing tours, a ten minute northern island tour for US$38 per person and a 20 minute southern island tour for US$75.

■ CAR RENTALS

St. Lucia's 500 miles (800 km) of roads, about half paved, provide ample opportunity to get around in a rental car and the driving, while often on winding and dipping roads, is easy. You need to be at least 25 years old to rent a car. Remember to stay on the left. Rentals start at about US$40 per day, but unlimited free mileage is not the norm. A temporary St. Lucian license is required and this is best obtained through the rental company, at a cost of EC$30 or US$12.

Rental companies include: Avis (Castries 809-452-2700, fax 453-1536; Hewanorra 454-6325, Vigie 452-2046), Budget (Castries 809-452-0233, fax 452-9362), Courtesy (Gros Islet 809-452-8140, fax 452-9566), CTL (809-452-0732, fax 452-0401), National (Castries 809-450-8721, fax 450-8577; Hewanorra 454-6699, Vigie 452-3050). For motorcycles try Wayne's Motorcycle Center (809-452-2059). No credit cards are accepted.

MONEY, HOURS AND COMMUNICATION

St. Lucia's currency, the Eastern Caribbean dollar, is currently pegged at EC$2.70 = US$1. U.S. dollars are widely accepted, Canadian dollars and British pounds to a lesser extent. Your change, however, will be in EC dollars and the exchange rate on the street will differ from that of the banks.

Most banks are open 8.00-12 Monday through Thursday and 15.00-17.00 on Friday and are located on the main streets of Castries, Pointe Seraphine, Rodney Bay, Soufriere and Vieux-Fort.

Major credit cards are accepted at car rental agencies, duty-free shops, larger hotels and larger restaurants. Craft stalls and small vendors will not accept them and may not even deal with traveler's checks. You can change money at banks, which will always give better rates than hotels.

Government hours are 8.30-12.30 and 13.30-16.30 Monday through Friday. Commercial hours are the same, plus 8.00-12.00 on Saturday. Some shops, particularly the duty-free shops at Pointe Seraphine, will remain open for cruise ships; most of St. Lucia, and this includes restaurants, closes down on Sunday.

Cable and Wireless phone cards are sold at select shops, banks, post offices and at Cable and Wireless on Bridge Street (809-452-3301) in Castries and in Vieux-Fort.

The international area code for St. Lucia is 809. Dial 1, then 809 and the seven-digit number. Since all telephone numbers in St. Lucia begin with 45, local calls are made by simply dialing the last five digits of the number.

You can find the General Post Office on Bridge Street in Castries.

ENTERTAINMENT

■ SPORTS

For deep-sea fishing, yacht charters and diving, the best place to start is the busy Rodney Bay Marina near Gros Ilet. For yacht charters call Tradewinds Yacht Charters (809-452-8424), Sunsail Stevens (809-452-8648), Via Carib Yacht Charters (Canada 514-982-6649). For deep-sea fishing try Mako Watersports (809-452-0412) and for diving call Buddies Scuba (Vigie Marina 809-452-5288) or Scuba St. Lucia (The St. Lucian Hotel 809-459-7355).

For tennis call the St. Lucia Racquet Club (809-450-0551) or the St. Lucia Yacht Club, which offers squash as well. Call Trim's Riding Stables in Gros Islet (809-452-8273) for horseback riding excursions.

The two golf courses on the island offer nine-hole challenges. Call the Cunard La Toc Hotel (809-452-3081) in La Toc and Cap Estate Golf Course (809-452-8523) in Cap Estate.

The Fitness Palace (809-452-0882), between Castries and Gros Islet, and Jazzercise (809-452-6853), at the Gablewoods Mall, offer workout equipment and aerobics.

Useful Addresses

■ TOURISM

St. Lucia Tourist Board:

❏ P.O. Box 221, Castries, St. Lucia, W.I.; (809) 452-4094 or 452-5968, fax 453-1121.

❏ 820 Second Ave., 9th floor, New York, NY 10017; 800-456-3984 or 212-867-2950, fax 212-370-7867.

❏ 4975 Dundas St. West, Suite 457, Islington, Toronto, Ontario M9A 4X4; 800-456-3984 or 416-236-0936, fax 416-236-0937.

❏ 421a Finchley Rd., London NW3 6HJ; 071-431-4045, fax 071-431-7920.

❏ Postfach 2304, D-6380 Bad Homburg 1, Germany; 06172-30-44-31, fax 06172-30-50-72.

❏ 53 Rue Francois I'er, 7th floor, Paris 75008; 47-20-39-66, fax 47-23-09-65.

❏ St. Lucia Hotel and Tourism Association, P.O. Box 545, Castries, St. Lucia, W.I.; 809-452-5978, fax 452-7967.

■ OTHER

❏ Emergencies, 999.

❏ Victoria Hospital, Hospital Road, Castries; 452-2421.

❏ Fitz St. Rose Medical Center, Micoud Street, Castries, 452-3333.

❏ Williams Pharmacy, Bridge Street, Castries; 452-2797.

❏ American Express, Carib Travel Agency, 20 Micoud Street, Castries; 452-2151.

❏ Federal Express, Bourbon Street, Castries; 452-1320.

St. Vincent and the Grenadines

Introduction

For many the word "Grenadines" invokes a powerful image of tropical micro-islands, scattered in a string over miles of translucent sapphire ocean. And it's true, that's exactly what they are, 30-plus islands and cays, ranging from the relatively large Bequia to the small and uninhabited Tobago Cays and even smaller rocks jutting out of the ocean. The chain stretches like stepping stones from the large St. Vincent to Grenada in the south; most of the Grenadines are politically linked to St. Vincent.

Due to the proximity of the Grenadines to each other, as well as their hundreds of accessible small coves, bays and reefs, the islands have been a favourite with yachtsmen, divers and tourists for years. Not so with the largest island, the St. Vincent mainland. This is changing, but not so rapidly that the island cannot be experienced in an non-hyped, natural state, without the glitter and glamour of mainstream tourist islands.

The Land

The 20 mile (32 km) St. Vincent Channel separates St. Vincent from its northern neighbour St. Lucia. The Grenadines, nearly 600 islands if you count rocks, sandbars and islets, stretch 45 miles (72 km) to the south, ending at, within the St. Vincent and the Grenadines border, Petit St. Vincent. Barbados lies some 100 miles (160 km) to the east.

St. Vincent measures 18 miles (29 km) north to south and 11 miles (18 km) at its widest east-west point. The land area is 133 square miles (344 sq km), about half the size of Dominica. The combined Grenadines add another 17 square miles (44 sq km) to the country's total.

St. Vincent's rugged volcanic terrain is dominated by a high central mountain range and a moderate range that reaches diagonally across the southeastern portion. The mountains are heavily forested and attract rain, producing numerous mountain streams and rivers. The windward east coast is irregular, with sharp cliffs, rocky beaches and rough surf. The western, leeward coast is full of small bays and inlets and a less dramatic coastline.

The northern section of the island is dominated by La Soufriere, a semi-dormant volcano looming 4,048 feet (1,234 m) above sea level. St. Vincent joins its sister islands in this regard—many have volcanoes and/or towns named, in one form or another, Soufriere, which is derived from the French soufre, for "sulfur." La Soufriere erupted in 1979, but adequate warning systems facilitated the full evacuation of the northern part of the island and no lives were lost. Property and crop damage, however, was extensive.

The Grenadines were also formed eons ago by volcanic activity, but are generally low-lying and less dramatic geologically than the mainland.

History

The history of St. Vincent and the Grenadines mirrors that of all the Windward Islands. The first inhabitants were the Stone Age Ciboney, who were followed by the relatively peaceful Amerindian Arawaks. The Arawaks, from South America, inhabited the southern Caribbean islands from 500 BC through the time of Christ and were, in turn, followed some 800 to 1,000 years later by the Amerindian Caribs, a warlike group which conquered virtually everyone in its path. The Caribs, who called St. Vincent Youroumei ("The Beauty of the Rainbows in the Valleys"), had eliminated the Arawaks by the time of Columbus' voyage to the New World in 1492.

Some historians claim Columbus never saw the island, while others say he at least charted it. Whichever the case, the Spanish did not make serious attempts to settle. Various other European explorers, busy settling neighbouring islands, had no success in rooting out the Caribs from their mountain and woodland strongholds. The French made a claim in 1626 and the English claimed St. Vincent in 1672, but neither were able to make any headway in routing the Caribs. The fierce tribe would hold onto the island for much longer than their unfortunate comrades in the north and south.

In 1675 a passing Dutch ship sank off the coast of Bequia and its survivors, mostly African slaves and a few Dutchmen, made it to St. Vincent. The Dutch did not survive the encounter, but the Caribs seem to have been more accepting of the Africans. They spared their lives and, ultimately, the two groups commingled. Later, more Africans escaped from neighbouring islands and made it to St. Vincent. They, too, contributed to the gene pool, adding to a growing mixed-race group of "Black Caribs." Caribs who had been driven off nearby islands also made it to St. Vincent, swelling the numbers of the so-called "Yellow Caribs."

As the Black Carib numbers increased, the Yellow Caribs felt the pressure. Friction, even battles, ensued between the two groups, until they finally asked Martinique's French governor to arbitrate their often violent rivalry. In 1700 he negotiated a physical division of the island, which proved only temporary. The two groups were soon fighting again. The original Caribs, however, had allowed the French to settle and farm parts of the island, probably as a bulwark against Black Carib incursion. The British also attempted to establish settlements, but were repelled by both Carib groups and by the French.

The difficulties in colonizing St. Vincent were further demonstrated by the 1748 Treaty of Aix-La-Chapelle, which in effect was a declaration of exasperation by the British and French. The treaty pronounced the island neutral, which is how it remained until the British and French once again resumed hostilities.

St. Vincent was ceded to Britain in 1763, which caused a Black Carib revolt, in what is known as the first of the Carib Wars. The French then intervened again in 1779, but the island reverted to England under the 1783 Treaty of Versailles. In the meantime the British managed to pressure the Black Caribs into signing various agreements that, in essence, relegated them to small parcels of land in the northern section of the island.

In 1795 the Black Caribs, organized and well-funded by a radical group of French rebels who had never intended to adhere to the Treaty of Versailles from the start, rose up again. The Second Carib War, also called The Brigands Wars, broke out. The Caribs gained land and fought valiantly, but were dealt a crushing blow when their Chief Chatoyer was killed in a battle at Dorsetshire Hill. Within a year the Caribs had been demoralized and, in 1797, they surrendered. The 5,000 surviving Caribs were rounded up and shipped to the British colonies now named Belize and Honduras, where their descendants live still. Black Carib survivors managed to escape to the St. Vincent hills and avoid deportation and their descendants can be found on the island today.

The British were clearly in charge by 1800. Sugarcane became the cash crop and, as plantations grew, more Africans were imported to work the land. By 1834, the year slavery was abolished, St. Vincent boasted several fairly large plantations, though nothing equal to the scale of neighbouring Barbados and islands to the north. Slavery's abolition brought Portuguese and then East Indian indentured laborers, as well as British and other laborers from nearby islands. The country, however, remained economically stagnant for the years into the 20th century. By this time arrowroot, a starchy tuber so-named for its use by the Caribs to treat arrow wounds, had surpassed sugarcane as the main crop. Today St. Vincent and the Grenadines is the world's largest producer of arrowroot.

St. Vincent and the Grenadines did not go into the 20th century, however, without drama. It came via La Soufriere, the northern coast's simmering volcano. The volcano's first recorded eruption was in 1718. In 1812 it erupted again, killing 56 people. But the 1902 eruption was its most destructive to date. The blast sent gases and clouds as far away as Barbados and rock and stones fell on Kingstown, in the south of the island. More than 2,000 died. A 1971 eruption was minor and another in 1979 forced the temporary evacuation of 20,000 people from their homes. Many of these people were descendants of the Black Caribs, defeated by Britain in the Second Carib War. No lives were lost, but substantial banana and arrowroot crops were destroyed.

St. Vincent and the Grenadines gained universal adult suffrage in 1951. In 1969 the islands became an associated state within the Commonwealth. Political parties had been formed by this time and the country received independence on 27 October 1979, the same year as La Soufriere's last blast. Later that same year the government, under Prime Minister Milton Cato, moved to quell strikes and a near-rebellion that were largely due to severe economic losses suffered after the eruption.

People and Culture

The disparate groups that settled St. Vincent and the Grenadines over the millennium have produced a multi-racial society that differs slightly from its island neighbours. The majority of the island's population of 112,000 is black, descended from slaves, but a substantial number of people are mixed-race descendants of Africans, Portuguese and East Indian indentured laborers, British workers and other assorted visitors. Today the Black Caribs account for two per cent of the population.

English is the island's official language. A Patois is spoken by most people, incorporating vocabulary and grammar from various African languages, French and some Spanish. The French influence is also seen in place names such as Sans Souci and Chateaubelair on the mainland, or Petit Vincent and Mayreau in the Grenadines. Carib names also appear on the map, such as the Grenadine island of Bequia or Commantawana Bay on St. Vincent.

The French influence shows up in the National Carnival Festival, "Vincy Mas." The carnival is held in July, thereby removing from it the pre-Lenten religious affiliation, but in all other respects it is a Caribbean carnival in the fullest sense. Calypso competitions, masquerades, parades, dancing and festivals mark the 11 day affair. If you're on the island during the two months preceding Vincy

Mas, you'll be able to hear the calypso competitions throughout the country, warming up for the big event in July.

Government and Economy

The economy of St. Vincent and the Grenadines is rooted in agriculture: banana, arrowroot, coconut and coconut by-products. Nearly 40 per cent of the island's land is arable and the soil, due to past volcanic activity, is fertile and rich. While agriculture employs many, nearly a fifth of the labor force of 70,000 is unemployed. Ninety per cent of the population, however, is engaged in some sort of agricultural activity, whether subsistence or for profit.

St. Vincent's bananas are given special market protection, due to the island's Commonwealth status, but this arrangement may end with the advent of the EEC. The government has given incentives to farmers to diversify to other crops, such as arrowroot, cocoa and citrus fruit. St. Vincent is the world's largest supplier of arrowroot, which is used as a food thickening agent, as well as an emulsifier and coating for industrial uses.

Tourism runs second to agriculture as the country's foreign exchange earner. Most tourists visit the Grenadines, although St. Vincent is getting more arrivals each year. The undersized airport, E.T. Joshua in Arnos Vale, limits the numbers that can arrive at any one time. Even at that, the country averages between 150,000 and 200,000 stopover visitors per year.

St. Vincent and the Grenadines is a parliamentary democracy within the British Commonwealth. The Queen is the nominal head of state, represented on the island by a governor general. The legislature is unicameral, an elected House of Assembly that includes 15 representatives and six senators.

Sights

About 300 miles (480 km) of paved road complete a near-circle around the island. Only the stretch from Richmond, on the leeward coast, to Fancy, on the northern side, is unpassable in sections. The Leeward and Windward highways run along the coast, passing small villages, inlets, bays, forests and dramatic cliffs rising from the sea.

The Windward Highway brings you to La Soufriere, the island's semi-active volcano in the north. The volcano's crater is one mile (1.6 km) in diameter and filled with water estimated at 1,670 feet (500 m) deep; the lake sprouted a small island near its center in 1971. The hike up to the crater, a sometimes strenuous climb, takes three hours. The trail begins near Georgetown, St. Vincent's second-largest town, after crossing the Rabacca Dry River near the Rabacca coconut plantation. The dry river was created from lava flow during the massive 1902 eruption. You'll hike through the plantation and a bamboo forest. The rim is nearly 4,000 feet above sea level and you might expect some mist, cool air, even rain. Alternate routes exist from the leeward-side villages of Chateaubelair or Richmond; these hikes are more scenic, but may take longer (ten miles or 16 km, still about three hours for the energetic) and can be rougher in places. Find a guide for these hikes in the villages. The cost should be US$25.

North of the La Soufriere turnoff is Owia Bay, site of the Owia Salt Pond. Owia is one of the Carib villages "given" to the group during the 18th century relocations. A stairway leads up a short hill to a small salt pond, where swimming is allowed.

The Falls of Baleine is also located in the north, past the road's end at Richmond. The usual way to get there is by boat—the views as you move along the coast are magnificent—which you can arrange by calling Dive St. Vincent (809-457-4714) or T's Tours Ltd. (809-457-1433). The cost of US$40 per person includes lunch and snorkelling along the way. After fording a stream, you'll reach the cascade, a rush of fresh water that falls about 60 feet (18 m) into a naturally formed bathing pool. You can also reach the falls by on a strenuous hike from the northern town of Fancy, another area relegated to the Black Caribs two centuries ago.

In the southern half of the island, past the airport on the Vigie Highway and heading east, is the town of Mesopotamia and the Marriaqua Valley, the heart of the island's agricultural industry, with miles of banana plantations, arrowroot fields, forests and streams. The nearby gardens and natural springs at Montreal (809-458-5452) offer a collection of exotic plants and trees. The view from these hills is worth the drive.

Heading north on the Leeward Highway, stop at Buccament Bay and turn inland. Here the Vermont Nature Trail weaves through a rainforest and a nearby reserve has been established for the protection of the St. Vincent parrot. You may see several rainforest dwellers, such as the black hawk and crested hummingbird.

Kingstown

The nation's capital is located in southwest St. Vincent, a few miles north of E.T. Joshua Airport in Arnos Vale. The town is set on a natural harbor and much of the dock and harbor area was built on reclaimed land. Downtown itself is easy to navigate, with several examples of colonial architecture and historic churches. A dozen blocks created by three streets, parallel to the bay and to each other, define the downtown area: Bay Street (Upper and Lower), Long Lane (Upper and Lower) and Grenville/Hallifax/Grand streets. Here you'll find banks, businesses, the police station, post office, stores, Cable and Wireless, small snack shops, taxi and bus stands and the tourism office.

Kingstown Market, open daily but especially busy on Friday and Saturday, is bordered by Bedford Street and Long Lane. Here you can buy anything from clothes, peanuts and newspapers, to fruits and vegetables. A block south is the New Fish Market and just east of downtown is the St. Vincent Craftmen's Center, a showcase for many island craftsman where you can choose from wood carvings, straw crafts, pottery, dolls and more.

St. George's Anglican Cathedral on Grenville dates to 1820 and its building was, in part, financed by the sale of Carib lands. Beneath the chandelier you'll find a stone memorial to the British officer who killed the Carib Chief Chatoyer in the Second Carib War. Across the street is St. Mary's Roman Catholic Cathedral (Assumption Cathedral), originally completed in 1828 and renovated in the 1940s. The dark cathedral is eclectic in styles, combining Moorish, Georgian and Romanesque influences. On the grounds are the presbytery and a school.

The police station was built in 1875 and the waterfront Cobblestone Inn is, not surprisingly, a cobblestone structure, built in 1810 and originally used as a sugar warehouse. The Tourism Department (809-457-1502, fax 456-2610) is located in a new complex on Upper Bay Street, on the waterfront.

The 20-acre Botanic Gardens, on the town's outskirts, were founded in 1765 and Vincentians claim they are the oldest in the Western Hemisphere—a claim also made by several other botanical gardens in the Caribbean. Still, the gardens have been around for a while and now sport extensive collections of exotic local and imported plants and trees. You'll see the original breadfruit trees brought from Tahiti by Capt. William Bligh (Bligh's famous mutiny on the Bounty occurred on his first voyage, in 1787. It was on his next attempt, in 1793, that he successfully transported the somewhat tasteless but substantial breadfruit—food intended for the slave population—to Jamaica and St. Vincent).

The Archaeological Museum, originally the home of the gardens' curator, now houses artifacts from the Amerindian period of St. Vincent and the Grenadines. Contact Dr. Earle Kirby, St. Vincent's resident history and archaeology expert (809-456-1787), for an entertaining and informative tour. Also on the grounds are Government House and a small aviary. The gardens are open daily until 18.00, but the museum is only open Wednesday mornings 9.00-12.00 and Saturday afternoons 15.00-18.00.

Just ten minutes outside of town is Fort Charlotte, built to guard Kingstown Harbor following the 1763 Treaty of Paris. There was, at the time, some threat from the Black Caribs and several cannon pointed inland. Originally fortified with three dozen cannon, the fort now has five. The views from here are marvelous; the Grenadines are visible to the south and, on a clear day, Grenada will stand out. The fort is administered by the National Trust (809-456-1060).

St. Vincent Practical Information

ACCOMMODATION

An extensive list of hotels is available through the St. Vincent and the Grenadines Hotel Association (see below). Hotels charge a ten per cent service charge and a five per cent government tax.

The government of St. Vincent and the Grenadines officially discourages camping, citing security problems.

❑ COBBLESTONE INN, P.O. Box 867, Kingstown, St. Vincent and the Grenadines, W.I. (809-456-1937) features 19 rooms in a circa 1810 sugar warehouse. The downtown location is excellent for exploring and you're close to the Grenadines Wharf, where ferries depart for the Grenadines. Moderate.

❑ VILLA LODGE HOTEL, P.O. Box 1191, Indian Bay, St. Vincent and the Grenadines, W.I. (809-458-4641, fax 457-4468) sits on a small hill overlooking Young Island, Bequia and the Grenadines. The rooms are simple and comfortable and the hotel has a pool; the beach at Indian Bay is right there. Moderate-luxury.

❑ INDIAN BAY BEACH HOTEL, P.O. Box 538, Kingstown, St. Vincent and the Grenadines, W.I. (809-458-4001) is small (14 rooms) and basic, but sits on Indian Bay beach. Don't miss the weekly barbecue. Moderate.

❑ YOUNG ISLAND RESORT, P.O. Box 211, Young Island, St. Vincent and the Grenadines, W.I. (809-458-4826, fax 457-4567, U.S. 800-223-1108) is actually a private island, about 670 feet (200 m) off the south coast's Villa Beach and Indian Bay. The 35-acre resort features private cottages that accommodate 60 guests, with watersports, pool and bar. A small ferry makes regular runs. Luxury.

EATING ON ST. VINCENT

In Kingstown stop at Basil's Restaurant at the Cobblestone Inn for West Indian creole cuisine. Aggie's Bar and Restaurant (809-456-2110) on Grenville features excellent creole and seafood specialties.

In the Villa Beach area the succinctly named French Restaurant (809-458-4972) has a reputation for some of the best French and seafood on the island. The seating is open air, on the beach. Lime N' Pub (809-458-4227) is on the beach across from Young Island. Rotis, grilled lobster, pizza, great place to relax with a cold one.

GETTING THERE

St. Vincent's E.T. Joshua Airport in Arnos Vale lands small inter-island aircraft and connections are made through neighbouring islands of Barbados (where you'll find a St. Vincent and the Grenadines information desk), St. Lucia, Martinique, Trinidad and Grenada, on LIAT (809-4578-4841 or 457-1821, Union Island 458-8230), Air Martinique (809-458-4528), Mustique Airways (809-458-4380) and SVG Air (809-456-5610).

Of the Grenadines, only Bequia, Canouan and Union Island have airstrips and immigration facilities. Night landing facilities are spotty and it is not always clear which islands are landing or not landing at night. The private islands of Mustique, Mayreau and Palm Island operate small airstrips, but are not entry points for St. Vincent and the Grenadines.

The departure tax from St. Vincent and the Grenadines is EC$20.

GETTING AROUND

■ PUBLIC TRANSPORT AND RENTALS

On St. Vincent taxis and minibuses operate on government-regulated fares, which can be found in a copy of the pamphlet "Discover St. Vincent and the Grenadines" at the airport or a tourist information center. Minibuses travel around the island and can be flagged down anywhere along the route. It's not always clear which vehicles are taxis and which are minibuses, since both can look the same, but this is half, or at least a quarter, of the fun. Minibuses depart from the market square in Kingstown for all points.

Island tours can be arranged through the Taxi Driver's Association (809-457-1807). Cost is about EC$35 per hour for a vehicle of four people. Other tour operators include Barefoot Holidays (809-456-9334) or Emerald Travel and Tours (809-457-1996).

Rental cars, which average US$35 per day, may be your best bet for travelling around St. Vincent. Driving is on the left. You must have a St. Vincent and the

Grenadines temporary driver's license to operate a vehicle, obtainable through the agency at a cost of EC$40. Call Avis (809-456-5610), Kim's Rentals (809-456-1884) or Sunshine Auto Rentals (809-456-5380).

Motorcycles and scooters can be rented through JG Agencies (809-456-1409) and Sailors Cycle Center (809-457-1712).

■ FERRIES

Travel to and among the Grenadines by ferry is not difficult, but somewhat complicated. Schedules are subject to change at any time, so keep abreast of the situation if that's how you decide to go. The ferries, which are reasonably comfortable and fun to boot, are found at the Grenadines Wharf in Kingstown.

On Monday and Thursday the MV Snapper makes a Bequia-to-Kingstown run at 6.00 and then turns around and travels from Kingstown to Bequia, Canouan, Mayreau and, lastly, Union Island. On Tuesday and Friday, the trip is in reverse, from Union Island to Mayreau, Canouan, Bequia and finally on to Kingstown. On Saturday the ferry departs from Kingstown at 10.30 and travels to Canouan, then on to Union Island. At 17.30, the ferry departs Union Island for a nonstop, five-hour trip to Kingstown.

The MV Admiral I (809-458-3348) and MV Admiral II (same phone) make daily runs from Kingstown to Bequia and back, only a one hour trip. Call for current schedules. Fares are also subject to change, but the Kingstown to Bequia fare is EC$10, to Canouan EC$13, to Mayreau EC$15 and to Union Island EC$20.

MONEY, HOURS AND COMMUNICATION

St. Vincent and the Grenadines use the Eastern Caribbean dollar, currently pegged at EC$2.70 = US$1. Most businesses accept U.S. and Canadian dollars, but this is not always the case. Banks can be found at E.T. Joshua airport (open Monday through Saturday, 7.00-17.00) and on the main streets of Kingstown and Georgetown, most open Monday through Friday 8.00-13.00 or 8.00-15.00, as well as Friday 15.00-17.00.

General business hours are Monday through Friday, 8.00-16.00, with an hour off for lunch and 8.00-12.00 on Saturday. Supermarkets may remain open all day. Government offices are open Monday to Friday, 8.00-12.00 and 13.00-16.15.

The General Post Office is located on Halifax Street in Kingstown and is open 8.30-15.00 Monday through Friday and 8.30-11.30 on Saturday.

The country uses the area code 809, which means from North America, dial 1 and 809, plus the seven digit number. Since all numbers in St. Vincent and the Grenadines start with 45, you simply dial the last five digits when making local calls. Cable and Wireless is located on Halifax Street.

For news of local events, pick up a copy of The News or The Vincentian (both EC$1), weekly tabloids found at small shops or vendor tables at the market.

ENTERTAINMENT

■ SPORTS

Given the proximity of the Grenadines, it's no surprise that sailing is a popular activity. This area and the Virgin Islands, which also hosts dozens of tiny cays and islands, have long been recognized as prime sailing spots. Most of the Grenadines offer docking facilities and amenities for sailors and a number of local charter companies provide boats, either bareboat or crewed. If you haven't made arrangements before you arrive, contact Barefoot Yacht Charters (809-456-9526, fax 456-9238) or the Lagoon Marina (809-458-4308) and CSY Yacht Charters (same phone) at the Blue Lagoon area of the southern coast.

Given the many underwater shelves and reefs weaving through and around the waters of the Grenadines, diving and snorkelling are excellent. In St. Vincent contact St. Vincent Dive Experience (809-456-9741), Caribe Divers (809-458-7270) or Dive St. Vincent (809-457-4714).

USEFUL ADDRESSES

■ TOURISM

St. Vincent and the Grenadines Department of Tourism:
❏ P.O. Box 834, Kingstown, St. Vincent and the Grenadines, W.I.;
   (809) 457-1502, fax 457-2880.
❏ 801 2nd Ave., 21st floor, New York, NY 10017; 800-729-1726, fax 212-949-5946.
❏ 100 University Ave., Suite 504, Toronto, Ontario M5J 1V6; 416-971-9666, fax 971-9667.
❏ 10 Kensington Court, London W8 5DL; 71-937-6570, fax 937-3611.
❏ Bruno Fink, Wurmberg Str. 26, D-7032 Sindelfingen, Germany; 70-31-80-62-60, fax 80-50-12.
❏ St. Vincent and the Grenadines Hotel Association, P.O. Box 834, Kingstown, St. Vincent and the Grenadines, W.I.; 809-457-1072.

■ OTHER
❏ Emergency, 999.
❏ Police, 457-1211.
❏ Kingstown General Hospital, 456-1185.
❏ Local information, 118.

❏ Reliance Pharmacy, Halifax Street, Kingstown; 456-1734.
❏ American Express, Caribbean International Travel Services, Granby Street, Kingstown; 457-1841.
❏ Federal Express, Halifax Street, Kingstown; 456-1649.

The Grenadines

The Grenadines, some 600 "islands" stretching 35 miles (56 km) from Bequia to Carriacou and surrounding islands north of Grenada, are the jewels of the southern Lesser Antilles. Most are rocks and small sand bars and only a few dozen can actually be classified as islands. Even fewer than that are occupied. Politically the islands are divided between the two countries, with St. Vincent administering the majority. By and large these islands are off the beaten track and, although they attract the majority of St. Vincent's tourists, they are certainly not overrun.

BEQUIA
Bequia (BECK-way), with a population of 4,900, is the largest of the Grenadines, some seven square miles (18 sq km) and nine miles (14 km) off the southern coast of St. Vincent. The name comes from the Carib word Becouya, meaning "Island of the Clouds." (Drive to the top of Mt. Pleasant and you'll see what they meant.)

Bequia's artisans craft the famous double-hull boats, known worldwide. The island was once a center for whaling and local boat builders and whalers took their cues from 19th century American whalers, who sailed the Caribbean in search of their livelihood. A small industry evolved and, in its heyday, the offshore cay of Petit Nevis became a whale processing center. The industry no longer exists, since many whales are protected by international law. Bequia's residents, however, are exempted from some restrictions, due to their status as indigenous people, and the hunt occasionally continues. Bequians still do it with hand-held harpoons and the island's premier whaler is the astonishing Athneal Olliviere, a septuagenarian, who last bagged a humpback in 1992. See the small museum at his home in Paget Farm, open Monday through Saturday 10.00-17.00 and Sunday 9.00-19.00; admission US$2. Whale jawbones frame the entrance.

The center of the island is forested and elevated and the coast is lined with small bays and inlets—plenty of great beaches. The best ones are: Princess Margaret Beach, just beyond Admiralty Bay; Lower Bay, with the Bequia Sailing Club; Friendship Bay, a long, quiet beach with a bar at the Friendship Bay Hotel;

and the isolated Spring Bay, lined with palm trees. The beach bar here is only sometimes open. Even more isolated, Hope Bay must be accessed by foot or boat. The island's hub is Port Elizabeth, a small town on Admiralty Bay. This is the center of activity for locals and yachties alike. Its main street is lined with shops, the Bayshore Mall, a bank, post office, police station, open-air and sheltered markets, taxi stand and the ferry dock. The Tourist Bureau (809-458-3286) is open 9.00-16.00 Monday through Friday and 9.00-12.00 on Saturday. Be sure to stop at the Bequia Bookshop (809-458-3905) for a wide selection of books (many cruising guides and charts), magazines and locally crafted scrimshaw and art.

Accommodation on Bequia consist of villas, guesthouses and a few small but unique hotels. For villa rentals contact Bequia Villa Rentals, P.O. Box 23, Bequia, St. Vincent and the Grenadines, W.I. (809-458-3393) or Friendship Bay Villa Rentals, P.O. Box 9, Bequia, St. Vincent and the Grenadines, W.I. (809-458-3222, fax 458-3840).

❑ PLANTATION HOUSE HOTEL, P.O. Box 16, Bequia, St. Vincent and the Grenadines, W.I. (809-458-3425, fax 458-3612, U.S. 800-223-9832, fax 212-599-1755, U.K. 045-383-5801, fax 383-5525) is set on 11 acres and a small beach, a 15 minute walk along the bay to Port Elizabeth. The main house is built in the old plantation style and the 25 rooms and cottages are spread over the property. Luxury. This is where you'll find Dive Bequia (809-458-3504, fax 458-3886, U.S. 800-851-DIVE), the best place on the island for your diving needs.

❑ THE FRIENDSHIP BAY HOTEL, P.O. Box 9, Bequia, St. Vincent and the Grenadines, W.I. (809-458-3222, fax 458-3840, U.S. 800-223-1108) fronts one of the island's nicest beachfronts and bays. All 27 rooms overlook the ocean and all have fans, but no air conditioning. The hotel is casual, relaxed and a great place for families. Find the Dive Paradise dive shop here. Moderate-luxury.

❑ JULIE'S GUEST HOUSE, Admiralty Bay, Bequia, St. Vincent and the Grenadines, W.I. (809-458-3304, fax 458-3812) features 19 simple rooms on Back Street in Port Elizabeth. All rooms have fans and private baths (six with hot and cold water, 13 with cold only). No credit cards are accepted. Budget.

❑ THE OLD FORT, Mt. Pleasant, Bequia, St. Vincent and the Grenadines, W.I. (809-458-3440, fax 458-3824), located on 30 acres atop Mt. Pleasant, dates to the 18th century. Peacocks, donkeys and rabbits meander about and the six rooms are simple—no phones or television. You can walk to Hope Bay from here. Ask owner Otmar Schaedle to show you a collection of antiques and artifacts he's unearthed on the property. Moderate-luxury.

For eats, THE FRANGIPANI (809-458-3255) is located at the hotel of the same name and is famous for being the birthplace of Prime Minister James "Son" Mitchell. Moderate. LE PETIT JARDIN (809-458-3318) in Port Elizabeth serves elegant French creole. DAWN'S CREOLE GARDEN (809-458-3154) on the Lower Bay beach features a weekend barbecue buffet with entertainment. Budget.

Getting around Bequia is not difficult. The J.F. Mitchell Airport lands interisland flights only (Mustique Airways, 809-455-5645, operates the flight from Kingstown to Bequia, EC$45 one-way) and is located at the far south end of the island. The airstrip is new and gleaming and was built on reclaimed land (turn off to the right past the airport for a long and secluded beach). A taxi to Port Elizabeth costs EC$25—about the most you'll pay to go anywhere on the island. Taxis on Bequia tend to be small, open-air pickup trucks outfitted with benches and canopies. The tourist booth in Port Elizabeth sometimes has rates available. For hotel pick-ups call Gideon Taxi (809-458-3760) or Sam's Taxi (809-458-3868). Minibuses run around the island and covered bus stops are scattered along major roads.

It may be important to arrange for a rental car prior to your arrival, particularly during high season or the annual Easter Regatta. Rates start at US$40 per day. Call Philmore's Rentals at Julie's Guest House (809-458-3304, fax 458-3812) in Port Elizabeth for a limited selection of small jeeps. Philmore will help you obtain the local license. You can hire a motorcycle from the Bequia Art Gallery (809-458-3722) in Port Elizabeth.

In addition to the two dive shops mentioned above, Sunsports (809-458-3577, fax 457-3031) at the Gingerbread Complex on Admiralty Bay can organize sailing, snorkelling, diving and other watersports. For a unique and informative excursion take a trip on the Friendship Rose (809-458-3202 or 458-3090, fax 457-3071). The offices are located at the Local Color Boutique, next to Barclays Bank in town. You'll see the Rose out in the bay. For many years Capt. Calvin Lewis ran the locally-built schooner as a mail boat and ferry between Kingstown, Bequia and other islands. Now he's retired and takes day trips to Mustique and the Tobago Cays and can tell you just about everything there is to know about the Grenadines. The Tobago Cays day trip costs US$65 per person, which includes lunch, drinks, snorkelling and a flight back to Bequia.

The increasingly popular Easter Regatta, held over the long Easter weekend, turns out to be a mini-carnival of sorts, with lots of beer drinking, amateur boat races (coconut boats), music, dancing and some bona fide sailing. The Bequia Sailing Club is the center of it all.

MUSTIQUE

Most guidebooks appear to be unable to mention Mustique (Mus-TEEK) without using phrases like "rich and famous" or dropping names such as Mick Jagger and Princess Margaret. Of course, we would never do that.

Eighteen miles (30 km) south of St. Vincent and five miles (eight km) southeast of Bequia, tiny Mustique is just three miles (four km) long and a bit over a mile (two km) wide at its widest. The attraction? Seclusion, exclusivity and a 12 mile (19 km) coastline with long, wide beaches. A favourite is Macaroni Beach on the Atlantic side. Offshore are several good snorkelling reefs and small cays, including Petit Mustique.

Mustique, a quasi-private island, has no real town, just villas, a guesthouse, a hotel, a couple of small stores, a church, petrol station, riding stables and a bar and restaurant. Once owned by a private investor, the island is now managed by the Mustique Company. The prime minister of St. Vincent and the Grenadines sits on the company's board and the government controls the island's internal affairs.

Villa rentals are handled by the Mustique Company, Mustique, St. Vincent and the Grenadines, W.I. (809-458-4621/2, fax 457-2551 or 456-4565).

The exclusive island offers only two public accommodation. THE COTTON HOUSE, P.O. Box 349, Mustique, St. Vincent and the Grenadines, W.I. (809-456-4777, U.S. 800-372-1323), a restored 18th century estate house, offers 22 rooms on Endeavor Bay. Luxury. FIREFLY GUESTHOUSE, P.O. Box 349, Mustique, St. Vincent and the Grenadines, W.I. (809-456-3414 or 458-4621) is small, just four rooms, but a good buy if you reserve in advance. No credit cards are accepted. Moderate.

BASIL'S BAR AND RAFT RESTAURANT is the public restaurant on the island, which makes it famous. On the western side's Britannia Bay, the bamboo and thatched-roof bar hangs right over the water.

CANOUAN

Small, quiet, croissant-shaped Canouan (CAN-oo-ahn) lies in the center of the Grenadines, between Mustique and larger Union Island. The get-away-from-it-all island, about 1,900 acres, features excellent beaches and reefs and is a good base for exploring the nearby islands, including the Tobago Cays. Yachts anchor in the small inlets surrounding the island.

THE CANOUAN BEACH HOTEL, P.O. Box 530, Canouan, St. Vincent and the Grenadines, W.I. (809-458-8888, fax 458-8875, U.S. 508-788-0306) features 43 rooms on a beach at the southwestern tip of the island, with great views of the southern Grenadines; you'll find tennis, watersports, a bar and restaurant here.

Luxury. THE CRYSTAL SANDS BEACH HOTEL, Grand Bay Beach, St. Vincent and the Grenadines, W.I. (809-458-8309) offers ten cottages on the beach. The village nearby is the island's center of activity. Moderate. VILLA LE BIJOU, Friendship, Canouan, St. Vincent and the Grenadines, W.I. (809-458-8025) is a small, ten room hotel on a hill, with great views and a short walk to the beach. No credit cards are accepted. Moderate-luxury.

For water sports contact Dive Canouan (809-458-8234).

Canouan has a small airstrip and ferry service from St. Vincent (schedule above).

MAYREAU

Secluded, privately owned Mayreau (MY-row), only 1.5 square miles (four sq km), with population of less than 200, lies 35 miles (56 km) south of St. Vincent. You can only get here by sea (see above), but this may be what you've been looking for. Ultra-isolated, with the Tobago Cays just offshore, you can't do much other than swim, snorkel, take trips to the islands and eat. You can't even drive, really. There are no proper roads, just paths, along which you'll see an old schoolhouse, a stone church and a small village.

Snorkelling and diving here and around the Tobago Cays is considered by some to be the best in the Grenadines.

You'll also see yachts anchored about the island and the Tobago Cays, a popular stop. A cruise ship stops once a week. Stay at SALT WHISTLE BAY CLUB (809-493-9609, Canada 613-634-1963, fax 613-384-6300), a 22-acre resort on the island's north side. The beach here is superb. Luxury. DENNIS' HIDEAWAY (809-458-8594), a three-room guesthouse and restaurant on Saline Bay, is a true hideaway. Moderate.

UNION ISLAND

Diminutive Union Island lies 36 miles (57 km) south of St. Vincent, within sight of Mayreau. The population of 2,500 lives in the two towns on the south coast, Clifton and the slightly larger Ashton, which sit in the shadows of Mt. Parnassus (nearly 700 feet or 210 m) and Mt. Olympus.

The island is a bit livelier than its neighbours, serving as the center of the southern Grenadines, but is, in many ways, detached. Political troubles arose when James "Son" Mitchell, a Bequian, became Prime Minister in a 1979 national election. A group of fifty Union Islanders revolted and demanded secession, but were instead arrested. The incident demonstrated just how close, but yet so far apart, these islands can be.

THE ANCHORAGE YACHT CLUB, Union Island, St. Vincent and the Grenadines, W.I. (809-458-8221, fax 458-8365) offers 21 bungalows, apartments and rooms and all available water activities on the island. Note the saltwater pool filled with sharks—this is not a swimming pool. Moderate-luxury. THE CLIFTON BEACH HOTEL, Clifton, Union Island, St. Vincent and the Grenadines, W.I. (809-458-8235) features 25 rooms overlooking Clifton Harbor, some bungalows with kitchenettes. Budget-moderate. LAMBI'S GUESTHOUSE, Clifton, Union Island, St. Vincent and the Grenadines, W.I. (809-458-8549) features six rooms and a restaurant, with occasional entertainment. No credit cards are accepted. Budget. SUNNY GRENADINES HOTEL, Clifton, Union Island, St. Vincent and the Grenadines, W.I. (809-458-8327, fax 458-8398) has 18 basic rooms, some with kitchenettes, and overlooks the harbor. Moderate.

Minibuses service only parts of the island, mostly between Ashton and Clifton.

For sailing charters call Captain Yannis (809-435-8451).

Union Island's airstrip houses immigration facilities. Flights to St. Vincent, Carriacou, Grenada, Guadeloupe, Martinique, Port of Spain, Barbados and St. Lucia are available on LIAT (458-8230).

PALM ISLAND

Just a mile off the Union Island shore, this was once called Prune Island. The island is private and tranquil, a secluded, one-resort getaway of 130 acres, with a beach circling the island.

Owner John Caldwell and his family have built 24 rooms in cabanas at their Palm Island Beach Club. Facilities include tennis, diving, a fitness path, open-air restaurant, bar and high tea at 16.00. Contact: Palm Island, St. Vincent and the Grenadines, W.I.; 809-458-8824, fax 458-8804, U.S. 800-776-PALM, fax 310-762-7283. To get there just sail on in, or fly to Union Island and the hotel staff will take you over in their launch.

PETIT ST. VINCENT

The country's southernmost island is another private, low-key and exclusive resort. We're talking deeply exclusive. Accommodation is in 22 luxury stone cottages set in tropical gardens. You raise a yellow flag from your cabana to let the staff know you'd like room service. This is considered by resort aficionados to be the most elegant private island in the Caribbean. Amenities include watersports, fine dining, you name it. Contact owner Haze Richardson II, Petit St. Vincent Resort, St. Vincent and the Grenadines, W.I.; (809) 458-8801, fax 458-8428, U.S. (800) 654-9326.

Grenada

Introduction

Grenada, the Island of Spice, has become a bit of a legend in its own time. The island has endured some of the most radical governments and changes over the Caribbean's past 50 years; Cuba, Haiti and Jamaica come to mind as similarly affected islands. Ronald Reagan's 1983 invasion—"rescue mission" and "intervention" were euphemisms used by his administration and, in fact, are the preferred nomenclature of Grenadians today—put the island on the map for many of us. Tourist travel to Grenada understandably slacked off for some years, but today has become an important income-earner for the island, signaling Grenada's not unreluctant acceptance of the region-wide boom.

The Land

Lush, green Grenada (Greh-NAY-da), together with the islands of Carriacou (CARRY-ah-koo), Petit Martinique (Petty Martin-EEK) and 30 smaller cays, form the State of Grenada's total land area of 140 square miles (362 sq km). Grenada proper, slightly smaller than neighbouring St. Vincent, measures 21 miles (34 km) long and 12 miles (19 km) at its widest point, a land area of 120 square miles (311 sq km). The 13 square mile (34 sq km) island of Carriacou is the largest of the Grenadines and lies about 20 miles (32 km) to the north; Petit Martinique, less than one square mile, is clearly visible just across Watering Bay, east of Carriacou.

The mountains of Grenada, created eons ago by underwater volcanic eruptions, dominate the island's interior. The highest point, Mt. St. Catherine, stands at 2,757 feet (830 m), while to the south, a dormant volcanic crater, Grand Etang, has become a national park and forest reserve.

At the foot of the mountains are drier coastal woodlands, mangrove and other swampland and fertile plains where bananas, coconut, fruits and vegetables and the island's famous spices, such as nutmeg, are grown. The southern and southeastern coasts are jagged and irregular, filled with small bays, inlets and peninsulas, while the leeward coast is smooth and offers several of the island's more popular beaches. The extreme northeast's Levera National Park features a large mangrove swamp and protected offshore reefs.

In the southwest St. George's, the capital, is fronted by a natural harbor, part of which is the crater of an ancient volcano. The old town is built in and around the base of Grand Etang and its street's steep dips and crests are reminiscent of, say, San Francisco.

The country's topography and rainforests create unique habitats for many plant and animal species. The Grenada dove, as well as assorted hummingbirds, parrots and warblers can be spotted. The mangroves and lowlands host exotic herons, coots and ruddies. The armadillo, often found in stew pots, is also emblazoned on Grenada's coat of arms. The opossum, or manicou in the local Patois, is also hunted. The usual lizards and frogs are found and imported Mona monkeys can be seen in the Grand Etang rainforest.

Carriacou—from a Carib word once spelled (not by Caribs) Kayryouacou, for "Land of Reefs"—is the largest of the Grenadines and irregularly shaped. A modest central range culminates in the 950 foot (285 m) High North in the north and Chapeau Carre to the south. The island's main town, Hillsborough, sits along a wide and calm bay on the island's leeward side. Several uninhabited offshore cays, including Sandy Island, Saline Islands, Large Island, Frigate Island and Mushroom Island, are visited by picnickers, fishermen and nesting birds.

Petit Martinique's one "peak" is a 500 foot (150 m) hill, located at the center of the island. The lowland coast is home to a mere 600 islanders, involved primarily in boat building and fishing.

History

Grenada's early history follows a pattern similar to that of many southern islands of the Lesser Antilles. The Stone Age Ciboney were its first inhabitants, followed by the Amerindian Arawaks and related tribes, who arrived in several waves from regions of South America from 500 BC until the time of Christ. Arawak artifacts and petroglyphs have been found near Victoria, on the northwestern coast, and at Levera, in the northeast. They were followed, or chased, by another Amerindian group, the warlike Caribs, who had either eliminated or assimilated the Arawaks by the time Columbus embarked on his late 15th-century journeys to the New World.

Columbus sighted Grenada on his third voyage in 1498. He charted it and named it Concepcion, but apparently never landed. Later, passing Spanish sailors called the island Granada, as its hills reminded them of the eponymous Spanish city. The Caribs, however, vigorously resisted early European colonization and it took 150 years before adventurers were able to establish a settlement on the island.

In 1650 the French governor of Martinique, du Parquet, sailed to the island with 200 colonists and, for trinkets and knives, purchased land from the Caribs. This proved to be a mistake for the soon-to-be-hapless aborigines. Once the French had a foothold on the island they took more and more and soon the Caribs and the French were at war. The Caribs' bows and arrows, however, were not equal to the French armaments and most were eliminated within months. The Caribs' involvement on Grenada culminated in a dramatic mass suicide; in 1651 forty Caribs threw their children, their women and themselves off a precipice, now called Caribs' Leap, at La Morne des Sauteurs (Leapers' Hill) in the north.

Thereafter the battle for possession of Grenada was waged between the British and French and reflected the ongoing European wars, as did similar battles throughout the Lesser Antilles.

The French built forts, including the impressive Fort George, which overlooks St. George's in the south. The island changed hands several times, until the 1783 Treaty of Versailles granted possession to the British. For nearly 200 years the island remained British, an involvement that created today's economic and demographic picture.

The British imported African slaves to do hard labor on the tobacco and sugar plantations. Nutmeg was introduced from the Dutch East Indies and became an important cash crop. Life for the slaves was harsh and the planters' cruelty, coupled with their increasing paranoia as the slave population grew to outnumber theirs by four- and five-fold, resulted in a slave rebellion in 1795. The revolt's leader, Julien Fedon, born of an African mother and French father, led a year-long uprising that left dozens of British landowners dead. When reinforcements arrived and the revolt was crushed, however, Fedon had disappeared—drowned, according to legend, while escaping.

In 1834 slavery was outlawed in the British colonies. The large sugar plantations fell to near-ruin, despite the importation of East Indian indentured laborers to bolster the sagging estates. By the end of the century sugarcane had taken a back seat to nutmeg and cocoa. Bananas were introduced and eventually became a major island industry.

The 1920s and worldwide depression affected Grenada both economically and politically. Throughout the Caribbean, poor labor conditions engendered the formation of labor unions, political parties and independence movements. Grenada was one of the first British islands to agitate for independence and many historians contend it was the work of one man, the enigmatic Eric Gairy.

Gairy, a Grenadian who had worked as a clerk in the Aruba oil industry, organized island-wide strikes and political agitation on Grenada in the late 1940s. When Britain granted universal adult suffrage in 1951, which allowed for the installation of local government, Gairy and his oddly acronymed Grenada United Labor Party (GULP) won with ease. For years GULP vied for power with the opposition Grenada National Party (GNP), led by Herbert Blaize.

By 1967 Britain had granted Grenadians a greater degree of autonomy and Gairy led the call for independence. Some Grenadians questioned whether independence was necessary at that point, but the charismatic and eccentric Gairy was able to rally enough support to dominate the movement.

Gairy portrayed himself as a mystic, the destined leader of Grenada. He was brash, once leading a calypso march through an opponent's political rally. As chief minister he was accused of corruption and was censured and suspended. He was fascinated by magic and UFOs and supported research in these areas. When faced with opposition he recruited a gang of armed enforcers known as the "Mongoose Squad."

Independence came in 1974, with Gairy at the helm, but the situation quickly deteriorated, due to the increasingly quirky leader's autocratic and heavy-handed tactics. While he was off the island in 1979, his government was ousted in an armed coup d'etat, led by the radical New Jewel Movement (Jewel is for Joint Endeavor for Welfare, Education and Liberation). Three people were killed in the coup, the first in the British Caribbean. New Jewel Movement installed Prime Minister Maurice Bishop, a lawyer, as leader of the Marxist People's Revolutionary Government (PRG).

Bishop's early rule was marked by increased social programs and marked improvements in the daily lives of Grenadians. However, when Bishop, a protégé of Castro, began to import Cuban military advisors and align himself with the Soviet Union, the Caribbean, the West and even factions within his own party began to worry. Tourism, until then on its way to becoming a major foreign exchange earner, dropped through the floor.

Then, in October 1983, a revolt within the New Jewel Movement deposed Bishop in the most extreme way. Bishop and several of his friends and advisors were murdered and within days the country plummeted to a state of anarchy. A week later a joint U.S.-Caribbean military force of 2,000 invaded the island to restore order—and to rescue American students of the threatened St. George's University Medical School. Bishop's killers were imprisoned and the Cuban military force, which had been building a military airstrip south of St. George's, was ousted.

Within a year an interim government, headed by Nicholas Brathwaite, had been installed and order restored. Many Grenadians today speak of the intervention in positive terms and there is a conspicuous pro-U.S. sentiment in many quarters of the country. In 1984 elections were held and Herbert Blaize, head of the coalition New National Party (NNP), was installed as prime minister.

Several opposition parties, including GULP, the Maurice Bishop Patriotic Movement (from New Jewel Movement) and factions within the NNP have formed and reformed over the years.

People and Culture

Culturally Grenadians take their cue from Africa, France and England and, to a lesser extent, from East Indian and other Asian cultures. The long history of British and French contention over the island, mingled with various African language holdovers, has created the island's mishmash Patois, although English is the official language.

Carnival takes its precedent from the French tradition and mixes it with African imagery. Grenada's Carnival takes place on the second weekend in August and involves weeks of preparation of costumes and feasts. Calypso singers hold local competitions that culminate in the finals in August and naming of the Calypso Monarch. The three days of Carnival are packed with masquerades, marches, feasts, parties and street dancing, featuring stock characters such as "Jab Jab Molassi" and "La Jab Bless," a molasses devil and she-devil, respectively.

Carriacou's Carnival takes place in February, during the traditional pre-Lenten season. Although smaller than Grenada's Carnival, it is no less energetic, featuring street parades, male/female impersonation shows and the spectacle of "Pierrots," in which characters dressed in period costumes recite Shakespeare —and "beat" each other with big sticks when a mistake is made.

Carriacou's "Big Drum" ceremonies also reflect its African heritage. Costumed dancers move to the beat provided by drums and "chac-chac" rattles. The drums, barrels or rum kegs topped with stretched goatskin, are played at weddings, funerals, boat launchings and festivals.

African religious beliefs are blended with established Western religions, such as Anglican, which dominates, as well as Methodist, Seventh-Day Adventists, Roman Catholic and others.

The population of Grenada is approximately 91,000; Carriacou, 11,000; and Petit Martinique, 600.

Government and Economy

Grenada is a parliamentary democracy and member of the Commonwealth, with Queen Elizabeth the nominal head of state, represented on the island by a governor general. A prime minister heads the ruling party and government, which consists of a 15 member House of Representatives, elected from the islands' parishes and districts and a 13 member appointed Senate.

Grenada's economy is dependent on overseas remittances and agriculture, which accounts for nearly 90 per cent of domestic exports. Grenada is the world's largest single producer of nutmeg and a third of the workforce is involved growing the spice. Other exports include mace (a nutmeg by-product) and other spices, bananas, cocoa and tropical fruit. Bananas are Grenada's second most significant export and farmers have enjoyed healthy trading status with the U.K., due to favourable export agreements. The introduction of the EEC may eliminate those trade agreements and Grenada will look toward other export markets. Some sugarcane is grown, but it is no longer a major crop.

Tourism has grown slowly and steadily since the 1983 military intervention. Following the restoration of democracy, U.S. aid increased. The 9,000 foot (3,000 m) airport at Point Salines opened in 1984, increasing the arrivals of international carriers. Some 90,000 visitors arrive by air annually. Cruise ship arrivals, since the turn of the century a popular way to visit Grenada, have increased from 80 ships in 1983 to 450, carrying 200,000 passengers, in 1993.

Sleepy Carriacou may not remain sleepy for long; from 1992 to 1993 the number of visitors to the island doubled. The total number of hotel rooms has increased from 588 in 1983 to nearly 1,500 in 1994.

Sights

BEACHES
The leeward coast, particularly the area south of St. George's, is the tourist strip, home of many of Grenada's beaches and hotels. There are, however, an estimated 45 beaches along the 80 miles (128 km) of Grenada's coastline.

Grande Anse, a long stretch of sand just south of St. George's, is the island's most popular hangout, particularly when cruise ships are in. South of Grand Anse is the smaller Morne Rouge Bay. Petit Cabrits and Magazin beaches south of the bay are also popular, as are the beaches at L'Anse aux Epines peninsula, east of the airport.

On the northern end of the island, the bay at Sauters is long and expansive. The beach at Levera, the national park, is sometimes rough, but fine for exploring. On the eastern windward coast stop at the scenic Menere and La Tante bays.

OTHER SIGHTS

Major roads in Grenada encircle the island, with the exception of the Grand Etang Road and several others that cut across the central mountains. Most roads are good shape, although stretches along the west coast are still dicey. Major repairs, with assistance from the U.S. and others, were underway during the 1980s and most have been completed.

Eight miles (13 km) north of St. George's is Concord Falls, the first of which is accessible either by car or a 45 minute hike from the main road. You'll find a changing room here. The second cascade is a half-hour hike from the first falls. Beyond the falls a trail leads to Fedon's Camp, once the headquarters of the 1795 slave-rebellion leader Julien Fedon and now a national landmark. You can hike to Grand Etang from Concord, a six hour excursion and not an easy one.

North of Concord is Dougaldston Estate and the town of Gouyave. This is the center of the nutmeg industry and the estate offers a tour of the spice factory. Nutmeg, as well as mace, cloves and cinnamon are dried and processed here and you can buy samples. The tour is free, conducted 9.00-16.00 weekdays. Gouyave, called "the town that never sleeps," is a fishing village and parish capital.

Heading north you'll come to Victoria, another small fishing village, which features an offshore rock with Amerindian petroglyphs.

In the far north is Sauters (French for "jumpers") and the 100 foot (30 m) cliff where, in 1651, a group of Caribs jumped to their deaths rather than submit to French encroachment. East of Sauters is Levera Bay and Levera Beach, part of a national park system, where you'll find hiking trails, mangrove swamps, swimming and snorkelling. The surf and currents can be rough, particularly between the shore and the privately-owned Sugar Loaf cay.

South of Levera is Lake Antoine, which has formed in a volcanic crater, and the River Antoine Rum Distillery. The 18th century distillery is one of the oldest in the islands and is still powered by a waterwheel. The rum is exceptional and you're invited to tour the estate.

Grenville is Grenada's second largest town and a busy port. Here you'll find several historical buildings, including the stone Anglican Parish Church and the post office. The town market is lively on Saturdays and a local spice factory is open to the public. Nearby is the old Pearls Airport, not in use since the completion of Port Salines International in 1984.

Inland is Mt. St. Catherine, Grenada's highest point at 2,757 feet (830 m). The climb to the mountain's summit starts at the village of Mt. Hope, west of Grenville. You first pass through old plantation land and forests, as well as the remains of a concrete delivery truck that made it up the mountainside, but didn't make it back down. The path follows a donkey trail to the summit, where you can see the Grenadines to the north.

Farther south, along the east coast, is La Sagesse Protected Seascape, an area of reefs, mangrove swamps and beaches.

The Grand Etang Road cuts across the island from St. George's to Grenville and is one of the island's more fascinating drives. The paved road winds and curves in places, through misty rainforest and drier woodlands and the views are breathtaking. The Grand Etang National Park visitors center describes the flora and fauna of the area, as well as the origins of the park's centerpiece, the Grand Etang, a shimmering 13-acre lake in the crater of an extinct volcano. You'll see the lake from the visitors center and several hiking trails, some difficult and some easy, begin here. The Morne la Baye Trail is short and not difficult. The Mt. Qua Qua Trail is difficult, over an hour in length. Off the Mt. Qua Qua Trail is a loop around the lake. You can also walk to Fedon's Camp and Concord Falls from here, an sometimes arduous hike of nearly six hours. The Forestry Headquarters (809-442-7425) is open 8.00-16.00 on weekdays.

From Grand Etang it's a drive or hike to the 50 foot (15 m) Annandale Falls, a popular swimming, picnicking and hiking area. The visitors center (809-440-2452) here is open 8.00-17.00 daily.

Much of the island is accessible without guides, but several outfits offer tours of the major sights as well as off-island tours of Carriacou and Petit Martinique. Prices, which include transport, drinks and sometimes lunch, range from US$20 to US$60 per person for groups of four or more. Call Arnold's Hike Grenada and Tour Grenada (809-440-0531 or 440-2213, fax 440-4118) or Henry's Safari Tours (809-444-5313, fax 444-4847).

St. George's

St. George's, one of the Caribbean's most picturesque towns, is fronted by a deep, natural harbor and a central inner harbor, the Carenage. The town's antique buildings, a blend of French colonial and English Georgian and Victorian architecture, were built in and around the hills at the base of the central mountains.

Port St. Louis was the area's first settlement, established by the French in 1650, in the area now known as The Lagoon. The French next built nearby Fort Royal, which was occupied in 1762 by the British, who named it St. George's.

The Carenage, shaped like a thumb, is the town's center of activity. Here you'll find the cruise ship docks, shops, the Grentel (Grenada Telephone) offices, the General Post Office, the Board of Tourism office (809-440-2279, fax 440-6637) and a cluster of restaurants and small cafes. The Carenage is a wonderful place to spend an hour or so and to start an exploration of the city. A statue, "Christ of the Deep," located at the head of the harbor, was presented to the Grenadian people by Italy's Costa Line for their help in rescuing passengers and crew from a burning cruise ship. Its inscription reads, "In Grateful Remembrance of the Fraternal Christian Hospitality Shown to Passengers and Crew of the Italian Liner Bianca C Destroyed by Fire in This Harbor on October 22, 1961." The ship, submerged in 170 feet (51 m) of water, is slated to become a marine national park.

Several buildings were burned in a serious fire on the Carenage in 1990 and still exhibit their scars. Water taxis are available for those who want to cross the Carenage on water rather than walk around it. The cost is EC$1 and worth it for the view.

The Grenada National Museum is located in the barracks and prison of a 1704 French fortification to the west of the Carenage. The museum contains exhibits of Amerindian artifacts and culture, a telegraph installed on the island in 1871 and one of the Empress Josephine's bathtubs. The museum is open 9.00-16.30 Monday through Friday and 10.00-13.30 on Saturday; admission, EC$1.

On the west side of town the Esplanade, with its fish and meat markets, runs along the ocean. A quick way to reach the Esplanade is through the Sendall Tunnel, built in 1895 to save donkeys laden with market goods from climbing over the hill. On Granby Street you'll find the large, sprawling and oft-photographed Market Square, busiest on Saturdays.

Fort George, a French fort built in 1705, now houses police headquarters. Some cannon are still in place and you can view the city from platforms. It was here that Maurice Bishop and his followers were murdered in 1983.

Along Church Street you'll find the impressive St. Andrew's Presbyterian Kirk, dating back to 1830, and St. George's Anglican Cathedral, which was completed in 1825. St. George's Catholic Cathedral, built in 1884, features a church tower dating back to 1818. York House is Grenada's seat of Parliament and the Supreme Court; next door is the 1780 Registry Building. The Methodist Church on Green Street is the city's oldest church, dating to 1820.

Marryshow House, on Tyrrel Street, was built early this century and is the home of Grenada's Folk Theater, which presents plays, dance and music. For a schedule of programs call 809-440-2451.

On the outskirts of town, several forts are open to the public. Forts Frederick and Matthew were started in 1783 by the French and later completed by their British occupants.

Practical Information

ACCOMMODATION

Hotels add a ten per cent service charge and an eight per cent room tax. Tax is also added to food and beverages.

❏ LASOURCE, P.O. Box 852, St. George's, Grenada, W.I. (809-444-2556, fax 444-2561; North America 800-544-2883) is an all-inclusive spa resort on Pink Gin Beach, near Point Salines, offering saunas, Swedish massages, salt loofah rubs, facials and seaweed wraps, as well as golf, tennis, fencing, archery and other eclectic sports. Luxury.

❏ RAMADA RENAISSANCE HOTEL, P.O. Box 441, St. George's, Grenada, W.I. (809-444-4371/5, fax 444-4800) is the largest hotel on Grenada, with 186 rooms, several bars, a swimming pool, two restaurants, gift shops and watersports, set on 20 acres by the popular Grand Anse Beach. Luxury.

❏ LA SAGESSE NATURE CENTER, P.O. Box 44, St. George's, Grenada, W.I. (809-444-6458, fax 444-4847) offers only three rooms, but the setting, an old plantation house on a bay in the southeast, is hard to beat. Facilities include a restaurant and bar, a nearby bird sanctuary and hiking trails. Moderate.

❏ MAMMA'S LODGE, P.O. Box 248, St. George's, Grenada, W.I. (809-440-1459, fax 440-7788) is located on the Lagoon Road near downtown St. George's. The small guesthouse offers nine rooms and is located near the famous MAMMA'S (809-440-1459) restaurant and bar. Easily one of the Lesser Antilles' top spots for unique West Indian cuisine, including manicou (opossum), armadillo, booby bird, sea urchin and "oil down," a breadfruit and coconut milk dish. Mamma, alas, has died, but her tradition of fine food remains strong. No credit cards at Mamma's. Budget.

EATING

❏ NUTMEG (809-440-2539) is located on the Carenage and very popular for lunch. Hamburgers, sandwiches and West Indian dishes are served. Moderate.

❏ RUDOLPH'S (809-440-2241), also on the Carenage, serves Continental and West Indian. The restaurant is closed Sundays and no credit cards are accepted. Moderate.

❏ THE RED CRAB (809-444-4424) in L'Anse aux Epines specializes in seafood, particularly lobster and crab dishes, and steaks, with indoor and outdoor seating. The restaurant is often crowded and features live music on Fridays. Moderate-expensive.

❏ MORNE FENDUE GREAT HOUSE (809-440-9330) at Sauters is the place to stop for lunch when touring the north of the island. The lunch buffet includes local recipes. Owner Betty Mascoll's pepperpot soup and nutmeg-laden rum punches are renowned. The four-room guesthouse, an old plantation house, is typically West Indian. No credit cards are accepted here and only lunch is served. Moderate.

GETTING THERE

Point Salines International Airport is serviced by BWIA (809-440-3818), British Airways (809-444-2796), American Airlines (809-444-2222), Air Canada and LIAT (809-440-2796).

Charter flights to and from various islands, including the Grenadines, are offered by Helenair (809-444-4401), Airlines of Carriacou (809-444-4425) and Aeretuyl (809-444-4732).

Daily flights from Port Salines to Carriacou Airport are available on LIAT. The trips takes 15 minutes and the cost is US$31 one-way, double for the round trip.

The departure tax from (but not between) Grenada and Carriacou is EC$35.

GETTING AROUND

■ PUBLIC TRANSPORTATION

Taxis are unmetered and rates, set by the government, are posted at hotels and the taxi stand at the Carenage. Add one-third to all rates after 18.00. For tours, renting a taxi will run US$15 per hour.

A water taxi service operates from the Carenage to Grand Anse, a nice way of making the short trip.

Inexpensive buses and minibuses, the typical West Indian wild ride through paradise, can be spotted by their individualized names ("Mannish" or "Jesus Mine"). Buses to the outer island depart from the Market and the Esplanade in St. George's, or you can flag them down along the road. Buses rarely run after 20.00 or on Sundays and holidays.

■ RENTALS

Rental cars are easy to organize and rates start at US$40 per day. This is the best way to tour the island. In St. George's call Avis (809-440-3936), Budget Rent-a-Car (airport 809-444-1620, St. George's 440-2778, fax 440-4174), Coyaba Car Rentals (809-444-4129) or MCR Car Rentals (809-440-5398, fax 440-6692). Maitland Motor Rentals (809-444-4022, fax 440-4119) rents Yamaha motorcycles as well as cars.

You'll need to purchase a local driving permit, which can be arranged by the rental company; the cost is EC$30. Remember to drive on the left.

■ FERRIES

Ferries run between the Carenage in St. George's and the Hillsborough jetty on Carriacou. The trip takes three to four hours, depending on the seas. The following have been operating for some time, but always check schedules: the Alexia II and Adelaide B depart Grenada to Carriacou at 9.30 Wednesday and Saturday, returning at the same time on Thursday and Monday. The Alexia III departs from Grenada to Carriacou at 9.30 Tuesday, 11.00 Friday and 7.00 Sunday, returning at 9.30 Wednesday and Saturday and 17.00 Sunday. The fare is EC$20 one-way, EC$30 round-trip.

The Little Desrine, Edna David and the Winnifred sail from Grenada to Trinidad at 19.00 Tuesday and return at 8.00 Friday. The Wisdom departs Carriacou for Union Island at 13.00 on Thursday and Monday.

MONEY, HOURS AND COMMUNICATION

The Eastern Caribbean dollar, Grenada's currency, currently trades at EC$2.70 to US$1. Many businesses will accept U.S. and Canadian dollars, but don't count on it. Credit cards and traveler's checks are accepted in most hotels, restaurants and boutiques, but not at the markets and small shops.

Money can be exchanged at hotels and banks, with banks giving the best rates. Banking are generally open 8.00-14.00 Monday through Friday and 14.30-

17.00 on Friday. Banks can be found on the main streets of St. George's, Grand Anse, Gouyave, Grenville, Sauters and Carriacou.

Regular business hours are 8.00-12.00 and 13.00-16.00 Monday through Friday and 8.00-12.00 on Saturday. For the most part, Grenada shuts down on Sunday, although some shops extend their hours to accommodate cruise ship traffic.

Grenada uses an 809 telephone area code. Offices of Cable and Wireless and Grentel (809-440-1000) are located on the Carenage. Open 7.00-19.00 Monday through Saturday and 16.00-18.00 on Sunday.

Grenada's newspapers are sophisticated and contain quite a bit of editorial comment and local and international news—surprising for an island of this size, perhaps not so surprising given its history over the past decade. Look for the weeklies *The Grenadian Voice, Grenada Today* and *The Informer*.

The General Post Office, on the Carenage, is open 8.00-15.30 Monday through Thursday and until 16.30 on Friday.

ENTERTAINMENT

■ SPORTS

For sailing charters go to The Moorings (809-444-4439 or 444-4549) at Secret Harbor or Seabreeze Yacht Charters (809-444-4924) in the Spice Island Marine Center on Prickly Bay, both in L'Anse aux Epines.

For deep-sea fishing call Evans Chartering Services (809-444-4422).

Favourite dives include the small cay called Kick 'Em Jenny, where coral and marine life are plentiful, and the Bianca C, the Italian liner that sank at St. George's. This second dive is for seasoned divers and strong swimmers only, as the currents are unpredictable and strong. Call Dive Grenada (809-444-4371, fax 444-4800) at the Renaissance Hotel, or Grand Anse Aquatics (809-444-4129) at the Coyoba Resort, both in Grand Anse, for diving information and rentals.

The Grenada Golf and Country Club (809-444-4128) at Grand Anse features a nine-hole course. The all-inclusive LaSource, also in Grand Anse, offers a private course.

USEFUL ADDRESSES

■ TOURISM INFORMATION

Grenada Board of Tourism:

❏ The Carenage, St. George's, Grenada, W.I.; 809-440-2279, fax 440-6637.
❏ 820 Second Ave., Suite 900-D, New York, NY 10017; 800-927-9554 or 212-687-9554, fax 212-573-9731.

❏ 439 University Ave., Suite 820, Toronto, Ontario M5G 1Y8; 416-595-1339, fax 595-8278.

❏ 1 Collingham Gardens, London SW5 0HW; 071-370-5164, fax 370-7040.

❏ Hotel Association, Ross Point Inn, Lagoon Rd., St. George's, Grenada, W.I.; 800-322-1753 or 809-444-1353, fax 809-444-4847, North America 800-223-9815, New York 212-545-8469.

■ OTHER

❏ Police, 911.

❏ Ambulance, 434.

❏ St. George's General Hospital, 440-2051/2/3.

❏ Mitchells' Pharmacy (open until 21.00), Grand Anse Shopping Center; 444-4845.

❏ Astral Travel and Tours, The Carenage; 440-5180.

❏ American Express, Church Street, St. George's; 444-2945.

❏ Federal Express, The Carenage, St. George's; 440-2206/1619.

Carriacou

The 13 square mile (34 sq km) island of Carriacou hosts a sparse population of 11,000, a tenth of whom live in Hillsborough, the capital. The rest live in the countryside, particularly in the village of Windward, which has a Scottish heritage, and in the L'Esterre area.

The island is low-lying and dry, a relaxing and easy place to explore. Several small bays and beaches, as well as outlying cays, are attractions. Carriacou means "Land of Reefs" and diving is also a big draw. Tanki's Watersport Paradise (809-443-8406) is one of several diving outfits on the island.

Carriacou was first settled by Arawaks and Caribs, then Frenchmen who, in the 17th century, used the island as a base for turtle hunting. Eventually the English and Scottish moved in and plantations grew. The main crop became cotton, followed by sugarcane, coffee, cocoa and indigo. Today's main industries are fishing, subsistence farming and, to a lesser extent, shipbuilding and repair.

The islanders have retained aspects of their African heritage, especially through their unique Big Drum dances. Other events include the traditional pre-Lenten Carnival and the popular August Carriacou Regatta.

Hillsborough, a long, ramshackle town, is built along Hillsborough Bay on the leeward side of the island. Here you'll find the tourism office, banks, a supermarket, bakeries, cafes, rum shops, an outdoor market, the jetty, the police station, the post office, a small seaside park and several guesthouses. The town is quiet and dusty, with a turn-of-the-century West Indian charm. Hurricane Janet whipped through the island in 1955 and islanders say things haven't been the same since. Indeed, much of Main Street appears to be under construction.

Stop in at the Carriacou Museum (809-443-8288), a branch of the Carriacou Historical Society, on Patterson Street. The museum, which also houses a library, displays Arawak and Carib artifacts, an old telephone exchange and photos of the hurricane damage. Curator Cassandra Cox Peters is a good source of information. The museum is open 9.30-15.45 Monday through Friday; admission is EC$5.

Also visit the scenic overlook and plantation ruins at Belair, or the Canute Calliste Art Gallery in L'Esterre. Calliste is a well-known folk artist and local personality. Tours can be organized through Carriacou Nature Tour & Trail Project (809-443-8064 or 443-7134) in Belvedere.

There are just a few hotels and half a dozen guesthouses on the island, most of them in Hillsborough. THE SILVER BEACH RESORT, Silver Beach, Carriacou, Grenada, W.I. (809-443-7337, fax 443-7156) sits on the beach with views to Union Island, with 18 units, some self-catering; a bar, restaurant and Silver Beach Diving (809-443-7882). Moderate. CASSADA BAY RESORT, Belmont, Carriacou, Grenada, W.I. (809-443-7494, fax 443-7672) has 14 units overlooking the White Island, Large Island, Saline Island and Frigate Island cays on the island's southern shore. Moderate. MILLIE'S GUESTHOUSE, Church Street, Hillsborough, Carriacou, Grenada, W.I. (809-443-7310, fax 443-8107) is new, located near the center of town. Budget. PEACE HAVEN GUESTHOUSE, Hillsborough, Carriacou, Grenada, W.I. (809-443-7475 or 443-8365), on Main Street, sits on the bay. Three of the six rooms share a bath and toilet. Budget. Near Peace Haven, the CALLALOO RESTAURANT (809-443-8004) is known for its West Indian cuisine.

Down Island Villa Rentals (809-443-8182) is the agent for local apartments and villas.

Carriacou Airport (809-443-7362) is located a few minutes drive west of Hillsborough. As a matter of fact, the road from Hillsborough to the south and west crosses the airstrip—it's a small one. LIAT (809-443-7362) connects the island with Grenada, Antigua, Barbados, Dominica, Trinidad, Union Island and several others, with stops. There are customs and immigration facilities at the airstrip.

Minibuses and taxis run all over the island and can be found at the jetty and market in Hillsborough. There are no real routes or schedules, but life manages to go on. Minibus fares average EC$2 and taxis charge set rates.

Rent cars through Barba's (809-443-7454) in Tyrrel Bay in Harvey Vale or at the Silver Beach Resort (809-443-7337).

Several helpful telephone numbers: Ambulance (774 or 809-443-7400), police and fire (809-443-7482), Tourist Board Office (on Main Street, 809-443-7948).

BARBADOS

TRINIDAD & TOBAGO

'Carnival in Port of Spain, Trinidad', by Melton Prior,
from The Illustrated London News, *May 5, 1888*

'A Spanish Buccaneer' from Esquemelin,
Pirates of America (1681)

Cricket, played Mustique style

Cattle boat, Hillsborough Bay, Carriacou, The Grenadines

(Above) Union Island, The Grenadines;
(below) Colourful gingerbread houses in Mustique

The Harbour of St Lucia, March 10, 1896

Barbados

St. LUCY
- North Point
- Archer's Bay
- Greenidge
- Animal Flower Cave
- Cuckold Point
- Nesfield
- Gay's Cove
- St. Nicholas Abbey
- Fustic
- Bentham's
- Morgan Lewis Windmill
- Six Men's Bay
- Farley Hill National Park & Barbados Wildlife Reserve
- **Speightstown**
- Belleplaine
- Long Pond
- **St. PETER**
- ▲ Mt. Hillaby
- **St. ANDREW**
- Gibbs Bay
- **St. JAMES**
- Mose Bottom
- Bathsheba Bay
- Orange Hill
- Welchman Hall Gully National Park
- **Bathsheba**
- Sandy Lane Bay
- **St. JOSEPH**
- Folkestone Underwater Park and Museum
- Conset Bay
- Holetown
- Villa Nova Plantation
- Bath
- **St. THOMAS**
- Harrison Cave
- **St. JOHN**
- Paynes Bay
- Jackson
- Ragged Point
- Ashford Bird Park
- Thorpe
- Gun Hill Signal Station
- **St. GEORGE**
- Barbados Zoo Park
- **St. MICHAEL**
- Cottage Vale
- Sunbury Plantation
- **St. PHILIP**
- Crane Bay
- Sam Lord's Castle
- Bulkeley
- Marchfield
- **Bridgetown**
- The Crane
- St. Michael's Cathedral
- Barbados Museum
- Sargeant
- **CHRIST CHURCH**
- Salt Cave Point
- Carlisle Bay
- Garrison Savannah Historic District
- Needham's Point
- ✈ Grantley Adams International Airport
- Hastings
- St. Lawrence
- Oistins
- Long Bay
- Oistins Bay
- Inch Marlowe Point
- South Point

Atlantic Ocean

N
↑

Constitution River

ST. JAMES = parish

0   5 km
0   3 miles

Caribbean Sea

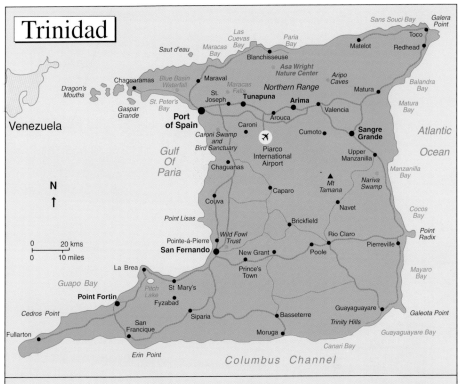

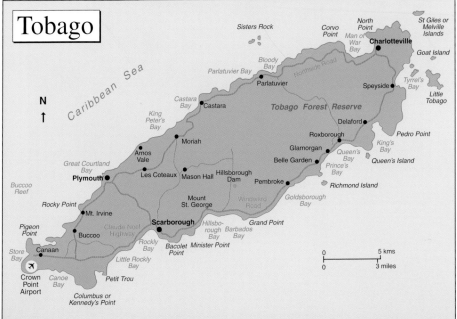

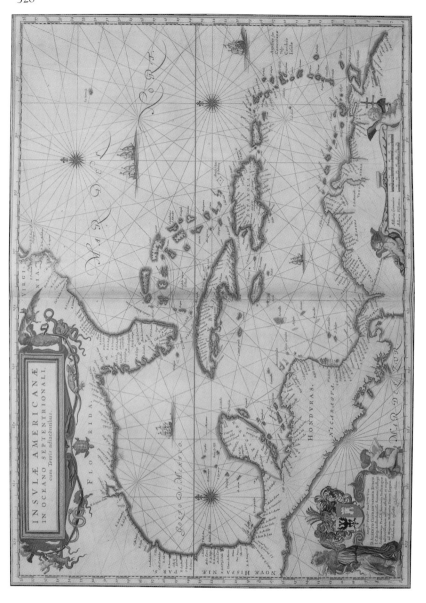

Barbados

Introduction

Barbados is, in some ways, an anomaly. In fact the island is not, technically, in the Caribbean at all—it lies outside the main Lesser Antilles chain, 180 miles (288 km) northwest of Trinidad, floating alone in the Atlantic Ocean like a stray pup.

Barbados was settled by Amerindian Arawaks and Caribs, who uncharacteristically abandoned it for unknown reasons. It was not, unlike its neighbours, visited by Columbus, but rather by Portuguese explorers, who made no substantive claim to the island. Subsequently, it became a British possession for its entire colonial history and today retains many British customs and sensibilities.

Further, Barbados is a relatively prosperous island, unpossessed of the pervasive, grinding poverty often seen in its Lesser Antilles neighbours. There still are, of course, the haves and the have-nots, yet high standards in education have resulted in high employment and numerous university graduates.

Yet, in most ways, Barbados is distinctly Caribbean. From its economy once based on sugarcane and slavery, to its fiercely fought politics, calypso-infused festivals and limpid, blue waters, the island is precisely at home.

The Land

The teardrop-shaped island, 21 miles (34 km) north to south and 14 miles (22 k) at its widest point, is an ancient one, older than its volcanic neighbours in the Windwards, and relatively flat. The highest point of its limestone-capped hills, Mt. Hillaby, reaches only 1,115 feet (335 m) above sea level. The hills tend to undulate rather than jut and tame valleys offer the perfect terrain for growing sugarcane, which Barbados did and does in abundance.

The windward eastern coast is pounded by the open Atlantic—on a map it appears concave, almost gutted—and features several spots with dramatic cliffs and hidden bays, particularly at Bathsheba. The southern and western coasts' calmer waters host most of the island's beachfront resorts and hotels.

The central sections of the island are characterized by rolling valleys, farmland and small settlements. Forests are dry and scrubby in places, dotted with open pastures, sugarcane fields and a few rivers and streams. The terrain, in a way, displays a uniformity that may disappoint anyone interested in mountain hiking or rainforest exploration.

History

Due to its isolated location, Barbados was removed from the wars and hand-changing between European powers that so disrupted life for the Lesser Antilles.

The island's first settlers were Amerindian Arawaks and later the warrior Caribs, whom the Portuguese explorer Pedro a Campos may have encountered when he first explored the island in 1536. Not much is recorded about early Portuguese and Carib encounters; it appears that the Portuguese did little with the island but populate it with pigs, intended for use by passing ships. And, importantly, they named it Los Barbados ("The Bearded Ones"), thought to refer to the aerial beardlike roots which hang from the island's fig trees.

By the time a party of 80 English settlers and their slaves landed on the island in 1627 the land was uninhabited. The English established a settlement at Holetown, on the western coast and set about cultivating the land. Indentured laborers from the working classes of Scotland and Ireland fled for Barbados and the Caribbean, under duress from the ongoing struggles between Oliver Cromwell and King Charles I. With a large labor force and terrain well-suited for sugarcane, plantations grew rapidly. The great plantocracies were in the hands of a few wealthy, often absentee, landowners.

In the eyes of many, Barbados came to define the industry. So great was the culture established around sugarcane and its byproducts that the word "rum" is thought to have been coined in the processing mills of Barbados. Some contend it is an abbreviation for the word "rumbullion," used to describe the effect of the alcohol on those who imbibed it.

The island's first governing body, the House of Assembly, was established in 1639 and today Barbados' legislature is the third oldest established government in the British Commonwealth. The planters were firmly entrenched by the 1650s, and the number of African slaves imported to work the sugarcane plantations—by then the island's sole industry—greatly outnumbered the Europeans. Harsh treatment, due in part to the planters' paranoia, succeeded in producing what the planters had hoped to avoid: slave rebellion.

In the late 17th and early 18th centuries slave revolts reverberated throughout the Greater and Lesser Antilles, with major uprisings in Jamaica, Haiti and Martinique. In Barbados slaves revolted in 1672, 1696 and 1702. Then, during

Easter 1816, a slave known as Bussa, from Bayley's Plantation in St. Philip, led the island's largest uprising to date. A tragically ironic rumor had spread among the slaves that emancipation had been granted, but that the plantation owners were refusing to comply. The revolt, and subsequent insurrections, were summarily and harshly squashed by the government. Sugar prevailed, as did slavery, until the 1834 abolition. Bussa is today honoured in a statue on the outskirts of Bridgetown.

After emancipation the freed slaves and their descendants drifted away from the sugarcane fields. Many went to work on canal construction in Panama, while others found work throughout the Caribbean and the Americas. The Barbados economy began to rely on remittances from these expatriate Barbadians. By the early 20th century the canal was completed and Barbados found itself in the same state as many of its neighbours—an economic backwash of diminishing importance to its colonial power, Britain, which was at that time dealing with the looming specter of European war.

As with many of the islands, the industrial revolution, war and the Great Depression combined to engender the growth of trade unions and political parties. Barbados's first large political party was the Barbados Progressive League, established in 1938 by Oxford-educated lawyer Grantley Adams. Through the work of this party and others universal suffrage came about in the Fifties. In 1958 Barbados joined the West Indies Federation, with Sir Grantley Adams as chief minister. The federation was dissolved four years later and subsequent agitation for independence led to elections. Independence was granted on 30 November 1966, with Errol Barrow serving as prime minister.

People and Culture

The 255,000 people of Barbados inhabit an island of 166 square miles (430 sq km), which makes for one of the highest population density rates in the Lesser Antilles—more than 1,500 per square mile.

The Amerindian influences on Barbadian (or Bajan, in the local dialect) culture were insubstantial. No place names and relatively few artifacts indicate their presence. Spanish and French influences seen on neighbouring Windward Islands were also negligible. The island sensibility is a product of two primary cultures, British and African. Nearly 80 per cent of Barbados' citizens are descendants of African slaves. The minority white population includes descendants of "poor whites" (in the past derisively called "red legs"), the Scottish Highlanders who fled to Barbados during Cromwell's purges and eventually settled in the northeastern Scotland District. A mixed-race group exists (and has grown) as it does on all islands where slaves were kept. East Indians and Asians live in small communities, mostly in Bridgetown.

British culture and customs are strong, so much so that the country has been described as "more English than England." Children attend school in crisp uniforms, white-wigged magistrates debate in court and cricket is played with a fervor that borders on the non-secular. The government infrastructure, the predominance of Anglicanism, the local architecture, the elaborate parade dress of the Royal Barbados Police Band and traditional afternoon tea all reflect British influence.

English, of course, is the country's official language, although a rapid Patois, which combines vocabulary and structures picked up from around the Caribbean and from Africa, is widely spoken.

Devotion to English, coupled with a West Indian sensitivity, is exhibited by several Barbadian literary lights, who have made their mark on regional and world literature. Novelist George Lamming, born in Barbados in 1927, often explores the dilemma of race and culture confronting Caribbean peoples living overseas. Lamming's works include a critically acclaimed first novel, *In the Castle of My Skin* (1953), and *Season of Adventure* (1960).

Frank Collymore (1893-1980), a poet and short story writer, was influential in the Caribbean literary scene during the heyday of 1930s nationalism. His volumes include *Beneath the Casuarinas* (1945) and *Flotsam* (1948) and a posthumous collection of short fiction, *The Man Who Loved Attending Funerals and Other Stories* (1993). Collymore's major legacy, however, may be the Barbadian literary magazine, *Bim*, which he established in 1942 and edited for most of his life. Over its long life (*Bim* is still published irregularly), the magazine has printed and promoted the work of major West Indian literary talents.

Edward Brathwaite, born in 1930, is known for poetry that incorporates West Indian rhythms and prose. His works include *Rights of Passage* (1967), *Islands* (1969) and *Sun Poem* (1982).

Several Bajan customs hearken back, if not directly to Africa days, at least to slave days. One is the continuing use of chattel houses, aptly named for people who were once regarded as property. Chattel houses were slave quarters, small wooden multi-roofed houses, often on stilts, that were designed to be moved from plantation to plantation as slaves were bought and sold. The design, though modified, is still used today.

Local theater groups perform plays and dances, often depicting the vagaries of love and life in the West Indies. Check the radio and newspapers for performances by Sistren, an all-female theater group who perform in the Bajan dialect. The National Cultural Foundation (809-427-2623) sponsors festivals throughout the year, including the National Independence Festival of the Creative Arts, a November festival that culminates in Independence Day (30 November) performances of music, dance, art and drama.

The annual Crop Over Festival is Barbados' nod to the sugarcane heydays. The July-August festival celebrates the harvest and features many of the lively excesses of the pre-Lenten carnivals of Trinidad and Tobago, St. Lucia and the French islands. From mid-July calypsonians perform around the countryside. The week of Crop Over features the crowning of the Calypso Monarch, a large Bridgetown Market day with local Bajan cooking and the climactic Kadooment Day, when masqueraders and singers pour into the streets of Bridgetown for parades, fireworks, dancing and drinking.

The Oistins Fish Festival takes place on Easter Weekend and celebrates Barbados' links to the sea with boat racing, fishing displays, fish-boning contests and food displays.

Government and Economy

Sugarcane and its byproducts were once the economic bedrock of the country; tourism has now taken its place as the country's major foreign exchange earner, contributing 12 per cent of the GDP and employing 13 per cent of the labor force. About 450,000 people visit the island each year, as well as an additional 433,000 cruise ship passengers. A third of the overnight visitors come from the U.S., with another 13 per cent from Canada, and they utilize the 150 hotels (14,500 beds) in the country. The government is currently spending US$6 million to remodel Bridgetown's cruise ship port area, adding some 20 duty-free and sundry shops.

Light manufacturing of clothing, furniture and electronic products accounts for a tenth of the domestic product, while agriculture, in which sugarcane is still the principal crop, represents less than ten per cent. Fishing is primarily a subsistence industry, with local fishermen providing for restaurant, hotel and local consumption.

Barbados' per capita income is one of the highest in the Caribbean, as is its literacy rate. The government pays tuition for all Barbadians attending the Cave Hill campus of the regional University of the West Indies. The country also hosts a teacher training college, a community college and a polytechnic institute.

Barbados is an independent member of the Commonwealth. The Queen is the titular head of state, represented on the island by a governor general. Parliament comprises two houses, an Lower House of Assembly with 27 elected members and an Upper House of Assembly with 21 appointed members. The government is led by a prime minister, who is leader of the majority party.

Sights

BEACHES

The southern and western coasts tend to be less rough than those on the windward side and, as a result, are where most of the tourism industry has set up shop. All beaches are public, but access to some is difficult due to hotels. Not all beaches have facilities, but many feature the ubiquitous pseudo-Rastafarians peddling their wares up and down the shore line. Annoying, but mostly harmless. A note: Barbados has experienced incidents of theft, pickpocketing and the like in and around tourist areas. While Barbados is not dangerous, you would be well-advised to lock your rental car, watch valuables at the beach and avoid walking along isolated stretches of beach at night.

The entire western coast, north of Bridgetown, is really one long beach. Route 1 runs along the coast from Bridgetown to north of Speighstown. Stop at Brighton, Gibbs Beach and Heywoods for good swimming.

South of Bridgetown is Carlisle Bay and another series of beaches, often fronted by hotels and apartments. Needham's Point is a favourite with locals. Accra Beach has some facilities and picnic tables and is often crowded, as are Miami Beach and Crane Beach. The eastern coast features several isolated spots, where the water is rough, but swimming is fine. Morgan Lewis Beach is a short walk from the East Coast Road.

OTHER SIGHTS

Those interested in nature hikes should start by contacting the Natural Areas Conservation Committee (tourism board, 809-427-2623, fax 426-4080), an umbrella group incorporating members of the Barbados Environmental Association, the Caribbean Conservation Association, the Society of Caribbean Ornithology and the International Council of Bird Protection. Numerous projects are on the boards, including preservation of the Graeme Hall Swamp in the south.

The Barbados National Trust (809-426-2421) organizes weekly Sunday hikes to historic plantation houses, sugar factory yards, natural sites and other places of interest. The hikes, which are free, start at 6.00 and conclude at about 15.30. An excellent road system and relatively accurate signs make getting around Barbados easy. The country is divided into 11 parishes, developed in the early days as administrative districts. Most roads lead to Bridgetown, passing through villages with such names as Easy Hall, Farmers, Retreat and Byde Mill.

Driving north from Bridgetown, on the Spring Garden Highway, you'll pass several rum refineries, the Lazaretto Gardens and national archives and the Cave Hill University of the West Indies campus, before arriving in Holetown. Holetown is the site of the first British landing on the island in 1627. The site apparently reminded the settlers of Limehouse Hole on the River Thames. Today it is a small but busy fishing village with some commerce. The landing is honoured each February with the Holetown Festival.

Nearby is the Folkestone Underwater Park and Museum. The reef here is protected and there's a fascinating underwater snorkelling trail. A Greek barge has been deliberately sunk and is home to many brightly colored, tropical fish. Glass-bottomed boats are available as well. A small museum and aquarium is open 10.00-17.00, Sunday through Friday; admission is BDS$1.

Farther north is Speighstown, a small harbor village used mainly during the sugar exporting days. North of the town is the Mount Gay Distillery, where Barbados' famous rum is produced. The distillery has been in operation since the 1800s and produces half a million gallons each year. Another Mount Gay distillery is located near Bridgetown. Tours are conducted 8.00-16.00 on weekdays.

In the center of the island are several sites worth a stop. Along Highway 2 you'll pass the Sharon Moravian Church, originally built in 1799 by the first missionary group to minister to the slave population. The church was destroyed by a hurricane in 1831 and rebuilt in 1833. Farther east is Harrison's Cave (809-438-6640/1), an underground complex with lighted, ochre-tinted stalactites and stalagmites, a 40 foot (12 m) water cascade and underground ponds. A daily guided tour is conducted by electric tram, starting at 9.30, and reservations are recommended. Admission is BDS$15 for adults, half that for children.

Farther north on the highway is the Flower Forest (809-433-8152), a landscaped botanical garden set on an old plantation. The garden features colorful and fragrant species from Barbados and from around the world—flower lovers shouldn't miss it. The views from here are breathtaking; visible to the west is Mt. Hillaby. The gardens are open daily, 9.00-17.00; admission is BDS$10 for adults, BDS$5 for children.

Continue north on Highway 2 to the Farley Hill National Park (809-422-3555), a botanical garden and 19th century plantation house with great views of the east coast. The admission is BDS$3 per car. Open 7.00-18.00 daily.

Across the highway, the Barbados Wildlife Reserve (809-422-8826) is a large mahogany forest with green monkeys, exotic birds and other animals roaming freely. Some, such as the alligator, are caged. Also on the grounds are an aviary and small natural history museum. Admission is BDS$10 for adults, BDS$5 for children; open 10.00-17.00 daily.

Sam Lord's Castle, on the southeastern coast, is now part of the Marriott hotel resort chain. Samuel Lord was a wealthy 19th century planter, rake and reputed land pirate. Lord plundered ships by hanging lanterns along the shore line to simulate the lights of a harbor settlement. When the ships ran aground, Lord and his crew would relieve them of their contents. The castle is something of an overblown attraction and more the centerpiece for the large and flashy resort than a historical site.

On Highway 3 the Andromeda Gardens (809-433-9261), another National Trust entity, are filled with flowers from around the world. Admission is BDS$8, children half price, and the gardens are open from 8.00 to sunset daily. Just north of Andromeda is Bathsheba, renowned for its crashing waves and rock cliffs.

The Barbados National Trust (809-426-2421), in addition to its Sunday Hikes, has created a Heritage Passport and Heritage Mini Passport, designed to give visitors access to a number of historical, cultural and ecological sites at discounted rates. The Heritage Passport allows entrance to National Trust sites, as well as the Welchman Hall Gully National Park, Gun Hill Signal Station, Codrington College, the Jewish Synagogue, Morgan Lewis Hill and the Sunbury Plantation and St. Nicholas Abbey greathouses. The passport costs US$35 and the mini passport costs US$18.

Bridgetown

Bridgetown, formerly "The Bridge" for the span over the Constitution River, was founded in 1628 by the Earl of Carlisle. The town houses a population of nearly 100,000, although the numbers belie its physical size—it does not seem large. Downtown, crowded with cars, taxis and buses, can be seen in a few hours. In places Bridgetown displays more concrete than West Indian charm. Still, it is a pleasant, negotiable city and the island's hub.

Eight highways, the main links to the country's parishes, leave the town center. The outskirts and suburbs of Bridgetown are older and feature the gingerbread and stone structures of plantation days.

The small inner harbor is known as the Careenage, where fishing boats and smaller pleasure craft dock alongside the walkway. You can, if you time it, buy fresh fish straight off the boats here. Between the wharf walkway and Broad Street, the main shopping area, is Trafalgar Square. The square's statue of the British naval commander Horatio Nelson has been a sore point for some time. Some Bajans feel the statue, which was erected in 1813, some 36 years before Nelson's Column was erected in London's Trafalgar Square, is reminiscent of the colonial past. Many have petitioned to have it replaced by a local national hero. In an odd compromise, the statue has been turned so that it no longer faces Broad Street. Near the statue is a memorial to Barbados' war dead and a dolphin fountain that commemorates the introduction of running water on the island in 1861.

On Broad Street, in addition to the many banks and businesses, are the Public Buildings, which include the upper and lower House of Assembly chambers. The building dates back to 1871.

Public markets can be found on Fairchild Street, on the south side of the Constitution River, and Cheapside, to the west of the Careenage. (For fresh fish, the market in the town of Oistins is a good bet.) James Street is lined with fruit and vegetable stands, often just boxes turned upside-down and laden with produce.

St. Michael's Cathedral stands on the site of the original Anglican church, first established in 1665 and destroyed or damaged by hurricanes in 1780 and 1831; the present church was completed in 1838. East of the cathedral is Queen's Park, formerly the residence of the commander of the King's forces in the West Indies. The Queens Park House is now a theater and small museum (open 9.00-17.00 daily). Note, as if you'd miss it, the massive baobab tree on the grounds, estimated to be more than 1,000 years old and measuring 61 feet (18 m) in circumference—the largest tree in the country. Baobabs are common in Africa, yet this one appears to predate the arrival of Europeans and slaves to the Lesser Antilles. No one knows how it landed on these shores.

North of the downtown area is Kensington Oval, one of four international cricket test grounds in the West Indies. Cricket is to Bajans as honey is to bears and nothing else, save perhaps politics, inflames the national passions like a good cricket match. Barbados has placed many a player on the West Indies test team, including the famous Sir Garfield Sobers.

Also north of downtown is the infamous Baxters Road, "the street that never sleeps," lined with the one-room, dimly-lit rum shops and small eating places that take on new life after midnight. Women sell fried fish cooked over open stoves and music blasts up and down the street. Definitely the after-hours place to be in Bridgetown, a slice of Bajan life with a few tourists in the mix.

South of town on Bay Street, the National Trust's Garrison Savannah Historic Area is a 17th century military complex with forts, monuments and military buildings. St. Ann's Fort, built in 1804, now houses the Barbados Defence Force. An amazing collection of cannon, some 30 in all, is displayed in front of the Main Guard. The Barbados Museum (809-427-0201, BDS$7 admission, open 10.00-18.00 Monday through Saturday), located in the old prison, features natural history exhibits, a map gallery and African artifacts. The small Cafe Musee here serves snacks and drinks. On Sunday and Thursday evenings the museum presents the folk-dance drama "1627 and All That." The show portrays aspects of past and present Bajan life through dancing, rollicking comedy and narrative skits and the evening includes drinks and a buffet dinner. Call for information.

The Harry Bayley Observatory (809-426-1317) in Clapham, the only observatory in the Caribbean, was built in 1963 and is the headquarters of the Barbados Astronomical Society. Open Friday evenings 20.30-23.30; admission BDS$5.

Practical Information

ACCOMMODATION
Contact the tourism authority (see below) or the Barbados Hotel Association (P.O. Box 711C, Bridgetown, Barbados, W.I.; 809-426-5041, fax 429-2845) for a more complete list of the country's accommodation. For rental villas and cottages contact the hotel association, Alleyne Aguilar & Altman (809-432-0840, fax 432-2147) or Bajan Services, Ltd. (809-422-2618, fax 422-5366).

Camping is not allowed on Barbados.

All hotels will add a five per cent tax and most will add a ten per cent service charge to your bill.

❑ BARBADOS HILTON, Needham's Point, St. Michael, Barbados, W.I. (809-426-0200) is one of the largest hotels on the island, with activities, sports and a fine beach; just minutes from Bridgetown. Luxury.

- ❏ SANDY LANE HOTEL, St. James, Barbados, W.I. (809-432-1311), an exclusive resort on the western coast, offers five bars, two restaurants, five tennis courts, watersports, a golf course and elegance. Luxury.
- ❏ BARBADOS BEACH VILLAGE, St. James, Barbados, W.I. (809-425-1440) is simple western coast hotel; you choose from rooms, cottages or apartments. Moderate.
- ❏ SANDY BEACH HOTEL, Christ Church, Barbados, W.I. (809-435-8000), on the crowded south shore between Bridgetown and Oistins, near dozens of restaurants and plenty of watersports. Moderate-luxury.
- ❏ ATLANTIS, Bathsheba, St. Joseph, Barbados, W.I. (809-433-9445) is removed from the madding crowd, with wonderful views of the open Atlantic. The rooms are simple, but the buffet meals are renowned. Budget-moderate.

EATING

Bajan cuisine is like, and unlike, West Indian creole found in the rest of the Lesser Antilles. A favourite is flying fish, which is almost the national dish. Dolphin, really a dorado, is no relation to Flipper. Black pudding, a spicy sausage made from pig's intestine and blood, is a popular holiday dish. Souse is pickled pig's head. Buljol is a French-influenced salad of salted cod, onion, tomato, lime and spices. Tasty conkies are made from cornmeal, coconut, sweet potatoes and spices, steamed in plantain leaves. Coucou is a side dish made from cornmeal or breadfruit, with okra, salt and butter. Jugjug, a traditional Christmas dish made with pigeon peas, meat and cornmeal, is believed to have originated with haggis, the Scottish dish.

Falernum, an alcoholic drink of rum, sugar syrup and lime juice, is similar to the ti punch of the French Antilles, with an extra essence of almond or vanilla.

- ❏ CARAMBOLA (809-432-0832) in St. James overlooks the ocean and is elegantly French. Expensive.
- ❏ RAFFLES (809-432-6557) in Holetown serves Bajan and Continental cuisine. Expensive.
- ❏ WATERFRONT CAFE (809-427-0093), on the Careenage in Bridgetown, is attractive for its location and its local food. Inexpensive.
- ❏ FISHERMAN'S WHARF (809-436-7778), also on the Careenage, upstairs, serves fish stuffed with crab and a unique Bajan fish pie. Moderate.
- ❏ BROWN SUGAR (809-426-7684), located at Aquatic Gap on Bay Street in St. Michael, a few minutes from Bridgetown, serves good Bajan cuisine. Moderate.

GETTING THERE

Grantley Adams International Airport (809-428-7101), ten miles (16 km) from Bridgetown, is a busy hub for the Caribbean, particularly the Windward Islands. The airport is large, newly renovated, with some of the best duty-free shopping in the Caribbean. You'll also find a bank, post office and car rental agencies.

Grantley Adams is serviced by American Airlines (809-428-4170), BWIA (809-426-2111), Air Canada (809-436-3835) and British Airways (809-428-0908).

Connections from other Caribbean islands are made by LIAT (Bridgetown 809-436-6224, airport 428-0986) and BWIA, as well as half a dozen local airlines serving the Caribbean and South America.

The departure tax is BDS$25.

GETTING AROUND

■ PUBLIC TRANSPORT

Taxis are available everywhere and are unmetered. The rates, a bit expensive by Caribbean standards, are set by the government and posted in both Barbados and U.S. dollars at most hotels and in the airport customs area. The new ABC Highway (named after three of Barbados' former leaders, Tom Adams, Errol Barrow and Gordon Cummings) connects the airport with the western coastal roads and skirts Bridgetown, making travel to that area easy and less expensive.

In Bridgetown taxis are located at Trafalgar Square, Independence Square and Lower Broad Street. There are stands at Accra Beach and Hastings Rock on the southern coast.

Buses, run by the government's Transport Board, are blue with a yellow stripe. Private minibuses are yellow with a blue stripe. Minibuses are otherwise identified by the booming reggae or calypso music ringing in your head and names like "Cobra," "Rambo" and the ominous "Killer."

Government buses cost BDS$1.50 to any location on the island, a good deal. You can catch them at Fairchild Street, Jubilee and Princess Alice Highway in Bridgetown and several places around the island. For a complete schedule call 809-436-6820.

Minibuses run from the River Bus Terminal (809-426-3967) to points east and southeast. From Temple Yard minibuses depart for points north and northeast and from Probyn Street they head to points south and central.

■ CAR RENTALS

Car rentals are easily found, but not always reasonably priced. Cost starts at US$45 per day for the small, open-air Mini Mokes (sort of like a beach buggy with smaller tires), to US$70 per day for larger cars. You'll have to get a temporary local driver's license for BDS$10 at a police station or the Ministry of Transport in Bridgetown or let the rental company arrange it for you.

The country, though small, features more than 800 miles (1,280 km) of paved road, most in good shape, although they might wind or end abruptly in places. Remember to drive on the left. For rentals call A&M (809-424-0469), Barbados Rent-a-Car (airport 809-428-0960), Double J Car and Moke Rentals (809-427-3155), National Car Rentals (809-426-0603) or Tropicar Rentals (809-425-5267).

Motorcycles and scooters are also a viable means of transportation and start at US$30 per day. Call Lynn's Rentals (809-435-8585) in Hastings, just south of Bridgetown, or Fun Seekers (809-435-8206) in Christ Church.

Bicycles are also available at Fun Seekers or at the succinctly named Bicycle Rentals (809-427-3995) in Christ Church. Cost is US$10 per day.

MONEY, HOURS AND COMMUNICATION

Barbados uses the Barbados dollar, first issued in 1973, and now fixed at a rate of BDS$2 = US$1. (Other currencies fluctuate against the U.S. dollar.) You can use U.S. and Canadian dollars in many transactions, but Barbados dollars will give you a better rate. Money can be exchanged at hotels and banks, with banks providing the better rate of exchange. Banking hours are generally 9.00-15.00 Monday through Thursday and 9.00-13.00 and 15.00-17.00 on Friday. The airport bank, Barbados National, is open daily from 8.00 until midnight, but only for arriving and departing passengers.

Travelers checks are accepted in many places and credit cards are almost universally accepted in hotels and larger restaurants. Call ahead, however, to check. Business hours are usually 8.00-16.00 weekdays and 8.00-12.00 on Saturday. Some supermarkets are open until 18.00 on Saturday and tourist shops often remain open for cruise ships. However, most of Barbados closes shop on Sunday.

The General Post Office and Philatelic Bureau is located in Cheapside, Bridgetown and open 7.30-17.00 weekdays. District post offices are found in each parish.

Barbados uses the international area code 809. The main office of Barbados External Telecommunications, a division of Cable and Wireless, is at Wildey, in St. Michael; here you can place calls and send faxes and telegrams. Another office on the Wharf in Bridgetown is also open to the public.

The nation's two daily newspapers, which also publish weekend editions, are the *Advocate* and the *Nation*. You'll also find weekly tabloids such as the tawdry *Weekend Investigator*. Tourist publications include *The Visitor* (free). *Caribbean Week*, a regional weekly, is published in St. Michael.

ENTERTAINMENT

■ SPORTS

The usual watersports suspects, such as waterskiing, windsurfing, harbor cruises, parasailing and snorkelling can be easily arranged through most hotels. Scuba diving is very good, though not as pristine as diving the unruffled waters of Dominica and Saba. The sunken Greek barge Stavronikita, at Folkestone, is submerged under 125 feet (38 m) of water and provides good diving. Call Dive Barbados (809-432-7090), The Dive Shop (809-426-9947) or Willie's Watersports (809-422-4900) for information about resort certification or diving excursions.

Tennis and other ball sports are found at most hotels. Golf is played at the 18-hole Sandy Lane Club (809-432-1145) in St. James or the 9-hole Rockley Resort (809-435-7873) and Heywoods (809-422-4900). The uncompleted Royal Westmoreland Golf and Country Club, in St. James, is scheduled to open soon.

To truly experience the Barbados spirit, catch a game of cricket. Games are held year-round and you can catch test matches at the Kensington Oval in Bridgetown from January through April. Check the newspapers for information.

Horseracing is another popular and emotionally charged event. The Barbados Turf Club (809-426-3980) runs races at the Garrison Savannah on alternating Saturdays from January to April and again from August to November.

SHOPPING

The airport and Broad Street in Bridgetown offer the best deals on duty-free items and crafts. Pelican Village, on Princess Alice Highway near the harbor in Bridgetown, contains a series of shops and an artisans' village. For art galleries, don't miss the Barbados Arts Council (809-426-4385) at Pelican Village and The National Cultural Foundation Gallery (809-427-2345) at the Queen's Park House.

Other items such as groceries, books, beer and sundries, are found around Bridgetown. Explore. Try The Cloister on The Wharf in Bridgetown for a large selection of books and magazines.

USEFUL ADDRESSES

■ TOURISM INFORMATION

Barbados Tourism Authority:

❑ P.O. Box 242, Harbor Road, Bridgetown, Barbados, W.I. (809-427-2623, fax 426-4080, also airport 428-9837 and Deep Water Harbor 426-1718).

❑ 800 Second Ave., New York, NY 10017 (800-221-9831 or 212-986-6516, fax 573-9850).

❑ 3440 Wilshire Blvd., Suite 1215, Los Angeles, CA 90010 (213-380-2198, fax 384-2763).

❑ 5160 Yonge St., Suite 1800, North York, Ontario M2N GL19 (800-268-9122 or 416-512-6569, fax 512-6581).

❑ 263 Tottenham Court Road, London W1P 9AA (441-636-9448, fax 637-1496).

❑ Rathenau Platz 1-A, 6000 Frankfurt am Main 1, Germany (069-28-08-82, fax 49-69-294-782).

❑ Caraibes 102, 102 Ave. Des Champs-Elysees, 75008 Paris (45-62-62-62, fax 331-4074-0701).

■ OTHER

❑ Emergency, 119.

❑ Ambulance, 426-1113.

❑ Fire, 113.

❑ Police, 112.

❑ Queen Elizabeth Hospital, 436-6450.

❑ Grantley Adams International Airport, 428-7101.

Trinidad and Tobago

Introduction

The Republic of Trinidad and Tobago is the Lesser Antilles' wild cousin, a country of deep and abiding passion and one of the most complicated in the chain. The nation has produced some of the world's most recognizable cultural icons; calypso and steelbands provide very nearly the universal Caribbean sounds and Trinidad's Carnival outshines all others in energy and pure bombast. Several eminent writers, such as V.S. Naipaul, Shiva Naipaul and Samuel Selvon and poet-storyteller Paul Keens-Douglas, were Trinidad-born. St. Lucian Nobel Prize-winner Derek Walcott wrote and produced several of his plays at the Trinidad Theater Workshop, which he established in Port of Spain in 1959.

Yet, beyond cultural exports, Trinidad and Tobago teems with modern successes—and disparities. It is a place of wealth and of abject poverty, both starkly evident in Trinidad's capital, Port of Spain. Christians, Muslims, Hindus, Asians, blacks and whites form a population that lives, if not always side by side, at least with a working degree of tolerance.

The Land

The sister islands of Trinidad and Tobago are the most southerly of the Lesser Antilles and the entire West Indies for that matter. Trinidad lies just seven miles (11 km) off the north coast of Venezuela, its nearest neighbour. The boot-shaped island, at 1,864 square miles (4,828 sq km), is the largest in the Lesser Antilles. Much of its topography resembles that of the Venezuelan mainland; the flora and fauna found on Trinidad, more so than on Tobago, are similar to species found in South America.

Half of Trinidad is forested. The Northern Range, stretching east to west, contains the island's highest point, Cerro del Aripo, at 3,085 feet (940 m). The range is thought to be part of a massive system extending from the Andes of South America to North America's Rocky Mountains. The center and south of the island, a flat plain, is the heart of the island's agricultural industry, of which sugarcane is the main crop.

The northern coast is hilly and green, host to many of the island's best beaches. Other sections of the coast can be rough and irregular and on the central Atlantic coast and western coast (on the Gulf of Paria) massive swamps are found. The western coast's Caroni Swamp is the site of a wildlife sanctuary, where one can see Trinidad's national bird, the scarlet ibis.

Tobago, Trinidad's zucchini-shaped sister 21 miles (34 km) to the northeast, is 26 miles (42 km) long by seven miles (11 km) wide, with an area of 116 square miles (300 sq km). The low-lying island is dominated by a central hill range with a high point of 1,860 feet (549 m). The central hills are largely a forest reserve and the island's coast is characterized by smaller hills, bays and stretches of sandy beach. The south of the island is flatter and home to the population centers of Plymouth and Scarborough, the capital, as well as the island's tourist activity.

History

Before various European explorers descended on the islands, Trinidad and Tobago was not an uncomplicated place. As early as 5,000 BC Amerindian groups had crossed the straits from Venezuela and inhabited Trinidad, which they called Iere or "Land of the Hummingbird." The largest groups were the Arawaks and Caribs, with several subgroups existing throughout the island. The Arawaks inhabited the south of the island and were relatively peaceful. The warrior Caribs lived in the north. They fought a lot. This is what they were doing when Columbus happened upon the island on 31 July 1493, during his third voyage.

Columbus landed and named the island "La Trinite." Some say this was in honour of the Holy Trinity, to which he had dedicated the voyage. Others believe it had to do with the three hills he first sighted as he approached the island. After claiming the island for Spain, Columbus sailed off and, two weeks later, he sighted Tobago, which is thought to have been called Tavaco by the Caribs. The word apparently refers to the native crop the Caribs grew and smoked, which we call tobacco, which came to us via Spanish. ("Tobago," a Spanish corruption of the Carib word, is pronounced to-BAY-go.) Columbus called the island "Concepcion" or possibly "Bella Forma." Whatever the case, Columbus did not land on Tobago.

Spanish colonization came slowly to Trinidad. Ongoing battles with Amerindians inhibited landings and permanent settlements. The first substantial colony was established in 1592. The Spaniard Don Domingo de Vera established the town of San Jose de Oruna and declared it the island's capital. A few years later, in 1595, Sir Walter Raleigh—part poet, part tobacco entrepreneur and part pirate—sacked San Jose and reduced it to rubble. The town, rebuilt in the early 17th century, is now called St. Joseph. (There are two St. Josephs on Trinidad, one on the southeastern coast and one west of Tunapuna, on the northern population corridor. The latter is the old capital.)

The Spanish were tenacious and hung onto their possession, seeing it primarily as a ready source of slaves. They were, as always, fired by the hope of finding vast amounts of gold, the legendary city of El Dorado. They knew it to be somewhere and would find it somehow. In the meantime they established mildly profitable tobacco and cocoa plantations.

Interaction between the Spanish and Amerindian groups was rife with violence and, eventually, disease. Dutch, French and British warships raided the island with regularity and even established small settlements. They also hammered away at the Amerindian groups and, reciprocally, were attacked. By the mid-18th century the island was already an amalgam of different nationalities and cultures, though nominally still in the hands of the Spanish.

By 1757 a Spanish governor had moved the capital from San Jose to the natural harbor on the northwestern coast. Catholic missionaries arrived and the Amerindians suffered even more because of their harsh proselytizing. Then Spain and Britain went to battle during the Napoleonic Wars.

An expedition under Sir Ralph Abercrombie captured the island for Britain. Fighting continued until Trinidad was finally ceded to Britain in 1802, under the Treaty of Amiens. By 1815 Tobago, which had changed hands numerous times, was also under British rule. Thus began the growth of the sugarcane industry and the accelerated importation of African slaves. By the 1820s the 35,000 Amerindians had been reduced to about 800. Today a community of Carib descendants numbering 300 lives in Arima, in northeastern Trinidad.

Abolition of slavery in 1834 caused a labor shortage, which was temporarily resolved by the introduction of indentured labor from East India. In 1846 a large number of Portuguese, fleeing religious persecution, were allowed to settle in Trinidad. Chinese were brought in during the late 19th century and Europeans, including Irish, Scots and Germans, emigrated to the island seeking employment. Workers from the smaller Caribbean islands also became part of the new labor force.

Britain's industrial revolution and the changing world order, brought about by World War I, spurred movements within the colonies for political representation and independence. Widespread worker unrest led to labor strikes, which in turn led to the formation of political parties. Universal adult suffrage was granted in

1946 and about that time the seminal figure in the modern-day Trinidad and Tobago political scene emerged from the dusty libraries of academia. Eric Eustace Williams received his doctorate from Oxford University, then became a lecturer at Howard University in Washington, D.C., where he published four books on West Indian social and political history, including the widely respected *The Negro in the Caribbean* (1940). Williams returned to Trinidad in 1944 to serve as a member of the Anglo-American Caribbean Commission. In the early Fifties he organized a series of lectures and demonstrations at Woodford Square, at Port of Spain's public library, that came to be known as the "University" of Woodford Square. It was at one of these lectures, in 1955, that he formed a political party, the People's National Movement (PNM), with the goals of reinfranchising Trinidad's black population and agitating for independence.

The PNM gained control of the legislative council and came to power in 1956, with Williams as chief minister. (The revered Williams would remain head of government until his death in 1981.) Trinidad joined the now-defunct Federation of the West Indies in 1958, but left in 1961 after Jamaica withdrew.

Trinidad and Tobago became an independent member of the Commonwealth in 1962 and a Republic within the Commonwealth in 1976.

Oil reserves discovered offshore had become an important industry during the early part of the century, but during the petroleum shortage of the 1970s Trinidad's resources suddenly turned to gold. Instant and seemingly unlimited wealth catapulted the nation to heady heights and the roads, hospitals, schools and social services of the republic became, at the time, more modern than any of the other islands of the Lesser Antilles.

Of course, times change. In the late Seventies the Middle East began releasing stockpiled oil and as world prices slipped, so did Trinidad's brightest economic prospect. The easy-flowing money of the Seventies had brought allegations of heavy-handed corruption and, in turn, voter mistrust. The PNM, in power since before independence, lost the 1986 election to the National Alliance for Reconstruction (NAR). However, the NAR's Prime Minister, A.N.R. Robinson, soon became unpopular by instituting cost-cutting measures and reducing social programs.

On a Friday afternoon in July 1990, a well-coordinated Muslim fundamentalist group stormed Port of Spain's Parliament building and the offices of Trinidad and Tobago Television, while simultaneously bombing the nearby police headquarters (the hulking shell looks much the same as it did that day). The group, called Jamaat al-Muslimeen and led by Bilaal Abdullah and Imam Yasin Abu Bakr, held the prime minister and several cabinet members hostage, while widespread riots and looting engulfed the streets of Port of Spain. Twenty people died and millions of dollars worth of property was damaged while the government negotiated with the Muslimeen. For days Trinidad remained in a state of anarchy, until finally the coup leaders surrendered with a full promise of amnesty, signed by the acting president. They were, however, immediately thrown in jail, where most remain today, pending numerous appeals.

The PNM was returned to power once again in 1991, headed by Prime Minister Patrick Manning.

People and Culture

Trinidadians like to say that they're descended from half the world, which may be as true as these types of statements get. The sister islands' population is 1.3 million, of which 41 per cent are of African descent, 41 per cent are East Indian and the remaining are of Chinese, Syrian, European and Mediterranean descent, or those of mixed ethnicity. Tobago's majority is black. Calling Trinidad and Tobago a bastion of racial harmony would be an overstatement, particularly between the majority African and East Indian populations. In many instances the groups tend to live in separate ethnic areas and mingling is done at work, in commerce and in social situations.

More than a quarter of the population live in Port of Spain and its environs. The main population corridor of Trinidad is the northern east-west swath from Port of Spain to Arima and along the north-south coast from Port of Spain to San Fernando.

One look at place names on a map of Trinidad will attest to the numerous languages that have passed through the island. Spanish names such as San Fernando, Rio Claro, Port of Spain and the derivative Trinidad reflect the earliest European influences. Earlier still, Amerindian names, such as Caroni, Chaguanas and Tobago, are reminders of the islands' first inhabitants. The French left Trinidad with Pointe-a-Pierre, Blanchisseuse and Roussillac and the English colonials named Claxton Bay, Flanagin Town and, of course, Waterloo. East Indian names are less frequent, belying the large population.

Likewise the languages of modern Trinidad reflect all these influences and more. English is official and, some say, spoken with a slight brogue. Dialect is fast and lyrical and peppered with bits of Spanish, French and African languages. The majority of the East Indian population is Hindu and some Hindi is still spoken. Urdu is spoken by some, but not all, Muslims. Spanish and some French Creole is spoken in pockets, particularly along the northern coast.

About a third of the population is Catholic, not surprising given the Spanish and French influences. A quarter of the population practices Hinduism; most are East Indians, although many East Indians have converted to Christianity. Islam is practiced by about six per cent of the population, Anglicans number 15 per cent and the rest practice various forms of Protestantism and other offshoots. Among them are Shango Baptists and Spiritual Baptists, which are heavily influenced by African spiritualism and practice. A small Jewish population also exists.

Of course, magic and other forms of mystical invocation inhabit the zeitgeist of modern Trinidad as deeply as western religion. Local folklore, festivals and, in particular, Carnival are replete with jumbies (ghosts or spirits), devils in disguise, the Lagahoo (a wolfman) and various characters both sinister and cynical. Orisha, the name derived from spirits and deities of the Yorubans of southern Nigeria, is combined with spiritual Christianity to invoke spirits through drumming. Obeah, magic widely practiced throughout the Lesser Antilles, has in Trinidad and Tobago also appealed to the mysticism of some segments of the East Indian population—Hinduism, with its multi-appendaged, elephant-headed gods and goddesses, lends itself well to magical imagery.

CARNIVAL

The festivals of Trinidad and Tobago have exported their fevers throughout the world. In particular, Trinidad's Carnival now ranks with New Orleans' Mardi Gras and Brazil's Carnival for the sheer energy and anarchic lunacy that fuel these pre-Lenten rituals. But it distinguishes itself from the New Orleans and Brazil festivals in two ways: calypso and steelbands.

Locals and visitors alike get into the fray, sometimes in ways you wouldn't want to tell your mother. Music, singing, dancing, licentiousness and bacchanalia become serious pastimes during Carnival season and the whole thing is so deeply infused with the national character that, for many, it is the main reason to visit. While this undervalues the rest of Trinidad and Tobago's attractions, a couple of days at Carnival is enough to persuade anyone that it is a prime cultural force of the nation.

So, what is Carnival and where did it come from?

Many trace the origins of Trinidad's Carnival to the French influences of the country's early history. In the 1700s the Spanish allowed the French to settle in certain parts of the country, no doubt due to a laissez-faire attitude on the part of the Spanish toward their possession—no gold, no bother. Before long the French population equaled that of the Spaniards. Beginning in 1783, the French organized a pre-Lenten festival lasting from Christmas until Ash Wednesday (the first day of Lent in Catholic doctrine). For half a century they celebrated with dinners, masquerade balls, concerts and hunting parties, clearly a more genteel celebration than Carnival as we know it today. They allowed their African slaves to surreptitiously celebrate as well and the slaves used the opportunity to parody their owners' mannerisms and styles of dress and dancing. This celebration caught on and became a popular and integral part of the culture and society of Trinidad and Tobago, lasting beyond the immediate influence of the French, throughout the period of British occupation.

After emancipation in 1834, Africans openly joined the celebration. This rapidly changed Carnival into a more raucous event—after all, the post-emancipation Africans had something to celebrate. They first developed "Canboulay," a portrayal of the practice of cannes brulees, the routine burning of cane in the sugarcane fields. The revelry included marching through the streets with lighted torches, singing and stick fights between "rival" groups of batonniers. At one point, Canboulay took place on August 1st (Emancipation Day), but later the Africans brought the celebration back to Carnival. It took place on Dimanche Gras, the Sunday before Carnival's final, two day explosion.

With that Carnival took to the streets and soon took on blatant African tones. The masquerades ("mas") marches became more complex, with satirical and sometimes overtly sexual stock characters such as the Jab Molassi (Molasses Devil), Jab Jab (a devil character with East Indian overtones) and the Moko Jumbie (a stilt dancer, often accompanied by a dwarf), all springing up from African-Trinidadian creole lore. Singing and chanting was in French Creole and, some say, languages from Guinea in West Africa. The beat of this music, which eventually developed into accompaniment for today's calypso, was culled from African drumming traditions and originally involved drums, "tamboo bamboo" percussion instruments and string bands. Drums were replaced by steel pans in the 1940s, after drums were condemned by the colonial government.

The Africanization of Carnival alarmed the upper-class whites, who gradually took to their homes, refusing to participate in the spectacle. And, as one would expect, participation among the masses increased.

Therein, and well into this century, the white colonials and upper class heaped scorn upon the Carnival celebrations. But this did not deter the libertines, who increasingly partied with vigorous dancing, masquerading and, perhaps most importantly, calypsoing.

So ingrained is Carnival with the character of Trinidad and Tobago, then and now, that riots broke out in 1881 when local authorities tried to quell Canboulay celebrations and rumor spread was that they were trying to shut down Carnival completely. In the 1940s opposition to Carnival's Sunday celebrations, a nod to Christianity's Sabbath, temporarily restricted the final days of the revelry to the last two days before Ash Wednesday.

Today, from Christmas until the weekend before Ash Wednesday, calypsonians throughout the country hold competitions for the best performances. Steelbands practice and elaborate "mas" costumes are fashioned by civic, work or other groups. Calypso competitions, featuring singers with names such as Shadow, Black Stalin and Calypso Rose, culminate on the Sunday before Carnival, Dimanche Gras, when a Calypso King and Queen, or Monarch, are chosen. On Jour Ouvert (also J'Ouvert, pronounced Jo-VAY), also called Carnival Monday, parades begin early and this is the day of flamboyant costumes, marches and the steelband competitions. Look to Queen's Park Savannah for the start of the action. The nights are filled with local parties and gatherings of dancers "wining," a particularly Trinidadian form of particularly suggestive dancing, at calypso and soca venues. On Tuesday the revelers pour back into the streets in costumes, accompanied by steelbands, calypso and soca trucks and not a small amount of rum, turning Port of Spain into what can only be described as a profoundly large party. Then, at midnight, the party winds down and Ash Wednesday begins Lent, ostensibly a period of atonement and cleansing for Catholics.

A word of warning: if you decide to attend Carnival, book your flight and hotel room now—everyone else who wants to come, including Trinidad and Tobago expatriates, is doing just that. And pay close attention to your personal possessions during Carnival— if there is ever a time when thieves and other unsavory types will look for easy targets, this is it.

OTHER FESTIVALS

Trinidadians complain that, due to the large number of ethnic communities in the nation, the constant stream of holidays—at least one for every month—makes it hard for anyone to get any work done. There is truth in the sentiment.

In October the East Indian community celebrates Divali, the festival of lights. The national religious holiday is Hindu in origin and honours Lakshmi, the goddess of light, beauty, love and riches. Throughout the countryside, thousands of tiny candles, deyas and white lights are lit in her honour. The holiday is accompanied by prayer, exotic East Indian feasts and low-key music and dancing. Hindus also celebrate Ramleema, honouring the life and teachings of Lord Rama.

Hosay, a Muslim festival observed in early June, began as a religious rite honouring brothers Hussein and Hossad, who were grandsons of Mohammed. Today it is a four-day cultural festival and includes elements of Hindu life, such as tassa drumming, and African life. The ceremonies of old included fire-walking and fire-eating, but today consist of role-playing the deaths of the brothers and singing and drumming.

Independence Day (31 August) and Emancipation Day (1 August) are accompanied by steelband competitions, parades and various local events.

The November Pan Jazz Festival is relatively new, dating from 1986, and is intriguing. There is some debate among jazz purists regarding the viability of pans as jazz instruments, but the fact is the event has received enthusiastic support from musicians and has in the past featured Dizzy Gillespie, Wynton Marsalis, the Stanley Turrentine Quintet and top pan artists such as Len "Boogsy" Sharpe.

Christmas is notable for its great food and festivities, which include the annual revival of parang music, a form associated with the country's Spanish heritage, involving caroling and accompaniment by guitar and mandolin. Parang is heard throughout the holiday season and in national competitions.

Government and Economy

Trinidad and Tobago became independent in 1962 and shifted to a republican form of government, with Commonwealth ties, in 1976. A non-executive president heads the republic, but power is vested in a prime minister, head of the majority political party. The legislature is bicameral, with an elected 36 member House of Representatives and an appointed 31 member Senate. Tobago, with an internally elected House of Assembly, has control over some of its affairs.

The Trinidad and Tobago economy is deeply entrenched, so to speak, in oil and natural gas, its main natural resources. The economy also includes some agricultural products and exports, such as sugarcane, cocoa, coffee and citrus fruit. About 14 per cent of the land is arable and agriculture employs 12 per cent of the labor force.

Mineral products, such as limestone, sand and gravel, are processed mainly for local use and some export. Asphalt, from the amazing Pitch Lake (the world's largest known reserve of natural asphalt) at La Brea, represents a significant natural resource for the country, but not in the world market.

The island's first exploratory oil well was sunk in 1857. Since then substantial oil and natural gas reserves have been discovered at offshore sites, which provide 75 per cent of total production. Nearly 80 per cent of the country's exports are petroleum and its by-products, which account for about one quarter of the gross domestic product.

When the oil economy boomed in the heady Seventies, Trinidad and Tobago became one of the wealthiest nations in the region. Overflowing government coffers doled out cash for infrastructure development and soon Trinidad and Tobago had modern roads, schools and hospitals. Most everyone had a car, maybe two, and the debilitating poverty that characterizes so many small Caribbean countries seemed as if it had become a distant memory. Then the OPEC nations released oil reserves and the Eighties became a time to wonder what happened to it all. The coffers were almost empty, due to unchecked spending and some sticky government fingers. This brought about changes in government and Trinidad and Tobago reconsidered the petroleum industry's one-sided effect on its economy.

An immediate reaction to several years of economic decline was the nation's decision to reschedule debts with the International Monetary Fund, which it did twice. Still unemployment rose to nearly 20 per cent. More effort was put into promoting tourism and that effort continues today. The government floated the Trinidad and Tobago dollar (TT$) in April 1993, which resulted in an immediate 34 per cent devaluation of the currency against the U.S. dollar.

Tourism continues to grow and today is primarily tiny Tobago's piece of the pie. Tobago currently hosts more than 1,000 hotel and guesthouse rooms and Trinidad, which accommodates large numbers of business travelers in Port of Spain, has 1,200. U.S. visitors account for the greatest number of overnight stays. The two-island nation saw an increase of seven per cent in its tourism numbers in 1992. Visitor arrivals for the two islands totaled 250,000 in 1993, still a small number relative to other Lesser Antilles islands.

Sights

BEACHES

Trinidad's beaches are best along the northern and eastern coasts. The surf can be rough at times and supervised beaches fly colored flags to indicate the conditions. Red is unsafe, yellow is sort of safe and white means splash to your heart's content.

Along the North Coast Road you'll find some of the island's most popular beach spots and the drive is breathtaking, through hills and dips with views of expansive ocean bays. The beaches mentioned below are public, with lifeguards, parking, changing facilities, showers and food kiosks. Most are free, although some charge a small fee to use the changing rooms.

Maracas Bay Beach is long, wide and possibly the island's most popular. Crowded on weekends and holidays, the beach is a half-hour drive from Port of Spain. A short hike into the hills south of Maracas Bay is the Maracas Waterfall, a 90 foot (27 m) cascade and fun spot for picnickers. A few minutes drive east of Maracas is the smaller Tyrico Bay, where camping is allowed. East of Tyrico, Las Cuevas Bay Beach is quiet and calm. The name refers to the many caves that are found in the area. Farther east are small and pleasant beaches at Blanchisseuse, Paria, Madamas Bay and Matelot.

On the east coast, from Manzanilla in the north to Point Radix in the south, is the lengthy and wide Manzanilla Bay. To the south, from Point Radix to Galeota Point, along the Mayaro-to-Guayguayare Road, you'll find Mayaro Bay, at ten miles (16 km) the longest beach on the island. This honky-tonk area features roadside kiosks, restaurants, hotels and guesthouses. Beaches at Vessigny in the south and Chagville (manmade, no lifeguards) in the northwest at Chaguaramas are also popular. Chaguaramas, the northwestern peninsula, was occupied by U.S. forces during World War II and many war-era buildings remain in place.

On Tobago the first stop is Pigeon Point, minutes north of the airstrip, where a good number of the island's hotels and other facilities are located. Area beaches include Store Bay and Sandy Bay. The Pigeon Point Resort offer facilities, but charges a fee to use them, adults TT$10, ages 6-12 TT$5 and under 6 free. The beach itself is free, as are all beaches in Trinidad and Tobago.

The town of Buccoo, also chock full of hotels and watersports facilities, is adjacent to Buccoo Bay and Mt. Irvine Bay, two fine swimming areas. Buccoo Reef is great for snorkelling.

To the north, the beach at Speyside features changing facilities and showers, and views of the famous bird sanctuary at Little Tobago Island, which can be accessed using local hotel facilities or by hiring local fishermen. Other Tobago beaches include King's Bay, near Roxborough, Man O' War Bay, near Charlotteville, and half a dozen others scattered around the island.

OTHER SIGHTS
■ TRINIDAD
Port of Spain, the cultural and administrative center of the country, is also the largest city in the Lesser Antilles. Its cosmopolitan promise and energetic street life give it a flair worth exploring for several days. This is a city where Christian churches, Islamic mosques and Hindu temples stand in close proximity, where a homeless beggar might stop a Mercedes Benz for handouts. The eclectic city architecture mixes Victorian with classic Caribbean wooden homes featuring gin-

gerbread fretwork and concrete office buildings with Gothic church towers. Port of Spain is lively, clean in places, dirty in others and generally safe; but watch yourself at night and don't travel to outlying areas without a specific destination. Port of Spain lies on the western coast's Gulf of Paria, sheltered from northeasterly winds by the Northern Range, surrounded by, alternately, suburbs and sloping hills, a natural harbor and the Caroni Swamp to the south. Downtown is laid out in a complicated system of one-way streets, making driving an endeavor that you may want to leave to taxi drivers. If you do drive, you'll find numerous small parking lots downtown (Frederick Street has several) that charge TT$3 per hour or TT$10 per day.

Queen's Park Savannah is the centerpiece, though not directly downtown, of the city. This sprawling 200-acre lawn is ground zero for Carnival activities and for festivities year-round. Ice cream kiosks, peanut and coconut vendors, joggers and strollers use the grounds, which is circumnavigated (about three miles or five km around) by busy one-way streets. The park is lined on its northwestern edge by a group of colonial mansions called The Magnificent Seven, built by wealthy families between 1904 and 1906. The mansions include Queen's Royal College, the residences of the Anglican and Roman Catholic bishops and Stollmyer's Castle, a reproduction of Scotland's Balmoral Castle. The architecture is diverse and mystifying, an odd reminder of wealth gone awry.

To the north of the Savannah are the Emperor Valley Zoo, Botanic Gardens and President's House. The zoo, which houses examples of Trinidad and Tobago's wildlife, is open 9.30-18.00 daily, admission TT$3. The gardens were established by Governor Woodward in 1820 and some claim they are the oldest botanical gardens in the Western Hemisphere. The gardens are a good introduction to local flora and exhibit many examples from South America and around the world. The president's official residence, as well as the prime minister's, are located on the gardens' grounds.

The National Museum and Art Gallery (809-623-5941), on Upper Frederick Street facing Memorial Park, is the place to stop for a complete background on Trinidad and Tobago. The free museum houses carnival costumes; displays about the coffee, coconut, sugarcane and printing industries; and a large section on the island's petroleum industry. Another chronicles the history of the aromatic, spicy Angostura Bitters, one of Trinidad and Tobago's best-known exports since 1824. The upstairs art gallery, housing local and international works, includes examples from the 19th century Trinidadian painter Cazabon. The museum is open Tuesday through Saturday, 10.00-18.00; no photos are allowed.

Woodford Square, at the heart of the city, is an important historical site. Named after former governor Woodford, it's where the late Eric Williams, Trinidad and Tobago's first prime minister and political dynamo, organized the 1950s series of lectures and demonstrations that came to be known as the "University" of Woodford Square. The park is still used for public discourse, Bible thumping and hanging out. This is a bustling place and residence of many of the city's homeless.

Bordering Woodford Square are Port of Spain's National Library (open weekdays, 8.30-18.00) and Trinity Anglican Cathedral, circa 1820, with architecture copied from London's Westminister Hall. Town Hall also borders the square.

Red House, the seat of Trinidad and Tobago's parliament, is the most imposing building on the square. The original parliament building burned down in 1903, during riots over proposed water-rate increases, and the present building dates to 1907. This was the site of the 1990 coup attempt and the charred police headquarters, destroyed by bombs during that attempt, is visible at its west end.

Two blocks south of Woodford Square, toward the docks, is Independence Square. Built along one of Port of Spain's first established roads, the square was once called Plaza de Marina. Refurbished in the early 1800s, it was named Independence Square in 1962. Today it is lined with sidewalk vendors, taxi and bus stands and dozens of small shops and bars. Surrounding the square are examples of colonial-era buildings, including the massive gothic Immaculate Conception Roman Catholic Cathedral at the east end. The construction of the cathedral began in 1816 and took 16 years. Express House occupies about a block on the south side of the square and has been both a cocoa warehouse and the home of Trinidad and Tobago's first newspaper. It now houses the Caribbean Communications Network (CCN) television and media organization.

Suburbs on the outskirts of town have an important role in Port of Spain's history. Laventille, a rough-and-tumble neighbourhood built into hills and dipping ravines, was where the first sounds of steelbands were popularized; in fact, many say the neighbourhood is the birthplace of the steel pan. The famous Desperadoes Panyard on Upper Laventille Road, established about 1945, may be the epicenter of pan music today. The current Desperadoes have been around since the 1960s, winning steelband competitions and carrying the sounds of Trinidad and Tobago worldwide.

St. James, the "city that never sleeps," lies north of downtown. This neon-laden, late night district is the place to go for a snack or drink, or whatever, after the rest of the city closes.

The Asa Wright Nature Center (809-667-4655), off the North Coast Road just past the village of Blanchisseuse, consists of nature displays, trails and a small inn. You can hike to Dunston Cave, home of a colony of the nocturnal oilbird, called the guacharo. Amerindian groups prized the birds for their fat, which they used for lamps and fires. Guided tours are available and the center is open daily, 9.00-17.00; admission is US$6.

The scarlet ibis, the national bird, makes its home at the Caroni Swamp and Bird Sanctuary, a half-hour drive south of Port of Spain. Part lagoon and part swamp, the sanctuary is most active at sunset, when hundreds of ibises and other birds come home to roost. Boat tours start late in the afternoon. You can organize a trip through tour operators at hotels or call authorized boat operators Winston Nanan (809-645-1305) or David Ramsahai (809-663-2207). The cost is TT$25 per person.

Chaguanas, south of Caroni Swamp, is the island's third largest city and home of writers and brothers V.S. Naipaul and Shiva Naipaul.

Farther south, San Fernando is the second largest city and industrial capital of the island. The town is a population center for East Indians. Belching oil refineries and sprawling industrial plants set the tone—this is not a pretty place, but definitely a slice of Trinidadian life. Nearby is the Pointe-a-Pierre Wildfowl Trust (809-662-4040), set on oil refinery land. The conservation trust features a learning center and walking trails and is a breeding area for local endangered species. The center is open 10.00-17.00, daily.

Heading south, past sugarcane and oil fields, you'll come to the amazing Pitch Lake at La Brea. The 109-acre bitumen lake, a viscous mass of warm tar, bubbles and boils indiscernibly like a rippled, gray-black sea of sludge. The center is an estimated 300 feet (100 m) deep and you can walk on the lake. Whether you'd want to is your choice, but there are guides available to explain the whole phenomenon—in fact, there are packs of guides, all willing to help you out for a price. Negotiate this before you set off on the lake with anyone. According to legend the lake engulfed an Amerindian tribe called the Chimans, who had offended the Good Spirit by eating hummingbirds. The Indians called the gooey stuff piche and it was here, in 1595, that Sir Walter Raleigh discovered that the lake's oozing pitch was ideal for caulking his ships. The asphalt has since been used in the building of roads. For a more thorough description of the lake, visit the display at the National Museum in Port of Spain; there is a small museum at the tar pit.

■ TOBAGO

Tobago is best seen by rental car, although taxis can do the job if you're willing to pay the price. The roads are generally good and, with the exception of a few small interior roads, marked well enough to get around. You can tour the island in a day, but if you'd care to linger, and you probably will, three days is better.

From Crown Point Airport, where rental cars and taxis are available, take the Claude Noel Highway to Scarborough, the island's capital. The town, population 18,000, is as busy as it gets on Tobago, which isn't very. The new Port Authority building, the largest structure in town, is the place to catch island buses. The rest of town consists of few banks, guesthouses, supermarkets, a mall and a large outdoor market. The 17-acre Botanic Garden is worth a stop. Fort King George, built by the British in 1779 in the hills above town, was the site of several battles with the French during the 18th century. It changed hands several times and was called Fort Castries from 1781 to 1793. Today you'll see a prison, barracks and armament ports, but the view is one of its best features. The Tobago Museum, located at the barracks house, houses military paraphernalia, Amerindian artifacts and documents from slave days. The museum is open 9.00-17.00 weekdays; admission is TT$3, children TT$1.

The Windward Road follows the southern coast, through small towns and villages, over steep hills and past small bays and inlets—a good introduction to the island. The Tobago Forest Reserve, located on the northeastern side of the island, is accessible by heading north at the small town of Roxborough or via any of the dozens of trails that crisscross and enter the reserve from all directions. The Roxborough-Parlatuvier Road crosses the heart of the reserve and the heart of the island. A good place to begin a hike is the Bloody Bay Recreation Site, a small rest-stop hut with a posted map of trails and striking views to Bloody Bay. The forest reserve was established in 1765 and is one of the oldest in this hemisphere.

Windward Road continues along the south coast to Speyside, where you'll find several nice beaches and Little Tobago Island, a 250-acre bird sanctuary. Charlotteville, a small, isolated and pleasant fishing town on the northeastern tip of the island, is the site of some of the island's best diving. Offshore is St. Giles Island, another bird breeding colony—the sea surrounding the island is rough and access is difficult.

In Plymouth ask someone to direct you to the 1783 tombstone of Betty Stiven and her child. The inscription reads: "She was a mother without knowing it and a wife without letting her husband know it except by her kind indulgences to him." Clearly, Ms. Stiven led a complicated life and the tombstone is a great source of mystery and local gossip.

At the southwestern tip of the island, the center for tourist activity, you'll find plenty of watersports facilities. Buccoo Reef is the island's best diving spot and a marine reserve.

At Turtle Beach Hotel and Grafton Beach Resort and other spots along the island's leeward coast, it is possible to see leatherback turtles laying eggs and nesting at night on the beaches. During the season, April through July and into August, the huge turtles lay upwards of 125 eggs at a time. Nearby hotels organize turtle-watching trips during the season.

Tobago's two-week Heritage Festival, held in late July, is an island-wide event that celebrates Tobago's African roots. Villages and towns celebrate by reenacting pivotal events in Tobago history, along with storytelling, feasts and costumed festivals.

Practical Information

ACCOMMODATION

The best bargains are found at small guesthouses and bed and breakfast homes, which are good opportunities for cultural exchange. The Bed and Breakfast Association of Trinidad and Tobago (P.O. Box 3231, Diego Martin, Trinidad, W.I.; 809-637-9329, fax 627-0856) lists more than 100 properties.

Camping is allowed in places, but not encouraged. Security is a problem. Check with the Tourism Development Authority for current approved camping facilities.

Larger hotels add a ten per cent service charge, plus a hefty 15 per cent value added tax (VAT). The VAT is sometimes added to guesthouse bills, but not always. Hotels and guesthouse rates during Carnival season are very steep and bookings should be made well ahead of time.

■ TRINIDAD

❏ TRINIDAD HILTON, P.O. Box 422, Port of Spain, Trinidad, W.I. (809-624-3211, fax 624-6133), on Lady Young Road overlooking Queen's Park Savannah, is within walking distance to downtown—if you've got some time and energy. The hotel is popular with business and convention types and features full facilities, including a large buffet breakfast. Luxury.

❏ HOLIDAY INN, P.O. Box 1017, Port of Spain, Trinidad, W.I. (809-625-3361) is on Wrightson Road, near the port and Independence Square, and therefore close to downtown. Luxury.

❏ KAPOK HOTEL, 16-18 Cotton Hill, St. Clair, Port of Spain, Trinidad, W.I. (809-622-6441, fax 622-9677, U.S. 800-333-1212), north of the Queen's Savannah heading out toward the Maraval suburb, is removed from the buzz of downtown. The rooms are simple but comfortable and the two restaurants, the Savanna and the Tiki, are excellent. Moderate.

❏ CARNETTA'S HOUSE, 28 Scotland Terrace, Andalusia, Maraval, Trinidad, W.I. (809-628-2732, fax 628-7717) is located just north of Port of Spain. Carnetta's is a five-room, family-run guesthouse, very much like home. The rooms feature private baths, television, phones and air-conditioning and the location is good for exploring the north coast. Moderate.

■ TOBAGO

❏ CONRADO BEACH RESORT, Pigeon Point, Tobago, W.I. (809-639-0145, fax 639-0755), located along the beach, offers a good location, no frills, but a good deal. Moderate.

❏ MOUNT IRVINE BAY HOTEL, P.O. Box 222, Tobago, W.I. (809-639-8871/2/3, fax 639-8800, U.S. 800-74 CHARMS), on the grounds of a 17th century sugar plantation at Mount Irvine Bay, is large by Tobago standards (over 100 rooms). The pool is huge and two tennis courts, gardens, a fine French restaurant and ocean views complete the picture. The hotel's 18-hole golf course is highly regarded. Luxury.

❏ ARNOS VALE HOTEL, P.O. Box 208, Scarborough, Tobago, W.I. (809-639-2881/2, fax 639-4629) features stucco cottages, a beach, pool, tennis courts and a dive shop. Luxury.

❏ JACOBS GUEST HOUSE (809-639-2271) in Scarborough has six rooms, two that share baths and only one with hot water. The rooms have fans and are clean and, really, at TT$50 (about US$10) per person, there's not much to complain about. Budget.

❏ BLUE WATER INN, Batteaux Bay, Speyside, Tobago, W.I. (809-660-4341 or 660-4077, fax 660-5195) is rustic, with no television, phones or air-conditioning—just simple rooms, some with kitchenettes, and nearly 50 acres of quiet grounds on a bay and beach. Moderate-luxury.

EATING

Trinidad's various cuisines—West Indian, East Indian, Chinese, various European and North American —are served up throughout the islands. East Indian restaurants often combine West Indian creole-style cooking, such as callaloo (leafy, green spinach stalks of the dasheen plant) and seafood with traditional items such as rotis, a flat bread filled with mutton or goat, or potato and peas and always curried to make you cry. Pelau is a rice and peas dish, sometimes prepared with meat.

You can find Subway, KFC and pizza joints in Port of Spain and most major towns (KFC is also one of the few open on Sundays). The cafeteria-style CALLALOO CAFE on Henry Street in Port of Spain is recommended for its creative East and West Indian dishes. CAFE SAVANNAH (809-622-6441), at the Kapok Hotel, serves up some of the best Trinidadian home-style cooking in town and is popular with locals. HOT SHOPPE on Mucurapo Street offers large rotis and East Indian takeout. VENI MANGE in St. James serves lunch only and the cuisine is West Indian creole, with lots of coconut bases and seafood.

On Tobago the road along Store Bay features several fresh seafood shacks, where you can buy lobster and other delicacies. Many of Tobago's hotels have fine restaurants, but try the DUTCHMAN'S COVE RESTAURANT, across from the Port Authority in Scarborough, for inexpensive, down-home cooking. DILLON'S, on the road to the airport in Crown Point, serves seafood. MISS JEAN'S (809-639-0563), at Store Bay, offers some of the best creole on the island.

Most smaller cafes and takeout restaurants do not accept credit cards.

GETTING THERE

Trinidad's Piarco International Airport (809-664-5196), 17 miles (27 km) east of Port of Spain, is served by major North American, European, South American and Caribbean airlines, including American Airlines (809-664-4661), Air Canada (809-664-4065), British Airways (809-625-1811), United (809-627-7000), ALM (809-625-1719), Guyana Airways (809-627-2753), Aeropostal (809-623-6522) and Trinidad's own BWIA (809-627-BWIA). LIAT (809-623-1837/8) is the best connection for neighbouring islands.

Tobago's Crown Point Airport (809-639-0509), eight miles (13 km) from Scarborough, can land international flights as well as smaller connections from Trinidad, a 15 minute flight. LIAT (809-639-0484) offers connections from Piarco and a direct connection from Barbados and BWIA offers direct service from Miami and Frankfurt. If Tobago is your final destination, it's best to try to book straight through to Crown Point and avoid Piarco altogether. Most round-trip tickets to Trinidad will tack on a Tobago leg for free, if you ask. Even if you only fly there for a day, it's worth it. Trips from Trinidad to Tobago take 15 minutes and cost US$35 round-trip by air, on either BWIA or LIAT.

Trinidad and Tobago's immigration laws are strict compared to other islands in the Lesser Antilles. Passports are required by everyone and visas are also required of nationals of Australia, India, Papua New Guinea, New Zealand, current and former communist/socialist block countries and others. Visas for stays of less than three months are not required for citizens of the U.S., Canada, France, Italy and the U.K. Check with your local authorities for visa requirements.

The departure tax, payable in Trinidad and Tobago dollars, is TT$75 per person.

GETTING AROUND

■ PUBLIC TRANSPORT

For a country of 1.3 million, the public transport system is sophisticated and fairly efficient. Most public transport vehicles are called "taxis" in one way or another and all public livery vehicles are identified by an "H" on the license plate.

Route taxis, usually cars, follow certain routes, as you'd expect, and charge per person. Route taxis operate in and around major population centers.

Maxi-taxis (minivans) operate along major roads between towns and are identified by large colored stripes—green for southern Trinidad, red for eastern Trinidad and yellow for Port of Spain.

In Port of Spain main transport stands can be found at Queen's Park Savannah, Woodford Square and Independence Square, which is the best place to start a journey. For taxi pick-ups call Bacchus Taxi (809-622-5588) or Queen's Park Taxi Stand (809-625-3002).

On Tobago the maxi-taxi color is blue; catch transport at the airport or in Scarborough near the public market or at Port Authority.

A ferry makes a daily (sometimes twice daily), five-hour run between Trinidad and Tobago. The single fare is TT$50 round-trip or you can opt for a cabin for two for TT$160. For ferry information contact the Port Authority in Port of Spain (809-625-4906) or in Scarborough (809-639-2181).

■ CAR RENTALS

Rental cars are not hard to find, except at Carnival time. Rates start at US$35 per day. At Piarco Airport try, among dozens of others, Singh's (809-664-5417, fax 627-8476) or Auto Rentals (809-669-2277, fax 675-2258). In town call Toyota Rent a Car (809-628-5516, fax 628-6808) or Automania (809-628-8503).

On Tobago call Alfred's Car Rentals (809-639-7448), Thrifty (809-639-8507) or Toyota Rent a Car (809-639-7495, fax 639-7482). The airport hosts ten or more agencies.

Bicycles (TT$25 per day), motor scooters and motorcycles (TT$80) can be rented from Greene's General Cycle (809-646-BIKE) in Arouca on Trinidad. In

Tobago, where the terrain and ambiance make them practical, at Modern Bike Rental (Union Village 809-639-3275) or Blossom Enterprises (Canaan, near the airport, 809-639-8485).

For rentals your valid license or international license will be fine for up to three months. Driving is on the left.

MONEY, HOURS AND COMMUNICATION

The Trinidad and Tobago dollar (TT$) was floated on the international market in 1993 and fluctuates daily against international currencies. Check local papers for the current rate. The recent average, however, has been TT$5.70 = US$1. You can exchange your money at hotels or banks, which are open 8.00-14.00 Monday through Thursday and 9.00-12.00 and 15.00-17.00 on Friday. The bank at Piarco Airport is open 6.00-22.00 daily.

Businesses open 8.00-16.00 Monday through Thursday and until 18.00 on Friday. Shopping malls remain open until 20.00 Monday through Saturday. Government offices are open weekdays, 8.00-12.00 and 15.00-16.30.

The international area code for Trinidad and Tobago is 809. You can pay with either coins or phone cards, which are available at banks, small shops or at Telecommunications Services of Trinidad and Tobago on Independence Square. You'll also find a TSTT office in Scarborough.

The main post office is located on Wrightson Road in Port of Spain, opposite the Holiday Inn, open 7.00-17.00.

The country's newspapers are among the most lively and trashy in the Caribbean. The dailies Trinidad Guardian and Daily Express are the best bets for local and international news and are found at any of about a hundred small vendors' stands throughout the cities.

USEFUL ADDRESSES
■ TRINIDAD AND TOBAGO TOURISM DEVELOPMENT AUTHORITY
❏ 134-138 Frederick St., Port of Spain, Trinidad, W.I. (809-623-1932/4, fax 623-3848).
❏ Piarco International Airport, 664-5196.
❏ NIB Mall, Scarborough, Tobago, W.I. (809-639-2125, fax 639-3566).
❏ Crown Point Airport, 809-639-0509.
❏ 25 W. 43rd St. Suite 1508, New York, NY 10036 (800-232-0082 or 212-719-0540, fax 212-719-0988).
❏ 8A Hammersmith Broadway, London W6 7AL, England (44181-741-4466, fax 741-1013).

■ OTHER

❏ Police, 999.

❏ Fire and ambulance, 990.

❏ Port of Spain General Hospital, 169 Charlotte Street; 623-2951.

❏ Scarborough Hospital, Tobago; 639-2551.

❏ Piarco International Airport, Trinidad; 664-5196

❏ Crown Point Airport, Tobago; 639-0509.

❏ Bhaggan's Pharmacy (open until 23.00), Independence Square, Port of Spain (627-5541).

❏ Federal Express, 31-33 Abercrombie Street, Port of Spain (624-0241 or 623-4070); Piarco International Airport (669-2672).

❏ National Carnival Commission, 92 Frederick St., Port of Spain, Trinidad, W.I. (623-7600 or 623-7510).

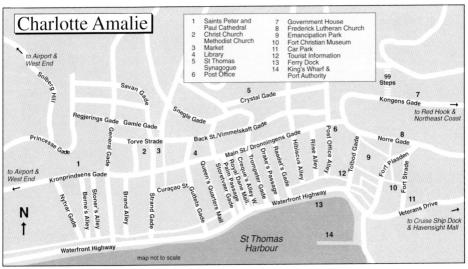

Charlotte Amalie

1 Saints Peter and Paul Cathedral
2 Christ Church Methodist Church
3 Market
4 Library
5 St Thomas Synagogue
6 Post Office
7 Government House
8 Frederick Lutheran Church
9 Emancipation Park
10 Fort Christian Museum
11 Car Park
12 Tourist Information
13 Ferry Dock
14 King's Wharf & Port Authority

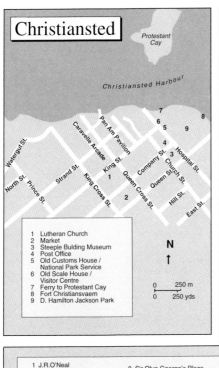

Christiansted

1 Lutheran Church
2 Market
3 Steeple Bulding Museum
4 Post Office
5 Old Customs House / National Park Service
6 Old Scale House / Visitor Centre
7 Ferry to Protestant Cay
8 Fort Christiansvaern
9 D. Hamilton Jackson Park

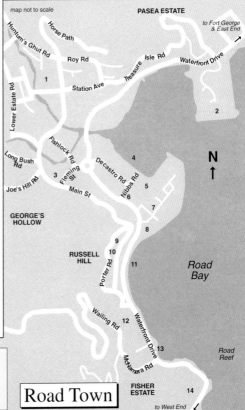

Road Town

1 J.R.O'Neal Botanic Gardens
2 Wickham's Cay 2
3 Library
4 Village Cay Marina
5 Wickham's Cay
6 Cable & Wireless
7 Tourist Board
8 Sir Olva George's Plaza
9 Virgin Islands Folk Museum
10 Post Office
11 Ferry DOck
12 Government House
13 Queen Elizabeth Park
14 Fort Burt Hotel

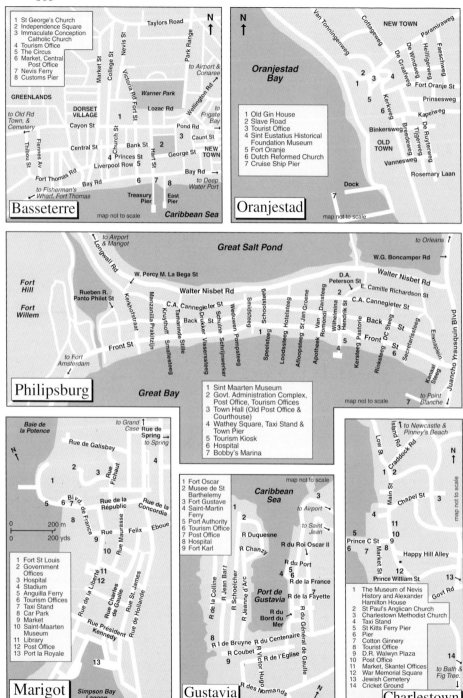

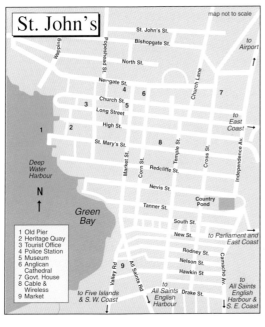

St. John's

map not to scale

St. John's St.
Bishopgate St.
North St.
Newgate St.
Church St.
Long Street
High St.
St. Mary's St.
Market St.
Corn St.
Redcliffe St.
Temple St.
Cross St.
Nevis St.
Tanner St.
Country Pond
South St.
New St.
Rodney St.
Nelson St.
Hawkin St.
Valley Rd
All Saints Rd
Drake St.
Camacho Av.
Independence Av.
Church Lane
Popeshead St.
Wapping

Deep Water Harbour

Green Bay

N

to Airport
to East Coast
to Parliament and East Coast
to All Saints English Harbour & S.E. Coast
to All Saints English Harbour
to Five Islands & S.W. Coast
to All Saints English Harbour

1 Old Pier
2 Heritage Quay
3 Tourist Office
4 Police Station
5 Museum
6 Anglican Cathedral
7 Govt. House
8 Cable & Wireless
9 Market

Plymouth

map not to scale

to St. Anthony's Anglican Church, Cork Hill, Old Towne & North
Church Rd
Lower Dagenham Rd
Shamrock Rd
Evergreen Road
Old Chapel St.
Marine Drive
Waterline St.
Parliament St.
Chapel St.
Strand St.
Houston St.
John St.
George St.
Harney St.
Peebles St.
Fort Ghaut

N

Caribbean Sea

Jetty

to St. George's Hill, Harris & Airport
to Wapping & Southwest

1 Tourist Office
2 Carib-World Travel
3 Methodist Church
4 Roman Catholic Church
5 Cable & Wireless
6 Post Office
7 Taxis
8 Clock Tower
9 Public Market

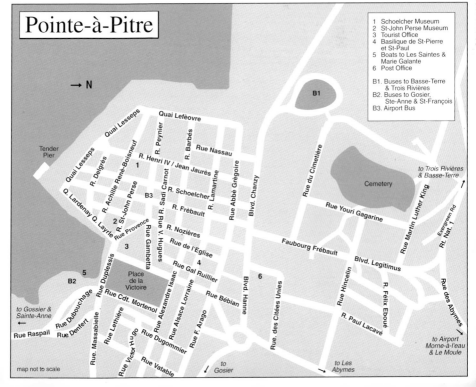

Pointe-à-Pitre

N

Tender Pier

Quai Lesseps
Quai Lesseps
Quai Lefèovre
Quai Lefèvre
R. Delgrès
R. Achille René-Boisneuf
R. St-John Perse
R. Peynier
R. Henri IV / Jean Jaurès
R. Barbès
Rue Nassau
R. Sadi Carnot
R. Schoelcher
R. Lamartine
Rue Abbé Grégoire
Blvd. Chanzy
R. Frébault
R. Nozières
Rue de l'Eglise
Rue Gal Ruillier
Rue Bébian
Q. Lardenay
Q. Layrle
Rue Provence
Rue Gambetta
Rue V. Hugues
Rue Alexandre Isaac
Rue Alsace Lorraine
Blvd. Hanne
Place de la Victoire
Rue Cdt. Mortenol
Rue Duplessis
Rue Dubouchage
Rue Massabielle
Rue Lethière
Rue Victor Hugo
Rue Dugommier
Rue F. Arago
Rue Vatable
Rue Raspail
Rue Denfert
Rue du Cimetière
Cemetery
B1
Rue Youri Gagarine
Faubourg Frébault
Blvd. Legitimus
Rue Martin Luther King
Rue Hincelin
R. Félix Eboué
R. Paul Lacavé
Rue des Abymes
Evergreen Rd
Rte Nat. 1
Rue des Citées Unies

to Gossier & Sainte-Anne
to Gosier
to Les Abymes
to Trois Rivières & Basse-Terre
to Airport Morne-à-l'eau & Le Moule

map not to scale

1 Schoelcher Museum
2 St-John Perse Museum
3 Tourist Office
4 Basilique de St-Pierre et St-Paul
5 Boats to Les Saintes & Marie Galante
6 Post Office

B1. Buses to Basse-Terre & Trois Rivières
B2. Buses to Gosier, Ste-Anne & St-François
B3. Airport Bus

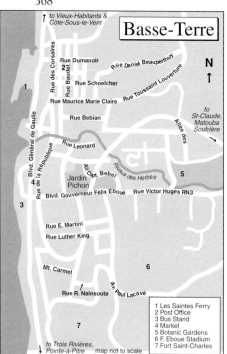

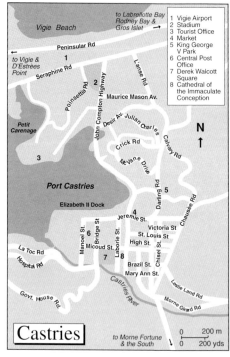

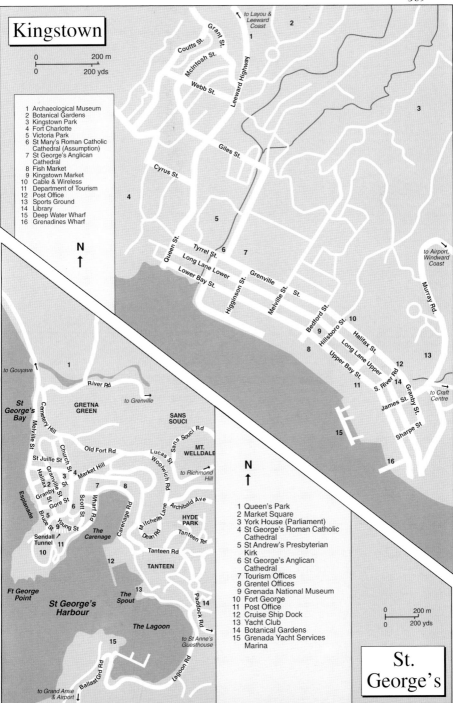

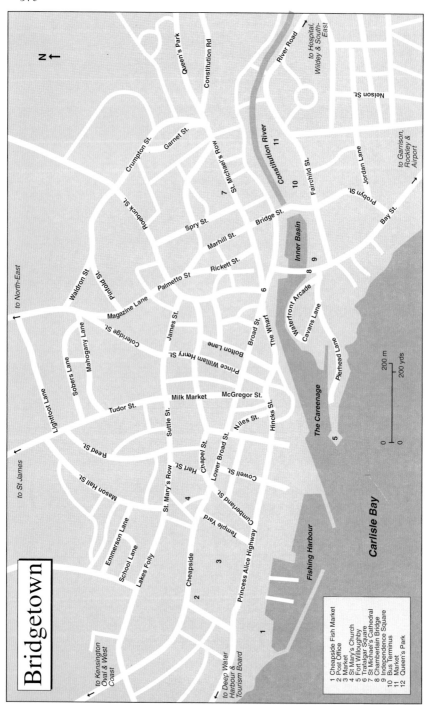

Bridgetown

N ↑

to Kensington Oval & West Coast

to St. James

to North-East

to Deep Water Harbour & Tourism Board

to Garrison, Rockley & Airport

to Hospital, Wildey & South-East

Queen's Park

Constitution Rd

River Road

Nelson St.

Crumpton St.

Garnet St.

St. Michael's Row

Constitution River

Fairchild St.

Jordan Lane

Probyn St.

Bay St.

Roebuck St.

Spry St.

Marhill St.

Bridge St.

Inner Basin

11

10

9

Waldron St.

Proud's St.

Magazine Lane

Palmetto St

Rickett St.

The Wharf

Broad St.

Waterfront Arcade

8

6

Mahogany Lane

Coleridge St.

James St.

Bolton Lane

Prince William Henry St.

Cavans Lane

Pierhead Lane

Sobers Lane

Lightfoot Lane

Milk Market

McGregor St.

The Careenage

5

Tudor St.

Suttle St.

Niles St.

Hincks St.

Reed St.

Mason Hall St.

Emmerson Lane

School Lane

Lakes Folly

St. Mary's Row

Hart St.

Chapel St.

Lower Broad St.

Cowell St.

Temple Yard

Cumberland St.

Princess Alice Highway

Cheapside

2

4

3

1

Fishing Harbour

Carlisle Bay

200 m

200 yds

0

0

1 Cheapside Fish Market
2 Post Office
3 Market
4 St Mary's Church
5 Fort Willoughby
6 Trafalgar Square
7 St Michael's Cathedral
8 Chamberlain Bridge
9 Independence Square
10 Bus Terminus
11 Market
12 Queen's Park

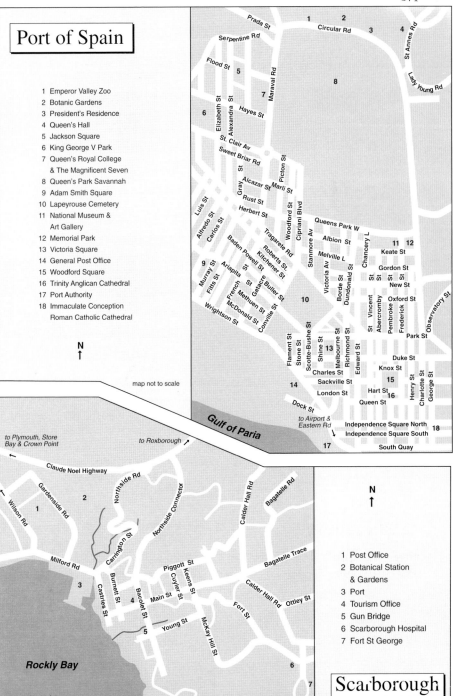

Recommended Reading

The recommended reading below represents a small portion of the large and fascinating body of work about the Lesser Antilles region and its people. A good source for new, used and first edition books on the Caribbean is: West Indies Books Unlimited, P.O. Box 2315, Sarasota, FL 34230 USA; 813-954-8601.

Bibliography

Gordon, R. *The Literature of the West Indies.* 20 vols. Gordon Press, 1977.

Miller, E. Willard and Ruby M. Miller, eds. *The Third World-Lesser Antilles: A Bibliography.* Vance Bibliographies, 1990. A concise (25 page) list.

Biography

Kennedy, Gavin. *Bligh.* Duckworth, 1978. The life and times of Capt. William Bligh, adventurer, dispossessed commander of the infamous Bounty and importer of the lifesaving breadfruit to the West Indies.

Wilford, John Noble. *The Mysterious History of Columbus: An Exploration of the Man, the Myth, the Legacy.* Alfred A. Knopf, 1991. Treatment of the often harsh, vain, but ultimately heroic man who, through one of the greatest mistakes ever made, brought European involvement to the West Indies and changed the course of world history.

Culture and Customs

Horowitz, Michael, ed. *Peoples and Cultures of the Caribbean.* Natural History Press, 1971. Dated, but contains interesting historical information.

Kurlansky, Mark. *A Continent of Islands: Searching for the Caribbean Destiny.* Addison-Wesley, 1992. Well-regarded treatise on the future of the Caribbean states and their cultures.

Walton, Chelle K. *Caribbean Ways: A Cultural Guide*. Riverdale Co., 1993. More than a list of do's and don't's, the work discusses the background of cultures and customs.

Description and Travel

The Cambridge Encyclopedia of Latin America and the Caribbean. 2nd edition; Cambridge University Press, 1992. Essential reference work for Caribbean region aficionados.

Cameron, Sarah and Ben Box, eds. *Caribbean Islands Handbook*. 5th edition; Passport Books, 1994. Solidly packed with practical information.

Dyde, Brian. *Caribbean Companion, the A to Z Reference*. Macmillan, 1992. Mini-encyclopedia and a good, practical guide to Caribbean terms, issues and personalities.

Literature

Abrahams, Peter. *Lights Out*. Mysterious Press, 1994. A tale of skulduggery and false imprisonment set against a Caribbean backdrop.

Allfrey, Phyllis A. *The Orchid House*. Three Continents, 1985. Sisters growing up in Dominica.

Anderson, John L. *Night of the Silent Drums*. Scribner's, 1975. Describes the 1733 St. John slave rebellion.

Barton, Paule. *The Woe Shirt: Caribbean Folk Tales*. Penmaen Press, 1980. A collection of West Indian folk tales from a Haitian goatherd and folklorist.

Bissoondath, Neil. *Digging Up the Mountains*. Viking, 1986. A collection of 14 short stories by a Trinidadian expatriate.

Burnett, Paula, ed. *The Penguin Book of Caribbean Verse in English*. Viking Penguin Books, 1986. Writers of and from the Caribbean.

Césaire, Aimé. Eshelman, Clayton and Annette Smith, translators. *The Collected Poetry.* University of California Press, 1983. Poetry from the famous Martiniquan poet, politician and proponent of the Négritude movement.

Césaire, Aimé and Charles Calixte. *Poems From Martinique.* Kraus, 1952.

Kincaid, Jamaica. *Annie John.* Farrar Straus Giroux, 1985. Novel of a young Antiguan girl's life and relationships, particularly with her mother.

Kincaid, Jamaica. *Lucy.* Farrar Straus Giroux, 1991. Familiar theme for followers of Jamaica Kincaid's work: a young girl's travails and loves in the islands.

Joseph, Lynn. *Coconut Kind of Day: Island Poems.* Lothrop, Lee & Shepard Books, 1990. Poetry for younger adults.

Joseph, Lynn. *A Wave in Her Pocket; Stories from Trinidad.* Clarion Books, 1991. A collection of short stories.

Lamming, George. *In the Castle of My Skin.* McGraw-Hill, 1954. The Barbadian writer's first novel, set amidst the island's pre-independence social awakening.

Michener, James A. *Caribbean.* Random House, 1989. Michener's epochal (and exhausting) tale of the settling of the Caribbean, from pre-Columbian to modern times.

Naipaul, Shiva. *The Chip-chip Gatherers.* Alfred A. Knopf, 1973. Chips-chips, tiny shellfish, are gathered by inhabitants of a small town in Trinidad; novel of village life, futility and class.

Naipaul, V.S. *A House for Mr. Biswas.* Alfred A. Knopf, 1983. Reprint of Naipaul's classic tale of Trinidadian society.

Naipaul, V.S. *The Mystic Masseur.* Viking Penguin, 1964. Comic novel of a failed Trinidadian schoolmaster and writer-turned-mystic masseur or healer. Naipaul's first book, published in 1959.

Ramchand, Kenneth, ed. *Best West Indian Stories.* Nelson Caribbean, 1982. An brief anthology of lesser-known but admirable Caribbean short stories.

Rhys, Jean. *Wide Sargasso Sea.* Norton, 1967. Presents the early life of the mysterious madwoman in Charlotte Bronte's Jane Eyre and portrays post-Emancipation Caribbean.

Selvon, Samuel. *Brighter Sun.* Dearborn Trade. Originally published in 1953, Selvon's tale concerns a 16-year-old Trinidadian bridegroom, Tiger, and Urmilla, his younger bride, as they piece together the puzzles of married life.

Shacochis, Bob. *Easy in the Islands.* Viking, 1985. Collection of short stories about life in the islands; winner of the American Book Award.

Shacochis, Bob. *Swimming in the Volcano.* Scribners, 1993. Novel of political intrigue, expatriate lust and love on the fictional island of St. Catherine.

Trillin, Calvin. *Travels With Alice.* Ticknor & Fields, 1989. Collection of travel essays from the quirky humorist, including several that deal with Lesser Antilles islands.

Walcott, Derek. *Omeros.* Farrar Straus Giroux, 1990. Omeros, Greek for Homer, is one character in this ambitious narrative of exile, spiritual travel and the redemption of place. Considered one of Walcott's most important works.

History

Course, A.G. *Pirates of the Western Seas.* Muller, 1969. Pirate fact and lore.

Dunn, Richard S. *Sugar and Slavery—the Rise of the Planter Class in the English West Indies (1624-1738).* University of North Carolina Press, 1972. Details the unpleasant marriage of slavery and the sugar economy in the culture of the West Indies.

Friends of English Harbor. *The Romance of English Harbor.* The Friends of English Harbor, 1969. History of Antigua's port, site of the famous Nelson's Dockyard.

Goldberg, Mark H. *Going Bananas: 100 Years of Fruit Ships in the Caribbean.* American Merchant Marine Museum Foundation, 1993. Banana boats also brought the first tourists from North America to the Caribbean.

Parry, J.H. and P.M. Sherlock and Anthony Maingot. *A Short History of the West Indies*. Macmillan, 1987. Accessible; one of the best histories of its kind.

Thomas, Gordon and Max Morgan Witts. *The Day the World Ended*. Stein and Day, 1969. The 1902 eruption of Mt Pelée, at Saint-Pierre, Martinique, was literally the end of the world for thousands.

Williams, Eric. *History of the People of Trinidad and Tobago*. Deutsch, 1964. Williams not only wrote the history, but, as the first leader of independant Trinidad and Tobago, was a major part of it.

Music and the Arts

Burgie, Irving, ed. *Caribbean Carnival: Songs of the West Indies*. Tambourine Books, 1992. Includes music and words.

Ekwene, Laz E.N. *African Sources in New World Black Music*. Toronto, 1972. Traces African influences in modern "black" music of the early part of this century.

Hamelecourt, Juliette. *Caribbean Cookbook*. Culinary Arts Institute, 1987. Recipes and references.

Hebdige, Dick. *Cut 'n' Mix: Culture, Identity and Caribbean Music*. Routledge, 1990. Mostly covers reggae; good chapter on Trinidadian music.

Sweeney, Philip. *The Virgin Directory of World Music*. Henry Holt, 1991. Forty pages on the Greater and Lesser Antilles, with information on many lesser known musicians.

Natural Sciences

Bond, James. *Birds of the West Indies*. Collins, 1960 edition. Author Ian Fleming took the name of this famous naturalist for his super-agent, 007.

Bourne, M.J., G.W. Lennox and S.A. Seddon. *Fruits and Vegetables of the Caribbean*. Macmillan, 1988. Pamphlet describing major Caribbean species.

Greenberg, Idaz and Jerry Greenberg. *Guide to Corals & Fishes of Florida, the Bahamas and the Caribbean.* Seahawk Press, 1977. Waterproof book with illustrations of warm-water coral and sealife.

Honeychurch, Penelope N. *Caribbean Wild Plants and Their Uses.* Macmillan, 1986. Uses of wild plants, from folk medicine to magic.

Social Issues

Abrahams, Roger D. *After Africa.* Yale University Press, 1983. Chronicle of Africans as slaves in the West Indies.

Davison, Robert Barry. *Black British: Immigrants to England.* Florida Atlantic University Press, 1972. Explores the impact of West Indian emigrants to the United Kingdom.

Patterson, Orlando. *Sociology of Slavery.* 1967. Slavery was the beast that pulled the West Indies economic cart and its resultant race and class problems are alive today.

Thomas, Clive Y. *The Poor and the Powerless: Economic Policy and Change in the Caribbean.* Monthly Review Press (Latin American Bureau, U.K.), 1988. Investigates some of the disturbing causes of trouble in paradise.

Periodicals

Caribbean Travel and Life. Box 6229, Syracuse, N.Y. 13217-7921. Bi-monthly glossy magazine.

Caribbean Week. Lefferts Place, River Road, St. Michael, Barbados, West Indies. Monthly newspaper covering Caribbean issues.

Index

38, 39, 46, 67, 69, 83, 84, 92, 114, 125-127,
130, 140, 151, 157, 158, 168, 183, 184,
200, 241, 243, 249, 256, 273, 285, 287,
302, 303, 331, 345, 346, 348, 349, 352
Spanish Town 83, 92
Statia 128, 130, 149, 151, 153, 155, 157-
165, 173
Steel band 27-29, 70, 85, 171, 185, 196,
209, 268, 344, 349, 351, 352, 356
Sugar 11, 14, 17-21, 23, 39-41, 46, 48,
67, 68, 79, 90, 91, 114, 115, 126, 140,
158, 159, 167, 169-172, 184, 187-189,
200, 203, 204, 210, 211, 213, 250, 257,
259, 262, 263, 272, 274, 286, 290, 303,
306, 314, 328-331, 333, 335, 339, 344,
346, 350, 352, 355, 357

Taino 14, 66
Tamboo-bamboo 28, 350
Telephone 122, 128, 178, 195, 208, 253,
268, 282, 313
Tête chien 242, 250
Tintamarre 125, 131, 132
Tobacco 15, 25, 39, 67, 114, 126, 158,
162, 184, 200, 244, 303, 345, 346
Tobago Cays 248, 297-299
Tortola 66, 68, 72, 73, 82-92, 95
Treaty of Aix-La-Chapelle 243, 286
Treaty of Paris 211, 243, 272, 291
Treaty of Utrecht 18, 169
Treaty of Versailles 169, 173, 200, 286,
303
Trinidad and Tobago 13, 14, 16, 17, 20-
27, 29, 32-34, 37, 38, 40-42, 44, 46, 48,
51, 52, 66, 84, 124, 186, 210, 272-274,
292, 312, 315, 329, 333, 344-364
Trois-Ilets 260, 263, 265, 268
Turtles 31, 42, 44, 75, 94, 270, 314, 359

Union Island 292, 293, 298, 299, 312, 315
United States 13, 21, 70, 126, 158, 160
US Virgin Islands 13, 14, 18, 30, 37, 44,
51, 65-82, 85-87

Valley, the (Ang.) 116, 118, 119, 121-123
Valley, the (B.V.I.) 83, 87, 88, 92
VC Bird Int'l Airport 182, 187, 193, 194
Venezuela 12-14, 16, 37, 49, 151, 152,
344, 345
Vigie Airport 279, 280
Villas 45, 46, 73, 75, 79, 88, 91, 93, 95,
119, 132, 141, 144, 152, 154, 175, 192,
197, 202, 205, 265, 278, 296, 298, 315, 338
Vincy Mas 287
Virgin Bank 65, 82
Virgin Gorda 72, 73, 82-84, 86-89, 92,
93, 95
Visas 52, 361, 362
Volcano 36, 37, 162, 167, 199, 202, 203,
210, 216, 241, 256, 260-262, 270, 276,
285, 287, 288, 302, 308, 375

Wallblake Airport 120, 121
Walcott, Derek 32, 34, 35, 273, 274,
278, 344, 375
West Africa 18-20, 24, 40, 47, 350
West African 25, 28, 30, 275
West Indies, Fed. of 84, 115, 272, 331
Winair 53, 72, 121, 133, 145, 155, 164,
176, 252
Windwardside 149, 152-156
World War I 21, 68, 140, 169, 179, 346
World War II 34, 69, 140, 185, 277, 354

Zemi 130
Zouk 27, 30, 212, 258, 273